Studies in the Greek New Testament

Studies in Biblical Greek

D. A. Carson
General Editor

Vol. 6

PETER LANG
New York • Washington, D.C./Baltimore • San Francisco
Bern • Frankfurt am Main • Berlin • Vienna • Paris

Stanley E. Porter

Studies in the Greek New Testament

Theory and Practice

PETER LANG
New York • Washington, D.C./Baltimore • San Francisco
Bern • Frankfurt am Main • Berlin • Vienna • Paris

Library of Congress Cataloging-in-Publication Data

Porter, Stanley E.
Studies in the Greek New Testament:
theory and practice/ Stanley E. Porter.
p. cm. — (Studies in Biblical Greek; vol. 6)
Includes bibliographical references (p.) and index.
1. Greek language, Biblical—Grammar. 2. Bible. N.T.—Language, style.
I. Title. II. Series.
PA817.P67 487'.4—dc20 95-22504
ISBN 0-8204-2858-2
ISSN 0897-7828

Die Deutsche Bibliothek-CIP-Einheitsaufnahme

Porter, Stanley E.:
Studies in the Greek New Testament: theory and practice/
Stanley E. Porter. - New York; Washington, D.C./ Baltimore; San Francisco;
Bern; Frankfurt am Main; Berlin; Vienna; Paris: Lang.
(Studies in Biblical Greek; Vol. 6)
ISBN 0-8204-2858-2
NE: GT

CONTENTS

PREFACE

This work owes its origins to a number of people who are to be thanked—or held responsible—for encouraging and helping the following research to develop over the last several years.

The first is those editors and publishers who accepted many of these chapters for publication, and who have now graciously offered permission for them to be presented below. I have made acknowledgment on the first page of each article that is reprinted. Although most of them are still recognizably the same as when they originally appeared, virtually all of them have undergone some form of revision, usually in terms of bringing references to secondary literature up to date. There have also been some changes in formatting, which I trust will make it easier to follow the flow of the argument.

The second person to thank is Dr. Heidi Burns, acquisitions editor for Peter Lang Publishing. I give her credit for asking every time we met at a conference whether I had another book for Peter Lang. After mulling this idea over for some time, and seeing the (at least to me) surprising amount of continuity in the following essays, I presented an outline of this volume to her. Practically by return mail I received a contract.

The third and most important person to thank is my wife, Wendy. I used to think that prefaces thanking wives were maudlin and overdone; now, if anything, that they are understated. The work of putting this volume together came at a particularly hectic time in our lives, with a recent transatlantic move, purchase of a new home, and adjusting to life abroad. It was she who helped me to find the time to get this finished, and to her the major credit for this volume must go.

I have for the most part used the abbreviations and format employed by the *Journal of Biblical Literature*, with a few modifications that should be self-evident.

INTRODUCTION

This volume, *Studies in the Greek New Testament: Theory and Practice*, presents a number of essays, all of which have been written within the last ten years, with several being previously unpublished. Although those previously published have appeared in a number of different journals and in a number of different formats, they are not nearly as uncoordinated as such a scenario would imply. All of these essays grow out of an abiding concern for the study and understanding of the Greek of the New Testament. Like few others, unfortunately, I have devoted a good portion of my academic career and research to the study of the Greek of the New Testament, as part of a larger hermeneutical and exegetical enterprise. That is, I have been concerned to bring the best insights of modern linguistics to the study of an ancient language, Greek, as part of an overriding concern to understand the world and people in which and by which this language was first used, especially as it appears in the Greek New Testament. The essays presented here are not the most technical ones that I have written in the course of my research (that kind of a collection will have to wait for another day). Instead, this volume bring together essays of two sorts, theoretical and practical, mutually complementary to the task that I have outlined above. Although most of the essays have appeared in print before, several of them have appeared in places that make their access more restricted than I would like. In some cases, people do not think to read the kinds of publications that these essays have appeared in as part of their general reading in the subject of New Testament studies, in others the journals have been too specialized or restricted in circulation to have come to the attention of a wider audience.

The first part of this volume contains a number of essays of a more theoretical sort. I admit that it is difficult to make a firm and fast distinction between theoretical and practical essays, and this volume well illustrates that difficulty, since in each essay there is at least a little bit of both. But the essays in this first part concentrate more on fundamental questions regarding understanding of the Greek of the New Testament. The first three essays attempt to outline my basic understanding of the Greek language, especially in terms of its grammatical structure, concentrating on the verbal system. In these essays I argue for the category of synthetic verbal aspect being the semantic feature that dictates Greek verbal usage, and show how this theory is different from other, earlier and perhaps better known models, such as those based on a temporal or *Aktionsart* understanding of the verb. The first essay presents a basic introduction to lexicography and grammar and uses these categories to look at the structure of Greek, as well as offering several examples of what is being said by invoking the grammatical category of verbal aspect. It is certainly pleasing to see that some of the fundamental work I have done in this area, along with important work by others both within the field of Greek language study and within the wider field of general linguistics, has led to continuing debate and discussion. Those who take a similar standpoint regarding the importance of verbal aspect are not agreed what this means, however, and this emerges especially in the second essay, where I defend my particular orientation to the subject. The third essay presents an assessment of teaching grammars of Greek in the light of recent work on verbal aspect. Rather than simply leave it to others to try to bring the theoretical discussion to bear upon the pragmatic issue of pedagogy, I have addressed some of these issues in this short essay, including evaluation of a number of the more recent grammars.

In the fourth essay, printed here for the first time, I discuss issues in biblical lexicography. Although most of the essays in this volume concentrate upon matters of grammar, lexicography is an area where there has been significant and necessary recent work, especially because of the UBS lexicon edited by J.P. Louw and E.A. Nida. In this chapter, I set out some principles for modern lexicography, ones not often followed by traditional lexicographers and hence not by the major tools used in current New Testament study, and then offer a supportive critique of the UBS lexicon.

In the final essay of the first part I discuss the nature of the Greek of the New Testament. Although this essay overlaps in some ways with the eighth chapter on whether Jesus spoke Greek, it is included here because it is a more general discussion of what kind of Greek is found in the New Testament, that is, whether it is of a pure *koinė* type, much like the rest of the Greek of the Hellenistic world, whether it is a form of Semitized Greek, because of translation or influence of the language milieu of Palestine, or whether it is some form of unique hybrid dialect, developed within the Church. Although this essay began as an introduction to essays by representative scholars who hold to the various views mentioned above, I have re-written the essay so that it offers a conspectus of the various opinions, focusing on particular scholars as representative. In some ways, this may be the most important essay in this volume, since it is my experience that scholars are constantly making judgments regarding the nature of the Greek of the New Testament (for example, stating that a particular structure is "Semitic") while knowing very little about the context in which such statements are made.

In part two of this book essays of a more practical sort are presented. The essays are arranged roughly in New Testament canonical order. Consequently, the first essay concentrates upon Matt 16:19, with a discussion of the periphrastic structure that has aroused so much discussion over the years. Some of the issues raised in this essay are re-visited in chapter eight when the language of Jesus is discussed. The second essay is a lexicographical study, in which the verb ἐγγίζειν, traditionally seen as a verb of motion, is discussed in the light of its Lukan usage. It is found that rather than primarily a verb of motion it is a verb of spatial or temporal location. This has significant implications for understanding Luke 18:35 in relation to its synoptic parallels. The third essay is concerned with whether Jesus ever spoke Greek. After briefly discussing the evidence for the use of Greek in Palestine, and using standard Gospel critical criteria, it is determined that there are several instances where Jesus may well have spoken Greek, including one passage (Mark 15:2 and parallels) where we may even have the very words of Jesus in Greek. The implications of this finding are tentatively explored. In the fourth essay, although the focus is not upon the actual language of the New Testament, the results of the study have serious implications for understanding the speeches in Acts. The programmatic statement of Thucydides in 1.22.1 regarding speeches is subjected to detailed scrutiny, exploring the various ambiguous elements of this crucial passage.

In the tenth and eleventh chapters, Romans 5 becomes the focus of attention. In chapter ten, an essay printed here for the first time, though summarizing material in some of my other recent work, I present evidence from the entire corpus of ancient Greek literature before the time of Paul concerning use of the verb καταλλάσσω. After discounting the religious importance of several passages often cited, and looking more closely at three passages in 2 Maccabees, I then discuss Paul's usage in Rom 5:10, attempting to place it in a larger context. This study involves both important lexicographical and grammatical discussion, well illustrating the importance of both dimensions of study for understanding. In chapter eleven, I return to Romans 5, but this time seeing it as exemplifying characteristics of ancient diatribe. Although diatribe is often discussed in terms of larger rhetorical patterns, this study focuses upon discussion of several important textual variants, as well as other features of the chapter, to show its diatribal character.

In chapter twelve, I have included an essay that had its origins in a discussion of Pauline ethics, but ethics that pays attention to the language in which ethical statements are expressed. Although the proposal regarding Wittgenstein's classes of utterances does not seem to me to offer a productive way forward in ethical discourse, including discerning the way to use Gal 3:28–29, it does exemplify in a poignant way the importance of paying attention to the way statements are formulated and how statements are subjected to various understandings.

In the thirteenth and final chapter, I take on a passage that continues to arouse much discussion, much of it not too informative. Few passages in the New Testament are subject to so much biased exegesis as 1 Tim 2:15. What I have attempted to do is to look at the several most important grammatical and lexical issues in the passage, not with the idea of justifying a particular theological position, but with the hope that through careful linguistic study understanding of the passage can be increased.

In the end, the goals of this volume are three. First, it is hoped that this collection of essays will help to increase understanding of several areas of importance in New Testament study, especially as these are focused on matters of grammar and lexicography as well as particular texts. Secondly, this volume is designed to reflect my position (at least at the time of writing and editing) on several of these issues. It would be foolish to hope that I could convince everyone of the rightness of each of my opinions, so that has never been the goal. Instead, these essays are an attempt in a continuing discussion to present a number of issues and to discuss them in some detail. It will be obvious that the issue of verbal aspect is one that I think is very important. It seems to me through the course of my continuing work that this is an area that merits continued and further study because its implications have only barely been touched upon. One frustration is that there is still a relatively small group of scholars who are aware of what the linguistic issues actually are in New Testament studies, and even fewer who can see the implications. Thirdly, perhaps naively, I am optimistic that these essays may interest others in exploring similar issues, either in conjunction with their current research interests, or as a new area of interest to which they would like to devote their time and energies. The study of the Greek of the New Testament is a highly rewarding area, and many of the most perplexing issues regarding the Greek language still await solution.

PART I THEORY

CHAPTER ONE

GREEK LANGUAGE AND LINGUISTICS*

1. *Introduction*

In his classic 1957 essay, "Is Exegesis without Presuppositions Possible?" Rudolf Bultmann answered resoundingly "No." The historical-critical method, Bultmann says, "is *the historical method* of interrogating the text," indeed, "exegesis as the interpretation of historical texts is a part of the science of history."[1] But most essential for Bultmann, and for a number of other New Testament exegetes, is the role of language. G.B. Winer's well-established grammar was entitled, in one of its several English versions, *A Treatise on the Grammar of New Testament Greek, regarded as a Sure Basis for New Testament Exegesis*.[2] As Bultmann says, "It belongs to the historical method, of course, that a text is interpreted in accordance with the rules of grammar and of the meaning of words."[3] J.P. Louw clarifies from the standpoint of modern linguistics: "In any communication there are always several layers of meaning which must be explored in order to understand what is meant." The three essential levels are "the word level, the sentence level, and the contextual level, involving not only the context of the text but the context of the total time-place setting."[4] This complex of factors has often been neglected in biblical studies.

---

* This essay is reprinted with the permission of T. & T. Clark Publishers, from *The Expository Times* 103 (1991–92) 202–208. The footnotes have been updated in places.

1 R. Bultmann, "Is Exegesis without Presuppositions Possible?" in *Existence and Faith: Shorter Writings of Rudolf Bultmann* (trans. S.M. Ogden; London: Hodder & Stoughton, 1960) 291, followed in many ways by, for example, O. Kaiser and W.G. Kümmel, *Exegetical Method: A Student's Handbook* (trans. E.V.N. Goetchius and M.J. O'Connell; revised edn; New York: Seabury, 1981) esp. 1–5, 30–36, 49–50.

2 (trans. W.F. Moulton; 3rd edn; Edinburgh: T. & T. Clark, 1882).

3 Bultmann, "Is Exegesis without Presuppositions Possible?" 291.

4 J.P. Louw, "Sociolinguistics and its Role in Text Analysis," in J.P. Louw (ed.), *Sociolinguistics and Communication* (UBS Monograph Series 1; London: United Bible Societies, 1986) 111, 112; cf. V.N. Webb, "Some Aspects of the Sociolinguistics of Bible Translation and Exegesis, and of Religious Language," in Louw (ed.), *Sociolinguistics and Communication*, 80. See also G. Downing, "Meanings," in *What about the New Testament?*

In 1961, James Barr published his *The Semantics of Biblical Language*,[5] making biblical scholars aware of some of their more obvious abuses of sound linguistic principles, such as contrasting Hebrew and Greek thought patterns on the basis of perceived linguistic differences, using questionable etymologies to establish lexical data, and confusing word and concept, to name a few. But the role of language in New Testament exegesis is much greater than simply correcting a few abuses carried to the extreme. It lies at the heart of serious and faithful textual analysis. Unfortunately, as late as 1975, Lars Rydbeck, a Greek grammarian commenting on the current state of research into New Testament Greek grammar, said, "today research into post-classical Greek in general and New Testament Greek in particular has come almost to a standstill." One of the reasons he gives for this is that "there is a prevalent but false assumption that everything in New Testament Greek scholarship has been done already."[6] That this situation continues to draw such comment is much to be regretted, since these same concerns were raised earlier by C.F.D. Moule in his 1952 Cambridge inaugural lecture, *The Language of the New Testament*.[7] His *An Idiom Book of New Testament Greek*, published in 1953,[8] was an important step in trying to remedy this situation, but his followers have not been many. In recent days, however, there has been increased interest in certain circles in the field of Greek linguistics. Much of this research has yet to permeate the entire discipline, but recent advances are worth being made aware of for their practical exegetical implications alone. In this chapter, I will attempt to describe a few of the more recent advances in Greek linguistics, draw out several significant points about one of the most exciting areas of research, Greek verbal structure, and conclude with several important guidelines for future research.

2. *Exegesis as Linguistics*

Exegesis as linguistics includes at least two major parts, lexis or the analysis of vocabulary, and grammar or the use of these words or the elements that make them up. Obviously, each of these areas could be treated at significant length, as each is being done by competent linguists. To prompt further reflection, however, I will introduce each of them briefly.

(Festschrift C.F. Evans; ed. M. Hooker and C. Hickling; London: SCM Press, 1975) 127–42; V.S. Poythress, "Analysing a Biblical Text: Some Important Linguistic Distinctions," *SJT* 32 (1979) 13–37.

5 (Oxford: Oxford University Press, 1961).

6 "What Happened to New Testament Grammar after Albert Debrunner?" *NTS* 21 (1974–75) 427.

7 (Cambridge: Cambridge University Press, 1952).

8 (2nd edn; Cambridge: Cambridge University Press, 1959 [1953]).

A. *Lexis or Vocabulary*

If as a result of Barr's work scholars are conscious of abuses of sound linguistic principles in the area of the lexicon, many will think that the task of linguistics is complete. But what is the method for study of vocabulary? The most widely used is the traditional lexicography of Liddell–Scott, and Bauer–Arndt–Gingrich–Danker.[9] This method works on the principle of translational equivalents or glosses. In other words, if we don't know what the word means we look it up, since the meaning of a word is what the dictionary says it is. Recent complaints that Liddell–Scott's or Bauer's lexicons are out of date because other words have been discovered which provide other translations do not either change this approach or solve the pressing problem of what meaning is all about. The lexicon is a vital tool, but it is all too frequently overlooked that the lexicon provides nothing more than a classification of meanings extrapolated from contexts. It does not establish meanings, which may be determined according to various criteria.

For example, a look at just a single linguistics book written as an introduction to the subject reveals the following definitions of meaning, each one of them directly applicable at least to the study of the lexicon.[10] There are others as well.

1. *Referential Theory*. The referential theory is one in which "the meaning of an expression is what it refers to, or stands for." This theory has had continuing currency, especially in an age which attempts to be very scientific, often in terms of the physical world. "Fido" means Fido your pet, and "dog" means

9 H.G. Liddell and R. Scott, *A Greek–English Lexicon* (rev. H.S. Jones with R. McKenzie, and E.A. Barber; 9th edn; Oxford: Clarendon Press, 1968); W. Bauer, *A Greek–English Lexicon of the New Testament and Other Early Christian Literature* (trans. W.F. Arndt and F.W. Gingrich; rev. F.W. Gingrich and F.W. Danker; 2nd edn; Chicago: University of Chicago Press, 1979).

10 J. Lyons, *Language, Meaning and Context* (London: Fontana, 1981) 30–31 for the following quotations. Several of the examples cited are suggested by G.B. Caird, *The Language and Imagery of the Bible* (London: Duckworth, 1980) 37ff., and E. Wendland and E.A. Nida, "Lexicography and Bible Translating," in J.P. Louw (ed.), *Lexicography and Translation* (Roggebaai: Bible Society of South Africa, 1985) 1–52. The lexicon has been the most widely written about area of New Testament Greek grammar. See also A.C. Thiselton, "Semantics and New Testament Interpretation," in *New Testament Interpretation: Essays on Principles and Methods* (ed. I.H. Marshall; Grand Rapids: Eerdmans, 1977) 75–104; *idem*, "Language and Meaning in Religion," in *New International Dictionary of New Testament Theology* (3 vols.; ed. C. Brown; Grand Rapids: Zondervan, 1978) 3.1127–32; M. Silva, *Biblical Words and their Meaning: An Introduction to Lexical Semantics* (2nd edn; Grand Rapids: Zondervan, 1994 [1983]); and D.A. Cruse, *Lexical Semantics* (Cambridge Textbooks in Linguistics; Cambridge: Cambridge University Press, 1986). See also ch. 4 in this volume, pp. 49–74.

either the class of dogs or the properties they all share. Thus, "the place where the lord your God shall choose as a dwelling for his name" (Deut 12:10) referred to Zion for Jews and Gerizim for Samaritans (John 4:20).

2. *Ideational or Mentalistic Theory*. The ideational or mentalistic theory is one in which "the meaning of an expression is the idea, or concept, associated with it in the mind of anyone who knows it." Related to the referential theory, this theory adds a mentalistic dimension, that is, an object brings to mind a meaning which is expressed via a linguistic sign. Thus σῶμα has a variety of meanings on the basis of the idea associated with it in the minds of users: the body of a person (Matt 6:25), or an animal (Jas 3:3), or a plant (1 Cor 15:37–38); heavenly bodies (1 Cor 15:40); the total person (Rom 12:1); slaves (Rev 18:13); reality (Col 2:17); human nature from a physical perspective (Rom 8:13), and a corporate entity consisting of various persons (Rom 12:5).

3. *Meaning-is-Use Theory*. For the meaning-is-use theory "the meaning of an expression is determined by, if not identical with, its use in the language." This theory has been supported by some recent philosophical thought. Greek κόσμος, while translated "world" in many instances, may be used of anything from the entire universe (John 17:5) to humankind (John 12:19) to a small subgroup of humankind (1 John 2:2), depending upon how it is used. This category is particularly important in determining meanings when grammatical forms are used in a variety of ways. For example, the so-called articular adjective, οἱ πολλοί, is used like a noun, as is the phrase οἱ περὶ Παῦλον, expanding the boundaries of the Greek lexicon to include items larger than the simple word.

4. *Truth-Conditional Theory*. The truth-conditional theory is one in which "the meaning of an expression is its contribution to the truth-conditions of the sentences containing it." This theory has been advocated by many recent linguists. Are the truth conditions, that is, the conditions under which an expression is true, of the phrase "kingdom of heaven" in Matthew the same as "kingdom of God" in Luke? If they are then the phrases might be considered to have the same meaning, or be synonymous.

There have been ardent supporters and critics of each of the above theories. For example, the major weakness of the first, referential theory, besides its placing supreme emphasis on the word and not the larger discourse unit, is its failure to be comprehensive and treat lexical items without physical referents, such as "beauty" or "round." In an attempt to overcome some of these difficulties, this theory has been promoted in an expanded form by the linguist John Lyons in terms of a referential-sense-denotation scheme, and has proved very helpful in a number of recent articles.[11] The second, the ideational or mentalistic theory, is subject to the same criticisms as the referential theory, and is most widely known from its abuse by, for example, the *Theological Dictionary of the New Testament*,[12] which Barr widely criticized (e.g. illegitimate totality transfer, when all ideas are heaped upon the single use of the lexical item).[13] The third theory, meaning is use, has become very popular of late, although it has been criticized for failing to provide a rigorous criterion for evaluation of meaning, as well as almost encouraging a blurring of traditional grammatical categories (e.g. noun, adjective, etc.). And the fourth, truth-conditional semantics, has become popular lately especially in terms of Chomskyan or transformational grammar, in which analysis tries to determine if basic phrases at the deep structure have the same truth-conditions. If they do, then their surface manifestations have the same meaning. This method has been widely criticized for a variety of reasons, but a major one is the number of assumptions which must be made, for example, about the human mind, apart from concrete linguistic data. I will not spend any more time on this important area of lexis, although it should be clear that determining something as apparently simple as the meaning of a word requires a solid and conscious methodological basis.

B. *Grammar*

Of more relevance here is the second area of linguistics, grammar. It has been expressed to me on more than one occasion, as Rydbeck has indicated, that it is unnecessary to investigate Greek grammar because all of the major problems were solved in the nineteenth century by grammarians who were dependent upon the Hellenistic Greek grammarians themselves. Those who know a little of the history of Greek language study will ask which of the two major schools of thought in the Hellenistic period is being referred to, Dionysius Thrax or the Stoics? This says nothing of the fact that most scholars have found the ancient grammarians woefully lacking in descriptive powers. And which school of thought in the nineteenth century, the time-based view or the one based on *Aktionsart*? The assertion that all of the questions have been answered usually reveals a lack of thorough acquaintance with the history of grammatical discussion and a lack of awareness of developments in the field of modern linguistics.[14]

---

[11] Included here would be F.S. Spencer, "Beyond Trench's Study of Synonyms," *ExpTim* 99 (1987–88) 140–44.

[12] (10 vols.; trans. G.W. Bromiley; Grand Rapids: Eerdmans, 1964–76).

[13] Barr, *Semantics of Biblical Language*, esp. 206–62.

[14] See D.D. Schmidt, *Hellenistic Greek Grammar and Noam Chomsky: Nominalizing Transformations* (SBLDS 62; Chico, CA: Scholars Press, 1981) 3–13, for a history of New Testament grammars. Cf. R.H. Robins, *A Short History of Linguistics* (2nd edn; London: Longman, 1979) esp. 9–44; J. Pinborg, "Classical Antiquity: Greece," *Current Trends in*

As any student of Greek knows, the verb lies at the heart of serious analysis of the Greek language, if for no other reason than the verb can do so much and consequently appears in so many different constructions. A verb form, for example, sometimes takes on characteristics of an adjective or a noun or even an adverb, besides performing more traditional verbal functions. Consequently, much of the recent work has concentrated upon the verb, and I wish to spend some time describing several recent developments. Currently, in the study of the Greek of the New Testament, there are at least four schools of thought regarding the use of its verbs, probably the most widely disputed and most interesting area for both pure linguistic analysis and theology.

1. *The Rationalists*. Winer, the German grammarian—a member of what is sometimes called the rationalist school—argued that virtually every use of a tense follows its so-called designated temporal function.[15] In other words, aorists and imperfects are past-referring, presents are present-referring, and futures are future-referring, although Winer acknowledges the use of the historic present in the Gospels, an anomaly in his system. This model has a number of obvious difficulties. For example, it leaves little room for so-called "gnomic" uses, such as Rom 5:7 ("on behalf of a good person perhaps someone indeed dares [τολμᾷ] to die"), and there can be no such things as non past-referring aorists, such as John 15:6 ("if anyone abides in me, he is cast [ἐβλήθη] out and burned [ἐξηράνθη]"). Whereas most scholars today disagree with this model on theoretical grounds, when it comes to actual interpretation many find the approach comfortable since it is similar to English and is still found in the vast majority of beginning Greek textbooks.

2. *Chomskyan Linguistics*. A second school of thought makes use of Chomskyan linguistics in one of its various forms, and is concerned to formulate the "rules" of the language by which the syntax of Greek, that is, its surface structure, is derived from kernel or basic sentences that reside in the deep structure.[16] Thus in Rom 1:17 ὁ δὲ δίκαιος ἐκ πίστεως ζήσεται ("the

---

Linguistics 13 (1975) 92–94; and R. Kühner and B. Gerth, *Ausführliche Grammatik der griechischen Sprache* (2 vols.; 4th edn; 1897; repr. Leverkusen: Gottschalksche, 1955) 1.129–200. See S.E. Porter, "Tense Terminology and Greek Language Study: A Linguistic Re-Evaluation," *Sheffield Working Papers in Language and Linguistics* 3 (1986) 77–86, reprinted and expanded as ch. 3 in this volume (pp. 39–48), for an assessment of beginning Greek grammars according to linguistic criteria.

15 Winer, *Treatise on the Grammar of New Testament Greek*, 330–50.

16 See, for example, Schmidt, *Hellenistic Greek Grammar*; J.P. Louw, *Semantics of New Testament Greek* (Chico, CA: Scholars Press; Philadelphia: Fortress Press, 1982), from whom the following example is taken (p. 105; but criticized by I. Ronca, *Acta Classica* 28 [1985] 102–103), and R. Wonneberger, *Syntax und Exegese: Eine generative Theorie der*

righteous by faith shall live") may reveal one of two "deep" structures: "righteous by faith" as the noun phrase, with "shall live" as the verb phrase; or "righteous" as the noun phrase, with "shall live by faith" as the verb phrase. Each reveals the same Noun–Verb deep structure, in which one has either an extended noun or an extended verb phrase. Overlooked without comment is that NV structure is only one possible word order of these Greek elements. But since truth conditions are the criteria for semantics in this model, further analysis is deemed unnecessary (the surface sentence has been translated into its most basic components), although quite possibly at the expense here of important insights into word order, as Stephen Levinsohn in his 1987 monograph, *Textual Connections in Acts*,[17] has shown, or at the expense of other factors. For example, is it obvious that a genitive phrase such as "love of God" is derived from the kernel sentence "God loves"? Or is it possible this phrase could mean "we love God," a very different kernel sentence? And how do we decide? This theory does not at first blush appear to be concerned with the verb. This is true, except that Chomskyan linguistics has derived its theoretical basis from and performed the great majority of its analysis upon English; consequently, English verbal categories of time, etc., are usually imposed upon Greek when this model is invoked.

3. *Aktionsart Theory*. A third school of thought is that verbs in Greek are based upon *Aktionsart*, that is, an objective description of action.[18] So a present verb represents linear action, an aorist represents punctiliar action, and the perfect represents the present result of a past action. This analysis of Greek grew out of comparative philological work of the last century, especially increased awareness of the relationship of Greek to other languages of common Indo-European descent, and has done much to push forward historical linguistics. But it also represents the point at which most grammatical work on the language of the New Testament stopped, as Rydbeck laments. This deeply enshrined view of grammar persists in large part because it is so widely disseminated through

griechischen Syntax und ihr Beitrag zur Auslegung des Neuen Testaments, dargestellt an 2. Korinther 5.2f. und Römer 3.21–26 (BBET 13; Bern: Peter Lang, 1979).

17 (SBLMS 31; Atlanta: Scholars Press, 1987).

18 The New Testament grammars that follow this school of thought are legion. See especially J.H. Moulton, *Prolegomena*, vol. 1 of *A Grammar of New Testament Greek* (3rd edn; Edinburgh: T. & T. Clark, 1908 [1906]); A.T. Robertson, *A Grammar of the Greek New Testament in the Light of Historical Research* (4th edn; Nashville: Broadman, 1934 [1914]); F. Blass and A. Debrunner, *A Greek Grammar of the New Testament and Other Early Christian Literature* (trans. R.W. Funk; Chicago: University of Chicago Press, 1961 [1896]); Moule, *Idiom Book*; N. Turner, *Syntax*, vol. 3 of *A Grammar of New Testament Greek*, by J.H. Moulton (Edinburgh: T. & T. Clark, 1963). One of the grammarians who was most crucial for the development of *Aktionsart* theory was K. Brugmann, *Griechische Grammatik* (ed. A. Thumb; 4th edn; Munich: Beck, 1913 [1885]) esp. 538–52.

the standard reference grammars, such as Blass–Debrunner and Robertson.

A crucial point in discussing the function of the Greek verb, especially in relation to the theory of *Aktionsart*, was reached in 1972, with the publication of an article by Frank Stagg, entitled "The Abused Aorist."[19] In it he showed many instances which apparently contradict *Aktionsart* analysis of the action. For example, sometimes a present verb is used where the action is not linear, for example Luke 19:13, where the verb "come" (ἔρχομαι) refers to a specific point of arrival; or an aorist is used duratively, for example John 2:20, with reference to the forty-six years building the temple (οἰκοδομήθη); or a perfect verb does not describe a past event with abiding results, for example John 1:15, where John bore witness concerning the logos and cried (κέκραγεν) saying that Jesus was the one he spoke of. And what of iterative aorists, for example 2 Cor 11:24–25, where Paul speaks of receiving thirty-nine lashes, being beaten three times (ἐραβδίσθην), and being shipwrecked three times (ἐναυάγησα)? Stagg also illustrated how interpreters have been led astray in their analysis of the Greek text by reliance upon outmoded conceptual frameworks. Yet abuses still persist. For example, Seyoon Kim unfortunately argues for the centrality of the Damascus road experience in Paul's theology on the basis of use of the aorist tense: "The aorist ἔλαμψεν [2 Cor 4:6] refers back to a definite point of time in the past, the moment of the Damascus event."[20]

4. *Verbal Aspect Theory*. A fourth school of thought—and one gaining greatly in influence—is that verbs in Greek function according to the semantic category of verbal aspect,[21] which is the speaker or writer's subjective view of a process

---

19 *JBL* 91 (1972) 222–31. Cf. C.R. Smith, "Errant Aorist Interpreters," *GTJ* 2 (1981) 205–26.

20 *The Origin of Paul's Gospel* (WUNT 30; Tübingen: Mohr–Siebeck, 1981) 7.

21 Most noteworthy are K.L. McKay, *Greek Grammar for Students: A Concise Grammar of Classical Attic with Special Reference to Aspect in the Verb* (Canberra: Australian National University, 1974); *idem*, "Syntax in Exegesis," *TynBul* 23 (1972) 39–57; *idem*, "On the Perfect and Other Aspects in New Testament Greek," *NovT* 23 (1981) 289–329; *idem*, "Aspect in Imperatival Constructions in New Testament Greek," *NovT* 27 (1985) 201–26; *idem*, "Style and Significance in the Language of John 21.15–17," *NovT* 27 (1985) 319–33; now *idem*, *A New Syntax of the Verb in New Testament Greek: An Aspectual Approach* (Studies in Biblical Greek 5; New York: Peter Lang, 1994); S.E. Porter, *Verbal Aspect in the Greek of the New Testament, with Reference to Tense and Mood* (Studies in Biblical Greek 1; New York: Peter Lang, 1989) esp. 75–109; now *idem*, *Idioms of the Greek New Testament* (Biblical Languages: Greek 2; 2nd edn; Sheffield: JSOT Press, 1994 [1992]) 20–49 and *passim*; B.M. Fanning, *Verbal Aspect in New Testament Greek* (Oxford Theological Monographs; Oxford: Clarendon Press, 1990). See reviews of the last two works in *ExpTim* 101 (1989–90) 346–47 and 103 (1991–92) 54. Fanning and I note our differences in Part I of S.E. Porter and D.A. Carson (eds.), *Biblical Greek Language and Linguistics: Open Questions in Current Research* (JSNTSup 80; Sheffield: Sheffield Academic Press,

or event. There are several important variations upon this school of thought, but those who hold this position believe temporal categories are not of primary concern in use of the verb. One of the problems with investigating tense distinctions in languages is that the names of tenses are based only on typical functions of the tenses concerned, and do not capture the full range of functions that a given form may express. This is potentially very misleading, because it is tempting to see the typical function that motivates the form name as *the* function, that is, to treat a short label as far more informative and exhaustive than it really is. For example, in English, the progressive present is used in contexts referring to present time: "I am reading this paper now," but what about "I am reading this paper tomorrow"? The verb form is exactly the same, but now I am referring to the future. This form has a variety of temporal uses, the present being one and the future being another equally legitimate.

There are two issues of special relevance in this discussion: temporal reference and kind of action. In Greek, "present" and "future" are temporal categories while "imperfect" and "perfect" are named according to the kind of action or the way the action is described. From this no one would suppose the relation between the "present" and "imperfect." And there is the "aorist," which some have characterized as being "without boundary," although this is hardly a helpful description. This leads to a useful and necessary distinction between verbal form and function. When Greek grammars speak of punctiliar presents, future presents, present aorists, they are speaking of two very different things. They are speaking of a verb form—that is, present, aorist, etc.—used in a certain function—that is, it refers to present time, future time, etc. But a phrase such as "present used of past time" still misses the basis of the Greek tenses, which is reference to describing the kind of action. Therefore tense categories should include some component to reflect this. Consequently, many scholars are turning to the category of verbal aspect. Greek can be neatly described as having three verbal aspects—the perfective (represented by the aorist), the imperfective (represented by the present/imperfect), and the stative (represented by the perfect/pluperfect).

There are various ways that these verbal aspects and their relationships may be described, some of them quite technical. But metaphors or analogies are often helpful to grasp a linguistic concept. Two must suffice here, although I list others elsewhere.[22] The first regards planes of discourse. This analogy is drawn from a spatial representation of the world. The planes of discourse can be divided into foreground and background. The Greek aorist is the "ground" or "background tense" and the Greek present/imperfect is the "figure" or

---

1993) 18–82. This volume is reviewed by J. Mateos in *FN* 7.14 (1994) 215–22.

22 See Porter, *Verbal Aspect*, 89–97 and 109, for technical discussion including markedness and a systemic linguistic display.

"foreground tense." In Greek often the basic narrative is laid down by the third person aorist, a common trait of the background tense, while the imperfect/present introduces significant characters or makes appropriate climactic references to concrete situations, typical of the foreground tense. When an extended description is given, the foreground tense is often used. Greek also has a third plane of exposition called the "frontground," providing a narrower range of the characteristic features of the figure tense, that is, it is discrete, well-defined and contoured, much more so than the present/imperfect and the aorist tenses. In Acts 16:1–5, the author uses the aorist to establish the basic framework of events: Paul arrived (κατήντησεν) in Derbe and Lystra, where there was a disciple named Timothy. The foreground aspect (imperfect) is then used to highlight a significant feature about this new character, Timothy: he was commended (ἐμαρτυρεῖτο) by the brethren. The background line then continues with the aorist (ἠθέλεσεν, ἐξελθεῖν, λαβών, περιέτεμεν). The reason for his circumcision is given with the frontground aspect, reinforced by the foreground aspect: for all knew (ᾔδεισαν [stative]) that his father was (ὑπῆρχεν [imperfective]) Greek. The matter of doctrine is obviously important in this passage, thus when the narrative continues, since the mission of Paul and his companions is related to teaching and building up churches, the foreground aspect is used (διεπορεύοντο, παρεδίδοσαν, φυλάσσειν) with the frontground aspect again employed to describe the dogma being guarded—the one determined (τὰ κεκριμένα) by the apostles and elders in Jerusalem. The successful result, again in the foreground aspect, is church growth (ἐστερεοῦντο, ἐπερίσσευον). The next narrative incident (16:6) continues with the background aspect (διῆλθον).

If each aspect represents the author's grammaticalized view of an event, it is also logical to ask what that picture might be. Let me draw the picture of a parade. If I am a television correspondent in the BBC helicopter flying over the parade, I view the parade as a process in its immediacy from a vantage outside the action as "perfective," that is, in its entirety as a single and complete whole. If I am a spectator sitting in the grandstand watching the parade pass by in front of me, I view the process from within, as "imperfective," that is, as an event in progress. And if I am the parade manager considering all of the conditions in existence at this parade, including not only all the arrangements that are coming to fruition but all of the accompanying events that allow the parade to be operative, I view the process not in its particulars or its immediacy but as "stative," that is, as a condition or state of affairs in existence. As Wallace says of how a linguistic feature such as verbal aspect is used by writers or speakers in organizing their discourses and consequently how it is interpreted by readers or hearers, "the speaker uses [linguistic] categories to structure an utterance…into more or less salient points, and the listener uses such categories as clues to interpreting the speaker's verbal picture."[23]

There are two important points to these analogies. (1) External temporal reference does not come into play here, for example, there is not necessarily anything inherently past about the perfective aspect. Because Greek does not grammaticalize time in its tense forms, some become uncomfortable and think that it means that Greek speakers did not know how to make temporal distinctions. This is clearly not the case, as seen from analysis of verb function in other, similarly structured languages or from Greek. Instead of grammaticalizing temporal reference, Greek relies upon temporal indicators, such as time words, reference to places and people, and discourse structures to establish temporal relations. (2) Although each aspect is describing the same set of circumstances, each contributes a unique perspective on the process, the speaker's subjective view of it. In Rom 8:11, when Paul says ὁ ἐγείρας Χριστὸν ἐκ νεκρῶν ("the one who raised Christ from the dead"), he views the resurrection of Christ as a complete event. When Paul uses the imperfective in 2 Cor 1:9 (τῷ θεῷ τῷ ἐγείροντι τοὺς νεκρούς ["the God who is raising the dead"]), he views the process as one that is in progress. And in 2 Tim 2:8 (Ἰησοῦν Χριστὸν ἐγηγερμένον ἐκ νεκρῶν ["Jesus Christ raised from the dead"]), the author emphasizes the state of Christ's risenness.

I hope that this summary of several schools of thought on the function of the Greek verb helps to show several of the key issues in the discussion, and one solution that I find particularly convincing and helpful. It directly addresses the several major shortfalls of previously proposed models of Greek verbal structure and it does a highly successful job of actually explaining the variety of Greek verbal function, including such things as the gnomic aorist, the historic present, etc.

3. *Conclusion*

Let me suggest several points to consider in discussing the grammar of Greek, or of any ancient language. My treatment here is not designed to minimize the importance of other exegetical questions that might be asked, but to show the importance of clear thinking about Greek grammar for New Testament exegesis.

First, of the writing of grammars there can be no end. English is the most widely written-about language in history. One would think that it would be relatively easy to construct a highly persuasive and complete grammar of

23 S. Wallace, "Figure and Ground: The Interrelationships of Linguistic Categories," in *Tense–Aspect: Between Semantics and Pragmatics* (ed. P.J. Hopper; Amsterdam: Benjamins, 1982) 214.

English since there is an abundance of native speakers to test any given theory. But theories continue to be created,[24] always attempting to have higher descriptive and explanatory powers. In this regard most ancient languages are greatly understudied, since the results of "modern" linguistic study have not yet been applied to them. It is here that much resistance has been found to appropriating the best insights of recent linguistics. Just because the languages are called ancient does not mean that the methods for studying them must be ancient also.

Secondly, no theory can ever hope to explain all areas of language usage to an equally satisfactory degree, since a grammar is not the language. As McKay says,

> Some apparent anomalies may be due to the incompleteness of our knowledge: for all the richness of extant Greek literature we need to remember that we have only selections of the language spread over many generations and a variety of dialects. The test of any hypothesis, therefore, is not that it resolves all doubts but that it offers the most consistent explanation, leaving few anomalies.[25]

The Greek language has a history extending over almost three millennia of change and development, and the remains of ancient Greek are quite large. The grammars of a language are of necessity static, but language is dynamic, always changing because the speakers and users of the language are always changing it as they use it.

The Greek future tense is a good example worth exploring. The future developed late, related in origin to the subjunctive. Semantically, it is related both to the subjunctive and optative and to the indicative, though it is not identical with any of them. Morphologically, it resembles the indicative, with a short connecting vowel, and has participles and infinitives, but it does not have subjunctive and optative forms. It may appear in contexts with future reference, although it also appears in commanding, descriptive, timeless and omnitemporal or gnomic contexts as well. Any grammar of Greek must account for this variety of factors.[26] Not all will be agreed on all the analyses.

Thirdly, there have been two distorting tendencies in analysis of Hellenistic and New Testament Greek. First, use of categories from Attic Greek has often

---

[24] Cf. J. Lyons, *Language and Linguistics: An Introduction* (Cambridge: Cambridge University Press, 1981) 43, who calls a language system a "theoretical construct."

[25] McKay, *Grammar*, 214. Cf. N.E. Collinge, "Some Reflexions on Comparative Historical Syntax," *Archivum Linguisticum* 12 (1960) 83: "If an economic description of the *valor* of a structure, or a systemic term found in it, leaks some few apparently intractable examples, it is immaterial whether these are resolved by the admission that the analyst cannot know the full context or by his allowing for a feature of *parole* (provided one or other admission is credible)."

[26] My proposal is in Porter, *Verbal Aspect*, 403–40.

distorted analysis of Hellenistic Greek as the standard language (*lingua franca*) of the Greco-Roman world, because scholars expected Hellenistic Greek users to display Attic competence. Because Hellenistic Greek speakers no longer grammaticalized, for example, the dual number does not mean that their language was in any way inferior to Attic Greek, which itself did not show uniform usage, much less that Hellenistic Greek speakers could not conceptualize duality. The same applies to numerous other changes in the language, for example reduced use of the optative. Secondly, many have analyzed the Greek of the New Testament as simply a veneer over Semitic thought-patterns. Recent work in bilingualism and investigation of language-use in the ancient Mediterranean world have shown the difficulty with such a conclusion. Many if not most inhabitants of Palestine were bilingual, with Greek the common language of the ancient Hellenistic world. There is little evidence that Semitic languages exercised any significant linguistic interference in the normal development of the Greek language. Paul's use of Greek to communicate with geographically scattered churches provides evidence along these lines.[27]

Fourthly, the peculiarities of a "purely epigraphic language"[28] must be taken into account. With any modern language native speakers play an important role in formulating its grammar. But for those languages with solely written remains problems are created on several fronts. First, the progressive and innovative force in language usage—the spoken usage—is removed from consideration and study. To some extent then all analysis of this usage is of a language that is by nature anachronistic and already dated, and in some instances even mannered and self-conscious. This applies to the papyri as well as (or perhaps especially) Polybius. Secondly, a selective and necessarily limited corpus remains. The epigraphic remains of Greek are larger than those of any other ancient language (and approximately ten times those of ancient Latin), which is to be applauded, but the parameters of even this corpus are finite.

Fifthly, formulation of a grammar must consider the difference between the items found within the language and translation into another language for analysis. As Henry Gleason says, "Translation is a very inadequate means of expressing meanings and must always be used with great caution."[29] Consequently, unnecessary problems are occasionally imposed upon the studied language on the basis of the presence of these problems in the language of

---

27 See Porter, *Verbal Aspect*, 111–61.

28 Collinge, "Some Reflexions," 79.

29 See H.A. Gleason, Jr., *An Introduction to Descriptive Linguistics* (revised edn; New York: Holt, Rinehart & Winston, 1961) 77. J. Lyons, *Structural Semantics: An Analysis of Part of the Vocabulary of Plato* (Publications of the Philological Society 20; Oxford: Blackwell, 1963) 97–99, esp. 98: translations (of terms for skills, etc.) "cannot claim to be adequate statements of meaning in any scientific sense."

discussion, or real problems in the language are overlooked because they are not problems within the language of discussion. For example, it is a commonplace among some grammarians that there is no meaningful difference between the Greek aorist and imperfect because the translation of these as preterites is identical in some languages, such as English or German. Or some grammarians posit punctiliar and durative presents in Greek on the basis of the simple and progressive English present used in translation. A classic example of over-reliance on supposed translational equivalents is J.R. Mantey's analysis of the periphrastic construction found in Matt 16:19 and 18:18. Mantey—arguing against what he sees as a Roman Catholic interpretation of the verses—claims that the future auxiliary and perfect passive participle should be translated as an English future perfect passive: that is, "shall have been bound/loosed," where future binding or loosing is the result of a first binding or loosing by God that has occurred before the time of speaking or writing. Mantey assumes that an English future perfect, like the Greek future perfect, conceives of a future event that comes about as the result of an event prior to the point of speaking or writing. But Mantey's understanding of the English tense is questionable, since the English future perfect is an absolute/relative tense. This means that there is an absolute reference to the future in relation to the speaker but a relative reference to the event that precedes this future event. Thus "I will have arrived next Tuesday and I am leaving tomorrow" is a legitimate use of the English future perfect which does not require reference to a past event with future result. Unfortunately, Mantey uses this English model to understand the Greek construction, which, as I have indicated elsewhere, is best interpreted without imposing this temporal framework.[30] English translation, therefore, as is so often the case, is not necessarily a reliable guide to understanding Greek tenses.

Much more could be profitably said about the fundamental, first level of linguistics. But what I have said should be enough to raise awareness that, for those interested in New Testament study, a critical understanding of the original language is a vital and necessary part of the discipline which has long been neglected, but which is ready for further exploration. There are some promising and worthwhile efforts being made.

---

30 J.R. Mantey, "The Mistranslation of the Perfect Tense in John 20:23, Mt 16:19, and Mt 18:18," *JBL* 58 (1939) 243–49. Cf. B. Comrie, *Tense* (Cambridge Textbooks in Linguistics; Cambridge: Cambridge University Press, 1984) 69–74; Porter, *Verbal Aspect*, esp. 471–74; *idem*, "Vague Verbs, Periphrastics, and Matthew 16:19," *FN* 1.2 (1988) 157–62, the entire essay of which is reprinted as ch. 6 in this volume, pp. 103–24.

CHAPTER TWO

IN DEFENSE OF VERBAL ASPECT*

1. *Introduction: Verbal Aspect in Greek Grammar and Linguistics*

The growth and development of an academic discipline is never completely straightforward. There are at least as many false starts as successful hypotheses, but the false starts are often forgotten. Like the stories of wars, the history of scientific discovery is written by the victors. To use the useful terminology of T. Kuhn, the history of discovery for virtually every discipline that considers itself to be scientifically rigorous is one of periods of normal science disrupted by often tumultuous paradigm shifts.[1] These shifts are rarely graceful, since there is not only the issue of accuracy (or truth) at play, but there are numerous personal, political and social issues at stake as well.

In this progression, digression, retrogression and further progression, there are several possible reactions that bear directly upon discussion of verbal aspect. One is to ignore work which stretches the traditional categories and to pretend that all is normal and that normal is in fact the way things are. It is disheartening to find that few recent biblical commentators include insightful comments upon Greek grammar, and especially verbal structure. Perhaps it is out of ignorance, or perhaps it is out of fear that many "assured" conclusions may not be so well grounded. Another reaction is to jump on any new

---

* This essay is reprinted with the permission of Sheffield Academic Press, from S.E. Porter and D.A. Carson (eds.), *Biblical Greek Language and Linguistics: Open Questions in Current Research* (JSNTSup 80; Sheffield: Sheffield Academic Press, 1993) 26–45. Slight adjustments have been made in the text in the light of its originally appearing as one of four chapters in Part I (pp. 18–82) on two recent works on verbal aspect, my *Verbal Aspect in the Greek of the New Testament, with Reference to Tense and Mood* (Studies in Biblical Greek 1; New York: Peter Lang, 1989) and B.M. Fanning, *Verbal Aspect in New Testament Greek* (Oxford Theological Monographs; Oxford: Clarendon Press, 1990). See the recent review of *Biblical Greek Language and Linguistics* by J. Mateos in *FN* 7.14 (1994) 215–22.

1 T. Kuhn, *The Structure of Scientific Revolutions* (2nd edn; Chicago: University of Chicago Press, 1970); cf. more recently V. Poythress, *Science and Hermeneutics* (Foundations of Contemporary Interpretation 6; Grand Rapids: Zondervan, 1988) esp. 39–49.

hypothesis as the answer to all questions, thus circumventing further fruitful enquiry. One is reminded of rhetoric regarding redaction criticism as the panacea for understanding all Synoptic difficulties. A third reaction is to recognize the validity of a new construct but—in resisting its full force—to make multifarious attempts to reconcile and harmonize the old perspective with the new. This pattern has been repeated numerous times in the history of scientific enquiry, and biblical studies is particularly susceptible to it, since it tends to be a reactionary discipline. Without analysing the basis of many of its current beliefs, it often attempts to incorporate new ideas into its existing structures, frequently failing to ask whether such a synthesis is methodologically possible (or even desirable). Elsewhere I have argued that work on reader-response criticism is of such a kind.[2]

The study of ancient languages, in particular of biblical languages, is experiencing a commendable—and I would say necessary—re-orientation in the light of developments in modern linguistics. As biblical scholars, we are at last responding to L. Rydbeck's call.[3] Modern linguistics is, as the name implies, a fairly recent discipline, delimited and developed within the twentieth century. Contrary to some, it cannot be equated simply with the ability to speak many languages (i.e. being a polyglot) or with the traditional concerns of classical philologists regarding the history of the language, the primacy of its literary remnants, and reconstructions of rather arcane etymologies. Instead, modern linguistics has its own assumptions (even if not all linguists agree what they are) and its own way of treating this phenomenon called language.[4] This is not the place to define these assumptions, except to say that most linguists are what might (for simplicity's sake) be called synthetic, viewing language as an autonomous system of interdependent structures, each warranting its own analysis but not fully comprehensible apart from those linguistic elements to which it is connected. This is a significant insight from modern linguistics, one which needs to be appreciated in examination of any language, including the Greek of the New Testament.[5]

For whatever reason—and speculation could be quite profitable—the

---

2 See S.E. Porter, "Why Hasn't Reader-Response Criticism Caught on in New Testament Studies?" *Journal of Literature and Theology* 4 (1990) 283–84.

3 L. Rydbeck, "What Happened to Greek Grammar after Albert Debrunner?" *NTS* 21 (1974–75) 424–27. I hope that the response is not in the direct shadow of Blass–Debrunner, however. See S.E. Porter, "What Should a Modern Grammar of an Ancient Language Look Like?: A Critique of the Schmidt Proposal for a New Blass/Debrunner/Funk," *Forum* (in press, still).

4 See R. Hudson, "Some Issues on which Linguists Can Agree," *Journal of Linguistics* 17 (1981) 333–43.

5 See S.E. Porter, "Studying Ancient Languages from a Modern Linguistic Perspective: Essential Terms and Terminology," *FN* 2.2 (1989) 147–72.

discipline of biblical studies hesitates to appropriate fully developments in other related and potentially productive areas of knowledge. These include, for example, sociology, literary interpretation of various kinds, psychology and modern linguistics. But recent developments in modern linguistics have been momentous and the pace and nature of its development continue. Recent research has moved beyond traditional linguistic concerns (e.g. phonology and morphology) into syntax, semantics, pragmatics, and discourse analysis, among other areas. As far as biblical studies is concerned, this research includes what may be called primary research, such as that by K.L. McKay and J.P. Louw into verbal aspect;[6] M. Silva, Louw and S.E. Porter into semantics;[7] D.D. Schmidt

6 K.L. McKay, "Syntax in Exegesis," *TynBul* 23 (1972) 39–57; *idem*, "On the Perfect and Other Aspects in New Testament Greek," *NovT* 23 (1981) 289–329; *idem*, "Aspect in Imperatival Constructions in New Testament Greek," *NovT* 27 (1985) 201–26; *idem*, "Style and Significance in the Language of John 21.15–17," *NovT* 27 (1985) 319–33; *idem*, *Greek Grammar for Students: A Concise Grammar of Classical Attic with Special Reference to Aspect in the Verb* (Canberra: Australian National University, 1974); *idem*, "Aspectual Usage in Timeless Contexts in Ancient Greek," in *In the Footsteps of Raphael Kühner* (ed. A. Rijksbaron *et al.*; Amsterdam: Gieben, 1988) 193–208; *idem*, "Time and Aspect in New Testament Greek," *NovT* 34 (1992) 209–28; and *idem*, *A New Syntax of the Verb in New Testament Greek: An Aspectual Approach* (Studies in Biblical Greek 5; New York: Peter Lang, 1994); J.P. Louw, "On Greek Prohibitions," *Acta Classica* 2 (1959) 43–57; *idem*, "Die Semantiese Waarde van die Perfektum in Hellenistiese Grieks," *Acta Classica* 10 (1967) 23–32; *idem*, "Verbal Aspek in Grieks," *Taalfasette* 15 (1971) 13–26; and *idem*, "Verbal Aspect in the First Letter of John," *Neot* 9 (1975) 98–104. I offer analyses of McKay's and Louw's work in *Verbal Aspect*, esp. 48–49 and 337–40. Although McKay was instrumental in providing the basis for further study of verbal aspect, a comment on p. 49 of *Verbal Aspect* summarizes my view of his theoretical basis: "His tacit equation of standard tense forms with aspectual categories is not argued explicitly." This is continued in his most recent work, including "Time and Aspect in New Testament Greek," where (though misconstruing several things that I state in *Verbal Aspect*) he essentially endorses my categories of analysis, even though he questions several examples (not always convincingly). See also J.W. Voelz, "Present and Aorist Verbal Aspect—A New Proposal," *Neot* 27.1 (1993) 153–64, reviving a theory found in his doctoral thesis and published in "The Language of the New Testament," *ANRW* II.25.2 (Berlin: de Gruyter, 1984) 944–50, 966–70 (refuted in Porter, *Verbal Aspect*, 63); and C.M.J. Sicking, "The Distribution of Aorist and Present Tense Stem Forms in Greek, Especially in the Imperative (Parts 1 and 2)," *Glotta* 69 (1991) 14–43, 154–70.

7 M. Silva, "The Pauline Style as Lexical Choice: Γινώσκειν and Related Verbs," in *Pauline Studies* (Festschrift F.F. Bruce; ed. D.A. Hagner and M.J. Harris; Exeter: Paternoster, 1980) 184–207; *idem*, *Biblical Words and their Meaning: An Introduction to Lexical Semantics* (2nd edn; Grand Rapids: Zondervan, 1994 [1983]); J.P. Louw, *Semantics of New Testament Greek* (Chico, CA: Scholars Press; Philadelphia: Fortress Press, 1982); S.E. Porter, "Is *dipsuchos* (James 1,8; 4,8) a 'Christian' Word?" *Bib* 71 (1990) 469–98; *idem*, *Καταλλάσσω in Ancient Greek Literature, with Reference to the Pauline Writings* (Estudios de Filología Neotestamentaria 5; Córdoba, Spain: Ediciones El Almendro, 1994). See also ch. 4 in this volume, pp. 49–74.

and J.T. Reed into syntax;[8] and Louw and E.A. Nida, along with many others, into discourse analysis;[9] among other contributors. There have also been a significant number of works of secondary research, "translating" modern linguistics for those who do not have the time, energy, inclination or requisite background for studying or developing primary works in linguistics.[10]

Verbal aspect is a notion of fairly recent provenance. For most linguists it falls under the category of semantics, in other words it is a category—no matter what its other linguistic properties—related to meaning. In this area, work in biblical Greek has not lagged far behind discussion of the topic in other linguistic circles.[11] B. Comrie did a tremendous service in his book, *Aspect*, first published in 1976. This was the first full-length monograph in English on the topic of verbal aspect,[12] followed by the useful monographs by Ö. Dahl and

---

[8] D.D. Schmidt, *Hellenistic Greek Grammar and Noam Chomsky: Nominalizing Transformations* (SBLDS 62; Chico, CA: Scholars Press, 1981); J.T. Reed, "The Infinitive with Two Substantival Accusatives: An Ambiguous Construction?" *NovT* 33 (1991) 1–27.

[9] J.P. Louw, "Discourse Analysis and the Greek New Testament," *BT* 24 (1973) 101–18; *idem*, *A Semantic Discourse Analysis of Romans* (2 vols.; Pretoria: Department of Greek, University of Pretoria, 1987); E.A. Nida *et al.*, *Style and Discourse, with Special Reference to the Text of the Greek New Testament* (Roggebaai: Bible Society of South Africa, 1983). For a survey of the field, see now S.E. Porter, "Discourse Analysis and New Testament Studies: An Introductory Survey," in S.E. Porter and D.A. Carson (eds.), *Discourse Analysis and Other Topics in Biblical Greek* (JSNTSup 113; Sheffield: Sheffield Academic Press, 1995) 14–35.

[10] These include works by M. Silva, *God, Language and Scripture: Reading the Bible in the Light of General Linguistics* (Foundations of Contemporary Interpretation 4; Grand Rapids: Zondervan, 1990), on general linguistics (see the short review by S.E. Porter in *JSNT* Booklist 45 [1992] 127); D.A. Black, *Linguistics for Students of New Testament Greek: A Survey of Basic Concepts and Applications* (Grand Rapids: Baker, 1988), on grammatical topics (he has written a number of articles using the methodology of Louw and Nida) (see the review by S.E. Porter in *CR* [1991] 172–73); A.C. Thiselton, "Semantics and New Testament Interpretation," in *New Testament Interpretation: Essays on Principles and Methods* (ed. I.H. Marshall; Grand Rapids: Eerdmans, 1977) 75–104, on semantics; P. Cotterell and M. Turner, *Linguistics and Biblical Interpretation* (London: SPCK, 1989), on semantics and pragmatics (see the review by S.E. Porter in *CR* [1991] 77–79); D.A. Carson, *Exegetical Fallacies* (Grand Rapids: Baker, 1984), on some of the linguistic errors of exegetes; and S.E. Porter, *Idioms of the Greek New Testament* (Biblical Languages: Greek 2; 2nd edn; Sheffield: JSOT Press, 1994 [1992]), in an intermediate level grammar.

[11] Two noteworthy articles deal with these topics in meaningful ways even though they were not perhaps fully aware of the larger linguistic issues: F. Stagg, "The Abused Aorist," *JBL* 91 (1972) 222–31; C.R. Smith, "Errant Aorist Interpreters," *GTJ* 2 (1981) 205–26. There are exceptions of course, in particular J. Thorley, "Subjunctive Aktionsart in New Testament Greek: A Reassessment," *NovT* 30 (1988) 193–211; *idem*, "Aktionsart in New Testament Greek: Infinitive and Imperative," *NovT* 31 (1989) 290–313.

[12] B. Comrie, *Aspect: An Introduction to the Study of Verbal Aspect and Related Problems* (Cambridge Textbooks in Linguistics; Cambridge: Cambridge University Press,

C. Bache.[13] McKay, whose publications on this topic began in 1965, has done the most significant work over the longest period of time on Greek, especially of the New Testament.[14] There are now two full-length monographs by Porter and B.M. Fanning (582 and 471 pages respectively) devoted to verbal aspect in the Greek of the New Testament or New Testament Greek, depending upon whose title one adopts.[15] (The difference in the titles is significant, because the first discusses the New Testament as one among many corpora of Hellenistic Greek texts, while the second treats the New Testament with few significant references to extra-biblical Greek and as a bit of an oddity in the linguistic panoply of the ancient world.)[16] Although the works were done in Great Britain

---

1976). Also of relevance is his *Tense* (Cambridge Textbooks in Linguistics; Cambridge: Cambridge University Press, 1985). My evaluation of Comrie's work is found in S.E. Porter, *Verbal Aspect in the Greek of the New Testament, with Reference to Tense and Mood* (Studies in Biblical Greek 1; New York: Peter Lang, 1989) 45–47, although his perspective was widely used in formulation of my linguistic model of verbal usage in ch. 2, pp. 75–108.

13 Ö. Dahl, *Tense and Aspect Systems* (Oxford: Blackwell, 1985), and C. Bache, *Verbal Aspect: A General Theory and its Application to Present-Day English* (Odense University Studies in English 8; Odense: Odense University Press, 1985). These two works proved highly instructive in formulation of my linguistic model of verbal usage, and the interplay between the use of individual tense-forms and their recurrence in various discourse types (see Porter, *Verbal Aspect*, 75–108). See also J. Forsyth, *A Grammar of Aspect: Usage and Meaning in the Russian Verb* (Cambridge: Cambridge University Press, 1970); and now H.B. Thelin (ed.), *Verbal Aspect in Discourse* (Amsterdam: Benjamins, 1990); R.I. Binnick, *Time and the Verb: A Guide to Tense and Aspect* (New York: Oxford University Press, 1991); C.S. Smith, *The Parameters of Aspect* (Dordrecht: Kluwer, 1991); H. Verkuyl, *A Theory of Aspectuality: The Interaction between Temporal and Atemporal Structure* (Cambridge: Cambridge University Press, 1993); and W. Klein, *Time in Language* (London: Routledge, 1994) 14–35, for a critical summary of discussion on time, aspect and *Aktionsart*.

14 Besides the works noted above, see K.L. McKay, "The Use of the Ancient Greek Perfect down to the End of the Second Century A.D.," *Bulletin of the Institute of Classical Studies* 12 (1965) 1–21; "On the Perfect and Other Aspects in the Greek Non-Literary Papyri," *Bulletin of the Institute of Classical Studies* 27 (1980) 23–49; "Aspects of the Imperative in Ancient Greek," *Antichthon* 20 (1986) 41–58. Louw's work precedes McKay's, but it was not published in places as accessible or in languages as widely known.

15 Porter, *Verbal Aspect in the Greek of the New Testament*, and B.M. Fanning, *Verbal Aspect in New Testament Greek* (Oxford Theological Monographs; Oxford: Clarendon Press, 1990). One needs only to look at the publication dates of the two works, and the substantial list of publications that anticipate them, to see that Fanning's statement that "NT verbal aspect has received no recent comprehensive treatment" (p. 6) is somewhat hasty. See my short review in *JSNT* Booklist 43 (1991) 127–28. The situation is unchanged by publication of McKay's *New Syntax of the Verb*.

16 The debate over the nature of the Greek of the New Testament is surveyed in S.E. Porter (ed.), *The Language of the New Testament: Classic Essays* (JSNTSup 60; Sheffield: JSOT Press, 1991), which collects statements by A. Deissmann, J.H. Moulton, C.C. Torrey, M. Black, J.A. Fitzmyer, H.S. Gehman, N. Turner, L. Rydbeck and M. Silva. The

(as was Comrie's), they were done independently, with neither seeing the other's work until published. As one might expect, since the two authors were analysing essentially the same primary material, and drawing upon the same traditions of research, the two works have similarities. But they have a significant number of differences as well.

2. *Areas of Agreement between Porter and Fanning*

As I see them, the works by Porter and Fanning have in common the following basic features. Since these features are treated similarly or at least are compatible with each other in a number of ways, I will not fully explicate them. They are, nevertheless, worth recounting. Both works realize the importance of the semantic category of verbal aspect for understanding the structure of the Greek verbal system, as well as its potential implications for exegesis. The Greek verb is seen as part of a coordinated system of verbal structure, so that talking about the aorist tense (for example) has implications for talking about the present tense and the perfect tense. Both works place their discussions within the context of the historical discussion of Greek grammar, in particular of verbs, and attempt to chronicle the progress of the discussion. Both works have a number of functional categories into which to place particular instances of a given verbal usage. The results of analysis of a number of passages are often consonant. For example, both Fanning and I have a place for gnomic (or as I prefer, omnitemporal) use of the tenses, where we list Jas 1:11 and 1 Pet 1:24 as gnomic aorists; for past use of the aorist tense and of the present tense (the so-called historic present), where we list numerous examples found in strategic places in narrative; for the future-referring use of the tenses, where we list Matt 26:45 and Mark 10:33 as examples of the future use of the present tense and John 13:31 and Jude 14 as examples of the aorist tense; for the present use of the aorist and present tenses; and the like. These functional categorizations are similar, even though our theoretical underpinnings may be distinctly different (more on this below). And these are not seen by us as surprising exceptions—and *usually* not (although more often for Fanning than for me) as Semitically motivated. Both recognize the importance of acknowledging the difference in the mood forms. Both treat the indicative uses of the various verb tenses, and devote rather lengthy sections to examining instances of usage of the verbs in non-indicative contexts. Both have discussions of the use of the imperative, where we are agreed that the oft-repeated distinction between aorist and present for inceptive and continuing action cannot be sustained (although we arrive at very different analyses of

introduction is reprinted as ch. 5 in this volume, pp. 75–99.

what the difference between the two is).

In fact, Fanning and I have very similar definitions of what verbal aspect is. I define verbal aspect as "a synthetic semantic category (realized in the forms of verbs) used of meaningful oppositions in a network of tense systems to grammaticalize the author's reasoned subjective choice of conception of a process."[17] In a linguistic situation, among the many choices that a language user must make is the conception of a process. An ancient Greek speaker had a choice of three verbal forms to grammaticalize three verbal aspects (note the relation of form and function): the aorist tense grammaticalized the semantic feature labeled "perfective," the present tense "imperfective," and the perfect tense "stative."[18] This language is not meant to imply that the choice by a language user was always (or ever!) conscious, but that the "choice" was presented or required by the structure of the verbal system of the language. In defining the semantic features of this system, my formulation utilizes contrastive substitution to illustrate that absolute temporal categories (such as past, present and future) are not grammaticalized by the verb forms even in the indicative mood and that a particular verbal aspectual semantic feature is grammaticalized by a given verb form. In this analysis, such significant instances mentioned above as the gnomic tenses, the historic present, and the like constitute important data that cannot be neglected. It is not only that such usage often goes beyond the parameters implied by the label given to a tense-form, since the names of the tense-forms are only markers, often formulated for various idiosyncratic reasons; it is also that such instances constitute legitimate and widely found verbal usage that must be semantically defined by the system. That semantic feature may indeed be shaped by use in a given context, but part of what using the form means is to have this particular meaning. The subjective factor involved means that the choice of verbal aspect rests upon the user, although patterns of usage, for example in various discourse types, mean that choice of verbal aspect is *not* random. The interpreter's latitude is circumscribed by the semantic features of the given form, and in this sense analysis of verbal aspect is objective.

Fanning's definition of verbal aspect is similar:

> Verbal aspect in NT Greek is that category in the grammar of the verb which reflects the focus or viewpoint of the speaker in regard to the action or condition which the

---

17 Porter, *Verbal Aspect*, 88.

18 It must always be remembered that these labels are given to the verbal aspect grammaticalized by a tense-form, and in no way are fully descriptive of their meanings or functions. It must further be remembered that the given terminology is to be interpreted within its respective context. I use the term "stative" within the context of the terminology of verbal aspect, and as elucidated in Louw, "Die Semantiese Waarde van die Perfektum in Hellenistiese Grieks"; cf. Porter, *Verbal Aspect*, 251–59.

> verb describes...
>
> To be more specific, aspect is concerned with the speaker's viewpoint concerning the action in the sense that it implicitly sets up a relationship between the action described and a reference-point from which the action is viewed...
>
> Thus, aspect has nothing inherently to do with temporal sequence, with procedural characteristics of actual situations or of verbs and verb-phrases, or with prominence in discourse. It is instead a rather subjective category, since a speaker may choose to view or portray certain occurrences by one aspect or another without regard to the nature of the occurrence itself.[19]

I have selected these areas of agreement in large part because they are areas that distinguish these "new" approaches to verb structure, and illustrate rightly the place that categories from modern linguistics can play in describing grammatical phenomena of ancient languages such as Greek. Traditional treatments typically (to make a gross generalization) looked at a particular tense-form in isolation, imposed absolute temporal reference upon it, were baffled by fairly commonplace "exceptions," and even fossilized study of Greek grammar with the rather absurd assertion that nineteenth-century comparative philology, or even the ancient Greeks themselves, had answered all of the "problems" of Greek grammar and linguistics. A slightly well-known (at least in some circles, none of them linguistic) professor once said this very thing to me.[20]

3. *Areas of Disagreement between Porter and Fanning*

Fanning and I are not far apart in our analyses of Greek verbal structure in so far as we recognize the importance of verbal aspect and have a fairly similar idea of what it is. But I do not want to minimize the significant differences in our treatments of verbal aspect and the Greek in which it appears, either. Many grammatical models can adequately treat a reasonably large number of common instances in a given language, but the difficult instances prove which is the most effective model and go the furthest to making the best grammatical rules. To the differences in our discussions of verbal aspect I now turn.

To refer back to the characteristic reactions I cited at the beginning of this chapter, my treatment perhaps comes across as one that appears to circumvent further discussion. I posit rather boldly a scheme for analysis of the Greek

19 Fanning, *Verbal Aspect*, 84, 85. He continues by referring to such things as procedural character and the nature of the action, both of which I dispute as relevant to a strict discussion of verbal aspect. That my criticism was not too wide of the mark is now confirmed by Verkuyl, *Theory of Aspectuality*, 33–67, who equates procedural analyses with temporal and ontological categories, not linguistic and aspectual ones.

20 See also Rydbeck, "What Happened to Greek Grammar," 427.

verbal system that does not suffer exceptions gladly, since I believe that—especially for ancient languages—one must begin from the dictum that where there is a difference of form there is a difference in meaning or function. In the period since my initial work on verbal aspect, and after having pursued much further research in this area, I believe now more than ever that I was essentially correct in my analysis of the Greek verbal structure as a coordinated system of three verbal aspects grammaticalized by three major tense-forms, in which temporal reference is not grammaticalized in either the indicative or the non-indicative mood-forms. The *three* verbal aspects (of which the future form is *not* one, as will be discussed below) are conveniently and explicitly analysed in a set of semantic oppositions, which I illustrate by way of a system network.[21] The semantic relation of the verbal aspects can also be discussed in terms of other useful metaphorical expressions, such as the visual analogy of a parade and the description of discourse prominence.[22] My subsequent research has taken forward several of my initial comments regarding discourse analysis.[23] The concept of verbal aspect—at least as I define it—has proved useful. Some of the results of this work appears in several journal articles, a forthcoming commentary on Romans, and my *Idioms of the Greek New Testament*, an

---

21 See Porter, *Verbal Aspect,* 109. The necessary theory behind systemic linguistics is discussed in the introduction, pp. 1–16.

22 See Porter, *Verbal Aspect*, 91–92, 92–93. Fanning (*Verbal Aspect,* 72) has stated that he believes that discourse functions are not the primary meanings of the verbal aspects, an idea in some ways mirrored in Silva's general comments on minimizing the exegetical significance of changes in tense form (*God, Language and Scripture*, 117–18). However, even in English, the aspectual choice between the progressive and simple forms of the verb in "When Sally got home, her husband was cooking dinner" and "When Sally got home, her husband cooked dinner" has meaningful semantic implications regarding the conception and sequence of events, as is ably (though unintentionally) proven by Silva (*Biblical Words and their Meaning*, 197–98). The difference between the two examples is the relation of Sally's arrival and her husband's cooking, with the first indicating that Sally's arrival is contemporaneous with her husband's cooking and the second indicating that Sally's arrival precedes her husband's cooking. The only difference in the two sentences is in the choice of verbal form, with the difference in meaning deriving from the difference in meaning between the progressive and simple past English tense-forms of "cook." These two forms have different meanings and to choose one over the other changes the meaning of the sentence. It is of course true that if one wishes to speak of contemporaneous action one uses the progressive form in the instances cited above, but rather than indicating that the choice of verb form is wholly predetermined, it is a strong argument for aspectual choice, with the choice of perspective on the action being grammaticalized into a particular verbal aspect.

23 Ch. 6 in Porter, *Verbal Aspect*, 291–320, regarding conditional structures, was an attempt in this area, since it illustrated how verbal aspect could be applied to units larger than the clause. But the premise was functioning throughout the entire work, as illustrated in ch. 2 in discussion of forms of discourse (pp. 102–107), among other places.

intermediate level grammar.[24] I believe that there is much to be said for the aorist serving as the background tense, the present as the foreground tense, and the perfect as the frontground tense in understanding many of the basic contours of units of discourse. Much more waits to be done regarding verbal aspect in various discourse types. Some of the potential for future research is well illustrated in the differences between the basic structures of narrative and exposition. In narrative the aorist tense or perfective aspect lays down a basic framework upon which more prominent items in the narrative—whether they be events or descriptions—are placed. In exposition, items are selected for description, analysis and the like, in which the present tense or imperfective aspect may be supported by the aorist tense or further heightened by the use of the perfect tense or stative aspect.

Fanning's treatment, it seems to me, falls victim to the last reaction noted above, that is, of feeling compelled to harmonize the new paradigm with the old. The result is a less than satisfactory synthesis. Fanning presents a revisionist view of the history of verbal aspect, going to great lengths to preserve the traditional categories and terminology. He stresses his belief that the comparative philologists of the nineteenth century were in actual fact discussing verbal aspect, even if they did not call it this or recognize it as such.[25] I find this highly problematic. Research in linguistics regarding the category of verbal aspect, as the technical term has come to be understood, while needing to acknowledge earlier work which may have foreshadowed or paved the way for verbal aspect, has changed the terms of discussion.[26] This is well illustrated by the important discussion between H. Jacobsohn and E. Hermann in 1926–33, in which Jacobsohn usefully distinguished between subjective aspect, which is very similar to what is now defined as verbal aspect in the linguistic literature, and objective *Aktionsart*, the notion central to much

---

24 For example, S.E. Porter and J.T. Reed, "Greek Grammar since BDF: A Retrospective and Prospective Analysis," *FN* 4.2 (1991) 143–64; S.E. Porter, "Greek Language and Linguistics (Keeping up with Recent Studies 17)," *ExpTim* 103 (1991–92) 202–208, reprinted as ch. 1 in this volume, pp. 7–20; *idem*, *Idioms of the Greek New Testament*, esp. ch. 1 on verb structure and ch. 21 on discourse analysis; S.E. Porter *et al.*, *The Book of Romans: A Grammatical–Rhetorical Commentary* (Leiden: Brill, forthcoming). The importance of verbal aspect in discourse analysis becomes more poignant as the importance of discourse analysis becomes increasingly acknowledged.

25 For example, Fanning, *Verbal Aspect*, 12.

26 Two names are important here, the first being G. Curtius (*Elucidations of the Student's Greek Grammar* [trans. E. Abbott; 2nd edn; London: Murray, 1875] 207–18) and the second being J.M. Stahl (*Kritisch-Historische Syntax des griechischen Verbums der klassischen Zeit* (Indogermanische Bibliothek 4; Heidelberg: Winter, 1907]). But their work was to a large extent ignored and did not have the redefining forcefulness it perhaps should have. It is clear that they are outside the mainstream of the discussion of their times.

earlier discussion.[27] Furthermore, the technical definition of verbal aspect is not readily compatible with the definition of the function and use of the verb tenses as typically conceived of in the pre-verbal aspect literature, as Fanning tacitly acknowledges in his critique of *Aktionsart*.[28] Fanning does not realize the full force of his criticism, for example, regarding the fact that the discussion of *Aktionsart* failed to consider its subjective nature (that is, it regarded the way the action transpired as objective) and made semantic judgments on the basis of the meanings of individual lexical items. Fanning has a vested interest in maintaining this line of continuity, since he devotes a large section of chapter 1 and all of chapter 3 to defining the effect of inherent lexical meaning upon the meaning of the verbal aspects.[29] The result is a conflation of grammatical and lexical semantic categories in which lexis takes predominance over grammar (Fanning does not really ask the question of what constitutes inherent lexical meaning). As Fanning recognizes, this methodology is surprisingly similar to the method found, for example, in the work of K. Brugmann,[30] in which he posited categories of meaning and then gave examples, some of them in Greek and some in German, without establishing firm Greek-based criteria for how one is to estimate whether use of a verb is iterative or punctiliar (to use categories from Brugmann) or unbounded or durative (to use categories from Fanning).[31] At this point it seems that any principled formal basis for discussing verbal aspect as a grammatical category that describes verbal structure as a coordinated system of tense-forms has collapsed.

Like McKay, Fanning assumes, but does not argue in any rigorous way, the traditional view that the tense-forms in the indicative mood and when used as participles are time-based.[32] This poses problems. One is the methodological

27 H. Jacobsohn, Review of *Vorlesungen*, by J. Wackernagel, *Gnomon* 2 (1926) 369–95, esp. 378–86; E. Hermann, "Objective und subjektive Aktionsart," *Indogermanische Forschungen* 45 (1927) 207–28; H. Jacobsohn, "Aspektfragen," *Indogermanische Forschungen* 51 (1933) 292–318.

28 Fanning, *Verbal Aspect*, 30–34.

29 Fanning, *Verbal Aspect*, 42–50 and 126–96 respectively.

30 K. Brugmann, *Griechische Grammatik* (ed. A. Thumb; 4th edn; Munich: Beck, 1913 [1885]) esp. 538–52.

31 This is not the place to discuss the apparent theological criteria which go into Fanning's categorization of verbs, so that he places verbs such as ἁγιάζω and ἁγνίζω, as well as verbs of "dying," into the category of climaxes, that is, verbs denoting instantaneous transitions. In the light of his treatment of usage in ch. 4, I believe that his statement on p. 127 n. 2 of *Verbal Aspect* is disingenuous.

32 For example, Fanning, *Verbal Aspect*, 29 and n. 71, 185, 198, 407; cf. McKay, *Greek Grammar*, 136–41, cf. 214–24. Several grammarians before the advent of verbal aspect argued that participles were non-temporal, including E.D.W. Burton (*Syntax of the Moods and Tenses in New Testament Greek* [3rd edn; Chicago: University of Chicago Press, 1900; repr. Grand Rapids: Kregel, 1976] 54 and *passim*) and A.T. Robertson (*A Grammar of the*

inconsistency it creates with his own definition of verbal aspect, which posits that it has nothing to do with temporal sequence. Another is the internal inconsistency with explaining—if his definition is correct—how the indicative functions as it does and how such examples as the future-referring use of the aorist participle are to be explained.[33] Fanning, it seems to me, is incapable of shedding a time-based perspective on verbs. This comes through transparently in his treatment of the perfect and the future tenses. Regarding the perfect tense Fanning strongly resists overthrowing the traditional conception of the tense as speaking of "a state or condition resulting from a completed action."[34] He goes so far as to say that the perfect is not an aspect like the aorist and present in his essentially two-aspect system, but combines three elements of meaning: tense, *Aktionsart* and aspect. According to Fanning's own terminology—in particular, his conflation of *Aktionsart* and aspect—this definition presents serious problems. The most significant is that it is flatly contradictory given his own definitions of *Aktionsart* (which I have argued is itself inherently contradictory)[35] and verbal aspect.[36] Regarding the future form, after citing several major positions, Fanning simply posits (he does not argue) that the future form is a "non-aspectual *tense* category."[37] He apparently means that rather than a category of *Aktionsart* or intention, it simply refers to future time. He does not consider paradigmatic peculiarities of the form, or views which discuss its relation to mood. I argue that the future form is not fully aspectual and neither an indicative nor a non-indicative mood form. It occupies a unique place in the Greek verbal structure.[38] In fact, Fanning provides enough evidence to have concluded similarly, if he had been able to free himself from the traditional categories.[39]

Greek New Testament in the Light of Historical Research [4th edn; Nashville: Broadman, 1934] 1111); cf. McKay, *Greek Grammar*, 219–20.

33 See Porter, *Verbal Aspect*, 385–87.

34 Fanning, *Verbal Aspect*, 103.

35 Porter, *Verbal Aspect*, 32–35.

36 It is interesting that the very useful article by Louw which disputes the traditional conception of the perfect ("Die Semantiese Waarde van die Perfektum"), and which I have used in my own redefinition of the meaning of the tense-form, is listed in Fanning's bibliography but not cited in his discussion of the meaning of the perfect.

37 Fanning, *Verbal Aspect*, 123.

38 Porter, *Verbal Aspect*, 403–49.

39 Fanning's traditionalist perspective is perhaps best summarized in a quotation from his *Verbal Aspect*, 196: "What is recommended for the interpreter of the NT is an understanding of the aspects as differences in the speaker's viewpoint concerning the occurrence, a general awareness of this range of other features which can affect aspect-function, and a sensitivity in looking for such features in texts where the use of one of the aspects may be important to interpretation. In many ways this is no different from the procedure to be followed in any area of exegesis: applying linguistic and historical

A second major difference between Fanning's work and mine is the role that modern linguistics plays. Fanning admits that he is not a linguist.[40] More importantly, I get an impression—it is only an impression, but it is a strong one—that linguistics is seen by Fanning as a tool. It is something that aids him in his task, but it remains a device that is selectively applied to the jobs to be done, and once the tool is worn out or is not useful or he does not know how to exploit it further he casts it aside. Now that the concept of verbal aspect has practical utility or the terminology is being widely employed, it is readily accepted by him and incorporated into his work. Just as *Aktionsart* as a name was thrown over when it was no longer au fait to use it, the same I suspect will happen to the term "aspect," as far as Fanning is concerned. But for Fanning the categories he uses for his actual discussion—that is, the practical framework regarding how the Greek verb functions—are unaffected by the conceptual categories of modern linguistics.

This can be seen in two important areas. First, when he actually discusses tense usage, Fanning's categories are the time-honoured ones employed by such grammars as Blass–Debrunner–Funk and Dana and Mantey, among others.[41] Why? Is it because these categories are sacrosanct, or fundamental in some intrinsic sense? No, they are not, even by Fanning's own terms; in other words, in the light of his own definition of verbal aspect, these categories must themselves be justified before they can be reintroduced into the discussion. They are merely enshrined by time and convention. Secondly, one notices that the explanations given for the various categories are for the most part in terms

sensitivity, along with a generous dose of common sense, to a broad array of contextual factors in order to construe the sense. What is to be avoided in any interpretive task is an atomistic approach to the text and its linguistic elements, and this is certainly true in regard to verbal aspect in NT Greek."

40 Fanning, *Verbal Aspect*, vi. However, he wishes for his book to be viewed as linguistic. By this he probably means that it is about language, as opposed to theology or history.

41 F. Blass and A. Debrunner, *A Greek Grammar of the New Testament and Other Early Christian Literature* (trans. R.W. Funk; Chicago: University of Chicago Press, 1961); H.E. Dana and J.R. Mantey, *A Manual Grammar of the Greek New Testament* (Toronto: Macmillan, 1955). Fanning's categories for the present indicative (*Verbal Aspect*, 198–240) are: progressive present, instantaneous present, iterative present, gnomic present, present of past action still in progress, conative present, futuristic present, historic present, perfective present; for the imperfect (pp. 240–53) are: progressive imperfect, customary or iterative imperfect, conative imperfect, inceptive imperfect; for the aorist indicative (pp. 255–82) are: constative aorist, ingressive aorist, consummative aorist, gnomic aorist, proleptic aorist, dramatic aorist, epistolary aorist; for the perfect indicative (pp. 290–305) are: perfect of resulting state, perfect of completed action, perfect with aoristic sense, gnomic perfect, proleptic perfect; for the pluperfect (pp. 305–309) are: pluperfect of resulting state, pluperfect of completed action, pluperfect with past stative meaning.

virtually identical to those of pre-verbal-aspect grammarians. A representative example is Fanning's treatment of the historic present.[42] He assumes that the vivid use, in other words, the transferring of past events into the present, is the function of the historic present (an explanation directly from *Aktionsart* grammarians),[43] and that it is simply a temporal transfer, not some sort of aspectual effect. His survey of significant discussions of the historic present is enviable, but there is no sustained attempt to discuss this usage in terms of the category of verbal aspect, which has been ruled out of play from the start. But how can this be? By Fanning's definition verbal aspect has to do with subjective choice of viewpoint and it seems that the historic present, if it is in fact used vividly, or if it is used as a narrative tense, or if it is simply a legitimate use of the Greek verb, requires some sort of explanation in (grammatical) aspectual or subjective terms.[44] Furthermore, linguists such as S.C. Levinson dealing with the area of pragmatics will be dismayed to know that they have taxed themselves over something as mundane as the epistolary aorist, which Fanning characterizes as "quite straightforward,"[45] something in fact which it is not.[46]

One's interpretative perspective does make a difference. The two earliest grammatical treatments of verbs, by the Greeks themselves (whom Fanning does not discuss), had two different perspectives on how to classify and categorize the Greek verb. Dionysius Thrax was concerned with the issue of time: his classificatory scheme lists the tenses we would call the imperfect, aorist, perfect and pluperfect as past tenses. But the Stoics recognized kind of action as important, classifying verb forms by meaningful pairs (or oppositions), such as present–imperfect, perfect–pluperfect. The aorist and future remained an enigma, but were placed in opposition, perhaps illustrating a common semantic misunderstanding.[47] The same categories of time and kind of action have more recent practitioners in the rationalists of the eighteenth and nineteenth centuries, who described verbs using highly time-bound categories,[48] and the comparative philologists (especially the New Grammarians) of the

---

42 Fanning, *Verbal Aspect*, 226–39.

43 For example, Brugmann, *Griechische Grammatik*, 555, 556.

44 Cf. Porter, *Verbal Aspect*, 189–98.

45 Fanning, *Verbal Aspect*, 281.

46 See S.C. Levinson, *Pragmatics* (Cambridge Textbooks in Linguistics; Cambridge: Cambridge University Press, 1983) 73–74; Porter, *Verbal Aspect*, 228–30.

47 See Porter, *Verbal Aspect*, 18–20 and 20–22, respectively.

48 See, for example, W.E. Jelf, *A Grammar of the Greek Language Chiefly from the German of R. Kühner* (2 vols.; 2nd edn; Oxford: James Henry Parker, 1851) 2.51–73; G.B. Winer, *A Treatise on the Grammar of New Testament Greek Regarded as a Sure Basis for New Testament Exegesis* (trans. W.F. Moulton; 3rd edn; Edinburgh: T. & T. Clark, 1882) esp. 330–31.

nineteenth century, who described verbs in terms of objective action.[49]

More recent examples are found in discussion of Rom 2:12 and 3:23. If one is using a time-based scheme, one may well look, for example, to J.D.G. Dunn, who in commenting upon the use of the aorist in 2:12 says: "Here the aorist (ἥμαρτον) is used, since at the final judgment the whole of life can be summed up as a single past event (though cf. 3:23 and 5:12)." At 3:23 Dunn says that the "aorist is used either because the perspective is that of the final judgment (as in 2:12, q.v.) or because the perspective is that of the decisive and universal character of man's fall (see further on 5:12)."[50] This reflects the perspective of many commentaries, in which a mixed number of time-based and occasionally *Aktionsart*-based comments is made (although the tension in Dunn's analysis between past and future, many events and singularity is palpable). Fanning lists Rom 3:23 as an example of the constative or complexive aorist used to "relate a *series* of repeated actions or states," in which the "multiple situations may be either iterative...or distributive... The aorist in either case indicates a summary or composite of the repeated situations."[51] I categorize Rom 2:12 as an instance of the timeless use of the perfective aspect (on the basis of the context and in the light of the indefinite relative pronoun). I categorize Rom 3:23 (and 5:12) as instances of the omnitemporal use of the perfective aspect (on the basis of the context and the use of πάντες).[52] To extend the implications of this analysis, it means that had the writer, Paul, chosen another tense-form (whether consciously or unconsciously is beside the point), for example the imperfect or present or even the perfect in some instances, the event he refers to would not have changed in and of itself but the aspectual semantics grammaticalized by the choice of another tense-form would have indicated a change in the writer's perspective. This would be true regardless of whether the change of tense-form

49 See, for example, Brugmann, *Griechische Grammatik*, esp. 538–41; and esp. J.H. Moulton, *Prolegomena* , vol. 1 of *A Grammar of New Testament Greek* (3rd edn; Edinburgh: T. & T. Clark, 1908 [1906]) 108–51.

50 J.D.G. Dunn, *Romans* (2 vols.; WBC 38A, B; Dallas: Word, 1988) 1.96, 1.167. Dunn's commentary is selected not because it is necessarily the worst offender, but because of its temporal proximity to Fanning's work and mine on verbal aspect and its claim to being a major commentary on the Greek text. Cf. the productive use of verbal aspect to discuss the notoriously difficult Rom 7:14–25 in M.A. Seifrid, *Justification by Faith: The Origin and Development of a Central Pauline Theme* (NovTSup 68; Leiden: Brill, 1992) 226–34, esp. 234. I know of now three recent commentaries that take seriously discussion of verbal aspect: M. Silva, *Philippians* (Chicago: Moody, 1988), D.A. Carson, *The Gospel according to John* (Leicester: Inter-Varsity Press, 1991), and R.H. Gundry, *Mark: A Commentary on his Apology for the Cross* (Grand Rapids: Eerdmans, 1993).

51 Fanning, *Verbal Aspect*, 258.

52 Porter, *Verbal Aspect*, 237, 222. Cf. [F.B. Denio], "Translation of the Aorist Tense in the Indicative Mood," *BSac* 41 (1884) 388.

resulted in a different translation in English.[53]

In keeping with my definition of aspect, I am less concerned with specifying precise temporal reference of a given tense-form (primarily because I do not believe that the verb forms in Greek grammaticalize absolute tense) than I am with explicating the semantic features that allow a given form to be used in a variety of contexts. It is clear in Dunn's case that he does not recognize the work of Stagg and others, much less of discussion of verbal aspect. He reflects the kind of understanding of Greek verbs found in elementary textbooks and the rationalist discussion of the eighteenth and early nineteenth centuries. His own comments illustrate that time-based categories are insufficient, however. Dunn never asks the important question of how these categories work together, quite possibly because the reference tools that he probably uses—such as Blass–Debrunner–Funk—do not ask these questions. What is perhaps more disappointing to see, but not entirely surprising in the light of my comments above, is that Fanning's treatment reads much like the discussion of *Aktionsart* found in nineteenth-century research. In other words, he shows more concern for the objective nature of the action than for the author's perspective on it. We cannot be dogmatic about the aorist as a past tense or as indicating one-time or punctiliar action, no matter how true we may believe the concepts to be (as Dunn illustrates), but neither can we see the aorist as reflecting objective action. The aorist, the present and the perfect tenses grammaticalize verbal aspects used by speakers to characterize processes, to make them, if you will, not simply to reflect them.

Many are willing to grant that modern linguistics has led to new ways of viewing language. One only needs to think of the fundamental re-orientation from diachronic to synchronic categories. It seems self-evident now—but this is because the categories of modern linguistics have had time to permeate our thoughts about language—that in analysing the Greek of the New Testament it is more important how the cases function in relation to each other or how the tenses form a system than whether the dative case is an amalgamation of three cases or the exact relation of the aorist to its Proto-Indo-European progenitor. The same re-orientation will become second nature in dealing with verbs as soon as the category of verbal aspect has had requisite time to permeate the linguistic vocabulary. By that I mean an accurate definition of the category. There will always be those who insist that the category is not viable; their

53 The difference between analysis of an ancient or epigraphic language and a modern language is often overlooked. The fact that speakers of, for example, modern English may know nothing about the workings of their language but can communicate in it has virtually no bearing upon the study of a language of which there are no native speakers and consequently there is no one with an innate knowledge of its system. All users of an epigraphic language must work from system to interpretation, whether or not they explicitly realize this.

insistence is the residual hesitance connected with any paradigm shift, according to Kuhn.

Not only is verbal aspect not simply *Aktionsart* in new clothing, or not simply another way of formulating the same temporal perspective on verbs, verbal aspect as a category of modern linguistics provides a new orientation to viewing the language itself. I would have preferred in my work merely to have defined the semantic force of, for example, the aorist or present or perfect tense and left it at that, a simple and elegant description of the semantics of the Greek tense-forms (I reject the notion that a grammatical analysis must have "practical" or exegetical value to be valid or worth discussing). But semantics implies pragmatics,[54] and since temporal and other categories were long-enshrined I was compelled to deal with such basic temporal notions as past, present and future. Along the way, I found it useful to include such terminology as omnitemporal and timeless, which place on the same plane categories that appear to be temporal but that expand the category to the point of breaking. One implies that a process cannot be pinned down to a specific time because it tends to happen all the time or at least regularly, and the other implies that a process cannot be pinned down to a specific time because there is no place on a timeline for such an event. The "truths" of theology and mathematics are of this sort.[55] Once this is understood, one becomes acutely aware that it is difficult to pin down in any exact way the relation between a language event and any absolute conception of past, present and future *time* as well. This is true of Greek, Hebrew, English and any number of other languages—some more extremely so than Greek. So time, at least as a linguistic category, is no more absolute than any other, and I would contend that it is not grammaticalized, that is, it is not enshrined by selection of a single tense-form in Greek, either in the non-indicative moods or in the indicative mood. The former has long been recognized by many serious students of Greek grammar, but the second moves beyond Fanning and even McKay. I am concerned to explicate what any of the verb tenses can be made by a speaker to do. The semantic category of verbal aspect can be imposed upon a process by a speaker, no matter when it may have occurred or how it may have actually occurred. This brings chills to some exegetes, because in their disjunctive (or tradition-bound) thinking they believe

---

54 The distinction between semantics (the meaning of a form) and pragmatics (what the form means in context) is a useful one to differentiate between the level of definition and application. In fact, I would go further and contend that application cannot occur until the semantic framework is firmly in place.

55 See J. Lyons, *Semantics* (Cambridge: Cambridge University Press, 1977) 680. Fanning obviously does not believe that these distinctions are worth making, since he conflates (or confuses?) the two. He defines the gnomic present in terms both of expressing "timeless, universal occurrences" and of representing "what occurs at *all* times' (*Verbal Aspect*, 208).

that this is another way of saying that the Greeks had no concern for time. I am in no way saying that time is unimportant. I am saying two things. The first is that when Greek speakers used a verb they had something other than temporal categories in mind with regard to what the verb form itself meant. They used the aorist form to mean one complex of things, and the present form to mean something else, and the perfect form for something else again. The second is that users could speak of when processes occurred, but they did not use verb forms alone to do so. They instead used various other tools in their language. For example, they would use deictic indicators such as temporal words or they would use discourse features, such as the type or kind of discourse.[56]

4. *Conclusion*

In conclusion, let me take this discussion beyond our two books. First, this is an important time in language study, since there is potential for rethinking many traditional categories in the light of work in theoretical and general linguistics. Secondly, the study of Greek, including that of the New Testament, is at a very promising point, when a new linguistic category—verbal aspect—is being analysed, assessed and even adopted. These new insights might well provide some of the needed impetus for renewing interest in the study of Greek at the undergraduate, theological college and seminary levels. Thirdly, this is an opportunity to go beyond the traditional strictures and confinements of discussion of the Greek of the New Testament to bring to bear a view of the language as a grammatical system, with all of the working parts functioning together. And verbal aspect, Fanning and I are agreed, should play a significant role in this linguistic revolution.

56 Porter, *Verbal Aspect*, 98–102; *idem*, *Idioms of the Greek New Testament*, chs. 1 and 21. See now J.T. Reed, "Identifying Theme in the New Testament: Insights from Discourse Analysis," in Porter and Carson (eds.), *Discourse Analysis and Other Topics in Biblical Greek*, 75–101.

CHAPTER THREE

TENSE TERMINOLOGY AND GREEK LANGUAGE STUDY: A LINGUISTIC RE-EVALUATION*

1. *Introduction*

One of the problems with investigating tense distinctions in languages is that the names for tense categories are based only on typical functions of the tenses concerned, and do not capture the full range of functions that a given category may express. This is potentially very misleading, because it is tempting to see the typical function that motivates the form name as the function, that is, to treat a short label as far more informative and exhaustive than it really is. In English, for example, the Progressive Present[1] is used in contexts referring to present time: "I am looking round the shop now" or "I am paying for this with change." But what about "I am going to the shop tomorrow"? The verb form is exactly the same, but suddenly the speaker is referring to the future. This can be analysed in several ways. Some might say there is something unusual about a Progressive Present that allows it to refer to the future (it is the Present of assured result, or some such thing), or better still, perhaps, this form has a variety of temporal uses, the present being one and the future being another equally legitimate. In fact, English speakers may use the Progressive Present form for future reference as much as if not more than they use the English Future form with *will*. (Similarly, for the future in the past: "I was going to the shop just now, but you stopped me" or "I was going to go eat there tomorrow, but I ran out of money.") These are pretty difficult to explain, except as various temporal functional uses of the Progressive form. Inherent in this discussion is differentiation of two issues—temporal reference and the kind of action referred to. While tense names in a language are based on some typical function, this function is usually not the only function of the form concerned, and speakers

* This essay first appeared in the *Sheffield Working Papers in Language and Linguistics* 3 (1986) 77–86. It has been updated in places and the references have been revised.

1 The convention of capitalizing formal names is followed throughout this chapter; see the body of the chapter for reasons.

risk causing considerable confusion if they fail to make clear, as they usually do, that the name only reflects one of several functions.

This brief chapter will examine the problem of tense terminology in relation to Greek, especially the Greek of the New Testament, with special reference to the benefit of clear terminology for language instruction, though it is hoped that what is said may have a wider application to similar problems in other languages. I will make three major points: (1) tense names can be confusing and even deceptive; (2) it is only too easy to mistake formal and functional grammatical categories and hence lack a proper basis for understanding verbal action; and (3) some relatively new categories based upon verbal aspect may alleviate much of the difficulty.

2. *Traditional Tense Terminology in New Testament Greek*

Turning now to New Testament Greek, A.T. Robertson and H.P.V. Nunn in the early 1900s recognized the problem of Greek tense terminology, but the problem seems to persist.[2] The "Present" and "Future" are temporal categories while "Imperfect" and "Perfect" are named according to the kind of action or the way the action is described. And the "Pluperfect" seems to combine both.[3] But who would suspect from this that, for example, the Imperfect is related to the Present? And then there is the "Aorist." Many grammarians say that this rubric comes from the Greek ἀ-όριστος, "without boundary" or "undefined." The term was first devised by the ancient Greek grammarians themselves, so that Dionysius Thrax links the Aorist and Future together, calling them both undefined.[4] Grammarians since have been fooled on more than one occasion into thinking then that the tense function itself is unspecified, but perhaps the Greeks themselves were fooled (if indeed they thought this). The Aorist verb defines an action (*Aktionsart*), or better by using the Aorist the speaker or writer conveys that an action is conceived in the mind in a certain way (aspect). The Aoristic action is not undefined either in itself or in the speaker's mind: rather a

---

2 A.T. Robertson, *A Grammar of the Greek New Testament in the Light of Historical Research* (4th edn; Nashville: Broadman, 1934 [1914]) 825; H.P.V. Nunn, *A Short Syntax of New Testament Greek* (5th edn; Cambridge: Cambridge University Press, 1956 [1912]) 66; and more recently D.A. Carson, *Exegetical Fallacies* (Grand Rapids: Baker, 1984) 69. Cf. also G.M. Bolling, "The Teaching of the 'Tenses' in Greek," *Classical Journal* 13 (1917–18) 104–10.

3 J. Lyons (*Semantics* [Cambridge: Cambridge University Press, 1977] 704) calls the term *pluperfect* "misleading."

4 In I. Bekker (ed.), *Anecdota Graeca* (Berlin: G. Reimer, 1816; repr. Graz, Austria: Akademische Druck- und Verlaganstalt, 1965) 2.638. Many grammars make reference to the etymology of the category.

suitable definition of its grammatical import has apparently eluded many grammarians both ancient and modern (note that they do *attempt* definitions). A simple solution to this problem of Greek tense terminology would seem to be to standardize the terms on the basis of temporal reference, but this will not work for several reasons, least of which is that time is of no direct consequence in the oblique or non-indicative moods. A second solution would be to realize that the Greek tenses are not primarily based upon a temporal understanding of verbal action and to reformulate the names accordingly. But, as this chapter shows, tense labels are rather seductive. Robertson regretfully remarks: "the names cannot now be changed, though very unsatisfactory."[5]

One of the most successful and pedagogically straightforward of all elementary New Testament Greek textbooks is that of John Wenham.[6] He is

---

5 Robertson, *Grammar of the Greek New Testament*, 826; cf. Carson, *Exegetical Fallacies*, 69.

6 J.W. Wenham, *The Elements of New Testament Greek* (Cambridge: Cambridge University Press, 1965). The following elementary grammars of New Testament Greek appear susceptible to the same kind of criticism to varying degrees: H.P.V. Nunn, *The Elements of New Testament Greek* (8th edn; Cambridge: Cambridge University Press, 1945 [1916]); J.G. Machen, *New Testament Greek for Beginners* (repr. Toronto: Macmillan, 1951); R. Summers, *Essentials of New Testament Greek* (Nashville: Broadman, 1950), and the recent revision of his work, D.A. Black, *Learn to Read New Testament Greek* (Nashville: Broadman, 1993 [2nd edn, 1994]); E.G. Jay, *New Testament Greek: An Introductory Grammar* (London: SPCK, 1965); E.C. Colwell and E.W. Thune, *A Beginner's Reader-Grammar for New Testament Greek* (New York: Harper & Row, 1965); R.W. Funk, *Beginning–Intermediate Grammar of Hellenistic Greek* (2 vols.; 2nd edn; Sources for Biblical Study 2; n.p.: Society of Biblical Literature, 1973) (Funk has many good points, especially regarding his understanding of the evolution of the language, but he is too tied to *Aktionsarten*); B.X. de Wet, *Learning Greek through the New Testament* (Durban: Butterworths, 1976); R.A. Martin, *An Introduction to New Testament Greek* (n.p., 1978); J.L. Story and C.I.K. Story, *Greek to Me: Learning New Testament Greek through Memory Visualization* (San Francisco: Harper & Row, 1979); M. Whittaker, *New Testament Greek Grammar: An Introduction* (revised edn; London: SCM Press, 1980); J.A. Hewett, *New Testament Greek: A Beginning and Intermediate Grammar* (Peabody: Hendrickson, 1986); J.H. Dobson, *Learn New Testament Greek* (revised edn; Stonehill Green, Swindon: Bible Society, 1992 [1988]); J.M. Efird, *A Grammar for New Testament Greek* (Nashville: Abingdon Press, 1990); F. Beetham, *An Introduction to New Testament Greek* (London: Bristol Classical Press, 1992); J. Swetnam, *An Introduction to the Study of New Testament Greek* (2 vols.; Rome: Pontifical Biblical Institute Press, 1992); L.W. Countryman, *The New Testament is in Greek: A Short Course for Exegetes* (Grand Rapids: Eerdmans, 1993); W.D. Mounce, *Basics of Biblical Greek: Grammar* (Grand Rapids: Zondervan, 1993). It is quite astounding that so many new grammars are being written, with so little new or insightful to commend them. Better than most recent attempts is K.H. Easley, *User-Friendly Greek: A Common Sense Approach to the Greek New Testament* (Nashville: Broadman & Holman, 1994).

Of the handbooks and intermediate grammars, H.E. Dana and J.R. Mantey, *Manual*

careful not to assume that the student knows much "grammar," so he begins with an introductory chapter on English. Here he notes that tense is concerned with both "the time at which an action takes place" and "the state or nature of the action." He then creates a grid with four kinds of action (continuous, simple, complete, continuous–complete) by three times (past, present, future) and thus has twelve "forms" in all.[7] While it probably is the case today that those learning Greek need a chapter such as this (adapted from Nunn, upon whom Wenham is based), may it not be ultimately misleading to try to teach students about the Greek verbal system in these terms, especially when Wenham himself states, "except for the future tense [but see below!], the tenses in Greek are concerned almost wholly with the nature and state of the action, and not with time"?[8] Wenham thus gives with the one hand (tense has temporal reference) and takes away with the other (Greek tenses do not have temporal reference). What is a student to think, except that when in a quandary he or she falls back on their native tongue? But English is really quite different from Greek, with English using primarily periphrastic tense forms, having analytic rather than synthetic aspect (that is, aspect is not tied to morphology), and maintaining temporal reference in most moods.

The real problem comes in Wenham's treatment of the individual tenses. His treatment of the Present focuses on translation, claiming that "two English equivalents are given for one Greek form of the Present tense. This is because there are more tenses in English than in Greek, and one Greek tense has to do the work of two English tenses."[9] The result of this, for the majority of (struggling) students, is to put an inordinate and unhealthy emphasis on translation. The goal of learning Greek, whether classical or New Testament,

---

Grammar of the Greek New Testament (repr. Toronto: Macmillan, 1955); C.F.D. Moule, *An Idiom Book of the Greek New Testament* (2nd edn; Cambridge: Cambridge University Press, 1959 [1953]); J.A. Brooks and C.L. Winbery, *Syntax of New Testament Greek* (Washington, D.C.: University Press of America, 1979); and J.H. Greenlee, *Concise Exegetical Grammar of New Testament Greek* (5th edn; Grand Rapids: Eerdmans, 1986 [1953]) are all problematic. More promising are M. Zerwick, *Biblical Greek illustrated by Examples* (trans. J. Smith; Rome: Pontifical Biblical Institute Press, 1963); D. Durie, *Greek Grammar: A Concise Grammar of New Testament Greek* (Canberra, Australia: privately printed, 1981); K.L. McKay, *A New Syntax of the Verb in New Testament Greek: An Aspectual Approach* (Studies in Biblical Greek 5; New York: Peter Lang, 1994); and R.A. Young, *Intermediate New Testament Greek: A Linguistic and Exegetical Approach* (Nashville: Broadman & Holman, 1994), who follows S.E. Porter, *Verbal Aspect in the Greek of the New Testament, with Reference to Tense and Mood* (Studies in Biblical Greek 1; New York: Peter Lang, 1989), which is also the basis of S.E. Porter, *Idioms of the Greek New Testament* (Biblical Languages: Greek 2; 2nd edn; Sheffield: JSOT Press, 1994 [1992]).

7 Wenham, *Elements of New Testament Greek*, 10–11.

8 Wenham, *Elements of New Testament Greek*, 10.

9 Wenham, *Elements of New Testament Greek*, 27.

whether for practical theology or scholarly endeavour, should not be to produce translational equivalents (there are plenty of excellent translations on the market) but to gain understanding of "how the language works"[10] and facility in thinking about texts in the original language, rather than seeing them through one's own or someone else's translational spectacles. (Can it be proved that either of these goals automatically follows from achievement of the other?) Wenham does not attempt to treat the Greek verb complex as a structured system here, but instead has isolated one tense and tried to find English equivalents. (Like many grammarians, he also separates the Indicative from the other moods.) But what of future uses of the Greek Present form, or past uses, or non-temporal uses? Arguments that these are not the primary functions (and this is a rather dubious numerical estimation) have already been seduced by deceptively simple terminology. Similar points could be made about treatment of other tenses (in what is, I repeat, a particularly straightforward and helpful textbook).[11]

---

10 See H.A. Gleason, Jr., *An Introduction to Descriptive Linguistics* (revised edn; New York: Holt, Rinehart and Winston, 1961) 77: "Translation is a very inadequate means of expressing meanings and must always be used with great caution." See also his "Linguistics in the Service of the Church," *Hartford Quarterly* 1 (1961) 15–16.

11 It is important to note that the advanced New Testament reference grammars are susceptible to the same criticism, with only E.D.W. Burton (*Syntax of the Moods and Tenses in New Testament Greek* [3rd edn; Chicago: University of Chicago Press, 1900; repr. Grand Rapids: Kregel, 1976]) coming close to presenting an integrated network of verbal dependence. On the other hand, F. Blass and A. Debrunner, *A Greek Grammar of the New Testament and Other Early Christian Literature* (trans. R.W. Funk; Chicago: University of Chicago Press, 1961 [1896]) 166–81, as well as in the German edition, *Grammatik des neutestamentlichen Griechisch* (ed. F. Rehkopf; 15th edn; Göttingen: Vandenhoeck & Ruprecht, 1979); J.H. Moulton, Prolegomena, vol. 1 of *A Grammar of New Testament Greek* (3rd edn; Edinburgh: T. & T. Clark, 1908 [1906]) 108–51; Robertson, *Grammar of the Greek New Testament*, 821–910; N. Turner, *Syntax*, vol. 3 of *A Grammar of New Testament Greek*, by J.H. Moulton (Edinburgh: T. & T. Clark, 1963) 59–89, are all based on essentially the same foundation—that of the comparative philology of the nineteenth century. Formulated first by Georg Curtius and perfected by Berthold Delbrück and Karl Brugmann, the New Grammarians posited (though they did not always follow this) that (1) the verb objectively refers to the kind of action depicted (*Aktionsart*), (2) this takes precedence over time of action, although time is still part of the semantic grid of the verb, and (3) the Greek language is to be studied as a natural and necessary development from Proto-Indo-European. Representative of the approach of the New Grammarians is K. Brugmann's *Griechische Grammatik* (ed. A. Thumb; 4th edn; Munich: Beck, 1913 [1885]). On the New Grammarians, see K.R. Jankowsky, *The Neogrammarians: A Re-Evaluation of their Place in the Development of Linguistic Science* (The Hague: Mouton, 1972).

Study of the major reference grammars and elementary textbooks of classical Greek shows that classicists, long plagued with the same problems, only recently have begun to discuss seriously the difficulties of tense. See especially K.L. McKay, *Greek Grammar for Students: A Concise Grammar of Classical Attic with Reference to Aspect in the Verb*

3. *Possible Solutions to the Problems of Tense Terminology*

Many may not have any problem with the terminological difficulties outlined above, since they have already confronted these problems through linguistics or language study of various kinds. For whatever reason, most who sense these problems are pretty well beyond rudimentary language instruction. For those just beginning study of an ancient language, however, the agony seems far removed from the ecstasy.

Let me briefly suggest three tentative ways of alleviating the difficulty of tense terminology. The first is to recognize the difference between verbal form and function. When Greek grammars speak of punctiliar Presents, future Presents, present Aorists, etc., they are speaking of two very different things. They are speaking of a verbal form—Present, Aorist, Perfect, Future—used in a certain function—that is, it refers to present time, future time, etc. Using the traditional tense terminology there seem to be two ways to avoid confusion. One would be to capitalize all form names and use small initial letters for functions. So the term "past Present" is a Present form used of past time. This provides a neat shorthand to keep the two categories separate, but it is just a shorthand and it only works in writing. The second suggestion is that perhaps the shorthand ought to be clarified. For example, "the Aorist form used of present time" and "the Perfect form used of past time" may take longer, but they are certainly clearer.

This once more shows up the difficulty of tense terminology in Greek, however. The phrase "Present used of past time" (or "with past time reference") still misses the basis of the Greek tenses, which is reference to how an action is depicted. Therefore, tense categories should include some component to reflect their reference to depiction of the action. McKay has done this partly when he labels the Present form the "imperfective."[12] But he does not need to keep the term Aorist either, since it is treated by grammarians as anything but undefined. (McKay should, it seems, eliminate the term Future as well, since he believes it constitutes an aspectual and not solely a temporal category.) The difficulties with this scheme, however, are self-evident. First, it eliminates the boundary between form and function so that the metalanguage requires an extra set of terms to refer to forms alone, and, secondly, it makes a too facile equation of form with function (though this equation seems warranted in Greek verbal usage).

The third solution is the most radical and yet probably the most promising: a

(Canberra: Australian National University, 1974); cf. J.M. Stahl, *Kritisch-Historische Syntax des griechischen Verbums der klassischen Zeit* (Indogermanische Bibliothek 4; Heidelberg: Winter, 1907).

12 McKay, *Greek Grammar*, 136.

reformulation of the description of Greek verbal usage on the basis of systematic application of the grammatical category of verbal aspect.[13] The traditional tense-form names may be retained to represent the formal paradigms as abstracted constructs that developed early in Greek usage and are now hallowed by tradition. But consistent functional names for the representative verbal conceptions of action must be devised as well.

Here is where the difficulty in terminology is perhaps most easily seen. Most grammarians want to define their functional categories as objective reflections of the kind of action depicted by the verb—that is, *Aktionsart*. This, however, does not seem to be at the heart of the Greek verbal system. Whereas once (in the mists of primeval Greek, Proto-Indo-European or somewhere) the verbal roots and suffixes may have had a particular controlling significance on verbal meaning, by at least the time of Homer, the primary grammatical category for the verb was aspect.[14] The roots and suffixes remained part of the lexical meaning of individual words and the kinds of action represented became as varied as there are different events, and as subjective to judge. This explains why efforts to describe present action as durative, linear, progressive, or iterative, defined in terms of temporal length, appear so odd in relation to the Aorist as punctiliar or single action. The categories are obviously being mixed. Instead when a Greek author selected a particular aspect he was subjectively deciding how he conceived of the "internal temporal constituency"[15] of a verbal process, with only secondary reference to its external temporal relation. Whereas this is subjective from the author's viewpoint, it is quite objective from the interpreter's.

Greek it just so happens maintains a surprisingly close correlation between tense categories and aspectual functions (sometimes called morphological or synthetic aspect), not wasting duplicate forms on the same functions or making single forms serve multiple functions.[16] This makes it all the more important to

---

13 A much fuller exposition of these categories is to be found in Porter, *Verbal Aspect*, esp. 75–109 but *passim*; cf. also B.M. Fanning, *Verbal Aspect in New Testament Greek* (Oxford Theological Monographs; Oxford: Clarendon Press, 1990).

14 The importance of aspect/*Aktionsart* as morphologically based (synthetic aspect) and already established in pre-Homeric Greek has been maintained by virtually every major grammarian of Greek: Curtius, Delbrück, Brugmann, Thumb, Stahl, Gildersleeve, Smyth, Chantraine, Humbert, Leroy, and McKay, followed by New Testament grammarians like Blass, Debrunner, Moulton, Robertson, and Turner.

15 B. Comrie, *Aspect: An Introduction to the Study of Verbal Aspect and Related Problems* (Cambridge Textbooks in Linguistics; Cambridge: Cambridge University Press, 1976); cf. P. Friedrich, "On Aspect Theory and Homeric Aspect," *International Journal of American Linguistics*, Memoir 23, 40 (1976) 18–20; C. Bache, *Verbal Aspect: A General Theory and its Application to Present-Day English* (Odense: Odense University Press, 1985).

16 J.L. Rose, *The Durative and Aoristic Tenses in Thucydides* (Language Dissertation 35; Supplement to *Language*; Baltimore: Linguistic Society of America, 1942) 43; cf. also

envisage the Greek verbal system as a network which encompasses, orders and arranges all the verbal functions. Greek can be neatly described as formally realizing three verbal aspects—the perfective (= Aorist), the imperfective (= Present and Imperfect), and the stative (= Perfect and Pluperfect). To give quick definitions of these let me draw the picture of a parade.[17] If I am in the BBC helicopter over the parade, I view it as "perfective." If I am sitting in the grandstand watching the parade pass in front of me, I view it as "imperfective." And if I am the parade manager considering all the conditions in existence at this parade, I view it as "stative." There are two important points to remember, however. External temporal reference does not come into play here, that is, there is not necessarily anything inherently past about the Aorist even in the Indicative (Indicative is a formal term, whereas its use in independent sentences may be described semantically as "assertive" or the like). And there is minimal confusion of forms. Therefore, when a Greek author selected a particular aspect correlating with a particular tense (Greek synthetic aspect is roughly the opposite of analytic aspect in English), he was choosing a particular overriding grammatical category (as opposed to others available in his system) to convey his conception of the process. Subsumed underneath this grammatical category is the particular manifestation of the lexical meaning of the verbal root and the temporal reference indicated by deixis.[18] As Lyons says, "Few parts of a language-system illustrate better than its aspect-system does the validity of the structuralist slogan: *Tout se tient* ('Everything hangs together'...)."[19]

4. *Conclusion*

This study of verbal aspect has great potential for understanding the Greek language at both elementary and advanced levels. First, the Greek language is not to be seen as a series of discrete, disjoint tenses but is to be viewed as a coordinated network of verbal choices. For example, the stative is the most complex, the least used and the most problematic for pragmatic interpretation. The perfective is the least important in the sense that it is the aspect used when

D.L. Bolinger, *Meaning and Form* (London: Longman, 1977) 1–20.

17 This illustration is dependent upon Isachenko, quoted in translation by A.B. Murphy, *Aspectual Usage in Russian* (Oxford: Pergamon, 1965) 21. The terms used in this chapter are intentionally similar to those used in discussion of aspect in Slavonic languages, though it is important to realize that these terms are only abbreviations for semantic features. Since a privative opposition between the perfective and imperfective aspects is not asserted, the latter need not have a negative connotation.

18 See S.C. Levinson, *Pragmatics* (Cambridge Textbooks in Linguistics; Cambridge: Cambridge University Press, 1983) 54–96.

19 Lyons, *Semantics*, 714.

no other is deemed necessary; it is the "ground" aspect,[20] though this is not to say that it is "undefined." It represents the facticity of an event conceived of as a whole, no matter its actual length of duration, and is well-suited to being juxtaposed to the other aspects. As noted above, most discussions of verbal usage do not conceive of the language systematically and hence treat all categories on the same plane. Secondly, it must be noted that certain semantic categories are formally grounded while others are not. The imperfective often refers to present time, but its aspect also allows past, future, and timeless reference, without grammarians having to resort to strained explanations of the use as "more vivid" or "more assured." The perfective is often used to refer to the past in the Indicative perhaps because of its view of the action as complete, but it may function with reference to present time, as well as being omnitemporal (i.e. gnomic) or timeless. It must be questioned, therefore, whether such categories as ingressive, effective and constative Aorist are grammatically legitimate. The form is, simply, the Aorist. Terminologically, these names tend to confuse form and function, as well as semantics and pragmatics. I believe such categories are better seen as lexical and contextual interpretations of a particular grammatical and semantic category. The "ingressive" ἐβασίλευσε ("he began to rule") is different in meaning from ἐκάθισε ("he began to sit") on the basis of lexis, not grammar. Many examples may be labeled constative or even effective just as well. After all, the number of objective classifications of events is potentially as great as the number of events themselves and need not be limited artificially to four or five.[21]

In conclusion, tense terminology in Greek has certain dangers that apparently have not been avoided over the years. Though there are some signs that New Testament grammars are making a conscious effort to understand the verb more clearly,[22] most elementary and more advanced grammars maintain

---

20 The use of this term comes from Gestalt psychology. See S. Wallace, "Figure and Ground: The Interrelationships of Linguistic Categories," in *Tense–Aspect: Between Semantics and Pragmatics* (ed. P.J. Hopper; Amsterdam: Benjamins, 1981) 201–23. These categories are useful for establishing and speaking of planes of discourse.

21 Contra Carson, *Exegetical Fallacies*, 72–74.

22 W.S. LaSor, *Handbook of New Testament Greek*. II. *Grammar, Synoptic Paradigms, Basic Vocabulary* (Grand Rapids: Eerdmans, 1973) §31.5, has a competent discussion of verbal aspect, but his method appears to be plagued with other difficulties; E.V.N. Goetchius, *The Language of the New Testament* (New York: Scribners, 1965), despite his promising references to modern linguistics, only has a rudimentary discussion of verbal aspect; J.H. Moulton, *An Introduction to the Study of New Testament Greek* (rev. H.G. Meecham; 5th edn; London: Epworth Press, 1955 [2nd edn 1903]) 121–29, actually provides the most comprehensive and well-reasoned study of any elementary New Testament Greek grammar to date. If account is taken of the fact that the discussion is in terms of *Aktionsart* (though he departs from this model occasionally), this could still provide a valuable resource for elementary study of the verb. See now the forthcoming S.E. Porter and J.T. Reed,

undifferentiated formal-functional terminology formulated around an at least misleading (if not erroneous) conception of the nature of the Greek verbal system. For the sake of both students and scholars alike, it is time that more attention was turned to improving and refining a suitable metalanguage in order to help grasp *inter alia* the aspectual nature of the Greek verbal network.

Fundamentals of the Greek New Testament (Biblical Languages: Greek 1; Sheffield: Sheffield Academic Press, 1996), for an attempt to deal with many of the problems raised above.

CHAPTER FOUR

LINGUISTIC ISSUES IN NEW TESTAMENT LEXICOGRAPHY

1. *Introduction*

Lexicography occupies an odd place within the whole endeavour of linguistics. For students of ancient languages, including students of the Greek of the New Testament, a lexicon is considered an essential tool. The same priority of lexicography is not true for many linguists.[1] Semantics—broadly defined as the study of meaning, in all of its complexity—comprises one of the essential components or divisions of linguistic investigation.[2] Many well-known linguists have devoted serious effort to the study of semantics, including (but certainly not restricted to) S. Ullmann, E.A. Nida, J. Lyons, D.A. Cruse, and others.[3]

1 I use the term "linguist" not in the usual British sense of one who studies languages (a polyglot), but in the sense of one who studies language from the standpoint of the discipline of linguistics as developed in the twentieth century. It is beyond the scope of this chapter to discuss the ways in which linguistics is related to study of the language before, for example, de Saussure, except to say that on the one hand linguistics is deeply indebted to previous philological exploration but on the other hand has distinguished itself by approaching and utilizing these data from a different perspective. It is this perspective that is explored in this chapter with respect to lexicography.

2 It is not altogether agreed what the other component or components are, some linguists seeing it as syntax, with others differentiating a third category of pragmatics. For now, to make such distinctions is beside the point.

3 S. Ullmann, *The Principles of Semantics* (Glasgow: Jackson, 1951); *idem*, *Semantics: An Introduction to the Science of Meaning* (Oxford: Blackwell, 1962); E.A. Nida, *Exploring Semantic Structures* (Munich: Fink, 1975); J. Lyons, *Semantics* (Cambridge: Cambridge University Press, 1977); D.A. Cruse, *Lexical Semantics* (Cambridge Textbooks in Linguistics; Cambridge: Cambridge University Press, 1986). Important works from a historical standpoint include M. Bréal, *Semantics: Studies in the Science of Meaning* (trans. H. Cust; preface J.P. Postgate; London: Heinemann, 1900 [1897]); C.K. Ogden and I.A. Richards, *The Meaning of Meaning: A Study of the Influence of Language upon Thought and of the Science of Symbolism* (10th edn; London: Routledge and Kegan Paul, 1952 [1923]); and more recent works: F.R. Palmer, *Semantics: A New Outline* (2nd edn; Cambridge: Cambridge University Press, 1981); G. Leech, *Semantics* (2nd edn; Harmondsworth: Penguin, 1980).

Although the study of semantics has taken great strides forward in the last thirty or forty years, it is still not agreed what place the lexicon plays in such analysis. For example, Ullmann early on put lexicography or dictionaries and how they are made outside the scope of semantics.[4] This has been the dominant position, even though lexicography has been made a central priority of such linguists as Nida and Louw.[5] Thus from the start there is a tendency even from a linguistic standpoint to distance lexicography from linguistics. This is not necessarily right or unchangeable, but it does have significant implications regarding the theoretical linguistic foundations of the subject. A second reason for the neglected place of lexicography is that it implies translatability, a proposition doubted by many linguists. It is not an accident that most linguistics textbooks do not include a chapter or section on translation, and for two reasons: it is not thought that translation is a quantifiably accurate form of indicator of understanding of the original language; and there is the question in many linguists' minds whether, even if translational equivalents can be given for individual words, natural languages are "intertranslatable at the level of sentences, statements or propositions."[6] The reason for this is that the use of a language is much larger than simply equating words from one language to another, but is based upon a view of language as a social activity—probably the most important social activity—governed by cultural norms.[7] Thus even the

4 Ullmann, *Semantics*, 30.

5 See E.A. Nida, J.P. Louw and R.B. Smith, "Semantic Domains and Componential Analysis of Meaning," in *Current Issues in Linguistic Theory* (ed. R.W. Cole; Bloomington: Indiana University Press, 1977) 139–67. See now J.P. Louw and E.A. Nida, *Greek–English Lexicon of the New Testament based on Semantic Domains* (2 vols.; New York: United Bible Societies, 1988); E.A. Nida and J.P. Louw, *Lexical Semantics of the Greek New Testament* (SBLRBS 25; Atlanta: Scholars Press, 1992); J.P. Louw (ed.), *Lexicography and Translation* (Roggebaai: Bible Society of South Africa, 1985); and J.P. Louw, "How Do Words Mean—If They Do?" *FN* 4.8 (1991) 125–42.

6 See J. Lyons, "*Structural Semantics* in Retrospect," in T.E. Hope *et al.* (eds.), *Language, Meaning and Style: Essays in Memory of Stephen Ullmann* (Leeds: Leeds University Press, 1981) 74 and 75. He is encapsulating the work in his *Structural Semantics: An Analysis of Part of the Vocabulary of Plato* (Publications of the Philological Society 20; Oxford: Blackwell, 1963), and explaining why he did not provide glosses for the Greek words (see pp. 97–99). See also H.A. Gleason, Jr., *An Introduction to Descriptive Linguistics* (revised edn; New York: Holt, Rinehart and Winston, 1961) 77; J.P. Louw, "What Dictionaries are Like," in Louw (ed.), *Lexicography and Translation*, 53–81.

7 Work by certain groups interested in Bible translation has tried to overcome some of these difficulties. See, for example, E.A. Nida, *Toward a Science of Translating with Special Reference to Principles and Procedures involved in Bible Translating* (Leiden: Brill, 1964); E.A. Nida and C.R. Taber, *The Theory and Practice of Translation* (UBS; Leiden: Brill, 1974), and a number of other works. It is at the least debatable whether a transformational framework is the solution (Nida–Taber, *Theory and Practice*, 39), especially since it clearly neglects the social dimension of language. Nida recognizes this in his essay,

vocabulary is organized according to the distinctions made by the language users, not its translators. We may believe that we know all that we need to do effective translation, but this factor must still be taken into consideration.

The situation is compounded by a tendency in New Testament studies to denigrate linguistics as an enterprise of relevance. Thus in a study exploring whether θεός is used of Jesus in the New Testament, involving a number of grammatical issues, including use of the article, there is virtually no mention of any of the relevant work in modern linguistics.[8] Whatever else New Testament studies consists of, it is a text—and consequently language—based discipline. Thus studies of the New Testament without concern for questions of language are an anomaly (or at least should be), and yet there is resistance to matters linguistic. For example, many degrees in theology of various sorts no longer require that Greek be studied. But it is not the students who are necessarily to blame here. To my mind it is often the students' teachers, in other words, we, who are to blame for failure to insist upon rigorous language study. It is noteworthy how many times lexicographical comments in books and articles speak of the "meaning" of a word as "X," often betraying that the author has no idea of the linguistic issues involved in such an apparently simple comment. There are even books attempting to deal with linguistic issues that apparently take a certain amount of pride in not being written by linguists or not using linguistic methods or terminology. Perhaps the most revealing way in which linguistics is marginalized in the discipline of New Testament studies is seen in the kinds of returns that are expected of it. Linguistic method is often dismissed because it has not produced startlingly new and different results than more conventional methods, but of course it is dismissed even more quickly when it produces any results that deviate significantly from the results of conventional exegesis. The result is an approach that "utilizes" linguistic method as a means of reinforcing or substantiating previously discovered results. This strikes me as more the product of an inherent conservative or even reactionary tendency in the discipline, than the result of rational consideration of the merits of linguistic study. Although it may be open to debate somewhere that a linguistic method is the best means to study other languages, can it be the case that New Testament Greek is the one language (if it is in fact best considered a separate language) that should *not* be studied in this way?

"Sociolinguistics and Translating," in *Sociolinguistics and Communication* (ed. J.P. Louw; UBS Monograph Series 1; London: United Bible Societies, 1986) 1–48. Functional grammars, such as systemics, have done a better job of recognizing this. See S. Dik, *Functional Grammar* (North-Holland Linguistics Series; Amsterdam: North-Holland, 1978) esp. 4–5.

8 M.J. Harris, *Jesus as God: The New Testament Use of Theos in Reference to Jesus* (Grand Rapids: Baker, 1992), including an appendix on the article.

2. *Traditional Lexicography*

Before discussing how and in what way a modern lexicon might be constructed, it would be wise to review the ways in which a traditional lexicon is organized and arranged, and some of the immediate questions that come to mind. Included here is a discussion of theological lexicography. This review is worth undertaking, if for no other reason than simply to ensure that we think a little about what our standard lexicographical tools provide.

The traditional lexicon follows a long-standing tradition of word-book making, dating back to the third millennium B.C., when bilingual word lists apparently were first used. In this sense the traditional lexicon is unchanged since earliest times, providing an alphabetically arranged vocabulary list (this is a convention, not a necessity) of one language, with supposedly equivalent words provided in another.[9] Of course, this immediately raises the question of which words should be included in the list. The words included are debatable along two lines: the stratum of usage (or register) and the class of word. For example, should names be included? Many linguists consider names to be words that can be used to refer but do not have sense. Those that carry negative connotations—such as Adolf and Nero—do so because of those to whom they have at one time been used to refer, not because of the name itself. As a further example, what about taboo words or slang words or other non-standard words? What of elitist words? One can see that a dictionary has potentially an important role to play in establishing standard vocabulary, on the basis of some words being included and others not.

There is the even more important task of determining how many distinct meanings a given word might have. Does a word have one distinct meaning with several different applications (that is, is it polysemous) or does it have several distinct meanings, revealing that it is two or more separate words (that is, is it a homophone or homograph)? This is related to the question: when is a word vague and when is it ambiguous? Practically speaking, should it then have only one or two or more dictionary entries? Lexicons divide over this issue, but there are clear implications. What about discussions of meanings? What is the value of the one or two words given in English as equivalents to a Greek word? I suspect that there is often more exegesis of the English word than of the Greek, in the sense that conceptual associations of the English term may well influence what one thinks about the Greek text. For example, the word "sin" has certain English associations that may or may not be part of Greek. And what if

---

9 The history of New Testament lexicography is discussed by J.P. Louw, "The Present State of NT Lexicography," in Louw (ed.), *Lexicography and Translation*, 97–117. On the problems of bilingual lexicography, see S. Wong, "Leftovers of Louw–Nida's Lexicon: Some Considerations Towards 'A Greek–Chinese Lexicon,'" *FN* 7.14 (1994) 137-74.

"sin" is the translation given for ἁμαρτία and παράπτωμα, as some lexicons have? Does that mean that these two Greek words mean the same thing? Translational equivalents are difficult to create, since they often bring as much baggage from the receptor language as from the original.

The problem of translational equivalents is compounded by the requirement that the equivalents be single words (or as near as possible) so as to facilitate glib sounding translations. But how helpful are these? For example, the use of "word" to translate λόγος in John 1:1 is to my mind highly problematic, since the result does not do much to aid in understanding of the text, especially since the translation has become institutionalized in English since Tyndale's translation (1524).[10] This comes very close to the problem discussed by R. Harris, when he calls for guidelines for translational semantics, otherwise one could simply provide *elephant* as the translation of "elephant."[11] The gloss must be explanatory according to a set of guidelines. A second consequence, however, is that these meanings are often treated as *the* meanings of a word. It must be remembered how lexicons are created. They are idealized representations and organizations of meaning based upon interpretative categorizations of the known data.[12] The wealth of material is narrowed down to a few supposedly equivalent words. In some ways this is a necessary convention, but one that has potential pitfalls. First, there is the possibility, even with an epigraphic language,[13] that new data will come to be recognized, for example in various papyri and inscriptions. The categories may need to be adjusted on the basis of this usage, rather than attempting to fit the usage to the known categories. There are no absolute boundaries to these usages. Secondly, in this process, the fact that the meanings are extrapolated from actual contexts is often forgotten. These contexts are often virtually obliterated in the lexicon and consequently often overlooked by its users, who treat the translational equivalents as a smorgasbord of meanings to sample, selecting the one that is most palatable.

---

10 1994 celebrated the 500th anniversary of Tyndale's birth. My comment is not meant as a slight of Tyndale—far from it. When Tyndale translated this, the first English translation from the original Greek, it was fresh and new—and so memorable that it has endured to today.

11 R. Harris, "Truth-Conditional Semantics and Natural Languages," in Hope *et al.* (eds.), *Language, Meaning and Style*, 22.

12 See the trenchant comments of A.C. Thiselton, "Semantics and New Testament Interpretation," in *New Testament Interpretation: Essays on Principles and Methods* (ed. I.H. Marshall; Grand Rapids: Eerdmans, 1977) 78–79.

13 N. Collinge makes an important distinction between a so-called dead and "purely epigraphic language," with the implication that those languages confined to written evidence are still worth studying ("Some Reflexions on Comparative Historical Syntax," *Archivum Linguisticum* 12 [1960] 79, cf. 79–82).

A good case in point is the treatment of prepositions. In Bauer's lexicon,[14] ἐν is defined in terms of four categories: (1) of place, (2) of time, (3) causal or instrumental, and (4) various other uses. Prepositions, most linguists think, fall into a category of words that cannot be placed alongside most other words because they are a certain kind of connecting word that has sense only. The UBS lexicon appreciates this problem and categorizes prepositions as "relational" and "case" words.[15] Apart from that, Bauer's definition reveals three different classifications of the "meaning" of ἐν. One is related to location in place or time (should these be differentiated?), another to means, and the other to some undefined category. It seems to me that these categories can only be defined by usage in context, not by something self-evident from ἐν apart from context, as the last category (various other *uses*) indicates. This raises the question of what role usage, both immediate (syntax) and remote (discourse), plays in lexicography, something often neglected.

There are two subordinate questions to be raised at this point. The first is with regard to something as fundamental as the meanings of words. Related to the question of polysemous and homophonous or homographic words (discussed above) is the issue of whether words have "basic" meanings.[16] This is not the same question as asking whether words have basic translations, which is often how the discussion is carried on. For the traditional lexicon there is the impression given—although I suspect that this reflects what is thought to be a reality in the makers' or users' minds—that words do have basic meanings, that is, that a given word will in virtually all instances share some sort of meaning related—if even by remote extension—to the basic meaning. The treatment of ἐν by Bauer reveals this in large part. In any ontological sense, of course words do not have basic or natural meanings, and they are not related to things from which they derive their meaning.[17] They do not have any meaning apart from speakers/writers of the language using them in certain ways and tacitly agreeing that certain contexts and conventions give them meaning. However, within a particular linguistic code or language game (the useful metaphors vary), let us say the varieties of modern English or the Greek of the New Testament, words do have conventional meanings and are not simply empty ciphers to be filled

---

14 W. Bauer, *A Greek–English Lexicon of the New Testament and Other Early Christian Literature* (trans. W.F. Arndt and F.W. Gingrich; rev. F.W. Gingrich and F.W. Danker; 2nd edn; Chicago: University of Chicago Press, 1979) s.v.

15 Louw–Nida, *Greek–English Lexicon,* xxv and Domains 89 and 90.

16 Thiselton ("Semantics and New Testament Interpretation," 83–84, following Ullmann) thinks there is, while Louw–Nida's *Greek–English Lexicon* is dubious (p. viii).

17 Onomatopoeic words are often cited as words whose meanings are directly derived from the things they denote. But the wide variance in how various language groups "hear" their animal noises shows that there is no facile correlation between the two.

anew on any given occasion.[18] A case in point is again the use of prepositions. In the sentence "I am ______ the house," the choice of preposition alters the meaning of the sentence, depending upon whether one uses "on," "in," "beside," "above," "at," or whatever. But this is only the case in terms of the range of prepositions and similar kinds of words available in English. If the language had only one preposition the situation would be entirely different. If it had only two, it would be different again. In other words, their semantic ranges would be different. The listing of ἐν in Bauer does not reveal this, but it seems to be the case that this is the way vocabulary is related in users' minds, in relation to the other possible words that they know in the language, not alphabetically and in isolation.

The second subordinate point, and one raised above, is with regard to grammatical information. For most lexicons this means the parts of speech, whether a word is a noun, verb, adjective, etc. These are categories derived from traditional grammar (that is, usually Latin categories). These words may also be categorized according to their function. But this immediately extends the discussion beyond the simple word to some larger context. However, words are virtually always used in a context larger than the single word, except in a lexicon. Even Bauer recognizes distinctions in meaning according to usage. But once such functional categories as, for example, agent, patient, instrument, etc., are used, word classes are apparently of minimal value regarding meaning (although they may well have value for morphology). A Greek verb in some of its various forms (such as the participle) may be used in virtually any of these roles. Even using traditional word classes, the participle can function as a member of most of these classes (and can be placed in several by morphology). The context must be determinative.

There is also significant "meaning" attached to the various morphological categories of Greek words that are not always conveyed by a lexicon. This is sometimes referred to as grammatical meaning, but this seems to imply that it is unrelated to lexis. This is not necessarily true. For example, although not everyone agrees on the meanings of the cases, moods or tenses, it is agreed that they mean something. So a noun in the nominative case may well mean something different from a noun in the dative case, and a verb in the indicative mood means something different from a verb in the subjunctive, and the aorist tense means something different from the present, etc. This is true even if we cannot translate these examples with a single equivalent word or any word at all. We have not gone beyond discussion of the word and we realize that there are some complexities that the lexicon does not usually or easily address. Periphrastic constructions—in fact, any units larger than the word—add a further complexity, since the periphrastic consists of two words that substitute

18 It is this that allows metaphor and irony to work.

for a simplex verb form.[19] Is the use of the participle καταλλάσσων in 2 Cor 5:19 periphrastic, and if it is what is its meaning? There is no indication given in Bauer that this is even an issue (or in the UBS lexicon). Isn't the meaning of this word, whether it is syntactically joined to an auxiliary verb or not, in this context or another, an important question regarding the use of this word?

A second function of the traditional dictionary is to provide the spelling and pronunciation of the words of a language (and accenting if it is a language such as Greek). This too is an important function, but the complexities involved are not often addressed. In fact, they are often dismissed, especially for ancient languages. But their being ancient languages is all the more reason to consider these factors. What derived forms should a lexicon include? Bauer is inconsistent. Related is the issue of variant spellings, such as first aorist endings attached to second aorist verb stems. Should a lexicon give variant spellings or only the agreed-upon regularized spellings? This raises the question of who determines the regularized spellings, and the status of variant spellings. The papyri well illustrate the tendency towards itacism during the Hellenistic period, in which there was apparently a tendency in pronunciation of vowels towards the high front vowel [i]. This is seen in a number of words, where *iota* is substituted for *eta*, etc. There is some virtue in maintaining the regular spellings in the lexicon, but this has undoubtedly influenced the conventions of pronunciation that are used in the teaching of Greek. Most teachers use the Erasmian system, which to some extent reflects classical and in particular Attic pronunciation (so far as such things can be determined), in order to preserve differences between *omega* and *omicron*, *iota* and other vowels, diphthongs and simple vowels, and *pi* and *beta*. This probably is not accurate pronunciation for the Greek of the New Testament era (although because of the Attic revival it may reflect the pronunciation of some of those who were later responsible for textual transmission).[20]

This may seem like a rather insignificant issue when one is concerned with lexicography, but it raises several very important questions regarding linguistic dialects and registers, and descriptive versus prescriptive language, important issues in sociolinguistics.[21] The lexicon presents words essentially on the same

---

19 This brief statement does not prejudge the many issues related to periphrastics.

20 See W.S. Allen, *Vox Graeca: A Guide to the Pronunciation of Classical Greek* (2nd edn; Cambridge: Cambridge University Press, 1974); S.-T. Teodorsson, *The Phonology of Ptolemaic Koine* (Studia Graeca et Latina Gothoburgensia 36; Gothenburg: Acta Universitatis Gothoburgensis, 1977); *idem*, "Phonological Variation in Classical Attic and the Development of Koine," *Glotta* 57 (1979) 61–75; K.J. Dover, "The Colloquial Stratum in Classical Attic Prose," in *Classical Contributions: Studies in Honour of M.F. McGregor* (ed. G.S. Shrimpton and D.J. McCargar; Locust Valley, NY: Augustin, 1981) 15–25.

21 See R.A. Hudson, *Sociolinguistics* (Cambridge Textbooks in Linguistics; Cambridge: Cambridge University Press, 1980) esp. 21–72; P. Trudgill, *Sociolinguistics: An*

level. Occasionally, one will find labels such as archaic, poetic, slang, colloquial, obsolete, etc. (although not many such labels in a Greek lexicon), but the dictionary presents the mass of words as if this were the full range of potential words for any given user. In theory this may be true, although the reality is quite different. These various levels of usage have different social implications, regarding when they are used and by whom. But a more important point, it seems to me, is that even if one knew all of the words in a language (including all of those being created to meet new situations), one would not consider drawing upon all of these words in any given context. There are some occasions where the language of business or commerce is required, some where formal language to a superior is necessary, some where informal language to a peer is proper, some where language to a subordinate is necessary, etc. One can imagine all sorts of different occasions where various kinds of language are more appropriate than others. Our knowledge of this information for most ancient languages is limited, although for Greek we apparently know enough to include more information in this regard than is usually provided. For example, we know that a different kind of vocabulary is used in Hebrews than in John's Gospel, Mark's Gospel or Paul's main letters. Or under σκύβαλα (used in Phil 3:8) some comment should be made regarding the shift to a colloquial if not slang level. Whereas the temptation is to ascribe such differences to varieties, the category of register is probably more accurate. Some generalizations can be made that indicate various strata of vocabulary. When the non-literary papyri and the Atticistic texts are considered, a fuller range is made possible.[22] Of course, the lexicon of an epigraphic language cannot do justice to the oral level, since all of our evidence—despite what we might think about the papyri, for example—consists of written sources. This is a necessary limitation but one that must be considered, nevertheless.

Thirdly, etymologies are often provided in lexicons.[23] True etymologies

---

Introduction to Language and Society (revised edn; Harmondsworth: Penguin, 1983) *passim*; J. Milroy and L. Milroy, *Authority in Language: Investigating Language Prescription and Standardisation* (London: Routledge and Kegan Paul, 1985) 1–28; M. Gregory and S. Carroll, *Language and Situation: Language Varieties and their Social Contexts* (Language and Society; London: Routledge and Kegan Paul, 1978).

22 On the concept of register along with dialect, see M.A.K. Halliday and R. Hasan, "Text and Context: Aspects of Language in a Social-Semiotic Perspective," *Sophia Linguistica* 6 (1980) 60–74; *idem*, *Language as Social Semiotic: The Social Interpretation of Language and Meaning* (London: Edward Arnold, 1978) 31–35. On registers in Hellenistic Greek, see S.E. Porter, *Verbal Aspect in the Greek of the New Testament, with Reference to Tense and Mood* (Studies in Biblical Greek 1; New York: Peter Lang, 1989) 152–53.

23 See below on theological lexicography for more discussion of this point. On historical linguistics, see T. Bynon, *Historical Linguistics* (Cambridge Textbooks in Linguistics; Cambridge: Cambridge University Press, 1977), where it will be noted that etymology plays a relatively small role in the field.

need to be distinguished from folk etymologies. True etymologies are a useful part of historical linguistics, that is, in tracing the origins and development of a word. They may even have some bearing upon the question of meaning. Unfortunately, much of what we know about Greek is of the folk etymological sort. Occasionally one hears statements to the effect that it is too bad that we do not understand the Greek language like Plato or Aristotle or other "real Greeks" did. I am not so sure that this is desirable. Plato in his "Cratylus" (*Crat*. 399C), full of all sorts of reflections on language, contains this fanciful etymology of the word ἄνθρωπος. He says that it comes from the verb ἀναθρεῖ ("look up") and ὄπωπε ("he has seen"), because it is only man who looks up and has seen. True etymologies are also to be distinguished from transparency. Transparency is the recognition that some words do in fact reveal their meanings through the composition of their component parts. For example, verbs of motion with prefixed prepositions are considered transparent (e.g. εἰσῆλθον "go in"). Transparency is not a category regularly utilized in biblical lexicography.

Nevertheless, there is a persistent tendency to use etymologies in an irresponsible way. As recently as 1974, one scholar stated, "In investigating the history of any word it is essential that we begin with its etymology [so far, acceptable though not recommended, but now things take a turn] and take its etymological meaning as the basic one. For if words mean anything at all [this is a point that needs definition], then the radical words, of whose elements a compound word is constituted, must surely disclose the fundamental meaning of that word."[24] A nice idea (I here play intentionally on the Latin meaning of *nice*, ignorant), but one that is highly problematic when one considers how people use language, apart from consideration of any principles of linguistic study. Not only are many etymologies unknown both now and to native users (remember Plato's opinion of ἄνθρωπος), but it overlooks the fact that apart from a very small group that may study such things these kinds of histories of words are unknown to the users of the language. If only those who knew the histories of their words could use those words we, like people of any language at any time, would be reduced to speechlessness.

A similar kind of argument is often used with the Septuagint.[25] Explanations of why a particular word is used in the Greek of the New Testament are often devised on the basis of Septuagintal usage. For example, some have argued[26] that ἐκκλησία is used to translate the Hebrew *qahal*, since it comes from *qol*, meaning "voice, call" (with the possibility of the influence of [k] and [l], an

24 C.C. Caragounis, "*Opsonion*: A Reconsideration of its Meaning," *NovT* 16 (1974) 36.

25 M. Silva, *Biblical Words and their Meaning: An Introduction to Lexical Semantics* (2nd edn; Grand Rapids: Zondervan, 1994 [1983]) 68–74.

26 See below on theological lexicography, since this is an example that G. Kittel uses, refuted by J. Barr.

unlikely suggestion), and since the Greeks had no single word for a religious community. This assessment tends to make ἐκκλησία into a technical theological term on the basis of the Septuagint, one that finds it difficult to explain not only Matt 16:18 and 18:18 (containing two different kinds of religious community) but Acts 19:32, where the word is used to refer to a hostile crowd. More likely is the fact that ἐκκλησία is used because it was a word for "gathering for a purpose," one instance of which might have been a Christian one.

As a last factor to consider, one must examine what is done in traditional lexicons regarding word relations, even such basic ones as synonymy or antonymy (there are other sense relations as well). Most people have a basic sense of the synonyms and antonyms of their language, but lexicons of ancient Greek, including Bauer's, virtually neglect this area. Abbott-Smith's lexicon does include information regarding synonyms, often in the form of a list.[27] But how does one decide how these items are related? Similar translational equivalents give the impression that the words are more or less complete synonyms. This is the impression that some of the older sources that purport to deal with synonyms give. For example, Trench appears to believe that βίος and ζωή are synonyms since they can be translated as "life."[28] This kind of approach often has some interesting outworkings. For example, there is the unexamined assumption that there are such things as true or complete synonyms in a language. Nevertheless, little if anything is done with antonyms or other kinds of sense relations. Thus there is little in the traditional lexicon to give the user an idea of how words related in meaning are related to each other.

In the light of what has been said above regarding the deficiencies of traditional lexicography, including its failure to develop a method that actually allows complex data to be adequately analysed by use of the lexical tools, traditional lexicography has left itself open to the development of theological lexicography. This may seem an archaic concept, but it was institutionalized in two lectures delivered at Cambridge in 1937 by G. Kittel himself, in which he outlined its programme.[29] Theological lexicography is essentially an attempt to

27 G. Abbott-Smith, *A Manual Greek Lexicon of the New Testament* (3rd edn; Edinburgh: T. & T. Clark, 1929).

28 R.C. Trench, *Synonyms of the New Testament* (1880; repr. Grand Rapids: Eerdmans, 1963) s.v.

29 G. Kittel, *Lexicographia Sacra* (London: SPCK, 1938), from whom the following examples are taken. Of course, Kittel's work and approach, especially as found in G. Kittel and G. Friedrich, *Theological Dictionary of the New Testament* (10 vols.; trans. G.W. Bromiley; Grand Rapids: Eerdmans, 1964–76, ET of *Theologisches Wörterbuch zum Neuen Testament* [Stuttgart: Kohlhammer, 1933–73]), were severely criticized by J. Barr, *The Semantics of Biblical Language* (Oxford: Oxford University Press, 1961). See also Silva, *Biblical Words and their Meaning*, 22–28; P. Cotterell and M. Turner, *Linguistics and*

describe words and their histories, especially those words with theological significance. The significance lies in the use of words that can be tied to definite historical events to which they bear witness. In other words, words are thought to bear witness to facts, with the facts behind these events, or the fundamental events, being even more significant than the words themselves. Language then exists not as a self-referring system but as a crystal through which to make concepts visible. For Kittel, genuine lexicography is the study of this relationship. For this purpose, the language that is analysed is the language of the New Testament treated as a distinct language heavily influenced by Semitic thought. Its development is seen to be completely distinct from that of other Greek and not to follow the kinds of patterns seen in the development of other languages. As evidence of this, δόξα is said to have become an entirely new word in the New Testament, changing from its classical meaning "opinion" to "glory of God."[30] The distinctives of secular Greek, as opposed to biblical Hebrew, are, in the minds of theological lexicographers, intimately connected to the particular ways of thinking of these people. Greek is static and cyclical, because of its use of adjectives and verbless clauses, whereas Hebrew is dynamic and linear, because of its focus upon the verb.[31] The discipline of New Testament studies has in the past been dominated and in fact continues to be influenced by theology, and in particular theological lexicography,[32] and I would say often at the expense of informed linguistic study. Numerous questionable assumptions and methods have been perpetuated under the veneer of lexicography, when what is really meant is theology. In some cases, the standard reference tools used in New Testament studies were written before the advent of and certainly before the development of modern linguistics. Of course, scholars cannot be held blameworthy of not using a not-yet-developed method, but neither should their conclusions be exalted or at the least held immune from criticism on that same account.

Biblical Interpretation (London: SPCK, 1989) 106–28. An improvement is C. Spîcq, *Theological Lexicon of the New Testament* (3 vols.; trans. J.D. Ernest; Peabody: Hendrickson, 1994 [1978, 1982]) esp. 1.vii–viii.

30 There are several problems with this analysis. First, the disjunctive thinking is evident, in which words are thought to be either pagan or Christian. Secondly, the semantic development of the word is neglected, from "opinion" to "high opinion" to "glory." Thirdly, the word is not used in the New Testament only of divine glory (Matt 6:29) but retains other senses. Fourthly, often the word is modified to indicate the divine ascription. On the concept of so-called Christian words, and the limited context in which they might appear, see S.E. Porter, "Is *dipsuchos* (James 1,8; 4,8) a 'Christian' Word?" *Bib* 71 (1990) 469–73.

31 See S.E. Porter, "Two Myths: Corporate Personality and Language/Mentality Determinism," *SJT* 43 (1990) 289–307, for discussion of how these characterizations are continued.

32 Theological lexicography was part of the biblical theology movement. See B.S. Childs, *Biblical Theology in Crisis* (Philadelphia: Westminster Press, 1970) 47.

Several of the assumptions of theological lexicography that have bearing upon serious lexicography warrant mention. Even those who do not share the agenda of the biblical theology movement can often be found subscribing to some of its ill-conceived tenets. For example, the idea of words bearing witness to facts was already disputed in philosophical thinking by Frege, who showed that there is no necessary correlation between the word and the thing. This is fundamental to the distinction between sense and reference (see below).[33] It is important to note that it is not a word that refers, but a language-user who uses a word to refer, otherwise it is simply an item in the lexical store.

The reliance upon etymology has been discussed above, but a classic instance that has died hard is J. Jeremias's thoughts regarding use of Aramaic *abba*.[34] Jeremias argued that it was a vocative form, probably going back to childish babble. The same word, according to Jeremias, was used by adults and children, so by the time of Jesus it had become an adult word, and thus, on the basis of its origin in child-language, was one that meant "daddy." All of this has been called into serious question.[35] The speculation on the origins of the sounds in childish babble is dubious (as is the idea that the sounds "pa" and "ma" are childish references to parents), besides the fact that it has no apparent relevance for the developed use of the word. This crucial link gone, Jeremias's case collapses. Besides the fact that many of Jeremias's Aramaic examples are too late to be of relevance for study of the New Testament, the fact that children and adults use the word does not necessarily imply an intimate use, especially when a sense of intimacy is totally lacking in many of the contexts. In the New Testament, the word *abba* is always glossed by ὁ πατήρ (Mark 14:36; Rom 8:15; Gal 4:6), never a diminutive. The article probably indicates emphatic usage, not being modified by "my" or another term of familiarity. The reliance upon a dubious etymology, motivated by theological interests, probably led Jeremias astray.

Concerning the relationship of word and concept, confusion still abounds, for example when an author refers to the "Johannine concept of logos" or the "concept of διακονέω."[36] The important consideration here, and a reason why C. Brown's *New International Dictionary of New Testament Theology* is

---

33 See W.T. Jones, *A History of Western Philosophy*. V. *The Twentieth Century to Wittgenstein and Sartre* (2nd revised edn; New York: Harcourt Brace Jovanovich, 1975) 148–50.

34 See, for example, J. Jeremias, *New Testament Theology: The Proclamation of Jesus* (trans. J. Bowden; NTL; London: SCM Press, 1971) 61–68, among several works; cf. also Kittel, *Lexicographia Sacra*, 14–16.

35 See J. Barr, "Abba isn't Daddy," *JTS* 39 (1988) 28–47.

36 The examples here are simply too numerous to mention, and to single out one or two would be unfair.

significantly better than Kittel's lexicon,[37] is that there may be many words that play a part in forming the Greek concept of love, ἀγάπη being only one of them. In fact, the Greek concept of something might even be represented by a scene in which there is no common lexical item. This is closely related to the problem of studying words in isolation, as if the individual words have theological meaning. Barr was clearly ahead of his peers when he said that "It is the sentence (and of course the still larger literary complex such as the complete speech or poem) which is the linguistic bearer of the usual theological statement, and not the word (the lexical unit)..."[38] In the extreme, there have been those who have wanted to write theologies of the prepositions, besides such problems as understanding the use of ἐκκλησία, and words for love. It is true that there are some important uses of the preposition ὑπέρ in the New Testament, but it seems to me that the significance is more fully appreciated when it is realized that substitutionary uses were part and parcel of common Greek usage, seen in instances in the papyri when, for example, one person writes "for" another,[39] than in some sanctified use of ὑπέρ that must neglect all of the more humdrum uses. From a linguistic standpoint these non-theological uses (if the term may be used) are every bit as important in establishing the usage of the word as the special instances. But the tendency has been to then read the theological sense into all of the uses, or to commit "illegitimate totality transfer" to use Barr's phrase. Similarly, G. Fee, in his recent work on the Holy Spirit, understands the use of πνεῦμα in Rom 1:9 as referring both to Paul's human spirit and to the Spirit of God at work in his own spirit. Not surprisingly, he cites the article in *TDNT* by E. Schweizer in agreement.[40]

Furthermore, theological lexicography takes an anthropomorphic or mystical view of language. Kittel says that the language of the New Testament has a single purpose, that is, the expressing of what has taken place. Kittel gives the idea that his is a kind of lexicography that is internal to the language and has penetrated to its core. He wants to link language to theology. But Kittel has language acting of its own accord, apart from the users of the language. Perhaps the writers wished to express this single purpose, but surely it was not the language itself. Where does this language live, where is it located and how does

---

37 C. Brown (ed.), *NIDNTT* (3 vols.; Grand Rapids: Zondervan, 1975–78). This is the translation of a German *Begriffslexicon*.

38 Barr, *Semantics of Biblical Language*, 263. Barr foreshadows the recent development of discourse analysis. See S.E. Porter, "Discourse Analysis and New Testament Studies: An Introductory Survey," in S.E. Porter and D.A. Carson (eds.), *Discourse Analysis and Other Topics in Biblical Greek* (JSNTSup 113; Sheffield: Sheffield Academic Press, 1995) 14–35.

39 See S.E. Porter, *Idioms of the Greek New Testament* (Biblical Languages: Greek 2; 2nd edn; Sheffield: JSOT Press, 1994) 176–77.

40 G.D. Fee, *God's Empowering Presence: The Holy Spirit in the Letters of Paul* (Peabody: Hendrickson, 1994) 485, citing E. Schweizer, *TDNT*, 6.435.

it accomplish its purposes? A. Deissmann's and J.H. Moulton's view is much more convincing when they find the vocabulary and syntax part of the common language, applied to tasks by its users.[41] Kittel ends up making language (to say nothing of theology) what it clearly is not or at least is not meant to be, and that is something that exists in isolation apart from language users. For Kittel, because "yoke" (ζύγος) is used of Christ's yoke, it must be a theological term, which will come as a surprise to many a beast of burden. Of 1 Thess 1:5ff., Kittel says that λόγος in 1:6 is "Word" (capital W), when in fact the article could simply indicate "this word" and refer to v. 5. Of εὐαγγέλιον, he argues that since εὐαγγελίζομαι translates Hebrew *basar* it must represent "procession of God," neglecting the fact that *basar* means "bringing news" good *or* bad in the Old Testament and minimizing the fact that in an inscription from Priẹne the noun refers to the good news regarding the emperor's birthday.[42]

3. *Modern Lexicography and New Testament Studies*

Once placed in this light, the shortcomings of traditional lexicography, including theological lexicography, become manifest. But what can be said of positive steps towards incorporating sound linguistic practice into modern lexical study? There is much to be said and there are various ways in which the subject may be examined. I will try to present some of the factors to be considered in modern lexicography, illustrated in terms of the recent UBS lexicon. I realize that there has been criticism of the execution of this project.[43] Some of this criticism is certainly valid, including the failure to treat as many examples as would be ideal,[44] and the relative lack of syntactical information.[45]

41 See A. Deissmann, "Hellenistic Greek with Special Consideration of the Greek Bible," 39–59, and J.H. Moulton, "New Testament Greek in the Light of Modern Discovery," 60–97, in S.E. Porter (ed.), *The Language of the New Testament: Classic Essays* (JSNTSup 60; Sheffield: JSOT Press, 1991).

42 Kittel, *Lexicographia Sacra*, 20–30 *passim* for examples. Cf. A. Deissmann, *Light from the Ancient East* (London: Hodder & Stoughton, 1927; repr. Grand Rapids: Baker, 1978) 366–67, referring to OGIS 1.458.

43 Most recently see J.A.L. Lee, "The United Bible Societies' Lexicon and its Analysis of Meanings," *FN* 5.10 (1992) 167–89, with response by J.P. Louw, "The Analysis of Meaning in Lexicography," *FN* 6.12 (1993) 139–48.

44 Of course the ideal number would be all instances, but then there would be the (already heard) criticism that their interpretations are not adequate. Several examples that I did not find were the use of παρεκτός in Matt 5:32, the use of μὴ ἐπί in Matt 19:9, discussion of πέτρος as "denoting" more than simply the name but a single rock, δίψυχος in Jas 1:8 (which I think is different from the use in 4:8), the use of κολλάομαι in 1 Cor 6:16, 17, and the use of καταλλάσσω in 2 Cor 5:19. These are some of my personal favourites, so the authors can hardly be held responsible for not including them. But it does indicate the

I would not always have made the same choices, created quite the same framework, or used the same terminology. But these are matters of execution. The concept, to my mind, is unimpeachable, and much to be welcomed. It makes the alternatives look to be the inadequate lexicons that they are. This is far from saying that this is the last word in lexicography, but so much has been gained by it that must be built upon rather than dismissed. The factors to be considered are based upon the principles of modern linguistics, and this provides some of the difficulty because, as mentioned above, some of these principles are quite different from those traditionally used.

Linguistics is a social science and uses a social-science methodology. This is not the kind of objectivist science of the nineteenth century that was confident that it could classify all data neatly into their various categories, but one that recognizes the role of the interpreter in formulating a testable hypothesis. Interpreters create models or theories in order to interpret what they have ascertained as important data. In fact, the theory is part of the determination of what constitutes important data. As Lyons states, "There is no such thing as theory-neutral and hypothesis-free observation and data collection."[46] Kempson has described the process by which linguists go about building an adequate model of a language. This applies to lexicography as well, when she says that "linguistics...is concerned, then, not with the mere collection of facts, but with the construction of a system of abstract concepts which will account most adequately for the particular properties which languages display."[47] However, with the development of linguistics into several major schools of thought (formalists vs. functionalists, etc.), some have wondered whether linguists have many assumptions in common. Hudson has shown that there is probably more in common than most realize.[48] For example,[49] linguistics is empirically based and explicit in its formulations. The strength of a theory is determined on the basis of which formulation is seen best to explain the available data. Traditional

---

huge task of creating a lexicon such as this, and the difficulties still confronting students of the Greek text.

45 This is beyond their stated purpose, but, as noted above and below, should be included in some form.

46 J. Lyons, *Language and Linguistics* (Cambridge: Cambridge University Press, 1981) 40.

47 R. Kempson, *Semantic Theory* (Cambridge Textbooks in Linguistics; Cambridge: Cambridge University Press, 1977) 1.

48 R. Hudson, "Some Issues on Which Linguists Can Agree," *Journal of Linguistics* 17 (1981) 333–43; but cf. R. de Beaugrande, *Linguistic Theory: The Discourse of Fundamental Works* (London: Longman, 1991) 1–5 and *passim*.

49 The following are developed in S.E. Porter, "Studying Ancient Languages from a Modern Linguistic Perspective: Essential Terms and Terminology," *FN* 2.4 (1989) 151–55. It is useful also to consider what modern linguistics is not, in terms of lexical study (see pp. 159–68).

and modern lexicography, as pointed out above, do not even necessarily agree on the data (what constitutes a lexical item or entry?) to say nothing of attempts to analyse the data. The UBS lexicon has been criticized for not making the kinds of fine distinctions that others desire. With the kind of history of theological lexicography and word by word analysis of much exegesis, it is not surprising to find this kind of criticism. But as Louw has recently pointed out, the ordering process is quite difficult: whereas one may lump data sometimes, one splits other data. What is more important is the grounds on which this is done.[50] Secondly, linguistics is systematic in approach and concerned with system in language. In many respects the system is the language, and this includes the lexicon as well as the grammar. This is a major point of weakness for conventional lexicography since the mere listing of words does not give a sense of how these words are arranged in the language or in the minds of its users. The modern lexicographer's task should be to report this structure systematically. As Lyons has stated, "the lexical structure of a language—the structure of its vocabulary—is best regarded as a large and intricate network of sense-relations: it is like a huge, multidimensional, spider's web, in which each strand is one such relation and each knot in the web is a different lexeme."[51] The UBS lexicon attempts this through the use of semantic domains. Thirdly, linguistics emphasizes synchronic over diachronic study (without neglecting the importance of diachronic study). Whereas much of traditional lexicography analyses the individual longitudinal fibers of the language-plant, modern linguists are more concerned with how the various strands are concurrently configured. The UBS lexicon takes the Greek of the New Testament as a "language," that is, as a self-contained linguistic system. Although the editors may well be open to other evidence, for all intents and purposes their exposition is of the Greek found in the New Testament. This is a limitation, in that it isolates this Greek from other varieties, but it also points out the difficulty in creating a modern lexicon in the light of the wealth of information available, especially in the ancient Greek papyri and inscriptions. Fourthly, linguists believe that linguistics should be descriptive not prescriptive. Traditional lexicons tend to be prescriptive (though not always helpfully) in several ways: they do not include non-standard language (although most New Testament Greek lexicons include all words), they mistake translational equivalents (glosses) for meanings, and they do not indicate how these words are used in relation to other words within the language. The UBS lexicon, through the use of semantic domains, attempts to indicate word relations, and works from the assumption that, while a gloss may be an appropriate translation in a given

50 Louw, "Analysis of Meaning in Lexicography," 140–41.

51 J. Lyons, *Language, Meaning and Context* (London: Fontana, 1981) 75.

context, lexical meaning is more difficult to describe.[52] With these principles in mind, it is worth exploring what this might mean for constructing a lexicon.

First, it must be recognized that meaning functions at various levels, and hence is a highly complex concept to define and use.[53] Traditional discussions imply too narrow an understanding of meaning, often in terms of finding a single translational equivalent or gloss and only basic—if any—other information. The meaning of even such an apparently simple thing as a single word—or better, a lexeme—goes far beyond a simple word for word substitute (I do not even attempt to get involved in the whole question of what constitutes a word or lexeme[54]). This is even evident in discussion of English words for which there are all kinds of associations. To give some idea of how difficult the concept of meaning is, one can turn to any introduction to linguistics. For example, in a recent linguistics book for students there are four definitions of meaning offered: referential theory, ideational or mentalistic theory, meaning-is-use theory, and truth-conditional theory.[55] These are only four possible definitions. An examination of a more advanced book reveals that the situation is in fact even more complex. For example, there are various ways of delimiting lexical hierarchies, including how one creates taxonomies and attempts to define various kinds of opposites (previously referred to as antonyms) and synonyms.[56] Thus the way in which meaning is defined and determined is a difficulty that must be faced.

To aid in discussion, it might be useful to recognize that at least the following five levels of meaning have relevance for study of the lexicon of the New Testament: lexical semantics or the "meanings" of words (the major topic of this chapter),[57] grammatical semantics (the meanings of such things as verb

---

52 See Louw, "How Do Words Mean," 139–41.

53 See, for example, Lyons, *Semantics*, 1–5 and *passim*; D. Bolinger, *Aspects of Language* (New York: Harcourt, Brace and World, 1968) 218–46; Cotterell–Turner, *Linguistics and Biblical Interpretation*, 77–105.

54 See discussion in J. Lyons, *Introduction to Theoretical Linguistics* (Cambridge: Cambridge University Press, 1968) 194–206; P.H. Matthews, *Morphology: An Introduction to the Theory of Word-Structure* (Cambridge Textbooks in Linguistics; Cambridge: Cambridge University Press, 1974) 20–36; Lyons, *Semantics*, 18–25; F. Palmer, *Grammar* (Harmondsworth: Penguin, 1971) 41–51; Cruse, *Lexical Semantics*, 49–83.

55 Lyons, *Language, Meaning and Context*, 30–31. These four theories are briefly discussed in ch. 1 in this volume, pp. 7–20.

56 See Cruse, *Lexical Semantics, passim*.

57 See, for example, Cruse, *Lexical Semantics, passim*; Lyons, *Semantics*, 174–335, 512–69; Thiselton, "Semantics and New Testament Interpretation," 75–93; J.P. Louw, *Semantics of New Testament Greek* (Chico, CA: Scholars Press; Philadelphia: Fortress Press, 1982); Silva, *Biblical Words and their Meaning*, esp. 101–69; D.A. Carson, *Exegetical Fallacies* (Grand Rapids: Baker, 1984) esp. 25–66; J. Mateos, *Metodo de Analisis Semantico Aplicado al Griego del Nuevo Testamento* (Estudios de Filología Neotestamentaria 1;

tenses/aspects, the case system, etc.),[58] sentential semantics or syntax (e.g. word and clause order),[59] pragmatics (the meanings of words in context),[60] and discourse.[61] "Meaning" can be found at each of these levels, but the meaning being discussed here is the kind that centres upon the word or lexical item, and hence the categories of lexical and grammatical semantics, since they focus upon the word, must be considered. Having said this, there is no way in which all five levels do not come into consideration. For example, how is it possible to speak of the lexical semantics of a word apart from envisioning its usage in a context? How is it possible to think of the meaning of a discourse without also considering the words it contains and how they are configured?[62] The editors of the UBS lexicon rightly recognize that the correct meaning of a word is the one that fits the context, whether that be textual or extratextual (although it is difficult to think of how much we know about the extratextual context of the

Córdoba, Spain: Ediciones El Almendro, 1989); Cotterell–Turner, *Linguistics and Biblical Interpretation*, 129–87.

58 See, for example, M.A.K. Halliday, *An Introduction to Functional Grammar* (London: Edward Arnold, 1985); Lyons, *Semantics*, 373–511; Matthews, *Morphology*, *passim*; B. Comrie, *Aspect: An Introduction to the Study of Verbal Aspect and Related Problems* (Cambridge Textbooks in Linguistics; Cambridge: Cambridge University Press, 1976); *idem*, *Tense* (Cambridge Textbooks in Linguistics; Cambridge: Cambridge University Press, 1985); F.R. Palmer, *Mood and Modality* (Cambridge Textbooks in Linguistics; Cambridge: Cambridge University Press, 1986); B.J. Blake, *Case* (Cambridge Textbooks in Linguistics; Cambridge: Cambridge University Press, 1994); J.P. Louw, "Linguistic Theory and the Greek Case System," *Acta Classica* 9 (1966) 73–88; S. Wong, "What Case is This Case? An Application of Semantic Case in Biblical Exegesis," *Jian Dao* 1 (1994) 49–73; Porter, *Verbal Aspect*, esp. 75–109, and chs. 1–3 in this volume.

59 P.H. Matthews, *Syntax* (Cambridge Textbooks in Linguistics; Cambridge: Cambridge University Press, 1981); K.J. Dover, *Greek Word Order* (Cambridge: Cambridge University Press, 1960); J.T. Reed, "The Infinitive with Two Substantival Accusatives: An Ambiguous Construction?" *NovT* 33 (1991) 1–27; S.E. Porter, "Word Order and Clause Structure in New Testament Greek: An Unexplored Area of Greek Linguistics Using Philippians as a Test Case," *FN* 6.12 (1993) 177–205.

60 S.C. Levinson, *Pragmatics* (Cambridge Textbooks in Linguistics; Cambridge: Cambridge University Press, 1983); Lyons, *Semantics*, 570–786; J.L. Mey, *Pragmatics: An Introduction* (Oxford: Blackwell, 1993).

61 R. de Beaugrande and W. Dressler, *Introduction to Text Linguistics* (London: Longman, 1981); G. Brown and G. Yule, *Discourse Analysis* (Cambridge Textbooks in Linguistics; Cambridge: Cambridge University Press, 1983); Halliday–Hasan, "Text and Context," 4–91; Porter, *Idioms of the Greek New Testament*, 298–307; D.A. Black *et al.* (eds.), *Linguistics and New Testament Interpretation: Essays on Discourse Analysis* (Nashville: Broadman, 1992); Porter–Carson (eds.), *Discourse Analysis and Other Topics in Biblical Greek*, Part I, pp. 14–116.

62 There are also idioms or "units" (so-called by the UBS lexicon in the index), in which the meaning of the string cannot be determined from its individual units or it behaves like a simple word.

New Testament at this stage).[63]

Several helpful constructs have been put forward by linguists to aid in this discussion. However, examination of a recent work in lexical semantics, such as the one by Cruse mentioned above, shows how complex the study of the lexicon can be. To get a sense of how such study might proceed, I will present a basic linguistic procedure for discussing the meaning of words. This is done not only to introduce the kinds of categories that must be considered, but to show how very different this procedure is from the one described above regarding traditional lexicography. Most linguists think that it is useful to make some sort of distinction between external and internal signification of words, that is, between how words can be used to signify entities that are extra-linguistic or outside the world of language and how they can be used to signify within the language in which they appear. Whereas traditional (and certainly theological) lexicography emphasizes the external dimension, linguistics rightly emphasizes the internal. There are various ways in which these distinctions are indicated. It is not my purpose here to arbitrate between them. Terminology such as denotation and connotation, sense and reference, and sense, reference and denotation are sometimes used.[64] The UBS lexicon uses designative or denotative and associative or connotative,[65] but this is not a happy set of choices. The impression is that denotation covers all of the meanings of a word and that connotation merely the associative meanings or the emotive bits left over. How does this correlate with the several schemes for meaning mentioned above? Does it make denotation a function of language rather than of language users? Where does reference fit in? Where does sense fit in? Does denotation cover names? Does it cover relation words and the like? If so, denotation seems to be a pretty blunt instrument. The authors' use of meaning and reference just further confuses a complex issue.

Although it is commonly thought—or at least stated—that words refer to things, this as Frege pointed out is not so, but has helped to perpetuate the difficulties found in theological lexicography. Words are not the things, and they do not emerge from or return to the thing, except that within a linguistic system the users of the language may use a word to signify a thing. When a speaker uses a word to speak of a thing, this can be called reference. Reference,

---

63 Louw–Nida, *Greek–English Lexicon*, xvi; Nida–Louw, *Lexical Semantics*, 12.

64 See Lyons, *Introduction to Theoretical Linguistics*, 424–34; *idem*, *Semantics*, 177–215; Cotterell–Turner, *Linguistics and Biblical Interpretation*, 77–90. For an application to biblical semantics, see M. Winger, *By What Law? The Meaning of Νόμος in the Letters of Paul* (SBLDS 128; Atlanta: Scholars Press, 1992) esp. 8–9, where he uses meaning and reference.

65 Actually the authors use a variety of terminology, also including reference and meaning. See Louw–Nida, *Greek–English Lexicon*, xv, xvii; Nida–Louw, *Lexical Semantics*, 7–8.

therefore, is a fairly specific task used to connect the world of language with the world outside of language, and a task that is not always going on, even when fairly common things that exist in the world are being spoken of. It is certainly not the part of lexical study that has priority either in learning a language or in determining its meaning (as Wittgenstein came to realize).[66] For example, when someone speaks of "cows," which "cows" are they referring to? It is probably good to recognize that signification in the world can refer either to specific items or to classes of items. It is when specific items are being spoken of that language users are using language to refer. What of language that is used to speak of classes of items that exist in the world, not in their particularity but in a more idealized realm? Some linguists prefer to call this denotation, when a word is used to speak of a class or type of thing. This category provides a link between the world of things and the world of language. Then there are the relations that words enjoy as part of a language system in users' minds. This is called sense. A word's sense is how a given word marks out its own territory in relation to the other words in a language, or at least in a given user's vocabulary. In these terms, apart from words such as names every word known to a user has a sense, or meaningful relations with other words, although it may not have referential capability. This does not make it less meaningful.

Some instances may help to illustrate. For example, when Paul uses the name of Timothy or Titus he is apparently referring to particular individuals. In 1 Corinthians 13 he argues that love (for which there is no referent as defined above, only denotation) takes priority over many other things that also have denotative capability. Prepositions are not used to refer or denote, but they form a system of relation words within a language, depending upon the number of prepositions. It is possible to think of a language with just two prepositions, one for direction and one for location, with the first often translated "to" and the second "on" or "in." Another language may have eighteen prepositions, two of which are often translated "to" and "on." This does not mean that these prepositions mean the same things to users of these two languages, even if translated similarly. In the first, the two prepositions divide up the entire field of prepositional functions and in the second only (let's say) one ninth of the semantic terrain. Each preposition must be understood in terms of the relations it maintains within the language in terms of its own language system.

The same kind of sets of relations exist for the vocabulary of any language. This raises the question of how sense relations can be established and quantified. There are many ways that this too has been discussed in the literature on semantics, but perhaps the most fruitful has been in terms of

---

66 Cf. J. Aitchison, *The Articulate Mammal: An Introduction to Psycholinguistics* (2nd edn; London: Hutchinson, 1983) 115–38, esp. 118–19; M.A.K. Halliday, *Learning How to Mean—Explorations in the Development of Language* (London: Edward Arnold, 1975).

semantic field theory, or semantic domains.[67] Semantic field theory recognizes that words do not appear in isolation but in contextual relations, and that language users use words to divide the world, experience, feelings, in fact all that they talk about, into various realms delimited by words. Thus the words of a language are not simply found in alphabetical lists but they are found grouped in users' minds according to the fields they occupy. One quick way to see the apparent correctness of this is to ask oneself to list the words one knows, proceeding alphabetically, versus to ask oneself to list the words one knows by meaningful fields, such as emotions, items of clothing, etc. There have been two ways of approaching this in New Testament studies. The first is Thiselton's, in which he speaks of the semantic range of a lexical item. By this he shows how a word may well be part of several semantic fields, such as πνεῦμα.[68] The other is Silva's, in which he exemplifies a semantic field by showing how a concept may be spoken of using various lexical items, such as the several verbs that help to make up the field of "knowledge."[69] Both perspectives are needed to grasp the importance of the concept. The concept of semantic fields or semantic domains is one that the UBS lexicon utilizes, taking into account both approaches.

But there seem to be at least two major difficulties with semantic field theory. These are besides the obvious difficulty—that this is not a theory-neutral framework but a construct used to understand the language. The first is determining what the semantic fields are. This requires first a comprehensive knowledge of the language, but secondly the admission that model building in linguistics is an interpretative exercise. Other interpreters may not agree on the same fields. Rather than abandon the exercise, however, it would seem to me that the way forward is to assess which fields provide for the largest number of meaningful categories, organize them in meaningful hierarchies, and have the fewest number of left over categories or concepts (my impression is also that the most successful model will recognize homographs without an overabundance of them, thus indicating an appropriate degree of generalization). Nida and Louw are aware of this possible criticism, and they have tried to explain their criteria in *Lexical Semantics*.[70] However, questions might still be raised regarding certain instances, such as relations (Domain 89) and case (Domain 90).

The second difficulty is quantifying the relations. Here componential

---

67 See Lyons, *Semantics*, 230–69; *idem*, *Structural Semantics*, *passim*; Cruse, *Lexical Semantics*, 15–20 and *passim*; Ullmann, *Principles of Semantics*, 152–70.

68 Thiselton, "Semantics and New Testament Interpretation," 90–91.

69 M. Silva, "The Pauline Style as Lexical Choice: Γινώσκειν and Related Verbs," in *Pauline Studies* (Festschrift F.F. Bruce; ed. D.A. Hagner and M.J. Harris; Exeter: Paternoster, 1980) 184–207.

70 Nida–Louw, *Lexical Semantics*, 107–14.

analysis has come into play.[71] Componential analysis theory states that the meaningful components or semantic features (or traits) of any lexical item can be specified, often in a hierarchy of specificity. Hence items may be compared on the basis of their components to determine in a quantifiable way the degree of similarity or difference between them. Although there has been much criticism of the concept of componential analysis[72]—and one must rightly recognize the interpretative factor present in determining and establishing the relations between the semantic features—to my mind this provides a serious step forward in being able to quantify semantic features rather than relying upon simple impressions, even if the components do not state all that there is about meaning. The UBS lexicon introduces distinctive feature notation in establishing their domains, and attempts to link the individual words to these, although this is done along informal lines.

The comments above suggest that more needs to be done in exploring the kinds of relations that obtain among words within a given vocabulary. Most are familiar with some of these categories, even though they may not be utilized, but it is worth bringing to mind the issues that surround their use. Meaning relations may be discussed in terms of paradigmatic and syntagmatic relations. Paradigmatic relations deal with the choices a language user makes to fill the same slot in a structure. For example, in the sentence "I ______ pizza" there are numerous words that might fit, including "love," "hate," "like," "crave," while there are a number of words that do not fit, either because they are not the right class of word (e.g. nouns, etc.) or they do not belong in this kind of relation, that is, they do not collocate with "I" and "pizza." Syntagmatic relations, concerned with such collocational relations, are discussed below. The relations among words of the same paradigm may be discussed in a number of ways.

1. Synonymy.[73] Even though the term synonym is thrown around fairly loosely, there is rarely sufficient recognition of the various kinds of synonymy. Synonymy is best spoken of in terms of a scale, that is, various degrees of complete and partial synonymy. There are very few complete synonyms found in language usage (apart from technical language), because such redundancy in vocabulary, in which two different words are used completely interchangeably in any context, is an intolerable luxury. Various degrees of partial synonymy exist when all factors indicate that either word would do in a given context.

---

71 See E.A. Nida, *Componential Analysis of Meaning: An Introduction to Semantic Structures* (The Hague: Mouton, 1975), following from his *Toward a Science of Translating*. See also M. Bierwisch, "Semantics," in *New Horizons in Linguistics* (ed. J. Lyons; Harmondsworth: Penguin, 1970) 168–82.

72 Some of the best is to be found in Lyons, *Semantics*, 317–35.

73 Cruse, *Lexical Semantics*, 265–94; Lyons, *Introduction to Theoretical Linguistics*, 446–53; Silva, *Biblical Words and their Meaning*, 120–26. Included here should also be contiguity.

Thus, in John 21:15–18, ἀγαπάω and φιλέω *may* be synonymous (although if one were translated "love" and the other "like," I do not think the difficulty would arise), but they certainly are not complete synonyms in Greek, not even in the New Testament (my own thinking is that the way they are used in John indicates that they are in fact not synonymous even here, since the change of word is noteworthy and brings the dialogue to a close). They may be partial synonyms being used completely synonymously in this context. Hence it is dubious for one to say, for example, that ἄλλος and ἕτερος and καινός and νεός are complete synonyms. Some have suggested that λόγος and ῥῆμα, ὁράω and βλέπω, and οἶδα and γινώσκω are synonyms in the New Testament.[74] This will not work. Could ῥῆμα have been used in John 1? I doubt it, especially with either the Greek philosophical or Old Testament conceptual background of the context. The perfect tense verb οἶδα simply cannot be a synonym of γινώσκω in any context where the passive voice is required, since οἶδα does not have a passive form, or where a form of γινώσκω other than the perfect tense is used. The UBS lexicon assumes that there are no true or complete synonyms (although their assertion lacks argumentation). This is apparently the case even if the words appear to be indistinguishable in denotative meaning, so long as the associative meaning differs.[75]

2. Opposites, including antonymy.[76] Opposition is used to describe a number of relationships, sometimes described as antonymy.[77] Opposites are words typically said to have some form of opposition in their meanings, which means that they must share at least one major semantic feature and hence be in the same semantic field. Often they will share more than one feature and differ on one significant feature. Hence "high" and "black" are not in opposition, since they have no shared semantic field. Opposites may be of various types: complementary, as in awake/asleep or dead/alive (Luke 15:24, 32); gradable, as in big/small or hot/cold (labelled antonyms by many linguists); or relational, as in buy/sell (1 Cor 6:20).[78]

3. Hyponymy or inclusion.[79] Hyponymy is similar to the scientific classification of genus and species and introduces a necessary hierarchy or third dimension to discussion of vocabulary items. In hyponymy, the co-hyponyms

---

74 D.A. Black, *Linguistics for Students of New Testament Greek: A Survey of Basic Concepts and Applications* (Grand Rapids: Baker, 1988) 126.

75 Louw–Nida, *Greek–English Lexicon*, xv.

76 Thiselton, "Semantics and New Testament Interpretation," 90–103, who provides useful examples. See also Lyons, *Introduction to Theoretical Linguistics*, 460–70; *idem*, *Semantics*, 270–80; Cruse, *Lexical Semantics*, 197–264.

77 E.g. Lyons, *Structural Semantics*, 61–69.

78 See S.E. Porter, "How Should Κολλώμενος in 1 Corinthians 6:16, 17 be Translated?" *ETL* 67 (1991) 105–106.

79 See Lyons, *Semantics*, 291–95.

are included in the superordinate term, but not vice versa. For example, words of asking may be represented in terms of the superordinate term αἰτέω, of which ἀπαιτέω, ζητέω and δέομαι are hyponyms (and co-hyponyms of each other). Languages do not always organize their hierarchies in the same way. For example, in English we do not have a superordinate term that would include flute player, doctor, woodworker, helmsman, etc. but Greek does, in the term δημιουργός. Hyponymy is very important because it adds this third plane or dimension to the conception of vocabulary. Whereas in most of the sense relations the individual words function on the same level, with hyponymy it is realized that there are priorities in the choice and use of vocabulary.

Syntagmatic relations are concerned with the elements on either side of a given item, that is, the linear chain of elements. Syntagmatic relations too are part of the meaning of a lexical item and constrain choice of lexical items, although we are perhaps moving into sentential semantics at this point. Nevertheless, there are two dimensions of syntagmatic relations worth noting. The first is collocation, in which the various types and kinds of word combinations are analysed. Thus, for Paul ἐκ πίστεως and ἐξ ἔργων readily collocate. They can be expected to be found together in Paul's writings. Collocation is often useful in determining the meaning of a word. For example, when a word is unexpectedly collocated with another word, this is to be noted, since it is different from the usual or regular pattern of collocation. Often words that link together help to specify lexical meaning. For example, in Mark 3:30 the collocation πνεῦμα ἀκάθαρτον eliminates many of the possible understandings of "spirit." The second syntagmatic relation is concerned with syntagmatic environments. This is where more precise syntactical information is given to help to delimit the meaning of a word. Rather than simply saying that a given verb takes a dative case object, a very important piece of information, designating syntagmatic environments is a way of differentiating what kind of subject or object a word might take (concrete, abstract, collective, etc.), whether a word is voiced, and if it is, what kinds of patients or agents are involved primarily or secondarily, and what kind of tense and mood alterations a verb is subject to. These several illustrations help to show that syntagmatic and paradigmatic relations operate together. Procedural rules are necessary to establish and define these relations, but they are operative nevertheless. It would be profitable to explore these, but the subject goes beyond the scope of this chapter.[80]

80 Systemic linguistics has emphasized the importance of such rules and procedures. See Porter, *Verbal Aspect*, 7–8, for discussion and bibliography.

4. *Conclusion*

In conclusion, the task of developing a lexicon is a large one. I have not been concerned with some of the more mundane but vital tasks of data gathering, etc., but I have tried to concentrate on method within a linguistic framework. It is evident that there is much to be done. It is not simply a task of refining the standard tools that are in existence so much as rethinking the procedures by which necessary new tools can be created. This is the daunting part of the task, since it (rightly) implies that much of what has gone on before—as valuable as it at one time may have been—must now be seen as the dated product of a previous way of thinking. New methods and procedures must be implemented. Some of these may not produce the kind of interpretative results that we have come to expect in the discipline (perhaps because we have placed too much emphasis upon the word, or because we have asked too many theological and not enough linguistic questions), but they may well prove to be more accurate understandings of the language of the New Testament.

CHAPTER FIVE

THE GREEK OF THE NEW TESTAMENT AS A DISPUTED AREA OF RESEARCH*

1. *Introduction*

What kind of Greek is the Greek of the New Testament—Semitic, *koiné*, transitionary, or something else? Since the first significant studies of Semitic influence on the New Testament published in the mid-seventeenth century, there has not been a lack of interest in the Greek language found in the New Testament, although the issues involved are diverse and not easily defined.[1] The topic includes treatment not only of the Greek found in the New Testament documents themselves, but of the languages current in first-century A.D. Palestine. Although the authors discussed in this chapter address both of these questions because of their close dependence upon each other, the major purpose of this chapter is to present summaries and assessments of several of the major statements of the twentieth century regarding what kind of Greek is found in the Greek New Testament.

Before analysing these statements in more detail, however, two caveats must be registered. First, any attempt to describe an entire century's worth of debate inevitably reflects the idiosyncrasies of its summarizer. This chapter is no exception. This recapitulation of thought attempts to present the opinions of scholars who speak for the major movements within this debate over the nature of the Greek of the New Testament during the last one-hundred years. Although I have chosen to discuss spokesmen who I believe should be represented, it is

---

* This essay is reprinted with the permission of Sheffield Academic Press, from S.E. Porter (ed.), *The Language of the New Testament: Classic Essays* (JSNTSup 60; Sheffield: JSOT Press, 1991) 11–38. Several significant adjustments have been made in the text in the light of its originally appearing as the introduction to a collection of reprinted essays by the major authors discussed in the chapter. I wish to thank Professor Jan Joosten of the University of Strasbourg for his constructive criticism.

1 For recent summaries of the debate, see E.C. Maloney, *Semitic Interference in Marcan Syntax* (SBLDS 51; Chico, CA: Scholars Press, 1981) 7–34; and J.W. Voelz, "The Language of the New Testament," *ANRW* II.25.2 (Berlin: de Gruyter, 1984) 894–930.

almost certain that someone else would have made a different selection, at least at a few points. Secondly, it is not always possible or even advisable to try to include everything that has been said by a given scholar or that represents the thought of a given position. Consequently, although I believe that I have included assessments of the most significant of these authors on this topic, I have chosen to do so by focusing upon one major writing by each one. Even though several of these authors are very well-known to the guild of New Testament scholars, many of the major issues discussed here are apparently unknown to a number of scholars, so I have in several instances chosen not to discuss in detail some of these authors' major works but have selected other statements for presentation. The result is a discussion which, I trust, will be broadly representative without being repetitious, inclusive but still definably focused.

The proposals regarding the nature of the Greek of the New Testament have ranged from positing a pure *koiné* derived directly from Attic Greek to a heavily Semitized translation Greek, and all points in between. Whereas there has been significant work in this area for well over the near one-hundred years surveyed by this chapter, many engaged in academic biblical studies are unaware of even the major contours of the debate. The result is often uncritical acceptance of a position which may not in fact be as well supported as some believe. Those who can recount the major positions of the last one-hundred years are all too aware that consensus on its many topics is still lacking. It is hoped that this chapter will serve both to provide a meaningful historical context in which discussion can continue and to clarify through examination of the history of discussion which questions are worth pursuing further and which questions are best laid to rest. The footnotes in this chapter are used to list bibliographical information for important sources, as well as to illustrate where some of the observations have been pursued by subsequent research. The literature on this topic is so immense that only a representative selection of more general works can be presented.[2]

2. *Proposals Regarding the Greek of the New Testament*

A. *The Greek Hypothesis*

Recent discussion of the nature of the Greek of the New Testament must begin with the work of the German scholar Adolf Deissmann. Beginning in his

2 I have placed this discussion within the larger framework of Greek grammar in S.E. Porter, *Verbal Aspect in the Greek of the New Testament, with Reference to Tense and Mood* (Studies in Biblical Greek 1; New York: Peter Lang, 1989). This introduction is dependent upon pp. 111–17, with my own assessment of the various positions on pp. 141–56.

Bibelstudien and *Neue Bibelstudien*, translated into English in 1901, and continuing with his *Licht vom Osten*, translated into English in 1910,[3] Deissmann was one of the first to make widely known the importance of the then fairly recently-discovered Egyptian papyri, as well as appreciate the importance of the Greek inscriptions, for the study of the Greek of the New Testament. Arguing against the views that New Testament Greek fulfilled classical standards or that it along with the Septuagint (LXX) was part of a "Biblical" Greek inspired by the Holy Spirit, Deissmann maintained that the Greek of the New Testament, like that of Egypt, was part of the body of popular Greek of the Hellenistic age. Recognizing the LXX as a translated document, he thereby discounted any "written Semitic-Greek" as ever being a spoken or literary language.[4] He recognized that certain portions of the Gospel material were translations from Aramaic into Greek, though he questioned the ability to reconstruct a *Vorlage* (unlike the case of the LXX). Most Hellenistic Jews,

---

3 *Bibelstudien* (Marburg: Elwert, 1895) and *Neue Bibelstudien* (Marburg: Elwert, 1897) were translated together as *Bible Studies* by A. Grieve (Edinburgh: T. & T. Clark, 1901) and *Licht vom Osten* (Tübingen: Mohr, 1908) was translated as *Light from the Ancient East* by L.R.M. Strachan (London: Hodder & Stoughton, 1910 [see *Expositor*, Seventh Series, 7 (1909) 97–110, 208–24, 352–57]); it went through several German and English editions.

4 This has been a topic of continuing debate. Some have questioned the purity of Alexandrian or Egyptian Greek, hence its validity as a standard for establishing the nature of Hellenistic Greek. One group has maintained that Alexandrian Greek came under Semitic (primarily Hebrew) influence because of the large Jewish population in the region. The papyri then already had a Semitic cast, hence their closeness to New Testament Greek. See, for example, G. Dalman, *The Words of Jesus: Considered in the Light of Post-Biblical Jewish Writings and the Aramaic Language* (trans. D.M. Kay; Edinburgh: T. & T. Clark, 1902) 17; R.R. Ottley, *A Handbook to the Septuagint* (London: Methuen, 1920) 165; and J. Courtenay James, *The Language of Palestine and Adjacent Regions* (Edinburgh: T. & T. Clark, 1920) 57–75. Another group has argued that the Alexandrian Greek of the papyri was influenced by Egyptian Coptic, which is, according to this view, similar syntactically to the Semitic languages. This would result in apparent linguistic similarities between New Testament Greek, influenced by Aramaisms, and the papyri, influenced by Coptic. See L.-Th. Lefort, "Pour une grammaire des LXX," *Muséon* 41 (1928) 152–60; J. Vergote, "Grec Biblique," *DBSup3* (ed. L. Pirot; Paris: Librairie Letouzey et Ane, 1938) cols. 1353–60; F. Gignac, *A Grammar of the Greek Papyri of the Roman and Byzantine Periods* (2 vols.; Milan: Istituto Editoriale Cisalpino, 1976, 1981) 1.46–48; *idem*, "The Language of the Non-Literary Greek Papyri," in *Proceedings of the Twelfth International Congress of Papyrology* (ed. D.H. Samuel; Toronto: Hakkert, 1970) 137–52; *idem*, "The Papyri and the Greek Language," *Yale Classical Studies* 28 (1985) 157–58. S.-T. Teodorsson argues against these positions, claiming that no other kind of Greek has ever been found in Egypt, thus there is no evidence of a previous "pure" Greek, no evidence of the creolization process that is implied, and no evidence of this Greek being considered to depart from the acceptable norms of Hellenistic Greek (*The Phonology of Ptolemaic Koine* [Studia Graeca et Latina Gothoburgensia 36; Gothenburg: Acta Universitatis Gothoburgensis, 1977] 25–35).

Deissmann maintained, knew Greek as a first language. Investigation of the New Testament documents must proceed, therefore, from their examination as philological artifacts, not of the literary language of the time but of the vast body of Hellenistic Greek, before application of secondary tests as to their Semitic "feel." As can be seen, Deissmann was surprisingly advanced in his consideration of the problems of multilingualism and linguistic development. Though he limited himself fairly exclusively to investigation of lexicographical items, Deissmann almost inevitably maintained that a lexical item of the New Testament could be paralleled in Hellenistic Greek.

Rather than discuss a portion from one of his better-known and more widely available works, including also his *The Philology of the Greek Bible* or *New Light on the New Testament from Records of the Graeco-Roman Period*,[5] perhaps a more suitable work is Deissmann's programmatic and influential "Hellenistisches Griechisch," from the well-known *Realencyklopädie für protestantische Theologie und Kirche*.[6] After dismissing several false definitions of the concept of "Hellenistic Greek," Deissmann settles on a definition of the language in use from 300 B.C. to A.D. 600 as the commercial language of the time. This Greek represents the collective written and spoken Greek of the period. After tracing various theories regarding the origin of this Greek, including the influence of the Attic dialect, Deissmann turns to particular features of the language. Deissmann distinguishes the language of the LXX from the Greek of the New Testament. He emphasizes that the clearest markers of the Hellenistic language occur in phonology and morphology, as well as vocabulary, where supposed New Testament meanings are shown to be characteristic of Hellenistic Greek. Deissmann admits that certain syntactical constructions appear to be unique to the Greek Bible, although he attributes many of these to restricted instances of translation Greek. He closes by raising the question of whether individual books of the New Testament reflect a more colloquial or literary kind of writing, claiming that the area requires further investigation. This wide-ranging essay reflects the major themes suggested by the debate over the nature of the Greek of the New Testament, handled with the fair-mindedness that was typical of Deissmann. He does not draw back from admitting Semitic influence where he sees it, although he does not lose sight of what he perceives as the larger linguistic milieu out of which the New Testament documents arose.

5 (trans. L.R.M. Strachan; London: Hodder & Stoughton, 1908 [see *Expositor*, Seventh Series, 4 (1907) 289–302, 425–35, 506–20; 5 (1908) 61–75]) and (Edinburgh: T. & T. Clark, 1907).

6 (vol. 7; ed. A. Hauck; 3rd edn; Leipzig: Hinrichs, 1899) 627–39. This essay appears in English translation as "Hellenistic Greek with Special Consideration of the Greek Bible," in S.E. Porter (ed.), *The Language of the New Testament: Classic Essays* (JSNTSup 60; Sheffield: JSOT Press, 1991) 39–59.

Deissmann's theories were soon applied more widely to grammar, as well as the lexicon, by James Hope Moulton, the Cambridge and Manchester scholar who was tragically killed in 1917 while crossing the Mediterranean. Moulton wrote a series of articles in the *Classical Review* and *Expositor*, his *Prolegomena*, vol. 1 of *A Grammar of New Testament Greek*, a significant portion of the *Accidence and Word-Formation*, vol. 2 of *A Grammar of New Testament Greek*, as well as a number of lesser-known but still valuable pieces.[7] *The Science of Language and the Study of the New Testament*, his inaugural lecture at Manchester University, and his "New Testament Greek in the Light of Modern Discovery" are not as well known as they deserve to be.[8] After examining volumes of papyri, Moulton found numerous parallels to many New Testament lexical items and grammatical constructions, some previously thought to be foreign to Greek. Recognizing the revolutionary character of Deissmann's discoveries, as well as Albert Thumb's similar philological findings,[9] Moulton concludes that biblical Greek, "except where it is translation Greek, was simply the vernacular of daily life," without "serious" dialectical differences and very much a predominant language in the bilingual environment of Palestine.[10]

In his "New Testament Greek in the Light of Modern Discovery," from

---

7 The following list is only representative: J.H. Moulton, "Grammatical Notes from the Papyri," *Classical Review* 15 (1901) 31–39, 434–42; 18 (1904) 106–12, 151–55; "Characteristics of New Testament Greek," *Expositor*, Sixth Series, 9 (1904) 67–75, 215–25, 310–20, 359–68, 461–72; 10 (1904) 124–34, 168–74, 276–83, 353–64, 440–50; "Notes from the Papyri," *Expositor*, Sixth Series, 3 (1901) 271–82; 7 (1903) 104–21; 8 (1903) 423–39 (many of his articles in *Expositor* 1908–1909 found their way into J.H. Moulton and G. Milligan, *The Vocabulary of the Greek Testament Illustrated from the Papyri and Other Non-Literary Sources* [London: Hodder & Stoughton, 1914–29]); *An Introduction to the Study of New Testament Greek* (2nd edn; London: C.H. Kelly, 1903) (this edition and subsequent ones reflect the view with which Moulton is associated, not the first edition of 1895); "Language of the New Testament," in *Dictionary of the Bible* (ed. J. Hastings; Edinburgh: T. & T. Clark, 1909) 528–30; *Prolegomena*, vol. 1 of *A Grammar of New Testament Greek* (3rd edn; Edinburgh: T. & T. Clark, 1908 [1906]) (with appendixes); *Accidence and Word-Formation*, vol. 2 of *A Grammar of New Testament Greek*, with W.F. Howard (Edinburgh: T. & T. Clark, 1929); *From Egyptian Rubbish-Heaps* (London: C.H. Kelly, 1916).

8 (Manchester: Manchester University Press, 1906) and *Essays on Some Biblical Questions of the Day: By Members of the University of Cambridge* (ed. H.B. Swete; London: Macmillan, 1909) 461–505. "New Testament Greek in the Light of Modern Discovery" is reprinted in Porter (ed.), *Language of the New Testament*, 60–97.

9 See, for example, A. Thumb, *Die griechische Sprache im Zeitalter des Hellenismus: Beiträge zur Geschichte und Beurteilung der KOINH* (Strassburg: Trübner, 1901); "Hellenistic and Biblical Greek," in *Dictionary of the Apostolic Church* (ed. J. Hastings; Edinburgh: T. & T. Clark, 1915) 1.551–60; "On the Value of Modern Greek for the Study of Ancient Greek," *Classical Quarterly* 8 (1914) 181–205.

10 Moulton, *Prolegomena*, 4, 5.

Essays on Some Biblical Questions of the Day: By Members of the University of Cambridge, Moulton begins by noting the changes of standpoint in study of New Testament Greek produced by comparative philology, the discoveries of papyri and inscriptions, the growth of interest in dialects of modern Greek, and the work of Thumb and Deissmann, as well as various opponents. Moulton argues for the homogeneity of the Hellenistic vernacular as the *lingua franca* of the Greco-Roman world, and against Semitic influence. In the second part of the essay, he analyses the various biblical writers. For example, he notes Luke's sense of style and conscious assimilation to the LXX, Paul's restricted yet significant contacts with Greek literature and philosophy, the literary quality of Hebrews, the artificial Greek of 2 Peter, the corrections of Mark's Greek found in Matthew, the simple Greek of the Johannine writings, interpretation of the odd Greek of the Apocalypse, and the (to him) obvious Aramaic background of Mark. Moulton concludes by recognizing the value of the papyri for understanding the vocabulary of the New Testament, and bemoaning the deleterious influence of classical presuppositions on the study of New Testament Greek. He pleads for recognition of the value of study of the Greek of the New Testament as a fitting introduction to the world and language of the Roman Empire. Whereas Moulton clearly built upon the work of Deissmann and others, he was an independent thinker in his own right, feeling free to suggest various places where recent discoveries aided in understanding the Greek of the New Testament. He was a rare man in combining the demonstrated abilities of a classical and comparative philologist, theologian and linguist. One can only speculate about the greatness of his contribution had he lived longer.[11]

B. *The Semitic Hypotheses*

Although Deissmann and Moulton were followed in their major precepts by many others,[12] as discussion below illustrates,[13] others found significant fault

11 M. Reiser (*Syntax und Stil des Markusevangeliums im Licht der hellenistischen Volksliteratur* [WUNT 2.11; Tübingen: Mohr–Siebeck, 1984] 2) contends that after the deaths of the significant advocates of the Greek-language hypothesis—Moulton, Deissmann and Thumb—the field was left open to those positing the Aramaic hypothesis.

12 Only a selection of names and representative works can be mentioned: H.St.J. Thackeray, *A Grammar of the Old Testament in Greek according to the Septuagint* (vol. 1; Cambridge: Cambridge University Press, 1909); L. Radermacher, *Neutestamentliche Grammatik: Das Griechisch des Neuen Testaments im Zusammenhang mit der Volkssprache* (HNT; 2nd edn; Tübingen: Mohr–Siebeck, 1925 [1911]); A.T. Robertson, *A Grammar of the Greek New Testament in the Light of Historical Research* (4th edn; Nashville: Broadman, 1934 [New York: Hodder & Stoughton, 1914]); G. Milligan, "The Grammar of the Greek New Testament," *ExpTim* 31 (1919–20) 420–24; *idem, Here and There among the Papyri* (London: Hodder & Stoughton, 1922); H.G. Meecham, *Light from Ancient Letters: Private Correspondence in the Non-Literary Papyri of Oxyrhynchus of the First Four Centuries, and its Bearing on New Testament Language and Thought* (London: Allen and Unwin, 1923);

with the Greek hypothesis. One of the major theories to reject Deissmann and Moulton's conclusions, and a theory with probably more longstanding support over the years—or at least more argumentative force than most others—maintains that the Gospels and at least the first part of Acts, and possibly Revelation, are directly dependent upon some form of Semitic language, probably Aramaic. This theory has progressed in several stages. A serious weakness of early attempts by, for example, A. Meyer, J. Wellhausen, E. Nestle, G. Dalman and F. Blass[14] was a failure to thoroughly support Aramaic reconstructions of the supposed original text. This shortcoming has been well-documented, even by proponents of the theory.[15] Later, armed with a

---

E.J. Goodspeed, "The Original Language of the New Testament," in *New Chapters in New Testament Study* (New York: Macmillan, 1937) 127–68; E.C. Colwell, *The Greek of the Fourth Gospel: A Study of its Aramaisms in the Light of Hellenistic Greek* (Chicago: University of Chicago Press, 1931); *idem*, "The Greek Language," in *Interpreter's Dictionary of the Bible* (Nashville: Abingdon Press, 1962) 2.479–87; P.W. Costas, *An Outline of the History of the Greek Language, with Particular Emphasis on the Koine and the Subsequent Periods* (Chicago: Ukrainian Society of Sciences of America, 1936; repr. Chicago: Ares, 1979); H. Koester, *Introduction to the New Testament* (2 vols.; Philadelphia: Fortress Press, 1982) 1.103–13; R. Browning, *Medieval and Modern Greek* (2nd edn; Cambridge: Cambridge University Press, 1983) 19–52; G.H.R. Horsley, "The Fiction of 'Jewish Greek,'" in *New Documents Illustrating Early Christianity*. V. *Linguistic Essays* (New South Ryde: Macquarie University, 1989) 5–40, who provides a very competent and detailed discussion of the major issues; and M. Silva (see below).

13 Suggestive modifications of their position have been made. For example, W.F. Howard, who completed vol. 2 (*Accidence and Word-Formation*) of Moulton's *A Grammar of New Testament Greek*, includes the appendix on Semitisms (pp. 411–85); A.J. Malherbe (*Social Aspects of Early Christianity* [London: Louisiana State University Press, 1977 (2nd edn; Philadelphia: Fortress Press, 1983)] 31–59) emphasizes the range of literary accomplishment of the New Testament documents; and Horsley ("*Koine* or Atticism—A False Dichotomy?" in *New Documents Illustrating Early Christianity*, 5.41–48) wants to ensure that Atticism as a phenomenon of Hellenistic Greek is given its due. The work of L. Rydbeck is to some extent a modification of Moulton and Deissmann's position (see below).

14 A. Meyer, *Jesu Muttersprache: Das galiläische Aramäisch in seiner Bedeutung für die Erklärung der Reden Jesu und der Evangelien überhaupt* (Freiburg: Mohr–Siebeck, 1896); J. Wellhausen, *Einleitung in die drei ersten Evangelien* (Berlin: Reimer, 1905) (in the first edition [pp. 7–43] he emphasizes the Semitic or Aramaic element standing behind the Gospels, while in the second edition [1911; pp. 7–32] he places slightly more stress on the Gospels as part of the *koiné*); E. Nestle, *Philologica Sacra: Bemerkungen über die Urgestalt der Evangelien und Apostelgeschichte* (Berlin: Reuther & Reichard, 1896); Dalman, *The Words of Jesus* (who recognizes this problem on pp. 43–71); and F. Blass, *Philology of the Gospels* (London: Macmillan, 1898).

15 See, for example, M. Wilcox, *The Semitisms of Acts* (Oxford: Clarendon Press, 1965) 1–12; "Semitisms in the New Testament," *ANRW* II.25.2, 979–86; and now "The Aramaic Background of the New Testament," in *The Aramaic Bible: Targums in their Historical Context* (ed. D.R.G. Beattie and M.J. McNamara; JSOTSup 166; Sheffield: Sheffield

wealth of supposed evidence on the basis of such criteria as apparent mistranslations, ambiguity in the Aramaic text, and parallels with the LXX, Charles C. Torrey, the Yale University scholar, argued vociferously that the Gospels, Acts 1–15, and Revelation were early translations from Aramaic originals. Rather than depicting the translators as bunglers, however, Torrey depicted, for example, the Gospel "writers" as pious men who did an admirable job of translation in an attempt to preserve "the wording of the original text," enabling reconstruction of the underlying original, though the final Greek may be, in Torrey's own words, "inexcusable" as idiomatic Greek.[16] Torrey wrote a number of important works, beginning with his now well-known early article in the C.H. Toy *Festschrift*, in which he responded directly to Moulton's work.[17] He continued his work in articles[18] as well as several books: *The Composition and Date of Acts*, *Our Translated Gospels: Some of the Evidence*, and *The Apocalypse of John*,[19] as well as *The Four Gospels: A New Translation*, in which he translated into English his reconstructed Aramaic text behind the four Gospels. Torrey was followed in many respects by other scholars such as C.F. Burney, J.A. Montgomery, M. Burrows and J. de Zwaan.[20]

The article by Torrey, "The Aramaic of the Gospels,"[21] is representative of his position. Although the article is a response directed at A.T. Olmstead,[22] it

Academic Press, 1994) 362–78, and especially the work of M. Black (see below).

16 C.C. Torrey, *The Four Gospels: A New Translation* (London: Hodder & Stoughton, n.d.) lviii, liv.

17 "The Translations Made from the Original Aramaic Gospels," in *Studies in the History of Religions* (Festschrift C.H. Toy; ed. D.G. Lyon and G.F. Moore; New York: Macmillan, 1912) 269–317.

18 A few of Torrey's articles include: "Fact and Fancy in the Theories Concerning Acts," *AJT* 23 (1919) 61–86, 189–212; "The Aramaic Origin of the Gospel of John," *HTR* 16 (1923) 305–44; "Julius Wellhausen's Approach to the Aramaic Gospels," *Zeitschrift der Deutschen Morgenländischen Gesellschaft* 101 (NS 26) (1951) 125–37; and "Studies in the Aramaic of the First Century A.D.," *ZAW* 65 (1953) 228–47.

19 (Harvard Theological Studies 1; Cambridge, MA: Harvard University Press, 1916), (London: Hodder & Stoughton, 1936), and (New Haven: Yale University Press, 1958).

20 See, for example, C.F. Burney, "A Hebraic Construction in the Apocalypse," *JTS* 22 (1920–21) 371–76; *idem*, *The Aramaic Origin of the Fourth Gospel* (Oxford: Clarendon Press, 1922); *idem*, *The Poetry of Our Lord* (Oxford: Clarendon Press, 1925); J.A. Montgomery, *The Origin of the Gospel according to St. John* (Philadelphia: J.C. Winston, 1923); M. Burrows, "The Original Language of the Gospel of John," *JBL* 49 (1930) 95–139; *idem*, "The Semitic Background of the New Testament," *BT* 2 (1951) 67–73; J. de Zwaan, "The Use of the Greek Language in Acts," in *The Beginnings of Christianity* (ed. F.J. Foakes Jackson and K. Lake; London: Macmillan, 1922) I.2.30–65; *idem*, "John Wrote in Aramaic," *JBL* 57 (1938) 155–71.

21 *JBL* 61 (1942) 71–85. This essay is reprinted in Porter (ed.), *Language of the New Testament*, 98–111.

22 A.T. Olmstead, "Could an Aramaic Gospel be Written?" *JNES* 1 (1942) 41–75.

gives a good sense of the kind of argumentation made by his supporters and opponents and a clear summary of the approach which Torrey himself took. Torrey claims first of all that much more Aramaic literature can be found than most suppose, including many documents translated into Greek from Aramaic originals. He discusses in some detail several of the more significant examples of translated Aramaic documents, and treats several books in Hebrew, which he characterizes as "learned *tours de force*." Then Torrey turns to questions regarding Aramaic and Greek in Palestine. Torrey sees no reaction against Aramaic in Palestine, but rather sees a negative attitude towards Greek. In response to Olmstead's question of whether an Aramaic Gospel could have been written, Torrey concludes that a Gospel could have been written in no other language but Aramaic. Hebrew would not reach the people and Greek would have been scorned. Instead, Torrey contends, the Aramaic of Palestine was a relatively homogeneous language from the seventh century B.C. through to the second century A.D. Having established the place of Aramaic, Torrey concludes by responding to critics of his theory of extensive mistranslation, taking several examples which (he argues) illustrate that the Gospels were originally written in Aramaic. This article, although brief in its several sections, contains what is essential in Torrey's position, including a justifiable context for discussion of Aramaic Gospels, an argument against the use of Greek, and a reassertion of his methodological soundness in relying upon mistranslation as an indication of Semitic sources.

As a herald of his position in this century, Torrey's approach was criticized even by later proponents of the same position. Though much of his writing is devoted to positing plausible reconstructions, the lack of an Aramaic *Vorlage* with which to compare his results leaves his conclusions tentative, as most readily admit. And many of his examples of mistranslations—upon which his theory so heavily depends—are open to objection. More recently Matthew Black, former principal of St. Mary's College and professor at the University of St. Andrews, Scotland, and Joseph A. Fitzmyer, former professor at the Catholic University of America, Washington, D.C., have attempted to answer a similar question, though they have been much more circumspect. They appreciate the varied Aramaic textual tradition, the tension between translation Greek and original Greek within the same texts, and the varied textual traditions of the New Testament. And their conclusions are stated cautiously, not polemically.[23]

---

23 Not all are as circumspect as Black and Fitzmyer. See, for example, F. Zimmermann, *The Aramaic Origin of the Four Gospels* (New York: Ktav, 1979) esp. 3–23; S.T. Lachs, "Hebrew Elements in the Gospels and Acts," *JQR* 71 (1980) 31–43; G.M. Lee, "Translation Greek in the New Testament," in E.A. Livingstone (ed.), *Studia Evangelica*, VII (Berlin: Akademie Verlag, 1981) 317–26; G. Schwarz, *"Und Jesu Sprach": Untersuchungen zur aramäischen Urgestalt der Worte Jesu* (2nd edn; Stuttgart: Kohlhammer, 1987).

Matthew Black was one of the most prolific writers on this topic (as well as others), and is legitimately well-regarded for his *Aramaic Approach to the Gospels and Acts*, which reached a third edition.[24] Rather than select a portion from this readily-available book, or choose one of the often highly-concentrated and focused articles which he wrote, I have chosen to summarize an article which reflects his concern for some of the broader questions regarding the relation of the Greek of the New Testament to forms of Aramaic: "Aramaic Studies and the Language of Jesus." This article is from a *Festschrift* to Paul Kahle,[25] a good friend of Black. The article conveys well the sense of entering into an ongoing dialogue on some of the significant issues concerning the nature of the Greek of the New Testament. The discussion reviews one school of research (represented by Kahle) into the kind of Aramaic used during the time of Jesus. Citing Kahle's most important works, including his two volumes on the Masoretes and his lectures on the Cairo Geniza,[26] Black describes the importance of Kahle's conclusion that the Aramaic represented by the Cairo Geniza was free from Hebrew influence and pre-dated the Onkelos tradition, which was not a representative Palestinian Aramaic but a mixed text. This was a bold conclusion at that time, and one which has been subsequently debated and evaluated. Black traces some of this discussion, responding to several scholars who have argued for modifications of Kahle's hypothesis. Even so, Black contends, Kahle's hypothesis about the Palestinian Targum tradition provides good information for studying the Aramaic of the New Testament period. Black recognizes that much more grammatical work is necessary to understand the Aramaic language more fully. Black proceeds to see how Kahle's theory has held up in the light of subsequent application to various texts, including finds from Qumran. In conclusion he applies his findings to the problem of the original language or languages of Jesus, which takes him into a few brief comments about the Hebrew language hypothesis presented by H. Birkeland (see below). Although studies of Aramaic have progressed since Black wrote his article, due in no small part to the work of Black and Wilcox, his former

---

24 A representative selection of Black's works bearing directly upon this topic includes: *An Aramaic Approach to the Gospels and Acts* (1st edn, 1946; 2nd edn, 1954; 3rd edn, Oxford: Clarendon Press, 1967); "The Recovery of the Language of Jesus," *NTS* 3 (1956–57) 305–13; "Second Thoughts—IX. The Semitic Element in the New Testament," *ExpTim* 77 (1965–66) 20–23; "The Biblical Languages," in *The Cambridge History of the Bible* (vol. 1; ed. P.R. Ackroyd and C.F. Evans; Cambridge: Cambridge University Press, 1970) 1–11.

25 *In Memoriam Paul Kahle* (ed. M. Black and G. Fohrer; BZAW 103; Berlin: Töpelmann, 1968) 17–28. This essay is reprinted in Porter (ed.), *Language of the New Testament*, 112–25.

26 P. Kahle, *Masoreten des Ostens* (BWAT 15; Leipzig: Hinrichs, 1913), *Masoreten des Westens*, II (BWAT 50; Stuttgart: Kohlhammer, 1930), and *The Cairo Geniza* (2nd edn; Oxford: Blackwell, 1959). See also H. Ott, "Um die Muttersprache Jesu: Forschungen seit G. Dalman," *NovT* 9 (1967) 1–25.

student,[27] the article gives a good idea of how the debate was conducted when studies of Aramaic documents in relation to the language of the New Testament were receiving much attention. The article also presents in clear fashion many of the forces and movements of the discussion, with a survey of the major proponents of the major theories.

It has long been agreed by scholars that Aramaic was the predominant language of Palestinian Judaism and almost certainly one of the languages, if not the primary language, of Jesus. Dalman's conclusion—that though Jesus might have known Hebrew, and probably spoke Greek, he certainly taught in Aramaic—has held sway with the majority.[28] The Aramaic hypothesis rests securely upon the fact that, though Greek was the language of the Greek and Roman Empires, it never fully replaced Aramaic (an important Semitic language brought back to Palestine after the exile) in Palestine, as evidenced by not only the biblical writings but a large amount of inscriptional, epistolary, papyric and literary evidence, especially from Qumran. It was once thought that Aramaic had entered a period of decline in the two centuries on either side of Christ's birth, but in the last fifty years many important discoveries have been made.[29] While it is likely that Jesus' primary language was Aramaic, this position is argued primarily by logical and historical inference, since Jesus is not recorded as using Aramaic apart from odd quotations (e.g. Mark 15:34). Also, the majority of texts are of literary quality, some quite late, while the inscriptional evidence (much of which could be Hebrew) is limited mostly to proper names.[30] Nevertheless, the theory that Jesus spoke primarily Aramaic has many important supporters, such as Wellhausen, Dalman, Joüon, Bardy, Black, Wilcox, Feldman, Torrey and Fitzmyer, to name only a few.[31]

---

27 On methodological questions, see S.A. Kaufmann, "On Methodology in the Study of the Targums and their Chronology," *JSNT* 23 (1985) 117–24.

28 G. Dalman, *Jesus–Jeshua: Studies in the Gospels* (trans. P.P. Levertoff; London: SPCK, 1929) 1–37; P. Lapide, "Insights from Qumran into the Languages of Jesus," *RevQ* 8 (1975) 483–86; Black, *Aramaic Approach*, 16 n. 1, cf. 47–49. For more detailed treatment of the issue of the language of Jesus, with discussion of passages where Jesus may have spoken Greek, see ch. 8 in this volume, pp. 139–72.

29 J.A. Fitzmyer and D.J. Harrington, *A Manual of Palestinian Aramaic Texts* (BibOr 34; Rome: Biblical Institute Press, 1978); K. Beyer, *Die Aramäische Texte vom Toten Meer* (Göttingen: Vandenhoeck & Ruprecht, 1984).

30 Recent comments on the methodology employed in Aramaic studies may be found in the neglected article by L.D. Hurst, "The Neglected Role of Semantics in the Search for the Aramaic Words of Jesus," *JSNT* 28 (1986) 63–80.

31 The works of many of these proponents have already been cited. Those who have not include: P. Joüon, "Quelques aramaïsmes: Sous-jacent au grec des Evangiles," *RSR* 17 (1927) 210–29; G. Bardy, *La question des langues dans l'église ancienne* (vol. 1; Paris: Beauchesne, 1948); L.H. Feldman, "How Much Hellenism in Jewish Palestine?" *HUCA* 57 (1986) 83–111.

Others have maintained, however, that some form of Hebrew, whether biblical or Mishnaic, had a far greater importance in first-century Palestine than is often suspected. M.H. Segal proposed that Mishnaic Hebrew, rightly considered the linguistic evolutionary offspring of biblical Hebrew, much evidenced in the Rabbinic writings and independent of Aramaic, was a prominent Jewish vernacular at all social levels from approximately 400 B.C. to A.D. 150.[32] The Judean Desert documents, including those from Qumran but especially the Hebrew Bar Kokhba letters, have given further credence to the theory of vernacular Hebrew. Although several scholars disagree with Segal over the exact nature of this Hebrew and its extent of use,[33] he has been followed to the extent that Mishnaic Hebrew is thought by many to have been a probable language of the first century and a possible if not probable language of Jesus, by T.W. Manson, J.A. Emerton, J. Barr, J.M. Grintz and C. Rabin.[34] Several scholars have argued concurrently that Hebrew sources lie behind several books of the New Testament. For example, K. Beyer has argued that the Johannine writings have a Hebrew and not an Aramaic *Vorlage*; J. Carmignac has posited a Hebrew original for the Synoptics; S. Thompson, following in a long tradition which includes R.H. Charles, posits a Hebrew source for Revelation; and G. Howard claims to have discovered an early, independent version of Matthew in Hebrew.[35] However, though Jesus may have known

---

32 See M.H. Segal, "Mishnaic Hebrew and its Relation to Biblical Hebrew and to Aramaic," *JQR* 20 (1908) 670–700, 734–37; *idem, A Grammar of Mishnaic Hebrew* (Oxford: Clarendon Press, 1927) 5–19. He is followed in his major formulations by H. Birkeland, *The Language of Jesus* (Oslo: Dybwad, 1954); E.Y. Kutscher, "Hebrew Language: Mishnaic," in *EncJud* (vol. 16; Jerusalem: Encyclopaedia Judaica, 1972) cols. 1592–93; *idem, A History of the Hebrew Language* (ed. R. Kutscher; Leiden: Brill, 1982) 115–20.

33 For example, Birkeland (*Language of Jesus*) contends that the Hebrew is a dialect of Mishnaic Hebrew overwhelmingly predominant at the lower social levels; Lapide ("Insights," 486–500) proposes that Mishnaic Hebrew was the bridge language between Hebrew and Aramaic in the Palestinian diglossic milieu (he relies on C.A. Ferguson, "Diglossia," *Word* 15 [1959] 325–40).

34 See, for example, T.W. Manson, *The Teaching of Jesus: Studies of its Form and Content* (2nd edn; Cambridge: Cambridge University Press, 1935); J.A. Emerton, "Did Jesus Speak Hebrew?" *JTS* NS 12 (1961) 189–202; *idem*, "The Problem of Vernacular Hebrew in the First Century A.D. and the Language of Jesus," *JTS* NS 24 (1973) 1–23; J. Barr, "Which Language Did Jesus Speak?—Some Remarks of a Semitist," *BJRL* 53 (1970) 9–29; J.M. Grintz, "Hebrew as the Spoken and Written Language in the Last Days of the Second Temple," *JBL* 79 (1960) 32–47; C. Rabin, "Hebrew and Aramaic in the First Century," in S. Safrai and M. Stern (eds.), *The Jewish People in the First Century* (2 vols.; CRINT 1.2; Assen: Van Gorcum, 1976) 1007–39.

35 K. Beyer, *Semitische Syntax im Neuen Testament* (vol. 1; 2nd edn; Göttingen: Vandenhoeck & Ruprecht, 1968) 17–18; J. Carmignac, "Studies in the Hebrew Background of the Synoptic Gospels," *ASTI* 7 (1968–69) 64–93; S. Thompson, *The Apocalypse and Semitic Syntax* (SNTSMS 52; Cambridge: Cambridge University Press, 1985) esp. 2–6, 108;

sufficient Hebrew to read Luke 4:16–39, and Hebrew was certainly in use in Palestine, at least by the Jewish leaders, the evidence for colloquial Hebrew—and for Hebrew lying behind the New Testament documents—is not sufficient to support the case made by Segal and others. Consequently, this view is not nearly as widespread as the Aramaic and Greek language hypotheses.

C. *The Revival of the Greek Hypothesis*

Other scholars have argued strongly for the predominant role of Greek in first-century Palestine and, hence, in the ministry of Jesus. Their arguments rest firmly on, among other facts, the role of Greek as the *lingua franca* of the Roman Empire, the trilingual nature of the Judean Desert documents, including Greek Bar Kokhba letters, and other remaining evidence, and most importantly the linguistic fact that the New Testament has been transmitted in Greek from its earliest documents. A number of scholars have argued in various ways that Greek was in widespread use in the multilingual society of first-century Palestine, including E.A. Abbott, A.W. Argyle, M. Smith, J.N. Sevenster, S. Lieberman, G. Mussies, K. Treu, M. Hengel, J.M. Ross, and especially N. Turner (see below).[36] There seems to be nothing to have prevented any Palestinian resident from learning Greek, certainly as a second and often as a first language, though the ability of the average resident is still an unquantifiable factor.[37]

R.H. Charles, *A Critical and Exegetical Commentary on the Revelation of St. John* (2 vols.; ICC; Edinburgh: T. & T. Clark, 1920) 1.cxliii; G. Howard, *The Gospel of Matthew according to a Primitive Hebrew Text* (Macon, GA: Mercer University Press, 1987).

36 Representative works of the proponents of this position include: E.A. Abbott, *Johannine Grammar* (London: A. & C. Black, 1906); A.W. Argyle, "Did Jesus Speak Greek?" *ExpTim* 67 (1955–56) 92–93, 383; *idem*, "Greek among the Jews of Palestine in New Testament Times," *NTS* 20 (1973–74) 87–89; M. Smith, "Aramaic Studies and the Study of the New Testament," *JBR* 26 (1958) 304–13; J.N. Sevenster, *Do You Know Greek? How Much Greek Could the First Jewish Christians Have Known?* (NovTSup 19; Leiden: Brill, 1968); S. Lieberman, *Greek in Jewish Palestine: Studies in the Life and Manners of Jewish Palestine in the II–IV Centuries C.E.* (2nd edn; New York: Feldheim, 1965); *idem*, "How Much Greek in Jewish Palestine," in *Biblical and Other Studies* (ed. A. Altmann; Cambridge, MA: Harvard University Press, 1963) 123–41; G. Mussies, "Greek in Palestine and the Diaspora," in Safrai and Stern (eds.), *Jewish People in the First Century*, 1040–64; *idem*, "Greek as the Vehicle of Early Christianity," *NTS* 29 (1983) 356–69; K. Treu, "Die Bedeutung des Griechischen für die Juden im römischen Reich," *Kairos* 15 (1973) 123–44; M. Hengel, *Judaism and Hellenism: Studies in their Encounter in Palestine during the Early Hellenistic Period* (trans. J. Bowden; London: SCM Press, 1974); J.M. Ross, "Jesus's Knowledge of Greek," *IBS* 12 (1990) 41–47.

37 The degree of Greek penetration of rural Palestine is discussed in A.H.M. Jones, *The Greek City: From Alexander to Justinian* (Oxford: Clarendon Press, 1940) 289–95; T. Rajak, *Josephus: The Historian and his Society* (London: Duckworth, 1983) 46–64; Hengel, *Judaism and Hellenism*, 58–65; Feldman, "How Much Hellenism."

In the midst of this discussion, with advocates for Aramaic, Greek, and even Hebrew, Joseph A. Fitzmyer's presidential address to the Catholic Biblical Association, "The Languages of Palestine in the First Century A.D.,"[38] was instrumental in giving perspective to the debate. Fitzmyer not only does an excellent job of representing the position with which he has become aligned, that is, appreciating the influence of Aramaic upon the Greek of the New Testament, but he does an excellent job of introducing the reader to the issue of the languages used in Palestine in the first century A.D.[39] Fitzmyer's survey combines in a highly readable way both a thorough and detailed discussion of the primary evidence for the use of Aramaic, Greek, Hebrew and Latin during the time of Jesus,[40] and several very important synthetic statements which draw upon the evidence to reach important conclusions. His footnotes may be mined for much useful material, as well.

Beginning with the most recent language on the Palestinian scene, Latin, Fitzmyer works his way back to the earliest, Hebrew, by way of Greek and Aramaic. Regarding Latin, Fitzmyer believes that it was used mostly by the Romans for official purposes. This is confirmed by inscriptions of various sorts, which are not abundant. Greek came to Palestine with the conquest of Alexander the Great, and the Hellenization which occurred was widespread, with the Greek language playing a part in it. Evidence of Greek influence includes names of towns and references to many Jewish-Greek writers, although little of their work is extant. Although Josephus provides some help, since he wrote in Rome, Fitzmyer turns to other evidence, including inscriptions and papyri. Regarding Jesus, it is probably true that he spoke Greek. Although he still believes that Aramaic was the most commonly used language in Palestine, Fitzmyer cautiously recognizes that Greek and Hebrew were used as well. Rejecting the theory that Aramaic was on the wane during the turn of the millennia, Fitzmyer argues on the basis of the Qumran discoveries, for example, that there was much literature being composed in Aramaic. But not only literary texts are to be found. There are also important inscriptions, some of them bilingual, although Fitzmyer finds no influence of Greek on Palestinian

---

38 *CBQ* 32 (1970) 501–31, reprinted in his *A Wandering Aramean: Collected Aramaic Essays* (Missoula, MT: Scholars Press, 1979) 29–56. This essay is also reprinted in Porter (ed.), *Language of the New Testament*, 126–62.

39 Many of Fitzmyer's major writings on this topic are collected in *A Wandering Aramean*, including "The Phases of the Aramaic Language," 57–84, and especially "The Study of the Aramaic Background of the New Testament," 1–27, which is highly recommended; and *Essays on the Semitic Background of the New Testament* (n.p.: Scholars Press, 1974). A more recent essay is "The Aramaic Language and the Study of the New Testament," *JBL* 99 (1980) 5–21.

40 See also E.M. Meyers and J.F. Strange, *Archaeology, the Rabbis and Early Christianity* (London: SCM Press, 1981) 62–91.

Aramaic, thus rejecting Kahle, Black, and Díez Macho's hypothesis regarding the Aramaic of the Palestinian Targums being from the first century A.D. (see above). Fitzmyer also sees a possible influence of Hebrew upon Palestinian Aramaic. As far as Hebrew is concerned, Fitzmyer believes that it was never fully supplanted by Aramaic. He expresses surprise regarding the paucity of inscriptional evidence, despite an abundance of literary texts. In response to Birkeland's proposal (see above), Fitzmyer calls for a cautious assessment. In a way for which he has become rightly heralded, Fitzmyer summarizes and evaluates a wealth of material, giving a fair and balanced analysis of the evidence for the four languages which vied for position in the linguistic milieu of first-century Palestine.

It is not possible to settle the various issues regarding the linguistic milieu of first-century Palestine, as Fitzmyer rightly notes, except to say that the archaeological, linguistic and sociological evidence seems to indicate that the region was multilingual, including at least Aramaic and Greek in widespread and frequent use, and Hebrew as a possible vernacular but certainly a written language, with Latin a fourth language used primarily by the Romans in political and administrative matters. Therefore, the likelihood that Jesus, along with most Gentiles and Jews, was multilingual himself is strong. As Fitzmyer says,

> the most commonly used language of Palestine in the first century A.D. was Aramaic, but...many Palestinian Jews, not only those in Hellenistic towns, but farmers and craftsmen of less obviously Hellenized areas used Greek, at least as a second language. The data collected from Greek inscriptions and literary sources indicate that Greek was widely used. In fact, there is some indication...that some Palestinians spoke only Greek... But pockets of Palestinian Jews also used Hebrew, even though its use was not widespread.[41]

D. *The Semitic-Greek Hypothesis*

Having agreed that Greek was a widely used language of first-century Palestine does not solve the problem of what kind of Greek is found in the New Testament, however. That topic remains one of widespread debate. A theory which has aroused more controversy than any other of late is that of Henry

---

41 Fitzmyer, "Languages of Palestine," in *Wandering Aramean*, 46. Many scholars mention the possibility of at least a trilingual community, including Dalman, Black, Rabin, Barr, Fitzmyer, Bardy, Sevenster, Birkeland, Emerton, Turner, Lapide, Rajak, Olmstead, and Meyers and Strange, among those already cited, as well as: R. Gundry, "The Language Milieu of First-Century Palestine: Its Bearing on the Authenticity of the Gospel Tradition," *JBL* 83 (1964) 404–408; H.F.D. Sparks, "Some Observations on the Semitic Background of the New Testament," *Bulletin of Studiorum Novi Testamenti Societas* 2 (1951) 33–42; H. Leclercq, "Note sur le grec néo-testamentaire et la position du grec en Palestine au premier siècle," *Les études classiques* 42 (1974) 243–55.

Gehman, a former Princeton professor, and Nigel Turner, a British scholar. The theory harks back to the late nineteenth century, when some (represented by H. Cremer[42]) believed that the New Testament was written in a unique Holy Ghost Greek. In their many significant works, Gehman concentrated upon the nature of the Greek of the LXX,[43] and Turner, while dealing most heavily with the New Testament, has also analysed apocryphal works.[44] Modifying the argument for a Holy Ghost language from the position advocated in the nineteenth century (to which Deissmann and Moulton responded), Gehman and Turner argue for a Jewish-Greek dialect in use in Palestine in the first century. Recognizing the Semitic element in the Gospels and other New Testament books, Turner claims that Semitic influence alone inadequately explains all the linguistic phenomena. Turner also asserts that the New Testament displays an "almost complete lack of classical standards in every author."[45] He therefore concludes that Jesus, as well as his disciples, the New Testament writers and possibly many others, used in regular conversation a Greek influenced by the Semitic languages spoken in Galilee at that time. In kind very similar to LXX Greek, Turner maintains, this Greek was very different from the Greek of the papyri; it "was a distinguishable dialect of spoken and written Jewish Greek."[46]

---

42 See H. Cremer, *Biblico-Theological Lexicon of New Testament Greek* (4th edn; Edinburgh: T. & T. Clark, 1895 [1867]), a translation from the German.

43 Gehman's works bearing on this topic include: "The Hebraic Character of Septuagint Greek," *VT* 1 (1951) 81–90 (reprinted in Porter [ed.], *Language of the New Testament*, 163–73); "Hebraisms of the Old Greek Version of Genesis," *VT* 3 (1953) 141–48; "Ἅγιος in the Septuagint, and its Relation to the Hebrew Original," *VT* 4 (1954) 337–48.

44 Of Turner's many works, the following warrant mention: "Were the Gospels Written in Greek or Aramaic?" *EvQ* 21 (1949) 42–48, where his ideas are taking shape; "The 'Testament of Abraham': Problems in Biblical Greek," *NTS* 1 (1954–55) 219–23; "The Unique Character of Biblical Greek," *VT* 5 (1955) 208–13; "The Relation of Luke I and II to Hebraic Sources and to the Rest of Luke–Acts," *NTS* 2 (1955–56) 100–109; "Philology in New Testament Studies," *ExpTim* 71 (1959–60) 104–107; "The Language of the New Testament," in *Peake's Commentary on the Bible* (ed. M. Black and H.H. Rowley; London: Nelson, 1962) 659–62; *Syntax*, vol. 3 of *A Grammar of New Testament Greek*, by J.H. Moulton (Edinburgh: T. & T. Clark, 1963) esp. 1–9; "Second Thoughts—VII. Papyrus Finds," *ExpTim* 76 (1964–65) 44–48; *Grammatical Insights into the New Testament* (Edinburgh: T. & T. Clark, 1965) 174–88 (reprinted in Porter [ed.], *Language of the New Testament*, 174–90); "Jewish and Christian Influence in the New Testament Vocabulary," *NovT* 16 (1974) 149–60; "The Literary Character of New Testament Greek," *NTS* 20 (1973–74) 107–14; "The Quality of the Greek of Luke–Acts," in *Studies in New Testament Language and Text* (Festschrift G.D. Kilpatrick; ed. J.K. Elliott; NovTSup 44; Leiden: Brill, 1976) 387–400; *Style*, vol. 4 of *A Grammar of New Testament Greek*, by J.H. Moulton (Edinburgh: T. & T. Clark, 1976) 1–10; "Biblical Greek—The Peculiar Language of a Peculiar People," in Livingstone (ed.), *Studia Evangelica*, 505–12.

45 Turner, *Syntax*, 2.

46 Turner, *Grammatical Insights*, 183.

Though Gehman suggests this may have been a temporary linguistic condition brought about by Jews passing from Semitic to Greek language, Turner believes that the period was not transitional nor the language artificial. In apparent common reaction with Turner to Deissmann, Black has even gone so far as to call biblical Greek "a peculiar language, the language of a peculiar people."[47]

Gehman's "The Hebraic Character of Septuagint Greek" was the first in a series of articles he published in *Vetus Testamentum* representing his position. The article is a little technical, relying on knowledge of both Greek and Hebrew, but the framework he sets for his discussion is highly instructive, with its direct focus upon the Greek of the LXX. Using a simple argument, Gehman begins from the premise that "The object of a translator obviously is to render a document clearly into the vernacular."[48] On the basis of apparent difficulties in the text of the LXX when compared to the Masoretic Hebrew text, as well as trouble in the idioms and constructions of the Greek itself,[49] and since "it is well-known that the Greek of the LXX is the koine" (though there are some differences), Gehman claims that "we can hardly avoid speaking of a Jewish Greek, which was used in the Synagogues and in religious circles." After introductory comments, in which he responds briefly to H.St.J. Thackeray's view of the Greek of the LXX, Gehman divides his discussion into two parts, the first treating syntactical and the second treating lexical items. In the first, he discusses various conjunctions, prepositions and pronouns, including such things as use of καί to introduce various dependent clauses, a temporal sense of ὅτι, and use of ἐν. He concludes that "the LXX is full of Hebrew idioms which

47 Black, "Biblical Languages," 11. See also W.H. Simcox, *The Writers of the New Testament: Their Style and Characteristics* (repr. Winona Lake, IN: Alpha, 1980); F.L. Horton, "Reflections on the Semitisms of Luke–Acts," in *Perspectives on Luke–Acts* (ed. C.H. Talbert: Edinburgh: T. & T. Clark, 1978) 1–23.

48 This premise has been widely criticized, in the light of the question of whether the translators in fact understood the original text. For discussion, see J. Barr, *The Typology of Literalism in Ancient Biblical Translations* (Göttingen: Vandenhoeck & Ruprecht, 1979) 15 and *passim*; J.A.L. Lee, *A Lexical Study of the Septuagint Version of the Pentateuch* (SBLSCS 14; Chico, CA: Scholars Press, 1983) 18. On translation in the ancient world, see S.P. Brock, "The Phenomenon of the Septuagint," in *The Witness of Tradition* (ed. A.S. van der Woude; Leiden: Brill, 1972) 11–36; *idem*, "Aspects of Translation Technique in Antiquity," *Greek, Roman, and Byzantine Studies* 20 (1979) 69–87; C. Rabin, "The Translation Process and the Character of the Septuagint," *Textus* 6 (1968) 1–26.

49 A recent discussion of these anomalies can be found in E. Tov, "Did the Septuagint Translators always Understand their Hebrew Text?" in *De Septuaginta* (Festschrift J.W. Wevers; ed. A. Pietersma and C. Cox; Ontario: Benben, 1984) 53–70. Comparison between Jewish writings originally in Greek and those translated shows a marked contrast, according to Lee, with the latter heavily Semitized. This argument was already stated by Deissmann (*Bible Studies*, 69 n. 1) and Thackeray (*Grammar*, 27–28), and, Lee contends, never refuted (*Lexical Study*, 14–15).

also involve a matter of syntax."[50] In the second part, he treats selected words. This article gives a wide-open look at how someone arguing for a Semitic hypothesis treats the evidence. Gehman hides nothing with respect to the basis for his position, going into detailed discussion of the examples he uses. This kind of evidence proved very important for Turner.

It is difficult to know which of Turner's many writings best represents his position. I have selected to discuss the final chapter, "The Language of Jesus and His Disciples," in his book *Grammatical Insights into the New Testament*, although I could have selected from a number of articles, some of them very narrowly focused and others very broad and general. In the concluding essay to his *Grammatical Insights*, Turner begins by recounting the possible languages which Jesus could have spoken. He acknowledges the hypothesis of Torrey regarding mistranslation but rejects it because of the lack of evidence regarding the kind of Aramaic used in Palestine during this time. And off-setting what he claims are clear examples of an Aramaic *Vorlage* are examples of characteristically Greek phrases. Turner also considers Hebrew, although he rejects Birkeland's hypothesis, since the evidence is against widespread use of Hebrew especially in a religious context. In support of Jesus' use of Greek are a number of distinctly Greek features, such as word-play, alliteration and lexical choice. In response to the paradox that, if Jesus spoke Greek, he would have had to use *koiné* Greek but the Gospels do not have a pure *koiné*, Turner responds by positing that the "hybrid" Greek of the Gospels was "a distinct type of Jewish Greek, which I would prefer to call biblical Greek, spoken by Jesus."[51] It is not inconceivable, Turner contends, that Jesus' language was influenced by all of the languages spoken in Galilee. Drawing upon his other grammatical studies, including work on the *Testament of Abraham*, Turner argues that this language was not a temporary phenomenon (as Gehman believed) but the normal language which Jesus spoke. In distinguishing his position from that of Moulton, Turner contends that the Egyptian papyri may well have been influenced by Semitic languages. Rather than Semitic documents lying behind the New Testament documents, however, Turner argues for the language of the New Testament as a form of symbolic representation, an iconography attesting to the pious devotion of its writers as they captured the sound of the Old Testament documents in Greek. Turner's essay provides much material for thought, as he attempts to find a balance between what he perceives as indisputable Semitic and Greek elements in the language of the New Testament, as well as the language of Jesus.

---

50 Gehman, "Hebraic Character," 81, 90, 87 for quotations.

51 Turner, *Grammatical Insights*, 182.

E. *Reassessing the Greek Hypothesis*

The above survey should convey some sense of the major issues of the debate that has occurred throughout this century. A broad generalization would claim that most scholars probably favour the Aramaic hypothesis, although many of them for no particular or definite reason, apart possibly from their educational training and a general tendency in New Testament studies today to privilege theories that advocate Semitic backgrounds. The Aramaic position remains strong, and many of its presuppositions are often assumed when taking a stance in critical work. But at the same time there has been much rebellion against this position, as well as reassessment of the Greek hypothesis of Deissmann and Moulton and the Semitic-Greek hypothesis of Gehman and Turner.

For example, Lars Rydbeck, a lecturer at Lund University in Sweden, is perhaps best known to English-speaking scholars for his challenging 1975 article in *New Testament Studies*, which called for a revival of the study of New Testament Greek.[52] But an arguably more important contribution has been Rydbeck's advocacy of a theory regarding the Greek of the New Testament. Although Rydbeck is in essential agreement with Moulton, in his book *Fachprosa, vermeintliche Volkssprache und Neues Testament* he desires to shift the categories somewhat by broadening discussion to include the "so-called people's language."[53] He asserts that the Greek of the New Testament shares a common grammatical base with all other *Fachprosa* (popular literature, papyri, scientific prose, etc.).[54] In his section entitled "On the Question of Linguistic

52 "What Happened to New Testament Greek Grammar after Albert Debrunner?" *NTS* 21 (1974–75) 424–27. See also his "Die 'Anstatt-Mentalität' bei der Erforschung griechischer Syntax," in *Greek and Latin Studies in Memory of Cajus Fabricius* (ed. S.-T. Teodorsson; Studia Graeca et Latina Gothoburgensia 54; Gothenburg: Acta Universitatis Gothoburgensis, 1990) 154–57.

53 *Fachprosa, vermeintliche Volkssprache und Neues Testament: Zur Beurteilung der sprachlichen Niveauunterschiede im nachklassischen Griechisch* (Uppsala: University of Uppsala; Stockholm: Almqvist & Wiksell, 1967). Pp. 186–99 appear in English translation in Porter (ed.), *Language of the New Testament*, 191–204. Rydbeck has been followed by L.C.A. Alexander, "Luke's Preface in the Context of Greek Preface-Writing," *NovT* 28 (1986) 48–74; *idem*, *The Preface to Luke's Gospel: Literary Convention and Social Context in Luke 1.1–4 and Acts 1.1* (SNTSMS 78; Cambridge: Cambridge University Press, 1993).

54 Several have raised objections to this characterization: e.g. H. Kurzová, "Das Griechische, im Zeitalter des Hellenismus," in *Soziale Probleme im Hellenismus und im römischen Reich* (ed. P. Oliva and J. Burian; Prague: n.p., 1973) 218–24, who disputes Rydbeck's denial that through the popular documents one can know the *Vulgärsprache* spoken during the Hellenistic period; E. Pax, "Probleme des neutestamentlichen Griechisch," *Bib* 53 (1972) 560–62, who questions the very concept of *Fachprosa*; and S.E. Porter, "Thucydides 1.22.1 and Speeches in Acts: Is there a Thucydidean View?" *NovT* 32 (1990) 124–27, who raises issues of dialect, register and content (this last essay is reprinted as ch. 9 in this volume, pp. 173–94).

Levels and the Place of the New Testament in the Contemporary Language Milieu [Zur Frage nach den Sprachschichten und der Stellung des Neuen Testaments im zeitgenössischen Sprachmilieu]," Rydbeck draws upon the detailed studies in the rest of his book in defending his position. Part one disputes the way the term "popular" has been used in traditional grammatical discussions, establishing the need for Rydbeck's own discussion of vernacular language using a more rigorous methodology. Part two establishes and defends the existence of an intermediate prose level, including treatment of such topics as the relation of spoken to written language. Rydbeck looks to a technical prose built upon an Ionic-Attic base as the widespread medium for written communication in the Hellenistic world, until the later classicizing influence took over. Part three concludes with eight theses which draw conclusions from the detailed grammatical discussions Rydbeck conducts throughout his monograph. Rydbeck concludes by introducing several areas for continued exploration, areas which some scholars have already taken up for further examination.

By discussing an appropriately synthetic essay by Moisés Silva, professor at Westminster Theological Seminary, Philadelphia, I bring this survey of scholarly opinion to a close. Silva has shown serious concern for issues of grammar and linguistics in several treatments of the Greek of the New Testament, including his essay "Bilingualism and the Character of Palestinian Greek."[55] Although he is a reserved advocate of the Greek hypothesis of Deissmann and Moulton, he attempts to provide a balanced perspective on the issues by illustrating that some of the disputes have arisen through imprecise language and the failure to make essential linguistic distinctions. There are two distinguishing features in his approach. First, Silva incorporates the categories of modern linguistics into his work, including the issue of bilingualism in sociolinguistics,[56] where he draws upon modern parallels. Secondly, he attempts to clarify the debate by subjecting the logic of various views to searching scrutiny. The article is structured in six parts. The first defends Deissmann, pointing out that much of the subsequent criticism directed towards

---

55 *Bib* 61 (1980) 198–219. This essay is reprinted in Porter (ed.), *Language of the New Testament*, 205–26. See also Silva's "Semantic Borrowing in the New Testament," *NTS* 22 (1975–76) 104–10; "New Lexical Semitisms," *ZNW* 69 (1978) 253–57; "The Pauline Style as Lexical Choice: Γινώσκειν and Related Verbs," in *Pauline Studies* (Festschrift F.F. Bruce; ed. D.A. Hagner and M.J. Harris; Grand Rapids: Eerdmans, 1980) 184–207; *Biblical Words and their Meaning: An Introduction to Lexical Semantics* (2nd edn; Grand Rapids: Zondervan, 1994 [1983]). See also G.H.R. Horsley, "Divergent Views on the Nature of the Greek of the Bible," *Bib* 65 (1984) 393–403; C.J. Hemer, "Reflections on the Nature of New Testament Greek Vocabulary," *TynBul* 38 (1987) 65–92.

56 See S.E. Porter, "The Language of the Apocalypse in Recent Discussion," *NTS* 35 (1989) 582–603, which is indebted to Silva's approach.

him—especially concerning signs of Semitic influence upon the New Testament—had been either anticipated or corrected by Deissmann, as well as Moulton. Silva observes that Turner is in fact very similar to Moulton in his position regarding the place and kind of Greek in use in the New Testament, though Turner disputes this. Secondly, Silva finds the term "dialect" to be problematic and adopts a definition from classical philology in which ancient Greece is seen to have had many regional dialects distinguished by essentially phonological and morphological features. Thirdly, Silva treats the issue of bilingualism, mentioning such factors as first and second language acquisition, prestige languages, and the important distinction of F. de Saussure between a language in and of itself (*langue*) and an individual user's language (*parole*). Silva contends that discussion of the Greek of the New Testament has been at cross-purposes because Deissmann and his followers have been discussing *langue*, arguing that the structure of Greek has been unaffected by Semitic languages, while those who have argued for Semitic influence have been discussing *parole*, citing features of individual language users which illustrate Semitisms. Fourthly, Silva responds to Gehman's article (see above) regarding Alexandrian bilingualism, refuting the idea of a transitional language. Fifthly, regarding Palestinian bilingualism, which is different from Alexandrian, Silva sees widespread evidence for use of Greek. Sixthly, Silva contends that discussion of biblical Greek must be concerned with style, that is, the features of individual usage of various authors. Silva resolves the dispute between those arguing for and against Semitic influence by seeking a compromise. Yes, he argues, there is a Semitized Greek style, just as there is a Christian English style, but no, there was no permanent influence upon the Greek language itself by Semitic languages, and in this sense Deissmann and Moulton were responsible in their conclusions.

3. *Conclusion*

The final word on the nature of the Greek of the New Testament has not been said, and it is questionable whether it ever will. Discussion of this issue will almost certainly continue if for no other reason than its outcome has serious consequences in several areas. For the student of ancient languages and cultures, examination of the Greek of the New Testament provides a window into the various forces at work in Palestine in the first century A.D. The period was one of widespread Hellenistic culture, yet a culture which came up against the force of equally proud cultural and religious heritages of local population groups. The times promoted widespread production of literary documents, including papyri and inscriptions, which provide instructive information regarding the development of the Greek language as well as the institutions of the Greco-Roman world. For the student of early Christianity, the answer to the question of the kind of Greek used in the New Testament documents has potential for determining which ideas were at play in the thinking of the writers of the New Testament, and whether biblical scholars should look to Greek or Jewish sources for the conceptual background of these ideas. The last fifty or so years of academic biblical studies have been dominated for the most part by a Jewish paradigm,[57] in which the major categories of thought have traditionally been traced to the Jewish background of the New Testament writers. It is interesting to see the correlation between this perspective and discussion of the nature of the Greek of the New Testament. I leave it to others to see if there is some sort of cause and effect at play. Just as there are signs of revival of the Greek hypothesis in study of the nature of the Greek of the New Testament, there are signs of increased attention to the Greco-Roman background of the New Testament documents.[58] It waits to be seen in which direction this recent discussion will proceed. For the student of linguistics, this discussion provides an interesting arena for honing and refining linguistic skills that are usually reserved for the study of modern languages.[59] The adaptation of modern linguistic methodology to the study of ancient languages requires some adjustments, especially in the weight given to epigraphic over oral evidence, since there are no native speakers by which to evaluate observations. But the complex interplay of the at least trilingual environment provides an interesting and intriguing context in which to study bilingualism.

By way of conclusion, I would like to state what I see as major issues still to be resolved in discussion regarding the Greek of the New Testament. As the survey above illustrates, there are many issues which call for further treatment, but I have selected four. First, there must be an increased awareness of the terms of the debate. My impression is that those who argue for a heavy Semitic influence upon the Greek of the New Testament for the most part are far less aware of the work of those who advocate little Semitic influence, than vice versa. For future progress, it will be incumbent upon all sides to be aware of the strengths and weaknesses of the various positions, and to re-examine the

---

57 Of course it is difficult to make such a sweeping generalization without recognizing that there have been many others who have looked to Greek background. This is, I believe, an accurate impression of the majority of work being done, however.

58 I cite, for example, work on the diatribe by S.K. Stowers (*The Diatribe and Paul's Letter to the Romans* [SBLDS 57; Chico, CA: Scholars Press, 1981]) and others, and work on more theological issues by J.L. Kinneavy (*Greek Rhetorical Origins of Christian Faith: An Inquiry* [New York: Oxford University Press, 1987]).

59 See S.E. Porter, "Studying Ancient Languages from a Modern Linguistic Perspective: Essential Terms and Terminology," *FN* 2.4 (1989) 147–72, which attempts to establish a workable methodology for thinking of ancient Greek in the light of categories of modern linguistics.

categories under discussion. Categories worth examining include Silva's helpful distinction between the structure of the language in and of itself and an individual's use of the language, or style, and Rydbeck's differentiation of kinds of prose writings. Scholars must be clear what the specific question is before they can be certain that they have found an appropriate answer.

Secondly, there must be a more nuanced method by which to evaluate the evidence that is marshalled. This will probably require less emphasis upon treatment of single examples of translation or mistranslation of individual lexical items and more concern for the cumulative evidence of the effect of a Semitic feature upon entire grammatical categories. In my work I have found it useful to distinguish between three kinds of data: instances of clear translation, for example where the author states the Semitic wording and then gives a rendering (e.g. Mark 15:34//Matt 27:46); instances of intervention, when a form that cannot reasonably be formed or paralleled in Greek must be attributed to the influence of a Semitic construction (e.g. temporal ἰδού in Luke 13:16); and instances of enhancement, when a rare construction that can be paralleled in Greek has its frequency of occurrence increased due to associations with Semitic literature (e.g. the adjectival attributive genitive in Rom 8:21). Whereas the third category plays a significant role in tracing diachronic change in a language, only the second constitutes what can legitimately be called Semitic influence, since it represents an incursion by Semitic language and not a linguistic change that can be accounted for within the recognizable parameters of Greek linguistic development.[60]

Thirdly, and in conjunction with defining a more nuanced method by which to evaluate the evidence, several other linguistic factors must be taken into account. One is to appreciate more fully the influence of the LXX as translation Greek upon the language of the New Testament. As suggested above, the LXX provides an important area of study, not only from a theological perspective but in terms of its linguistic influence upon the New Testament writers since it appears to have been their Scripture.[61] Their familiarity with the text and the possible influence of its language upon their writing needs to be examined in more detail. This will require not only study of the language of the New Testament but closer attention to the Greek of the Septuagint both in terms of its characteristics as translation Greek and in terms of its integrity as a literary document or documents written in Greek.[62] A second factor to explore in more detail is the difference represented by Alexandrian and Palestinian bilingualism, that is, the difference between someone who may have had Greek as a first

60 Porter, *Verbal Aspect*, 118; "Language of the Apocalypse," 587.

61 See, for example, W.G. Most, "Did Luke Imitate the Septuagint?" *JSNT* 15 (1982) 30–41; Porter, *Verbal Aspect*, 145–47.

62 There has long been a need for both suitable reference tools for study of the kinds of Greek of the LXX and exegetical commentaries upon the Greek text.

language and been translating out of a Semitic language, such as Aramaic, and someone who may have had Aramaic as a first language and been translating from that language into another.[63] Each of these issues adds to the complexity of speaking about issues of bilingualism.

Fourthly, literacy in the ancient world, an area which is only recently receiving the kind of attention it deserves, must be considered. Written documentation in various forms became increasingly important in the Hellenistic world as communication and the need for keeping of records spread beyond local confines. Since study of ancient languages is incumbent upon the study of written documents, no matter how these are conceived as giving insight into the spoken registers, it is all too easy to get a distorted view which either overestimates or underestimates the extent of literacy in the ancient world. Errors in both extremes have been made, promoted in large part due to the difficulty in gathering and assessing the evidence. One recent estimate is that at the most approximately 20% to 30% of the males in a given Hellenistic community would have been literate (with women probably less literate). Literacy is directly related to the educational system of the time, which was primarily focused upon the city rather than the country and tended to privilege males, especially those with money.[64] The papyri provide interesting information at this point. For example, a number of texts make reference to one writing for another, because the author of the letter is illiterate.[65]

With this historical perspective in mind, as well as an agenda for future study suggested, there are several possible responses the reader might have to the debate. Perhaps one side in the debate has proved convincing, in which case the reader will approach further studies from a new or at least reinforced methodological perspective regarding the influence of Semitic languages upon the Greek of the New Testament. More likely, however, is the alternative that, even if one is not fully convinced by one side or another, the reader will gain a greater appreciation for the history and importance of this on-going debate, and

63 Porter, *Verbal Aspect*, 154–56.

64 See W.V. Harris, *Ancient Literacy* (Cambridge, MA: Harvard University Press, 1989), for a recent incisive study of this area. He treats the classical period on pp. 65–115 and the Hellenistic era with its educational system on pp. 116–46 (the statistic of 20% to 30% literacy comes from p. 141). See also Hengel, *Judaism and Hellenism*, 58–106.

65 For example P.Tebt. I 104.39–40 (92 B.C.): ἔγραψεν ὑπὲρ αὐτοῦ Διονύσιος Ἑρμαΐσκ[ου / ὁ προγεγραμμένος διὰ τ]ὸ αὐτὸν μὴ ἐπίστασθ[αι γρά]μματα; and P.Hamb. I 4.14–15 (A.D. 87): ἔγραψεν ὑπὲρ αὐτοῦ φαμένου μὴ / εἰδέναι γράμματα Ἰσίδωρος νομογράφος; cf. B.G.U. VII 1579.27–28 (A.D. 118/19). See Harris, *Ancient Literacy*, 146 n. 145, for other examples. On the relation of this phenomenon to the New Testament, see R.N. Longenecker, "Ancient Amanuenses and the Pauline Epistles," in *New Dimensions in New Testament Study* (ed. R.N. Longenecker and M.C. Tenney; Grand Rapids: Zondervan, 1974) 281–97; and E.R. Richards, *The Secretary in the Letters of Paul* (WUNT 2.42; Tübingen: Mohr–Siebeck, 1991).

will perhaps wish to explore the sources discussed above in more detail. The goal has not been to argue unfairly for one perspective over another but to bring to the attention of a wider constituency some of the central questions regarding the nature of the Greek of the New Testament, so that in approaching the text of the New Testament and responding to those who have commented upon it one's scholarship will be better informed and enhanced.

PART II PRACTICE

CHAPTER SIX

VAGUE VERBS, PERIPHRASTICS, AND MATTHEW 16:19*

1. *Introduction*

> καὶ ὃ ἐὰν δήσῃς ἐπὶ τῆς γῆς ἔσται δεδεμένον ἐν τοῖς οὐρανοῖς, καὶ ὃ ἐὰν λύσῃς ἐπὶ τῆς γῆς ἔσται λελυμένον ἐν τοῖς οὐρανοῖς (whatever you might bind upon the earth is expected to be in a state of boundness in heaven; and whatever you might loose upon the earth is expected to be in a state of loosedness in heaven; Matt 16:19)

Few passages with periphrastic verbs have generated so much discussion as Matt 16:17–19.[1] Focusing on noteworthy literature since 1950, when Cullmann's significant book appeared, this chapter aims to determine how much can be learned about this passage on the basis of its context and grammar, and then to explore the implications of grammar for exegesis and theology. These two considerations provide a fairly neat division of the chapter into two major parts.

---

* This essay is reprinted with the permission of Ediciones El Almendro de Córdoba, Spain, and the editor of the journal *Filología Neotestamentaria*, Professor Jesús Peláez, from *Filología Neotestamentaria* 1.2 (1988) 154–73. Several slight adjustments have been made in the text. The analysis of this passage is placed in another interpretative context in ch. 8 in this volume (pp. 139–72) on the language of Jesus.

1 W.J. Aerts (*Periphrastica: An Investigation into the Use of Εἶναι and Ἔχειν as Auxiliaries or Pseudo-Auxiliaries in Greek from Homer up to the Present Day* [Amsterdam: Hakkert, 1965] 96) says Matt 16:19 contains "pregnant examples." For an insightful history of interpretation and bibliography, see J.A. Burgess, *A History of the Exegesis of Matthew 16:17–19 from 1781 to 1965* (Ann Arbor: Edward Brothers, 1976) *passim* (there is a noticeable dearth of significant studies of the periphrastics); O. Cullmann, *Peter: Disciple, Apostle, Martyr: A Historical and Theological Study* (trans. F.V. Filson; 2nd edn; London: SCM Press, 1962) 164–76; M. Wilcox, "Peter and the Rock: A Fresh Look at Matt 16:17–19," *NTS* 22 (1976) 73 n. 1; and M.J. Wilkins, *The Concept of Disciple in Matthew's Gospel: As Reflected in the Use of the Term Μαθητής* (NovTSup 59; Leiden: Brill, 1988) esp. 178–79, 185–98 (except on the issue of the periphrastic). There are no significant textual issues of concern. See K.L. Schmidt, ἐκκλησία, *TDNT*, 3.519–20.

2. *The Context and Grammar of Matthew 16:19*

A. *Context*

The ongoing debate over authenticity of this verse has usually focused on the supposed Semitic elements in the passage. Whether the words are genuine or not (see the appendix on authenticity for a survey of current opinion), the passage appears in its Gospel context as part of Peter's confession.[2] Jesus says to Peter that he is blessed, or favoured of God, because mortal humans ("flesh and blood," possibly a common Jewish[3] or Rabbinic[4] expression) did not reveal Jesus' identity to him.[5] Whether this is the first moment of Messianic recognition or whether v. 18 is the occasion when Jesus gave Peter his name is unknown and probably indeterminable. A tendency to Petrine exaltation by the early church would affect these questions, though it does not lessen the necessity of interpreting the scene in its present literary context. More important is the actual wording.

An examination of one instance of possible Semitic background must suffice. Though there is some debate about the meaning of כיפא and πέτρος,[6] virtually every scholar sees word-play here.[7] The question is whether the word-play works in Aramaic alone or in Greek as well.[8] In Aramaic Jesus would have

---

2 Cf. Mark 8:27–30 and Luke 9:18–21, where the confession is treated similarly: Jesus follows with a prediction of his suffering.

3 So D.A. Carson, "Matthew," in *The Expositor's Bible Commentary* (11 vols.; ed. F.E. Gaebelein; Grand Rapids: Zondervan, 1984) 8.367. Cf. 1 Cor 15:5; Gal 1:16; Eph 6:12; Heb 2:14.

4 So H.L. Strack and P. Billerbeck, *Kommentar zum Neuen Testament aus Talmud und Midrasch* (6 vols.; Munich: Beck, 1961–65) 1.730–31.

5 ἀπεκάλυψέν σοι follows the pattern of many transitive verbs in Hellenistic Greek by omitting the direct object. ἀποκαλύπτω appears in the New Testament eight times transitively (Matt 11:25; Gal 1:16; 2 Thess 2:6; and Matt 11:27; 16:17; Luke 10:22; 1 Cor 2:10; Phil 3:15), the first three where the direct object is necessary, the last five where it is not. Of the five, only one takes the object (Phil 3:15).

6 See J.A. Fitzmyer, "Aramaic Kepha' and Peter's Name in the New Testament," in *Text and Interpretation: Studies in the New Testament Presented to M. Black* (ed. E. Best and R.McL. Wilson; Cambridge: Cambridge University Press, 1979) 121–32.

7 See Wilkins, *Concept of Disciple*, 174–75, esp. 189–91, but who argues for the Aramaic solution.

8 Cullmann (*Peter*, 192–93; πέτρος, *TDNT*, 6.106; πέτρα, *TDNT*, 6.98–99) claims that the pun cannot work in Greek, while P. Lampe ("Das Spiel mit dem Petrus-Namen—Matt. xvi.18," *NTS* 25 [1979] 227–45) and P.E. Hughes ("The Language Spoken by Jesus," in *New Dimensions in New Testament Study* [ed. R.N. Longenecker and M.C. Tenney; Grand Rapids: Zondervan, 1974] 141), followed by R. Gundry (*Matthew: A Commentary on His Literary and Theological Art* [Grand Rapids: Eerdmans, 1982] 333–34), claim that the pun works only in Greek.

said, "You are כיפא (rock)[9] and upon this כיפא (rock) I intend to build my church." כיפא is Peter's Aramaic name used elsewhere of him in the New Testament in its Greek form, κηφᾶς (John 1:42; 1 Cor 1:12; 3:22; 9:5; 15:5; Gal 1:18; 2:9, 11, 14). While many scholars would argue that the word-play does not work well in Greek because two different Greek words are used (hence most explain Jesus' statement on the basis of an Aramaic original), perhaps it works for the following reason. πέτρος, a masculine noun, is the name given to Simon, but it is usually interpreted to mean a "stone,"[10] while πέτρα, a feminine noun, is often used for a mass of rock.[11] Jesus thus says, "You are πέτρος (a name for an individual male and a single stone) and upon this πέτρα (firm foundation of stone) I intend to build my church." This accounts well for the alternation in Greek words, unnecessary if it merely translates the same Aramaic word, and it accommodates general Greek usage of the two words.[12] Despite the alternation of terms, however, it seems clear from the parallelism that Jesus intends to found his church upon Peter himself,[13] though early exegetes, as well as a few more recent ones, have argued for such things as

---

9 B. Chilton (*Targumic Approaches to the Gospels: Essays in the Mutual Definition of Judaism and Christianity* [Lanham, MD: University Press of America, 1986] 80 n. 31) claims, citing Dalman and Taylor, that "*Ptr*, however, is an Aramaic term borrowed from Greek which appears in Aramaic with the meaning 'foundation.'"

10 Euripides, *Her.* 1002: πάντα κινῆσαι πέτρον, "to leave no stone unturned." Cf. Sophocles, *O.C.* 1595, where it means a boulder used for marking boundaries. See H.G. Liddell and R. Scott, *A Greek–English Lexicon* (rev. H.S. Jones with R. McKenzie, and E.A. Barber; 9th edn; Oxford: Clarendon Press, 1968) s.v.

11 Euripides, *Ion* 936: πέτρα κεκρόπια, "the Acropolis."

12 Lampe ("Das Spiel mit dem Petrus-Namen," 242–45) argues against the כיפא/πέτρος equation and for a folk etymology by early Christians that maintained classical distinctions between πέτρος and πέτρα, thus arriving at a view similar to the one I have expressed. If the two Greek words are treated as synonymous, paronomasia or merely literary variation may explain the alternation. Cullmann (πέτρα, *TDNT*, 6.95) claims that the two Greek words are often interchangeable (though he notes a difference in content); Fitzmyer ("Aramaic Kepha'", 131) suggests that the feminine form is a literary variant; and O. Betz ("Felsenmann und Felsengemeinde [Eine Parallele zu Mt 16:17–19 in den Qumranpsalmen]," *ZNW* 48 [1958] 49–77) points to conceptual parallels from the Qumran literature. He is disputed by W.D. Davies (*The Setting of the Sermon on the Mount* [Cambridge: Cambridge University Press, 1964] 228–30).

13 So most modern scholars, except for C.C. Caragounis, *Peter and the Rock* (BZNW 58; Berlin: de Gruyter, 1990) esp. 88–113, who also argues for two differing underlying Aramaic words. See R. Brown *et al.*, *Peter in the New Testament* (Minneapolis: Augsburg, 1973) 92; Wilkins, *Concept of Disciple*, 191–94. Note that the use of the future form οἰκοδομήσω ("I will build") gives Jesus' statement an expectative sense; contra many scholars who posit a strictly future-referring sense. See S.E. Porter, *Verbal Aspect in the Greek of the New Testament, with Reference to Tense and Mood* (Studies in Biblical Greek 1; New York: Peter Lang, 1989) 409–16, on the semantics of the future form.

Peter's confession, Peter's faith, or even Christ himself.[14] I will return to this question in section 3.

B. *Grammar*

Virtually every discussion of Matt 16:17–19 seems to mention sooner or later the periphrastic constructions in v. 19. It is here that attention will initially be focused. There have been several analyses of the structure of v. 19, most of which affirm the unity of at least the two conditional clauses.[15] Verse 19a continues Jesus' instruction to Peter, saying that his intention is to give him the keys of the kingdom of heaven (or plural, heavens). Carson notes the shift of metaphor from Peter being the foundation to being the gatekeeper,[16] though Jeremias is probably correct in emphasizing that in biblical and Jewish usage handling the keys implies full authority.[17]

1. *Definition of Periphrasis.* The periphrastic construction has been a long-neglected grammatical phenomenon, primarily because it has been thought by most classicists to give little insight into the literary nature of the Greek language.[18] Before discussing this particular instance, I would suggest the following explicit formal criteria for determination of periphrasis in general. A periphrastic construction contains, first, a form of the aspectually vague auxiliary verb εἰμί (not γίνομαι or ἔχω, since they are not aspectually vague). Aspectually vague verbs are those very few verbs which "lack choice" in their formal paradigm, in that they are confined to a single stem form and hence offer

---

14 The Church Fathers up to the Reformers, as well as more recent commentators, have posited such things as: Peter's confession (Origen, Eusebius, Ambrose, Theodore of Mopsuestia, John Chrysostom, A.H. McNeile [*The Gospel according to St. Matthew* (1915; repr. Grand Rapids: Baker, 1980) 241]), Peter's faith (Luther, Calvin, Zwingli, A.B. Bruce [*The Synoptic Gospels* (5 vols.; Expositor's; repr. Grand Rapids: Eerdmans, n.d.) 1.224]), Christ himself (Origen, Augustine, W.C. Allen [*A Critical and Exegetical Commentary on the Gospel according to St. Matthew* (ICC; 3rd edn; Edinburgh: T. & T. Clark, 1912) 176]), the preaching office (Melanchthon), or Jesus' teaching (Gundry [*Matthew*, 334]). See Brown *et al.*, *Peter*, 93 n. 216; Cullmann, *Peter*, 168; Wilkins, *Concept of Disciple*, 191–92; J.D.M. Derrett, "'Thou Art the Stone and upon the Stone...'" *Downside Review* 106 (1988) 276–85.

15 See, for example, C.F. Burney, *The Poetry of our Lord* (Oxford: Clarendon Press, 1925) 115; Brown *et al.*, *Peter*, 95; J. Jeremias, κλείς, *TDNT*, 3.749–50, who posits a high Semitic influence; and Wilkins, *Concept of Disciple*, 186–87.

16 Cf. Rev 9:1–6; 20:1–3. Carson, "Matthew," 370.

17 Isa 22:22; Rev 1:18; 3:7. Jeremias, κλείς, *TDNT*, 3.750. On the kingdom in Matthew, see G.E. Ladd, *A Theology of the New Testament* (Grand Rapids: Eerdmans, 1974) 57–90; and J.D. Kingsbury, *Matthew: Structure, Christology, Kingdom* (Philadelphia: Fortress Press, 1975) 152–60.

18 See K.J. Dover, Review of Aerts, *Periphrastica*, *Gnomon* 40 (1968) 87.

no corresponding aspectual opposition.[19] Secondly, a periphrastic construction contains a participle in grammatical agreement with its referent, which participle may either precede or follow the auxiliary but cannot be separated from it by anything other than elements completing the participle (such as adjuncts or complements; this is apart from postpositive conjunctions, of course). According to this understanding of periphrasis, the auxiliary places the periphrasis in its proper modal or attitudinal category, while the participle conveys its verbal aspect (as well as voice).[20]

2. *Traditional Opinions on the Periphrastic Constructions in Matthew 16:19.* There are two major competing opinions on the meaning of the periphrastic constructions in Matt 16:19.

a. Since his article in the 1939 issue of *JBL*, and again in an article in 1973, Mantey has been a strong proponent of the view that the future auxiliary and perfect passive participle should be translated as an English future perfect passive, that is, "shall have been bound/loosed,"[21] where a future event is the result of a first event which has occurred before the time of speaking or writing. He argues this along four main lines. (1) He cites a number of Greek grammarians who state that the perfect tense refers to the continuing results of a past action.[22] (2) Though not all perfect-tense verbs maintain this temporal construct (some refer to past time, others refer to the present, while some may even refer to the future), he claims that "sound exegesis requires that the regular usage of tenses be given the benefit of the doubt..."[23] (3) He cites several grammars to reinforce his view that the future perfect refers to an action to be completed in future time. (4) He cites a number of passages in the New

19 See S.E. Porter and N.J.C. Gotteri, "Ambiguity, Vagueness and the Working Systemic Linguist," *Sheffield Working Papers in Language and Linguistics* 2 (1985) 105–18, on the issue of verbal ambiguity.

20 The issue of periphrasis is covered in detail in Porter, *Verbal Aspect*, 441–86; cf. pp. 75–109 on the general theory of verbal aspect. See also now S.E. Porter, *Idioms of the Greek New Testament* (Biblical Languages: Greek 2; 2nd edn; Sheffield: JSOT Press, 1994) 45–49.

21 J.R. Mantey, "The Mistranslation of the Perfect Tense in John 20:23, Mt 16:19, and Mt 18:18," *JBL* 58 (1939) 243–49 (Mantey has many extraneous arguments in his efforts to counter sacerdotalism); "Evidence that the Perfect Tense in John 20:23 and Matthew 16:19 is Mistranslated," *JETS* 16 (1973) 129–38. In the latter article Mantey depends heavily on a Th.D. thesis by his student W.T. Dayton, though he again cites much evidence with far greater rhetorical than substantive weight. Mantey is followed by N. Turner, *Grammatical Insights into the New Testament* (Edinburgh: T. & T. Clark, 1965) 80–82; W.F. Albright and C.S. Mann, *Matthew* (AB 26; Garden City, NY: Doubleday, 1971) 197; Gundry, *Matthew*, 335; Wilkins, *Concept of Disciple*, 197; and tentatively Carson, "Matthew," 370–72.

22 He cites the following grammarians: Kühner, Smyth, Hadley and Allen, Goodwin, Jelf, Burton, and Robertson.

23 Mantey, "Mistranslation," 245.

Testament (Luke 5:20, 23; 7:47; 1 John 2:12; esp. John 20:23), as well as other Greek writings, as parallels (see below). Using a rough-and-ready definition of periphrasis, in which the participle and εἰμί are "unquestionably" periphrastic when side-by-side but non-periphrastic when they have one or more words between them,[24] Mantey argues that in Matt 16:19 and 18:18 (as well as John 20:23) instead of a simple future passive ("will be bound/loosed")[25] the future perfect passive shows that Christ was elevating his disciples to the rank of scribes who were to interpret God's will to humanity: "This passage does not teach that God concurs in men's conclusions; but rather it teaches that those who live in accordance with Christ's directions will decide to do just what God has already decided should be done."[26] In other words, humanity will ratify decisions already made in heaven.

b. Cadbury, responding to Mantey in the same 1939 issue of *JBL*,[27] agrees that the perfect tense usually indicates a "situation already existent at some time contemplated in the sentence," but disputes Mantey's assertion that the time referent is the same as that of the other verbs in the sentence, since the major examples are found in the "apodosis of a general condition,"[28] a conditional sentence which is difficult to evaluate temporally. Citing several examples (1 John 2:5; Jas 2:10; Rom 14:23; 13:8), as well as referring to major grammarians,[29] Cadbury claims that this type of conditional construction may refer to future action (e.g. John 20:23; Rom 7:2; 1 Cor 7:39; Xenophon, *Anab.* 1.8.12) but does not do so here. He concludes that Matt 16:19 and 18:18 "seem to imply a permanent condition rather than a condition prior to the time of the relative clause,"[30] and thus should be translated "shall be once for all" (in contrast to John 20:23, "shall be at once").[31] He concludes by showing that several examples in the New Testament (Mark 2:5, 9; Luke 7:47, etc.) make impossible Mantey's reading of a perfect as referring to a past action preceding the time of speaking.

---

24 Mantey, "Mistranslation," 248.

25 So C.F.D. Moule, *An Idiom Book of New Testament Greek* (2nd edn; Cambridge: Cambridge University Press, 1959) 18; G. Maier, *Matthäus-Evangelium* (2 vols.; Bibel-Kommentar; Neuhausen: Hänosler, 1979) 1.573; F.W. Beare, *The Gospel according to Matthew: A Commentary* (Oxford: Blackwell, 1981) 351; J.D.M. Derrett, "Binding and Loosing (Matt 16:19; 18:18; John 29:23 [sic])," *JBL* 102 (1983) 112.

26 Mantey, "Mistranslation," 246.

27 H.J. Cadbury, "The Meaning of John 20:23, Matthew 16:19, and Matthew 18:18," *JBL* 58 (1939) 251–54.

28 Cadbury, "Meaning," 251.

29 He cites the following grammarians: Blass and Debrunner, Moulton, Robertson, Burton, and Winer.

30 Cadbury, "Meaning," 252.

31 Cadbury, "Meaning," 253.

3. *A New Understanding of the Periphrastics in Matthew 16:19*. Matthew 16:19 is problematic for interpretation whichever view above is adopted. On the basis of research into periphrastic constructions in Greek, I suggest the following understanding.

a. The construction is clearly periphrastic, since it consists of a future form of the aspectually vague auxiliary verb εἰμί and a perfect passive participle in the configuration mentioned above. In Matt 16:19 and 18:18 the mode is one of expectation—with the prospect of fulfilment—of a hypothetical event, that is, binding and loosing. Attempts to establish future temporal implicature (that is, future temporal implications of a particular stretch of discourse in context) on the basis of the future verb form alone are not acceptable,[32] since the future form in Greek is best understood as semantically conveying a modal sense related to that of the subjunctive.[33]

b. The perfect passive participle is best understood as aspectually designating the state or condition of being bound or loosed,[34] without implicature of either the temporal construct that Mantey and many grammarians posit or the strictly adjectival sense that Turner, McKay and Moule suggest.[35] McKay has established that, *pace* Chantraine and a host of followers, the perfect form was very much alive in Hellenistic Greek for a good many centuries after the writing of the New Testament.[36] Even if a perfect participle is used "adjectivally," which is one of the common functions of a participle, especially with the stative aspectual semantic feature, its verbal aspect is not necessarily neutralized. This is further confirmed by the fact that δέω and λύω are both found with relatively complete sets of forms in the New Testament.[37]

32 Turner, *Grammatical Insights*, 80.

33 So P. Bonnard, *L'Évangile selon Saint Matthieu* (CNT; 2nd edn; Neuchâtel: Delachaux et Niestlé, 1970) 245. On the modality of the future form, see V. Magnien, *Le futur grec*. II. *Emplois et origines* (Paris: Honoré Champion, 1912) esp. v–vii; J. Humbert, *Syntaxe grecque* (Collection de philologie classiques 2; Paris: Klincksieck, 1945) 151–53; tentatively A. Rijksbaron, *The Syntax and Semantics of the Verb in Classical Greek: An Introduction* (Amsterdam: Gieben, 1984) 33; and now Porter, *Verbal Aspect*, 403–39.

34 J.P. Louw ("Die Semantiese Waarde van die Perfektum in Hellenistiese Grieks," *Acta Classica* 10 [1967] 23–32) convincingly argues against a tradition which defines the perfect in terms of a temporal construct. Cf. also Porter, *Verbal Aspect*, esp. 251–59.

35 Turner, *Grammatical Insights*, 80–82; *idem*, *Syntax*, vol. 3 of *A Grammar of New Testament Greek*, by J.H. Moulton (Edinburgh: T. & T. Clark, 1963) 81–82; K.L. McKay, "On the Perfect and Other Aspects in the Greek Non-Literary Papyri," *Bulletin of the Institute of Classical Studies* 27 (1980) 23–49; Moule, *Idiom Book*, 18.

36 McKay, "On the Perfect," 23–49; *idem*, "The Use of the Ancient Greek Perfect down to the End of the Second Century A.D.," *Bulletin of the Institute of Classical Studies* 12 (1965) 1–21; contra P. Chantraine, *Histoire du parfait grec* (Collection linguistique; Paris: Honoré Champion, 1927) *passim*.

37 δέω is only found in the New Testament in the present stem in the stereotyped forms

Thus Turner's view of the perfect in its original sense as being stative agrees with the understanding of the periphrastic advanced here, glossed "shall be in a state of being bound or having boundness," without explicit reference by verb form alone to when this event might occur. Not only is any presupposition of a rigid temporal scheme unsupportable, but any undue emphasis on the permanence of the state (i.e. "once for all") cannot be posited here on the basis of the participle alone.[38] This lessens the importance of much of the debate regarding the permanence of the Petrine office. The state is *in effect*, without alluding to the time of its inception or termination.

c. Cadbury is correct in emphasizing the importance of the conditional or conditional-like statement for determining temporal implicature. The third class conditional—usually with the subjunctive and ἐάν or its equivalent in the protasis and almost any verb in the apodosis—posits a hypothetical situation and specifies its logical fulfilment.[39] An internal logical order is all that can be posited for the conditional or conditional-like statement apart from temporal deictic indicators. Jesus in essence states, "if something might be bound (subjunctive) upon the earth, then the consequence is a state of boundness in heaven, and if something might be loosed (subjunctive) on earth, then the consequence is a state of loosedness in heaven." The opposition of heaven and earth must be considered in section 3 before temporal implicature can be more closely established.

d. An examination of the parallel examples cited by Mantey is in order.[40] He contends that they endorse his position, but they are perhaps more reasonably interpreted according to the explanation of periphrasis given above in this chapter.

Lysias 22.19: ἐὰν δ' ἀζημίους ἀφῆτε, πολλὴν ἄδειαν αὐτοῖς ἐψηφισμένοι ἔσεσθε ποιεῖν ὅ τι ἂν βούλωνται. This more likely means, "if you might free them unpunished, then you will be in a state of having voted them freedom to do whatever they might want," rather than that they were given freedom before their remission. Note the third class conditional construction, which merely posits a hypothetical event.

δεῖ, etc., and δέον, though other conjugations of the present were current in Hellenistic Greek. See Liddell–Scott, *Greek–English Lexicon*, s.v.

38 Contra Allen, *Matthew*, 177; apparently followed by Cadbury, "Meaning," 253.

39 See B.T. Koppers, *Negative Conditional Sentences in Greek and Some Other Indo-European Languages* (The Hague: Westerbaan, 1959) esp. 91. Cf. J.L. Boyer, "Third (and Fourth) Class Conditions," *GTJ* 3 (1982) 163–75; Porter, *Verbal Aspect*, 301–11; and *idem*, *Idioms of the Greek New Testament*, 261–63.

40 See also, for example, Epictetus 2.22.37, where the periphrasis is parallel to simple future forms. For other examples of Hellenistic usage of future perfect periphrastics, see E. Mayser, *Grammatik der griechischen Papyri aus der Ptolemäerzeit* (2 vols.; Berlin: de Gruyter, 1906–38) 2,1.225.

Lysias 12.100: ὅσοι μὲν ἂν τούτων ἀποψηφίσησθε, αὐτῶν θάνατον κατεψηφισμένους ἔσεσθαι ("whoever of you would vote [to acquit] them, they [regarding the condemned] will be in a state of being condemned [by vote] to their death"). In this conditional-like statement, the logical consequence of acquittal is said to be condemnation to death, with no indication of a previous event of condemnation contemplated.

Lucian, *Phal.* 1.1: και τοῖς ἄλλοις ἅπασι δι' ὑμῶν ἀπολελογημένος ἔσεσθαι. In context the message of Phalaris, conveyed by messenger, is that he feels that if (fourth class conditional) he clears himself he will stand cleared through the Delphians and before all the other Greeks. Surely, it does not mean that if he clears himself he will be ratifying a decision to be cleared before he actually undertakes his effort to exonerate himself.

B.G.U. II 596.11–13 (1st–2nd century A.D.?): τοῦτο οὖν ποίη/σας ἔσῃ μοι μεγάλην / χάριταν κατ[α]τεθειμ[έ]νος ("if/when/after you do this, you will be in a state of having bestowed on me a great favour"). The same interpretation holds for this sentence, where the aorist participle may be interpreted as forming the protasis of a conditional-like statement.

P.Paris 14.49–50 (2nd century B.C.): τούτου δὲ γενο/μένου ἔσομαι βεβοηθημένος ("if/when/after this happens, I will be in a state of being helped"); 8.22–24 (129 B.C.): τούτου / δὲ γενομένου ἔσομαι τετευχυῖα τῆς / παρά σου ἀντιλήψεως ("if/when/after this happens, I will be in a state of reception of help from you"). Both of these constructions close letters, and, as above, use the aorist participle to set up a conditional-like statement. Even if the aorist participles refer to previous events, the logic of the conditional establishes any continuing sense, not the perfect participle alone.

e. Care must be taken not to formulate conceptions of Greek tenses on the basis of translation into English. Mantey, to some extent Cadbury, and others, seem to posit that an English future perfect conceives of a future event that comes about as the result of an event prior to the point of speaking or writing. Comrie, in his recent work on tense, has shown that the English future perfect is an absolute/relative tense. This means that there is an absolute reference to future time in relation to the speaker but a relative reference to the event that precedes this future event.[41] Thus "I will have arrived next Tuesday, and I am leaving tomorrow" is a legitimate use of the English future perfect that does not require reference to a past event with future result. English translation, therefore, as is so often the case, is not necessarily a reliable guide to the understanding of Greek tenses. As already noted above, Greek differs at several points from English in relation to the use of verbal aspect, the use of aspectually vague auxiliary verbs, and grammaticalized temporal reference.

---

41 B. Comrie, *Tense* (Cambridge Textbooks in Linguistics; Cambridge: Cambridge University Press, 1985) 69–74.

In conclusion, therefore, I note that the sense of heaven ratifying earth's decision, a point to be considered further in section 3 below, seems fairly clearly established,[42] and thus I render the passage by the following gloss: "whatever you might bind upon the earth (if such a binding event were to occur), this is expected to be in a state of boundness in heaven; and whatever you might loose upon the earth, this is expected to be in a state of loosedness in heaven."

3. *The Exegesis and Theology of Matthew 16:19*

In this part of the chapter, I would like to mention several exegetical and theological issues that impinge upon our understanding of the passage: the issues of binding and loosing, heaven and earth and the passive voice, and Petrine authority. These are fairly substantial issues, which can only be discussed briefly in terms of the grammatical context established above.

A. *Binding and Loosing*

Derrett, in a fairly recent article, may be right that in context the concepts discussed needed no explanation for the original readers.[43] But that makes the problem of determination no less real for the twentieth-century reader. Several possible interpretations have been suggested.[44]

1. *Rabbinic Thought.* On the basis of a suggested Semitic linguistic parallelism, many scholars have looked to contemporary Rabbinic thought.[45]

a. Strack and Billerbeck cite *b. M. Qat.* 16a containing אסר and שרא (Aramaic) meaning "to ban or acquit members of the community," though they admit this is the only place they have found where the two terms occur together with this personal meaning.[46]

b. The two terms are found more frequently in doctrinal contexts referring to prohibiting or permitting according to the halakah or rules of conduct.[47]

---

42 Cf. McNeile, *Matthew*, 243; D. Hill, *The Gospel of Matthew* (NCB; London: Oliphants, 1972) 262.

43 Derrett, "Binding and Loosing," 112.

44 See W.G. Thompson, *Matthew's Advice to a Divided Community: Mt. 17,22–18,35* (AnBib 44; Rome: Biblical Institute Press, 1970) 89–93.

45 See Burgess, *History*, 62–64, tracing proposals back to the eighteenth century.

46 Strack–Billerbeck, *Kommentar*, 1.739. Jeremias (κλεῖς, *TDNT*, 3.751) claims this meaning is grounded in the juridical use.

47 E.g. *m. Yeb.* 1.4 where the school of Shammai permits (מתירים) a brother to marry his concubine and Hillel forbids it (אוסרים). Strack–Billerbeck, *Kommentar*, 1.738–41, esp. 739 and 740.

Thompson rightly notes that reliance on one instance of the personal meaning is tenuous (though it must be said that it is not impossible), while the common legal meaning depends upon a juridical context.

2. *Opposition as a Statement of Comprehensiveness*. A view that has not gained much popular support holds that the opposition of antithetical elements is common to the literature of a large number of societies and derives its meaning from the opposition as a comprehensive statement of the factors involved. Hence in Matt 16:19 Peter is said to hold all power.[48] Perhaps this reflects a Rabbinic tendency to hyperbole. In any case, Thompson's critique of this argument aptly points out that the idea of totality must mean totality of something, and this has yet to be defined.

3. *Isaiah 22:22*. Emerton argues for direct dependence upon Isa 22:22 (MT): "And the key of the house of David will I lay upon his shoulder; so he shall open, and none shall shut: and he shall shut and none shall open."[49] Arguing that Aramaic was the language of the early Matthean church, and that the original saying followed the order of verbs in Isaiah (where verbs one and four, and two and three are the same, whereas in Matthew one and two, and three and four are), פתח was translated by λύειν to capture the sense of "loosing,"[50] and אחד (the word used in Aramaic for סגר), which is more difficult, was translated by δεῖν either in the sense of shutting people up (though Matthew has an impersonal object) or simply to contrast the familiar "loosing."[51] Thompson argues that Emerton's reconstruction, as he admits, is conjectural and does not account fully for the Matthean context,[52] while Basser claims in his response to

---

48 G. Lambert, "Lier–délier: L'expression de la totalité par l'opposition de deux contraires," *Vivre et penser* (*RB*) Third Series (1943–44) 91–103; J.B. Hofmann, "Zum Wesen der sog. polaren Ausdrucksweise," *Glotta* 15 (1927) 45–53.

49 ופתח ואין סגר וסגר ואין פתח. The targum reads: ויפתח ולית דאחיד וייחוד ולית דפתח. Cf. Derrett, "Binding and Loosing," 113, who claims there "is no OT phrase which precisely agrees."

50 See Gen 43:27; Job 39:5; Ps 51:21; Isa 5:27; 14:17; 58:6; Jer 47:4 LXX.

51 J.A. Emerton, "Binding and Loosing—Forgiving and Retaining," *JTS* NS 13 (1962) 325–31. See his slightly different explanation of the origin of John 20:23 (pp. 328–30). He is followed by Chilton, *Targumic Approaches*, 75–77.

52 In a related theory, A. Díez Macho ("The Recently Discovered Palestinian Targum: Its Antiquity and Relationship with the Other Targums," in *Congress Volume* [VTSup 7; Leiden: Brill, 1960] 222–45, esp. 231; cf. G. Vermes, "The Targumic Versions of Gen 4:3–16," *ALUOS* 3 [1963] 109, who reconstructs an original Aramaic version of Matt 16:19; 18:18) has proposed that the Aramaic *sh^{e}ri*, meaning "loose" or "forgive," is related to Matt 16:19 and 18:18 (and John 20:23). *Targ. Ps.-J.* (Num. 30) offers a partial parallel when establishing laws about the vows taken by women (esp. vv. 6, 9, 13), though the contexts are not identical (Thompson, *Matthew's Advice*, 192–93).

Derrett that Rabbinic treatments of Isa 22:22 do not refer to the binding and loosing of persons at all but to Rabbinic interpretation of Scripture and legal pronouncements. He discounts this view on the basis that no special permission would have been needed to be given either to the rabbis or to the disciples to perform this function.[53]

4. *Greek Phrasing*. Perhaps trips so far afield are not necessary to establish the meaning of "binding and loosing." As Thompson says, "at the level of imagery, the opposition between bind and loose is very natural and immediately evident..."[54] The linking of the two concepts is found in Josephus (*War* 1.5.2 §111), where he refers to the Pharisees as ingratiating themselves to the empress Alexandra so that they might "loose and bind" (λύειν τε καὶ δεσμεῖν).[55] The concepts themselves have parallels in Jesus' teaching, especially Luke 11:52 (cf. Matt 23:13): Jesus warns the lawyers because they take the key (κλεῖδα) of knowledge (or that is knowledge) and thus prevent others from entering (presumably) the kingdom. They load down people with incredible burdens and deprive them of knowledge of the kingdom. In Matt 16:19, therefore, Jesus may be seen as establishing his "church" on Peter. To Peter are given the keys of the kingdom so that rather than the lawyers it is now he who opens or closes the kingdom to men, via the church.[56] The outcome of this commission is seen then in such significant passages as Acts 2:14–39 and 3:11–26, where Peter, along with one or more of the eleven, is depicted as helping to add many to the church, and Acts 4:11–12 and 8:20–23, where the kingdom is shut up from men. Similar passages depicting the work of other apostles, such as Acts 8:5–6, 27–40, might also be included. Matthew 16:19a seems, therefore, to be in some way parallel to v. 19bc, which is perhaps epexegetic or specifying what is entailed in possessing the keys of the kingdom. Though the neuter pronoun ("whatever") makes it difficult to decide whether

---

53 H.W. Basser, "Derrett's 'Binding' Reopened," *JBL* 104 (1985) 297–99.

54 Thompson, *Matthew's Advice*, 189.

55 This example was apparently first cited by W. Whiston (*The Works of Flavius Josephus* [4 vols.; London, 1806] 3.263 note) in a note to his translation: "Here we have the oldest and most authentic Jewish exposition of binding and loosing, for punishing or absolving men, not for declaring actions lawful or unlawful, as some more modern Jews and Christians variously pretend." Later this passage in Josephus was cited with the variant δεῖν by Strack–Billerbeck (*Kommentar*, 1.738), but discounted by F. Büchsel (δέω, *TDNT*, 2.60 n. 8). Büchsel dismisses the example since it clearly refers to imprisonment, but the point here is that the linking of the concepts is not foreign to Greek, as Wilcox notes ("Peter," 81 n. 1).

56 Brown *et al.* (*Peter*, 97) give the following possible options for this function: baptismal discipline, post-baptismal or penitential discipline, excommunication, exclusion from the eucharist, the communication or refusal of knowledge, legislative powers, or power of governing. See also Wilkins, *Concept of Disciple*, 196–97, who argues for authority to grant entrance into the kingdom, although for different reasons.

people or laws are the objects of the verbs (18:18 seems to include people), "binding and loosing" probably includes at the least a juridical meaning on the basis of Greek, Old Testament and Rabbinic parallels, easily seen as implying a metaphorical application to behaviour that would include and exclude from personal membership in a body,[57] in this case the "church" or kingdom.

B. *Heaven and Earth, and the Passive Voice*

There are two major opinions worth considering on the issue of the meaning of heaven and earth and the use of the passive voice.

1. *Divine Passive*. Jeremias argues that the passive voice of the perfect participles is a substitute for the divine name, with Jesus following the custom of the time in speaking of God's action by means of circumlocutions.[58] Thus he renders the verse, "What you bind on earth God will recognize to be bound (at the Last Judgment), and what you loose on earth God will recognize to be loosed (at the Last Judgment)."[59] Jeremias not only imposes a rigorous temporal framework on the statements (presumably on the basis of the future verb forms) but he has neglected the obvious contrast between heaven and earth. A temporal scheme might be posited, but a stringent scheme referring to the judgment is made unlikely not only by the use of the future verb but by the conditional-like construction that links the two concepts.

2. *Spheres of Existence*. A second and better possibility is that "heaven" and "earth" refer to spheres of existence. The contrast is found elsewhere in Matthew,[60] and stresses the opposition between the two realms.[61] Debate over the inauguration of the kingdom falls outside the concern of this passage, since Jesus asserts no more than that the expected consequence of an act of binding or loosing in the earthly realm, the realm of the church, if such an act might occur, is the state of boundness or loosedness in the heavenly sphere. In the sense that heaven is God's realm the participle is probably a divine passive, though the

57 E. Schweizer (*Church Order in the New Testament* [trans. F. Clarke; SBT; London: SCM Press, 1959] 59) says the two meanings cannot be separated from each other.

58 J. Jeremias, *New Testament Theology: The Proclamation of Jesus* (trans. J. Bowden; NTL; London: SCM Press, 1971) 9. Curiously he only lists δέω in 16:19 and 18:18 as unique to Matthew as divine passives, not λύω (p. 11).

59 Jeremias, κλεἰς, *TDNT*, 3.751. In *New Testament Theology*, 9, he renders ἐν τοῖς οὐρανοῖς as "with God," which could be interpreted quite differently.

60 Matt 5:34–35; 6:10, 19–20; note that these use the singular form of heaven, like 18:18. Thompson (*Matthew's Advice*, 189) notes that the compound phrase "heaven and earth" (e.g. Matt 5:18; 11:25; 24:35; 28:18) signifies a totality. Cf. Allen, *Matthew*, 177, who claims the opposition is "merely literary."

61 ἐπί with γῆ and ἐν with οὐρανός follow the general pattern, except for Matt 5:34–35.

agent does not appear to be nearly so important as the state that results.

C. *Petrine Authority and the Church*

It might strike some readers as theologically presumptuous to grant an individual authority over human destiny, and make even God responsive to human decision-making. Without getting too inextricably mired in the theological morass, several observations can be made. (1) No interpretation of the periphrastics can totally dismiss the question of Petrine authority. (2) Whereas this passage fits well with Matthew's theme of human participation in the kingdom,[62] it is unwise to read more into it than is warranted. In Matt 16:18 Jesus says he intends to build his church on Peter and in 16:19 the keys of the kingdom are said to be intended for him.

1. *The Role of Peter*. There are essentially three views of Peter's role in the founding of the church.[63]

a. A few scholars argue that Peter "is the supreme Rabbi in whom resides the final interpretation (the power 'to bind and to loose') of the New Law given to the New Israel ('my [i.e. the Messiah's] Church') by Christ."[64] In a full treatment, Bornkamm argues that the authority to bind and loose refers to Peter's teaching authority, and his role as "fundamental for the existence of the church and for her stability and continuance during the eschatological afflictions..."[65] This authority derives from the teaching of Jesus entrusted to Peter and obligatory for the whole church, even for sentencing at the last judgment.[66]

b. An alternative, put forward strongly by Strecker,[67] is that Matthew does

---

62 See Matt 4:19, fishers of men; 5:13, salt; 5:14–16, light; 10:6–42, preaching; cf. 28:18–20.

63 See J.D. Kingsbury, "The Figure of Peter in Matthew's Gospel as a Theological Problem," *JBL* 98 (1979) esp. 67–68; Wilkins, *Concept of Disciple*, 180–83, 194–95.

64 B.H. Streeter, *The Four Gospels: A Study of Origins* (London: Macmillan, 1924) 515.

65 G. Bornkamm, "The Authority to 'Bind' and 'Loose' in the Church in Matthew's Gospel: The Problem of Sources in Matthew's Gospel," in *Jesus and Man's Hope*, I (Pittsburgh: Pittsburgh Theological Seminary, 1970) 46. Cf. also C. Kähler, "Zur Form- und Traditionsgeschichte von Matth. XVI.17–19," *NTS* 23 (1977) 44–45, 46, 50.

66 Kingsbury ("Peter," 69–72) makes a case for Peter's importance in Matthew, emphasizing: reference to Peter (Petros) in 16:17–19, etc.; prominence given to Peter in disciple lists (10:2) and a host of events; Matthew's excision of Peter's not knowing what to say at the transfiguration (17:1–8; cf. 9:61); and Peter's significant statements (17:4; 19:27; 26:33, 72).

67 G. Strecker, *Der Weg der Gerechtigkeit: Untersuchung zur Theologie des Matthäus* (2nd edn; Göttingen: Vandenhoeck & Ruprecht, 1966) esp. 203–205. This view is also presented by R. Walker, *Die Heilsgeschichte im ersten Evangelium* (Göttingen: Vandenhoeck

not show "ein spezifisches biographisches Interesse an der Person des Petrus... Es fehlen auch die Verbindungslinien, die eine biographische oder psychologische Entwicklung andeuten können." Matthew is much more concerned with representing the life of Jesus, with Peter as spokesman for the other disciples, a representative disciple with all his many faults clearly enunciated.[68]

c. A convincing mediating view has recently been articulated by Kingsbury, who recognizes that though in some cases Peter may seem to be singled out as a prominent figure, or at least a spokesman for the other disciples, he falls squarely within the circle of disciples. Kingsbury sees support in the following facts: (1) virtually everything Matthew writes of Peter he writes of the other disciples,[69] (2) he eliminates two references to the inner group of disciples,[70] and (3) Peter is not mentioned specifically in any of Matthew's Easter stories. Instead Peter has what might be called "salvation-historical primacy."[71] He is the first disciple called (Matt 4:18–20; 10:2–4) and in Matt 16:16, therefore, is the one to make the significant confession that Jesus is the Messiah, the Son of God. Though not a unique confession (cf. 14:33), it has special significance here, since it elicits Jesus' blessing (note forms of address of Peter, including αὐτῷ, σοι, and Simon's full name in v. 17; cf. 3:16), leads to the consequential statement about Peter as the rock (note emphatic κἀγώ, σοι and σύ with εἶ in v. 18) and prompts establishment of the church.[72]

If Kingsbury is correct, arguments about Peter's failure to live up to his supposed commission are of relatively little importance.[73] On the one hand, the passage may be saying nothing more than that Peter, with the apostles, has the authority to "bind and loose" in relation to the church or kingdom, without making any assertion about infallibility in other areas or in general. In this case,

---

& Ruprecht, 1967) 118, who stresses Peter's "Sprechrolle" for the disciples = church; and Gundry, *Matthew*, 334–35.

68 Strecker (*Weg*, 204–205) notes that these failings are taken over from Mark.

69 For example, being called by Jesus: 4:18–22; showing fear: 14:30–31; 8:25–26; faith and doubt: 14:28, 31; 28:17; requesting explanation of a parable: 15:15; 13:36; confessing Jesus: 16:16; 14:33; being pronounced blessed: 16:17; 13:16–17; receiving divine revelation: 16:17; 11:25; exercising authority of "binding and loosing" or "church discipline": 16:19; 18:18; experiencing a Christophany: 17:1, 5; receiving teaching on forgiveness: 18:21–22, 35; taking offense at Jesus: 26:31, 33; and failing to watch when tempted: 26:38, 40–41, 43, 45. Kingsbury, "Peter," 72–73.

70 Matt 9:23, cf. Mark 5:37–38; Matt 24:3, cf. Mark 13:3.

71 Kingsbury, "Peter," 74.

72 See Brown *et al.*, *Peter*, 105–107, esp. 106–107; Wilkins, *Concept of Disciple*, 178–79, 187ff. Kingsbury ("Peter," 74–76) seems to minimize Peter's role, even after his assertion of his primacy in salvation history.

73 T.W. Manson (*The Sayings of Jesus* [London: SCM Press, 1947] 203) suggests this; contra Schmidt, ἐκκλησία, *TDNT*, 3.523.

it would appear that confession of Christ provides the necessary basis for acts of binding and loosing. On the other hand, as Hill asserts, any authority of Peter may be confined to his "special juncture" in God's history, "and its repetition in the bishops of Rome is quite another matter and hardly a legitimate deduction."[74] Peter played a significant role in the early church (Acts 1–12) by preaching the Gospel to Jews (Acts 2:14–36) and gentiles (Acts 10:23b–48), but he too was under authority: he was sent out by other apostles (Acts 8:14), was held accountable by the Jerusalem church (Acts 11:1–18), and was rebuked by Paul (Gal 2:11–14).[75] When v. 18 speaks of the church and Peter, the church is probably meant to be viewed as a continuing body, since it is spoken of as resisting the assault of the "gates of Hades." But whereas the function that Peter performs may also be construed to continue (teaching authority, discipline, etc.), it is not possible to substantiate from this passage that the role of a single individual is perpetuated, still less as an infallible or authoritarian figure.[76] While this removes any thought of personal infallibility or authority being based on this passage, it still gives the ongoing church an awesome responsibility. The use of the future and subjunctive verbs is limited modally to expectational/projective constructs in establishing the church, giving the keys, and instituting the power to bind and loose. Granted that the hypothesis is confirmed, the result is in some sense obligatory, but the authority to bind and loose, while initially entrusted to Peter and the apostles,[77] is apparently perpetuated through the group of believers, that is, the church, not the individual, as Matt 18:18 seems to confirm.

2. *The Church.* In the context of Matt 16:17–19 "my church"[78] does not need to be seen as anything more than an idealized assembly or gathering of Jesus'

---

74 Hill, *Matthew*, 262; cf. also Cullmann, *Peter*, 218–23.

75 See Carson, "Matthew," 368–69.

76 Cullmann (*Peter*, 212–17), as well as Bonnard (*L'Évangile selon Saint Matthieu*, 245), argues against the idea of Petrine succession. Brown *et al.* (*Peter*, 83 n. 189) note that "In the exegesis of the Church Fathers and, indeed, even of the medieval theologians (including Thomas Aquinas) surprisingly little attention was focused on this text for establishing the authority of the Roman church."

77 Note that Matthew lacks any explicit expansion of this group, as Luke includes in, for example, 9:1–6.

78 The word ἐκκλησία only appears in Matt 16:18 and 18:17 in the Gospels, though parallel terms can be found. As Schmidt (ἐκκλησία, *TDNT*, 3.520) says, "the statistical data have no more cogency here than in 1 Pt., where the slogan ἐκκλησία does not occur, but what the ἐκκλησία stands for is richly described by other expressions from the OT." He cites, for example, ποίμνη/ποίμνιον (Matt 26:31; John 10:16; Luke 12:32; Acts 20:28); ἡ αὐλὴ τῶν προβάτων (John 10:1); ἀρνία μου (John 21:15); τὰ προβάτιά μου (John 21:16–17). Contra Schweizer, *Church Order*, 21.

followers,[79] a group which by metonymy Satan or, better, death (is there the prospect of immediate death?) cannot be expected to overcome.[80] Reference to Hades might suggest the church as an eschatological kingdom,[81] but the church or community and kingdom, though closely connected in Matthew, as well as in the Old Testament and Qumran literature,[82] need not be equated and certainly the church need not be conceived of as wholly eschatological,[83] especially if

---

79 The following words have been suggested as lying behind use of ἐκκλησία: biblical Hebrew פהל, בית or עדה, Rabbinic Hebrew צבור or כנסת ישראל, or Aramaic קהלא, צבורא, or כנישתא. See Schmidt, ἐκκλησία, *TDNT*, 3.524–25. Gundry (*Matthew*, 335) claims no Semitic tradition lies behind the Greek since it is purely Matthean redaction. Many commentators posit that use of the word ἐκκλησία must evidence later Matthean redaction, usually on the basis of the word's low number of occurrences in the Gospels (see e.g. B.P. Robinson, "Peter and his Successors: Tradition and Redaction in Matthew 16.17–19," *JSNT* 21 [1984] esp. 90–91). But they may be unnecessarily imposing an overly restricted definition dependent upon usage in Paul and Acts that refers specifically to the church as an organized, formal institution, instead of recognizing a process of lexical conservatism. The Greek word ἐκκλησία, originally meaning simply a meeting or gathering of people (e.g. Herodotus), during the Attic period could be used of the authoritative Athenian political body (see Plato, *Gorg*. 452E, 456B; Thucydides 2.22.1; esp. inscriptions) or it could refer to other assemblies gathered for various purposes (see Euripides, *Rhes*. 139; Xenophon, *Anab*. 1.3.2). This more general meaning, only possibly supported by a Hebraic or biblical influence (esp. Psalms and possibly Ben Sira), seems to have been constricted to refer to early Christian gatherings and then was applied to the whole church (the even wider usage also persisted: e.g. Acts 19:39). See A. Hilhorst, "Termes chrétiens issus du vocabulaire de la démocratie athénienne," *FN* 1.1 (1988) 29; J.Y. Campbell, "The Origin and Meaning of the Christian Use of the Word ΕΚΚΛΗΣΙΑ," *JTS* 49 (1948) 130–42; M. Silva, *Biblical Words and their Meaning: An Introduction to Lexical Semantics* (2nd edn; Grand Rapids: Zondervan, 1994 [1983]) 26, 79.

80 J. Jeremias (ᾅδης, *TDNT*, 1.148–49) proposes a cosmological interpretation of "Hades," but this has not commanded assent (see Chilton, *Targumic Approaches*, 76). Wilkins (*Concept of Disciple*, 194 n. 95) suggests a passion prediction. H. Conzelmann (*An Outline of the Theology of the New Testament* [trans. J. Bowden; NTL; London: SCM Press, 1969] 33) takes a different tack, arguing that Jesus' eschatology does not fit the concept of an organized church, so that if Jesus considered himself Messiah the saying must be inauthentic. This is argued against by A. Richardson (*An Introduction to the Theology of the New Testament* [London: SCM Press, 1958] 307) and Albright–Mann (*Matthew*, 195–96), who note that a "messiah without a messianic community would have been unthinkable to any Jew" (p. 195).

81 So Hill, *Matthew*, 262. Cf. Allen, *Matthew*, 179.

82 On the ambiguity of בית, meaning community/temple/kingdom in, for example, 2 Sam 7:13 and 4QFlor 1:2, 10, see G.J. Brooke, *Exegesis at Qumran: 4QFlorilegium in its Jewish Context* (JSOTSup 29; Sheffield: JSOT Press, 1985) 86–87/91–92, 112; and B. Gärtner, *The Temple and the Community in Qumran and the New Testament: A Comparative Study in the Temple Symbolism of the Qumran Texts and the New Testament* (SNTSMS 1; Cambridge: Cambridge University Press, 1965) esp. 31–32.

83 Schmidt, ἐκκλησία, *TDNT*, 3.522.

"gates of Hades" is metaphorical for death.[84] Perhaps there is a parallelism here, with church and earth, and kingdom and heaven. The close connection between the two spheres, not clearly articulated in terms of temporal relation, would revolve around the commission to tend to the keys through binding and loosing.

D. *Matthew 18:18*

How does what I have said above apply to Matt 18:18? Much of it applies directly, especially concerning the periphrastic construction within a conditional or conditional-like statement. Whatever one's view of Matthew 18 and the church,[85] the major opinions treat 18:15–20 as a whole, concerned with some form of discipline for those who sin.[86] Verses 15–17 are apparently concerned with the procedure to be taken when a member of the community sins, and vv. 18–20 offer two proverbial statements applied to it. The introductory formula of v. 18 ("truly I am saying to you") seems to link the verse with the previous pericope, a common use of the phrase in Matthew (cf. Matt 18:3, 10, 13). In contrast to 16:19, 18:18 has plural objects and plural subjects for the verbs. Perhaps these clauses are less well connected to their context than those in 16:19,[87] where the singular verb agrees with reference to Peter. The plural verbs, as well as the reference to binding and loosing, are not so obvious in their meaning, unless we see 18:18 as a "special application" of 16:19 addressed not to a single individual but to all the disciples (v. 1) as the leaders called upon to enforce standards in this newly formed group, called the church.[88] This, however, does not alleviate the potential problem of the relation between the stringency of 18:15–20 and the apparent emphasis on forgiveness in the parable of the lost sheep in Matt 18:12–14 and the teaching on forgiveness in Matt 18:22ff. As far as origins are concerned, that is, which verse is the source of the other, there are no clear indications whether Matthew has applied to the disciples words spoken to Peter, or vice versa,[89] whether the words are

---

84 Carson, "Matthew," 370. He cites parallels in canonical Old Testament literature (Job 17:16; 38:17; Pss 9:13; 107:18; Isa 38:10), noncanonical literature (Wis 16:13; *3 Macc* 5:51; *Pss. Sol.* 16:2) and pagan literature (Homer, *Il.* 9.312; *Od.* 11.277; Aeschylus, *Ag.* 1291; Euripides, *Hec.* 1).

85 See Thompson, *Matthew's Advice*, 2–4, esp. 193–94; and Bornkamm, "Authority," 42–43.

86 Hill (*Matthew*, 276) suggests either excommunication or ratification of a disciplinary measure.

87 Contra F. Büchsel, δέω, *TDNT*, 2.61.

88 Carson, "Matthew," 374; cf. Bornkamm, "Authority," 46. Several scholars see a specific community (as opposed to the idealized group of 16:19) referred to here: e.g. Schmidt (ἐκκλησία, *TDNT*, 3.526) and C.H. Dodd (*New Testament Studies* [Manchester: Manchester University Press, 1953] 57–58), who notes however that in the early church the local community in Jerusalem and the catholic church were the same.

89 Thompson, *Matthew's Advice*, 94. He notes that Matthean doublets may have two

independent and come from the ministry of Jesus himself, or whether they are both later creations or redactions by an early Petrine community.

4. *Conclusion*

I would not pretend to have solved the many enigmas of Matt 16:19, though I hope I have set at least a plausible agenda for a better understanding of several of the most significant issues. I have concentrated on interpretation of the periphrastic construction. This, like most grammatical issues, introduces serious methodological questions that must be confronted before further textual analysis is possible, and sets interpretative limitations for a given passage. The question of authenticity, while certainly interesting and important for unraveling other Gordian knots, can be set aside in struggling with the grammatical issues (although see the appendix below). Word-play on Peter's name, while possible in Aramaic, is likely in Greek, pointing to at least a Greek formulation of the discourse at some early stage. Peter's role in the formation of the church, while certainly significant, cannot be institutionalized on the basis of this passage alone, but rather points to a primary though not exclusive function. Any theological constructs, it seems, must first consider the periphrastic construction in its several elements: the more modal than strictly future-referring nature of the future form of the auxiliary εἰμί; the stative rather than temporally-schematized verbal aspect of the perfect participle; and temporal implicature on the basis of the discourse deixis of the conditional statement.

APPENDIX ON THE AUTHENTICITY OF MATTHEW 16:19

Burgess notes that attacks on authenticity of Matt 16:19 began in 1781.[90] In recent times, the most notable person to argue against the authenticity of this passage perhaps has been Bultmann,[91] who claims that the words, put in the mouth of the risen Lord, go back to an early Aramaic tradition of a Palestinian church that looked to Peter as its founder and leader. Their origin must be early on account of the word-play on Peter's name that, he claims, can occur only in Aramaic, reference to "gates of Hades" (v. 18; see Isa 38:10), and

different meanings, e.g. 10:40 = 18:6; 5:29–30 = 18:8–9.

90 Burgess, *History*, 42; cf. 42–49 and *passim*.

91 R. Bultmann, *The History of the Synoptic Tradition* (trans. J. Marsh; revised edn; Oxford: Blackwell, 1968) 138–40, 258–59; followed by, for example, Manson, *Sayings*, 204, 201–205; Brown *et al.*, *Peter*, 83–101; Robinson, "Peter," esp. 86–87; and J. Lambrecht, "'Du bist Petrus'—Mt 16,16–19 und das Papsttum," *SNTU* 11 (1987) 5–32.

eschatological reference to the church's salvation.[92] More recently Wilcox, though recognizing that the dialogue rests on "ancient traditional material going back to the primitive Church if not to Jesus himself," has proposed that "in its present form it is a piece of Matthean redaction" using an early "stone"/"rock" tradition, reflected in 1 Pet 2:8 and Rom 9:33 (possibly Eph 2:20) and perhaps originating in several Old Testament passages (e.g. Ps 117:22–23; Isa 8:14; 28:16; possibly Dan 2:34; 7:13), which links Jesus with the "rejected stone." This tradition, available in Greek and Aramaic, was reinterpreted to identify the church with the stone on the basis of word-play on Peter's Greek name (πέτρος).[93]

Several scholars have maintained the authenticity of the passage. Responding to the claim that the use of ἐκκλησία is the major objection to authenticity, Cullmann stresses the Jewish origin of the term (see, for example, Acts 7:38) meaning "people of God," and argues similarly for the rock imagery (e.g. Dan 2:34ff., 44ff.) and "building" metaphor (e.g. Num 12:7; Ruth 4:11; Amos 9:11). On the basis of kingdom-language and parallels illustrating Jesus' eschatological concern, Cullmann claims there is nothing that indicates Jesus did not speak these words, though they probably were spoken in a passion-story context. In fact, Cullmann believes that John 21:15ff. reflects a common source for Matt 16:17–19, Luke 22:31–34, and John 6:66ff.[94]

One of the most interesting of recent contributions to the debate comes from Meyer,[95] who argues along slightly different lines for the authenticity of the words in context. He concentrates on the following points. (1) The Gospels are united in stating that Peter received his name from Jesus (Mark 3:16; Luke 6:14; John 1:42), though they do not stress such an event. The other New Testament references are in agreement (1 Cor 1:12; 3:12; 9:5; 15:5; Gal 1:18; 2:9, 11, 14; Acts 1–15), with only Matt 16:17–19 providing a plausible explanation for the naming. (2) The complex of themes (Messiah/Son of God/building of temple) coordinates with v. 16 and the Caesarea Philippi pericope, thus answering the question of who Jesus is. (3) The lack of parallels

92 The list is supplemented by Wilcox, "Peter," 73–74, 79: the expression "flesh and blood" meaning "man"; "my Father in heaven"; the name "Simon Barjona"; the formula μακάριος εἶ; "binding and loosing"; opposition of "heaven and earth"; and asyndeton opening v. 19. He disputes many of these.

93 Wilcox, "Peter," 87–88.

94 Cullmann, *Peter*, 176–217, esp. 190–91; followed by Richardson, *Introduction*, 309. For specific critique of Cullmann's proposal that these verses originated in a passion-story context, see R.H. Gundry, "The Narrative Framework of Matt 16:17–19," *NovT* 7 (1964–65) 1–9; and more generally M.D. Goulder, *Midrash and Lection in Matthew* (London: SPCK, 1974) 383–86.

95 B.F. Meyer, *The Aims of Jesus* (London: SCM Press, 1979) 185–97; followed by Carson, "Matthew," 366–67; Wilkins, *Concept of Disciple*, 185–86.

does not of itself prove or disprove authenticity, even if Mark has priority, which is unlikely in this section, according to Meyer. In fact, the Lukan and Johannine parallels (Luke 9:18–20; John 6:69) attest common tradition through the shared phrase τοῦ θεοῦ. (4) Vocabulary in Matt 16:17–19—"reveal" (Matt 11:25–26); "flesh and blood" (Matt 5:3ff.; 11:6; 13:16); "gates of Hades" (Matt 6:13); "binding and loosing"—need not be construed as part of a post-resurrectional saying. (5) Many redactional elements predate Matthew's redaction, like "my heavenly Father" (v. 17); "the reign of heaven" (v. 19); and use of the name "Peter." (6) The word "church" may refer not to an isolated sectarian community but to the community of "eschatological Israel."

CHAPTER SEVEN

"IN THE VICINITY OF JERICHO": LUKE 18:35 IN THE LIGHT OF ITS SYNOPTIC PARALLELS*

1. *Introduction*

At Luke 18:35, the author (called Luke for purposes of clarity) has apparently redacted his source, Mark 10:46 (//Matt 20:29), quite heavily.[1] Mark's relevant wording reads: "And they came (ἔρχονται) to Jericho. And as he was going out (ἐκπορευομένου) from Jericho and his disciples and a great multitude, the son of Timaeus, Bartimaeus, a blind beggar, was sitting beside the road." Luke retains very little of the wording, using instead ἐγένετο δὲ ἐν τῷ ἐγγίζειν αὐτὸν εἰς Ἰεριχώ. Worth noting are the following changes. First, Mark's two directional references indicating going away from Jericho—"out" (ἐκπορευομένου) and "from" (ἀπό)—are completely eliminated in Luke. Secondly, although the phrase εἰς Ἰεριχώ is retained, in Luke it follows a

---

* This essay is reprinted with the permission of the Editor-in-Chief, from the *Bulletin for Biblical Research* 2 (1992) 91–104. The format has been changed slightly.

1 For the sake of discussion and in the light of the majority of scholarly opinion, I assume that the Markan version is redacted by Luke. That this is reasonable for this passage is seen in the light of Lukan differences regarding language, phrasing and geography, where Matthew and Mark are in closer harmony than the more distinctive Lukan account (see below for discussion of details). This is not the position of all, however. For example, H. Riley posits that Mark conflates his Matthean and Lukan sources (B. Orchard and H. Riley, *The Order of the Synoptics: Why Three Synoptic Gospels?* [Macon, GA: Mercer University Press, 1987] 70–71). Although this perhaps fits R. Bultmann's analysis in which he posits that the Synoptics tend to add details (*The History of the Synoptic Tradition* [trans. J. Marsh; revised edn; Oxford: Blackwell, 1968] 213, 316), this is far from certain. If Luke's account does not have a sense of motion, then conflation has not occurred. The presumption rests with those who see Matthew as abbreviating his Markan source to only one directional indicator, and Luke as changing his reference to a spatial indicator. Movement from Luke's verb of location to two similar accounts with verbs of motion is very unlikely (see below for arguments to support the above analysis of Luke). That the sources and directions of influence in the Synoptic accounts are complex is demonstrated by B. Chilton, *Profiles of a Rabbi: Synoptic Opportunities in Reading about Jesus* (Atlanta: Scholars Press, 1989) esp. parts 1 and 2.

different verb from the one in Mark, coinciding with changes in number. Luke introduces ἐγγίζειν in place of Mark's verb of motion, ἔρχονται. Thirdly, Luke introduces his distinctive ἐγένετο ἐν τῷ plus infinitive phrasing.[2]

According to traditional interpretation of this verse, Luke apparently contradicts Mark and Matthew.[3] Mark tells of Jesus' healing of Bartimaeus on the way out of Jericho, an understanding which Matthew at 20:29–34 appears to follow. But as Haenchen states, "Nach Mk spielt sich diese Heilungsgeschichte ab, als Jesus Jericho verlässt, nach Lk (18,35), als sich dieser Stadt näher."[4] As a consequence, there have been numerous attempts either to bring these two accounts into some meaningful harmony or to explain why it is that Luke so clearly stands against his apparent source. It must be recognized, however, that McNeile's position—that Luke's relation to Mark "admits of no harmonization"[5]—has carried the day with the majority of scholars.

2. *Proposed Solutions Regarding Luke 18:35 and its Parallels*

A few of the proposed solutions regarding Luke 18:35 and its parallels warrant mention, nevertheless.[6] Augustine simply argued that there were two separate healing accounts, with one blind man healed on entrance and the other on exit (Augustine, *Quaest. Evang*. 2.49). This solution eliminates the apparent directional discrepancy, while suggesting a whole new set of problems focused upon the very similar wording of the two accounts throughout the rest of the pericope. This solution has not commended itself to many, if any, major recent commentators.

Calvin proposed that the blind man, Bartimaeus, saw Jesus on the way into the city of Jericho but was unable to attract his attention. On Jesus' way out of the city, with the help of a friend, he did attract Jesus' attention and was

2 S.E. Porter, *Verbal Aspect in the Greek of the New Testament, with Reference to Tense and Mood* (Studies in Biblical Greek 1; New York: Peter Lang, 1989) 120–26, esp. 124. This kind of construction occurs in 54 of its 63 instances in Luke–Acts, and 38 of these in the Gospel. Parallel references occur at Luke 1:8, 9:33, 11:27, 17:14, 24:51 with the present infinitive, and 24:30 with the aorist infinitive.

3 I am not concerned with the difficulty over how many were healed. This problem is not nearly so difficult as the one treated in this chapter.

4 E. Haenchen, *Der Weg Jesu* (Berlin: Töpelmann, 1966) 370. See also G.N. Stanton, *The Gospels and Jesus* (Oxford: Oxford University Press, 1989) 151.

5 A.H. McNeile, *The Gospel according to St. Matthew* (1915; repr. Grand Rapids: Baker, 1980) 291; contra (too facilely?) Z.C. Hodges, "The Blind Men at Jericho," *BSac* 12 (1965) 328.

6 See A. Plummer, *The Gospel according to S. Luke* (ICC; 5th edn; Edinburgh: T. & T. Clark, 1901) 429–30; cf. *idem, An Exegetical Commentary on the Gospel according to St. Matthew* (1915; repr. Grand Rapids: Baker, 1982) 282–83.

healed.[7] Consequently, the healing actually occurred on the way out of Jericho. Whereas Mark and Matthew only mention the blind man upon the occasion of his healing, Luke mentions that the blind man was present on both Jesus' entrance and his exit. This theory has recently been revived by Blomberg, utilizing redaction criticism:

> Probably Luke has just abbreviated Mark, as he does consistently elsewhere, leaving out the reference to the departure from Jericho. Mark after all begins his passage in agreement with Luke, by reporting that Jesus first came *to* Jericho, but his style is somewhat inelegant in stating that "they came to Jericho and as he is going out of Jericho..." (Mk. 10:46). Luke therefore improves the style by excising the latter clause, so that one must not press him to mean that the miracle narrated in 18:36–43 occurred immediately after the action of verse 35. Luke simply records Jesus' arrival, Mark presupposes his entrance into and exit from the town, which Luke omits, and then both describe the healing as Jesus was on his way out. The blind man would have sat by the roadside, as beggars customarily did, all the while (18:35), but would only have realized the significance of the passing visitor when crowds were accompanying him upon his departure (18:36). The type of gap which must be presupposed between verses 35 and 36 is hinted at by Luke's omission of any mention of crowds as Jesus was entering, and is consistent with the type of literary abridgement which occurs throughout the gospels...[8]

But this interpretation surely is strained, since one must infer a period of time when Jesus was in Jericho, even though the text of Luke does not make reference to it. No one reading Luke's Gospel by itself would be able to imagine this as the sense of the passage.

A third solution is that there were two known Jerichos a few miles apart.[9] Archaeological evidence is clear that the site of New Testament Jericho (Tulul Ab el-'Alayiq), which was enhanced and built up by Herod, is different from the site of Old Testament Jericho (Tell es-Sultan; cf. Josephus, *War* 4.8.3 §459;

---

7 J. Calvin, *A Harmony of the Gospels Matthew, Mark and Luke* (vol. 2; trans. T.H.L. Parker; ed. D.W. Torrance and T.F. Torrance; Grand Rapids: Eerdmans, 1972) 278; and tentatively F. Godet, *A Commentary on the Gospel of St. Luke* (New York: Funk & Wagnalls, 1887) 415.

8 C.L. Blomberg, *The Historical Reliability of the Gospels* (Leicester: IVP, 1987) 128–29; cf. also G.L. Archer, *Encyclopedia of Bible Difficulties* (Grand Rapids: Zondervan, 1982) 332–33.

9 P. Ketter, "Zur Lokalisierung der Blindenheilung bei Jericho," *Bib* 15 (1934) 411–18; Godet, *Luke*, 415; N. Geldenhuys, *Commentary on the Gospel of Luke* (NICNT; Grand Rapids: Eerdmans, 1951) 467; W.F. Arndt, *The Gospel according to St. Luke* (St. Louis: Concordia, 1956) 387; tentatively D.A. Carson, "Matthew," 8.435, and W.L. Liefeld, "Luke," 8.1006, in *The Expositor's Bible Commentary* (11 vols.; ed. F.E. Gaebelein; Grand Rapids: Zondervan, 1981).

cf. *Ant.* 15.4.2 §§96–103; 15.4.4 §§106–107).[10] This theory holds that all three Gospel writers place the healing event on Jesus' trip between the Old Testament site and the New Testament site. Mark and Matthew speak of Jesus' walking away from the Old Testament city and Luke speaks of Jesus' walking towards and into the New Testament city. This theory is damaged by the lack of any clear evidence that the long-abandoned Old Testament site was even known as the city of Jericho, despite the presence of an important perennial spring. The evidence to this point indicates that it was probably merely a tell, at best only sparsely populated.[11] There is the further difficulty that any reader of the text would have had difficulty knowing which site was being referred to in any one of the accounts.

A fourth solution is that Luke 18:35 was originally part of the Zacchaeus story, which is unique to Luke, but that Luke interposed the healing of the blind man and wrote a new introduction at 19:1.[12] This solution is implausible, since it posits that the Lukan ἐγένετο construction was part of pre-Lukan material.

A fifth solution is that

> The alteration may have been made simply to accommodate the Zacchaeus incident which takes place in Jericho, and which Luke wishes to place after the healing of Bartimaeus as a climax to the series of incidents. At the same time, Luke avoids separating the Zacchaeus story from the following parable, which also comes from his non-Marcan material. . .[13]

This solution is perhaps enhanced if one recognizes the movement of Luke's Gospel; Jesus is travelling towards Jerusalem, his city of destiny. Any movement which does not point towards this final goal, especially in relation to Jericho, a city so near to Jerusalem, is eliminated.[14] Of course, this solution may

---

10 On New Testament Jericho, see J.L. Kelso and D.C. Baramki, *Excavations at New Testament Jericho and Khirbet En-Nitla* (New Haven: American Schools of Oriental Research, 1955) esp. 5–19; and J.B. Pritchard, *The Excavations at Herodian Jericho, 1951* (New Haven: American Schools of Oriental Research, 1958) esp. 56–58.

11 See K.M. Kenyon, *Digging up Jericho* (London: Benn, 1957) 264; *idem*, "Jericho," in *Encyclopedia of Archaeological Excavations in the Holy Land* (ed. M. Avi-Yonah; Englewood Cliffs, NJ: Prentice-Hall, 1976) 2.564, followed by most archaeologists since. For a recent survey, see J.R. Bartlett, *Jericho* (Grand Rapids: Eerdmans, 1982) chs. 6 and 7.

12 See T. Schramm, *Der Markus-Stoff bei Lukas: Eine Literarkritische und Redaktionsgeschichtliche Untersuchung* (SNTSMS 14; Cambridge: Cambridge University Press, 1971) 143–44. He follows B.S. Easton, *The Gospel according to St. Luke* (Edinburgh: T. & T. Clark, 1926) 277.

13 I.H. Marshall, *The Gospel of Luke* (NIGTC; Grand Rapids; Eerdmans, 1978) 692.

14 See J.A. Fitzmyer, *The Gospel according to Luke X–XXIV* (AB 28A; Garden City, NY: Doubleday, 1985) 1211. C.F. Evans (*St. Luke* [London: SCM Press, 1990] 657) notes that Jericho is the first town mentioned by Luke since 9:51, and is not actually on the natural or direct route from Galilee to Judea via Samaria, except if the Markan account (see esp.

well explain why Luke has done what he does but it does not reconcile the apparent contradiction. For many this is in fact not a problem.[15]

3. *A Solution Based upon the Verb Ἐγγίζειν*

Since the meaning appears clear in Luke 18:35, few have taken time to examine in detail the particular wording of the important Lukan introduction to the healing pericope. The Lukan introduction in 18:35 by all accounts sets the stage for Luke's description of the miraculous healing, as well as bringing the Lukan account into apparent conflict with Mark and Matthew. Perhaps one of the reasons that commentators have not pursued the linguistic issues is the disparaging comment made by Plummer in his commentary. He claims that "The translation, 'When He was not far from Jericho,' i.e. as He had just left it (Grotius, Nösgen), is perhaps the worst device for harmonizing Lk. with Mt. and Mk. The meaning of ἐγγίζειν is decisive; and there is the εἰς in addition."[16] But as most scholars are all too well aware, the exact meaning of ἐγγίζειν is open to some debate, as is the sense of εἰς. I do believe, however, that Plummer is correct that ἐγγίζειν does not mean "he had just left." Instead, I wish to argue that, at least as far as Luke is concerned, ἐγγίζειν is not exclusively or even primarily a verb of motion, as it is usually interpreted; in some of its instances it is a verb of location, either in time or in space. Luke 18:35, therefore, speaks of location, not movement. Not only is this analysis compatible with evidence found in the standard lexica, but this sense can be widely substantiated by examination of the evidence in Luke–Acts, including use of the verb in so-called kingdom passages, use of the verb in other passages, and use of the preposition εἰς.

A. *Ἐγγίζειν in Kingdom Passages*

The spatial locational sense of ἐγγίζειν is supported by a brief statement in Preiske's entry in *TDNT*. He says that "A very different use of ἐγγίζειν and ἐγγύς as indications of time and space is also to be found, esp. in Lk. and Jn. Ἐγγίζω is used...with the dat[ive] to indicate place and movement...or with εἰς...," where he cites Luke 18:35.[17] Much of the difficulty that has bedeviled

10:1) is being followed; cf. E.P. Sanders and M. Davies, *Studying the Synoptic Gospels* (London: SCM Press, 1989) 39–40.

15 See, for example, M. Goulder, *Luke: A New Paradigm* (2 vols.; JSNTSup 20; Sheffield: JSOT Press, 1990) 2.672–74.

16 Plummer, *Luke*, 430; cf. J. Reiling and J.L. Swellengrebel, *A Translator's Handbook on the Gospel of Luke* (Leiden: Brill, 1971) 611: "*eggizó eis* followed by the name of a town means 'to approach,' 'to come into the neighborhood of.'"

17 H. Preiske, ἐγγύς, *TDNT*, 3.331–32.

examination of ἐγγίζειν has come about because of its theological significance, in particular with reference to the issue of the coming of the kingdom. On the one hand, Dodd argued vociferously for so-called realized eschatology, claiming that forms of ἐγγίζειν and φθάνειν are both verbs which indicate arrival.[18] On the other hand, Kümmel and more recently Mattill argue for the sense in the New Testament of imminence though not arrival, claiming that ἐγγίζειν and φθάνειν are both verbs which indicate that something is at hand though not fully present.[19] This is not the place to venture any proposals regarding the concept of the kingdom, except to say that recent discussion has arrived at what amounts to a more widespread consensus: there are statements in the Gospels, including Luke's Gospel, which are compatible with the kingdom as present (e.g. Luke 11:20; 17:21) and the kingdom as still expected (e.g. Luke 11:2; 13:28–29).[20]

This debate has some relevance for the discussion of this chapter, since Luke 10:9, 11 are the two places in the Gospel where forms of ἐγγίζειν are used in terms of kingdom. Luke 10:9 is paralleled by Matt 10:7, and may well pick up Mark 1:15, which Luke omits in his parallel (Luke 4:15). Luke reads (at vv. 9 and 11): ἤγγικεν [ἐφ' ὑμᾶς v. 11 omits] ἡ βασιλεία τοῦ θεοῦ. This passage has been discussed numerous times. Although Fitzmyer suggests that Luke 10:9 is the same as Mark 1:15, he resists the force of the Markan passage, as well as the Lukan passage. He says with reference to the Lukan passage that the kingdom "has drawn near to you," that is, "in the very preaching of it by the disciples sent out by Jesus." This seems to imply a present reality, although Fitzmyer claims to follow Kümmel, James Robinson and others in understanding it to mean "has approached, has drawn near."[21] The Markan passage precedes the statement that the kingdom is come with the words πεπλήρωται ὁ καιρός. As Robinson recognizes, Mark 1:15

18 C.H. Dodd, *The Parables of the Kingdom* (revised edn; New York: Scribners, 1961) 28–30.

19 W.G. Kümmel, *Promise and Fulfilment: The Eschatological Message of Jesus* (trans. D.M. Barton; London: SCM Press, 1957) esp. 19–25; A.J. Mattill, Jr., *Luke and the Last Things: A Perspective for the Understanding of Lukan Thought* (Dillsboro, NC: Western North Carolina Press, 1979) 71–76, 168–76.

20 See as recent examples: R.H. Stein, *The Method and Message of Jesus' Teachings* (revised edn; Louisville: Westminster/John Knox, 1994) esp. 69–81; D.C. Allison, Jr., *The End of the Ages Has Come: An Early Interpretation of the Passion and Resurrection of Jesus* (Philadelphia: Fortress Press, 1985) 101–14; G.R. Beasley-Murray, *Jesus and the Kingdom of God* (Grand Rapids: Eerdmans, 1986) 71–218; R. O'Toole, SJ, "The Kingdom of God in Luke–Acts," in *The Kingdom of God in 20th-Century Interpretation* (ed. W. Willis; Peabody: Hendrickson, 1987) esp. 154–55, 157–59.

21 Fitzmyer, *Luke X–XXIV*, 848, with bibliography; cf. Kümmel, *Promise and Fulfilment*, 23–24, although his argument regarding whether two different Greek verbs would have translated the same original Aramaic behind Luke 10:9 and 11:20 is beside the point.

> consists in an announcement of what has happened: πεπλήρωται, ἤγγικεν... But the exclusive use of the perfect tense (v. 15) to announce the nearness of a future eschatological consummation is worthy of note. For even though we must understand ἤγγικεν to mean "has drawn near" rather than "has come," it still refers to something having taken place: the times have shifted, the kingdom is now near because it has moved from a vague distance to a near position, a shift which has already taken place.[22]

Much easier to understand and accept is Hengel's simple translation: "The time is fulfilled and the kingdom of God is here."[23] Regarding Luke 10:9 and 11, Marshall relies upon Mark 1:15 and Luke 11:20, where a parallel is found. He believes that the point of Luke 10:9 and 11 is the same as 11:20: "the power of the kingdom has drawn near to those to whom it is being preached and may be received by them if they respond to the message... In Mk. 1:5 the nearness is more temporal, whereas here it is more spatial."[24] This linkage of temporal and spatial proximity is worth noting. This evidence creates at least the possibility that ἐγγίζειν may be used with the sense of spatial or locational proximity in Luke 18:35.[25]

B. *Ἐγγίζειν in Luke–Acts*

An examination of the other places where ἐγγίζειν appear in Luke–Acts is now in order.[26] First, I will treat several examples that appear to have an arguably evident spatial-locational sense.[27] Secondly, I will discuss several more difficult examples. Thirdly, I will mention Luke 18:40. It is not necessary for me to prove that ἐγγίζειν has a clear spatial-locational meaning in every instance, only that there are enough clear cases so that it can be recognized that the locational sense is one of the legitimate senses of the word.

---

22 J.M. Robinson, *The Problem of History in Mark* (SBT 21; London: SCM Press, 1957) 24, with bibliography (unchanged in Philadelphia: Fortress Press, 1982, p. 72).

23 M. Hengel, *Studies in the Gospel of Mark* (trans. J. Bowden; Philadelphia: Fortress Press, 1985) 53 and n. 82.

24 Marshall, *Gospel of Luke*, 422, with bibliography; cf. also *idem*, *Luke: Historian and Theologian* (Grand Rapids: Zondervan, 1970) 133–34. Allison agrees (*End of the Ages*, 104). Cf. D.C. Allison, Jr., "A Plea for Thoroughgoing Eschatology," *JBL* 113 (1994) 651–68.

25 Cf. the statements in D.E. Hiebert, *Mark: A Portrait of the Servant* (revised edn; Chicago: Moody, 1979) 262: "still others hold that Luke's language simply means that Jesus was 'near' or in the vicinity of Jericho when the healing took place"; and 262 note: "The original in Luke could quite literally be rendered 'in his being near unto the city.' This would agree with either an entry or a departure from the city." He does not give evidence for his informal references.

26 Luke–Acts contains 23 of the 40 instances of ἐγγίζειν in the New Testament.

27 Examples with potential temporal-locational senses include: Luke 21:8 (//Mark 13:6; Matt 24:5); Luke 21:20 (no meaningful parallels); Luke 21:28 (no meaningful parallels).

1. *Spatial-Locational Usage*

a. Luke 7:12 (no parallels). Luke narrates that Jesus went (ἐπορεύθη) to the city of Nain, and his disciples and a crowd went (συνεπορεύοντο) with him. ὡς δὲ ἤγγισεν τῇ πύλῃ τῆς πόλεως, the dead body of the widow's son was carried by. Use of ἐγγίζειν follows use of two verbs of motion. The use of the aorist, ἤγγισεν, after ὡς, along with the dative object, following two verbs of motion, is certainly compatible with the idea that Jesus was located at the gate when the body was brought by. Use of the aorist form of ἐγγίζειν after ὡς is uniquely Lukan.[28]

b. Luke 15:25 (no parallels). In the parable of the prodigal son, Jesus reportedly says that the older son was in the field and, ὡς ἐρχόμενος ἤγγισεν τῇ οἰκίᾳ, heard the music and inquired of his father. Use of ἐγγίζειν follows a verb of motion, a dependent adverbial participle. Following the verb of motion, the aorist form after ὡς and preceding the dative object is certainly compatible with the idea that the older brother was located near the house when he heard the music.[29]

c. Luke 19:29 (//Mark 11:1; Matt 21:1). The Markan parallel reads καὶ ὅτε ἐγγίζουσιν εἰς Ἱεροσόλυμα εἰς Βηθφαγὴ καὶ Βηθανίαν... This usage helps to demonstrate a spatial-locative sense for ἐγγίζειν. Although the sense of "drawing near" might be plausible, in the light of the fact that Jerusalem is still a ways off, it is better to see the author as saying that they were now in the area of Jerusalem, etc. Luke seems to understand his source in this way. He substitutes a verb of motion to cover the entire trip to Jerusalem, but uses ἐγγίζειν as part of a typically Lukan construction[30] to describe their proximity to Bethphage and Bethany: ἐπορεύετο ἔμπροσθεν ἀναβαίνων εἰς Ἱεροσόλυμα. καὶ ἐγένετο ὡς ἤγγισεν εἰς Βηθφαγὴ καὶ Βηθανία (Luke 19:28–29). That this verb is one of spatial proximity is reinforced by Marshall's observation that in fact "Bethany was further away from Jerusalem than Bethphage."[31] With this verb Luke introduces nothing which distracts from his depicting Jesus as heading towards Jerusalem.

d. Luke 19:37 (no parallels at this point). In describing Jesus' "triumphal entry," Luke says that as he went (πορευομένου) the crowd was strewing their garments in the road. ἐγγίζοντος δὲ αὐτοῦ ἤδη πρὸς τῇ καταβάσει τοῦ ὄρους τῶν ἐλαιῶν, they began to praise him. Since Jesus' movement is established by

---

28 See Plummer, *Luke*, 198. In this instance, Plummer claims that the καί introducing the apodosis of ὡς δὲ ἤγγισε "must be omitted in translation" since the translation with "then" would be "too strong."

29 Fitzmyer, *The Gospel according to Luke I–IX* (AB 28; Garden City, NY: Doubleday, 1981) 658, recognizes a spatial sense for ἐγγίζειν.

30 Contra Schramm, *Lukas-Stoff*, 145–46.

31 Marshall, *Gospel of Luke*, 712. If Plummer (*Luke*, 445) is correct that Bethphage is not a village but a whole district which includes Bethany, then the point is even better made.

the preceding verb of motion, and the following clause establishes what the crowd did at a certain place, ἐγγίζειν at this point, along with the locative phrase, could well have a locational sense: "when Jesus was located there, at the descent."[32]

e. Luke 22:47 (//Mark 14:45; Matt 26:49). In Mark and Matthew the verb equivalent to ἐγγίζειν is a verb of motion.[33] Mark and Matthew narrate that Judas came with a crowd, and then they include a body of descriptive material before stating that Judas came up to Jesus, spoke to him, and then kissed him. Luke, however, has abbreviated Mark to the simple sequence that Judas was going before (προήρχετο) the crowd καὶ ἤγγισεν τῷ Ἰησοῦ φιλῆσαι αὐτόν, and then Jesus spoke to Judas. Luke relies upon the verb of motion found in Mark 14:43 (//Matt 26:47). With the dependent infinitive (of purpose?), ἐγγίζειν may very well be locational, that is, Judas was there to kiss Jesus. This is true even if Judas does not actually kiss him, being interrupted by Jesus' statement.[34]

f. Luke 24:15 (no parallels). On the road to Emmaus the narrator says that, while the travellers were walking along and discussing, Jesus ἐγγίσας συνεπορεύετο with them. ἐγγίζειν is used as a dependent aorist participle, here preceding a verb of motion, and makes better sense as a verb of location than as one of motion. Jesus must be proximate to them before he can join along with them.[35]

g. Luke 24:28 (no parallels). Further on in the Emmaus narrative, it says that καὶ ἤγγισαν εἰς τὴν κώμην οὗ ἐπορεύοντο. ἐγγίζειν is best seen as a verb of spatial location to avoid the redundant use of verbs of motion. As Marshall suggests, it could well be rendered "they arrived at" the village where they were going.[36]

These examples are characterized by several features worth noting. One of the most pronounced is that ἐγγίζειν is found in the syntactical environments of verbs of motion, although this is not required for the sense. In several of the cases, in fact, interpretation is made far more difficult if ἐγγίζειν is seen as a verb of motion. As a verb of spatial location, it often describes the consequences of a previous movement. This is not to deny that ἐγγίζειν has a

32 See Plummer, *Luke*, 447, who takes the πρός phrase as epexegetic, rendered "at the descent."

33 Cf. C.E.B. Cranfield, *The Gospel according to St. Mark* (CGTC; Cambridge: Cambridge University Press, 1972) 437, who notes that the verb of motion "can be defended as referring to Judas' arrival at the place as opposed to his actually approaching Jesus."

34 See Marshall, *Gospel of Luke*, 835. There are a number of textual variants which try to establish that Judas did kiss Jesus, but since some of the language interposed echoes Mark 14:44, harmonization is probably the explanation.

35 Cf. Plummer, *Luke*, 552: "He overtook them."

36 Marshall, *Gospel of Luke*, 897.

relationship to verbs of motion, since location may well imply movement towards a position. But the sense of motion is not central. With respect to a spatial-locational sense, the following examples seem decisive—Luke 7:12: "when he was located at the gate of the city"; 19:29: "when he was in the vicinity of Bethphage and Bethany"; and 24:28: "they were near the village where they were going."

The same results can be found for the book of Acts.[37] Acts 9:3: This construction is noteworthy on several accounts. First, ἐγγίζειν is used after a verb of motion, and secondly, the construction with ἐγένετο is altered so that the verb of motion in the ἐν τῷ phrase is placed before the finite verb: ἐν δὲ τῷ πορεύεσθαι ἐγένετο αὐτὸν ἐγγίζειν τῇ Δαμασκῷ. Acts 22:6: More regular is this passage in which Paul is reported as narrating the same event as described in 9:3: ἐγένετο δέ μοι πορευομένῳ καὶ ἐγγίζοντι τῇ Δαμασκῷ. The spatial-locational sense avoids redundancy with the verb of motion. Acts 10:9: A verb of motion also precedes ἐγγίζειν in this narrative: ὁδοιπορούντων ἐκείνων καὶ τῇ πόλει ἐγγιζόντων. Whereas the construction might mean that Cornelius's servants were on their way *and* approaching the city, it might instead mean that Cornelius's servants, having gone on their way, were now in the vicinity of the city when Peter went up on his rooftop. Acts 21:33: τότε ἐγγίσας ὁ χιλίαρχος ἐπελάβετο αὐτοῦ. Whereas the chiliarch certainly approached Paul before taking hold of him, the larger context casts doubt upon the sense of motion of ἐγγίζειν. Verse 32 says that the chiliarch was already in motion down towards the crowd. It makes better sense, therefore, to see ἐγγίζειν as a verb of location, since it was only when the chiliarch was in the vicinity of Paul that he could grab him. Acts 23:15: In their plot to kill Paul, the Jews reportedly told the chief priests that ἡμεῖς δὲ πρὸ τοῦ ἐγγίσαι αὐτὸν ἕτοιμοί ἐσμεν τοῦ ἀνελεῖν αὐτόν. The NASB, for example, translates this "and we for our part are ready to slay him before he comes near the place," supplying "the place." This is perhaps correct, but the sense of urgency is better maintained if ἐγγίζειν is a verb of location.

2. *Difficult Examples*. Several examples in Luke are more difficult, in large part because they do not have verbs of motion at hand or such clear spatial-locational indicators in their contexts. But these verses also can be explained along locational lines for ἐγγίζειν.

a. Luke 12:33 (//Matt 6:20). Matthew uses διορύσσουσιν instead of ἐγγίζειν. There are two ways of looking at the parallels between the Lukan and Matthean versions. On the one hand, the parallelism may be between Matthew's "where neither moth nor rust consumes" and Luke's "no moth destroys," and Matthew's "where thieves do not break in and steal" and Luke's ὅπου κλέπτης

37 Acts 7:17 is not treated, since it has a potential temporal-locational sense.

οὐκ ἐγγίζει. On the other hand, the parallelism may be between Matthew's "where thieves do not break in" and Luke's ὅπου κλέπτης οὐκ ἐγγίζει, and Matthew's "and steal" and Luke's "and no moth destroys." In either case, the immediacy of the warning is made clearer if ἐγγίζειν is understood as locational, that is, with the thief at hand, nearby.[38]

b. Luke 15:1 (no parallels). The transitional nature of this usage without Synoptic parallels is difficult.[39] But the context gives credence to the locational sense. In v. 2 the Pharisees and scribes are said to be grumbling over Jesus' being with the tax collectors and sinners. With this the complaint, it makes sense that in v. 1 Luke says that the tax collectors and sinners ἦσαν...αὐτῷ ἐγγίζοντες...ἀκούειν αὐτοῦ. They were located near Jesus for the purpose of (or possibly resulting in) their hearing him.

c. Luke 19:41 (no parallels). The transitional nature of this usage without Synoptic parallels is difficult. The phrasing is typically Lukan (ὡς ἤγγισεν). Although the sense of motion might be present, the following construction allows for the locational sense: "seeing the city, he wept over it, saying..." The implication is that only as he was in the vicinity could he observe.

d. Luke 22:1 (//Mark 14:1; Matt 26:2). The parallels to Luke establish that at the time of Jesus' reported instructions to his disciples the passover was two days away. Neither Mark nor Matthew uses ἐγγίζειν, Mark having ἦν and Matthew γίνεται. Whereas Luke may have introduced ἐγγίζειν to mean that the passover was approaching, there is another explanation. Luke uses a more expressive locative verb than ἦν or γίνεται and eliminates the specific temporal indicator, placing the chief priests and the scribes' machinations within the proximate time period of the passover.

3. *Luke 18:40.* A final concluding example makes the spatial-locational sense almost certain for Luke 18:35; the example is Luke 18:40. It is surprising that more attention has not been drawn to the presence of ἐγγίζειν within the story of the healing itself. After the blind beggar is told that Jesus of Nazareth is passing by (παρέρχεται), he begins to shout until those in front of him rebuke him. But he continues crying out σταθεὶς δὲ ὁ Ἰησοῦς ἐκέλευσεν αὐτὸν ἀχθῆναι πρὸς αὐτόν. ἐγγίσαντος δὲ αὐτοῦ ἐπηρώτησεν αὐτόν... The genitive absolute almost assuredly has to be taken as "when he [the blindman] was near," not "when or while he was approaching." First, Jesus is already near the beggar when the beggar begins shouting (note the preceding verb of motion). Secondly, Jesus is speaking to the blind beggar, something not easily imagined

38 Cf. Fitzmyer, *Luke X–XXIV*, 983, who translates: "*where no thief gets near to it.* I.e. to steal it."

39 Cf. W.R. Farmer, "Notes on a Literary and Form-Critical Analysis of Some of the Synoptic Material Peculiar to Luke," *NTS* 8 (1961–62) 303, who claims that the phrase at the beginning of the section is not Lukan.

from much of a distance in the light of the circumstances. The Synoptic accounts (Mark 10:50–51; Matt 20:32) have motion by either of the parties stopped before the dialogue begins.

C. *The Preposition Εἰς*

The third issue concerns the preposition εἰς, and how it could be compatible with a spatial-locational sense. When analysing the prepositions, one must not fall victim to a simple gloss. The spheres to which the prepositions apply often have broad overlap. For instance, the prepositions ἐν, εἰς and πρός have a wide semantic overlap.[40] Whereas ἐν is often used locatively, this does not mean that other prepositions cannot be used with a locative sense as well. And this sense is well-established for εἰς. Cranfield, for example, argues that during the Hellenistic period εἰς in many contexts had lost its directional sense, so that it is used synonymously with ἐν.[41] One need not go so far as to eliminate the directional sense to note that εἰς can be used locationally: for example, Matt 5:39: strike on (εἰς) the cheek; 27:30: strike on (εἰς) the head; Mark 8:23: spat on (εἰς) his eyes; 11:8: garments were strewn in (εἰς) the road; 13:3: he was sitting in (εἰς) the Mount of Olives; 13:9: you will be struck in (εἰς) synagogues; 13:16: the one who is in (εἰς) the field (//Matt 24:18 with ἐν); Luke 9:61: those in (εἰς) my house; 11:7: they are in (εἰς) bed; Luke 14:10: sit in (εἰς) the lowest place; John 1:18: in (εἰς) the bosom of the father.[42] BAGD in fact cite Luke 18:35 with the meaning "in the vicinity of, near, to."[43]

The analysis of these passages in Luke–Acts indicates that whatever one might think of the sense of motion connected to ἐγγίζειν, there are distinct cases in which a spatial-locational sense is paramount. These are indicated especially clearly in contexts where ἐγγίζειν is used in relation to a verb of motion, although the locational sense is found in other contexts as well. In these instances, the sense of motion often results in a strained or forced understanding.

---

40 See C.F.D. Moule, *An Idiom Book of New Testament Greek* (2nd edn; Cambridge: Cambridge University Press, 1959) 67–69; and now S.E. Porter, *Idioms of the Greek New Testament* (Biblical Languages: Greek 2; 2nd edn; Sheffield: JSOT Press, 1994) esp. 153.

41 Cranfield, *Mark*, 52 on Mark 1:9. Grammarians differ on the amount of overlap between εἰς and ἐν, although virtually all admit that overlap is present.

42 BAGD, 228 1.c, also cite several papyri: P.Ryl. II 145.13 (A.D. 38): he gave many blows to (εἰς) every part of his body; P.Tebt. I 39.32 (114 B.C.): they injured my wife on (εἰς) the right hand; and Arrian, *Anab*. 2.26.4: hit on (εἰς) the head. N. Turner (*Syntax*, vol. 3 of *A Grammar of New Testament Greek*, by J.H. Moulton [Edinburgh: T. & T. Clark, 1963] 254) lists P.Oxy. VI 929.13 (2nd–3rd centuries A.D.): all these things were in (εἰς) the brown tunic.

43 BAGD, 228, 1.b. They also cite Matt 21:1; Mark 11:1; and Luke 19:29 (see above on all three).

4. *Luke 18:35 and the Spatial-Locational Sense of Ἐγγίζειν*

Having established that ἐγγίζειν may have a spatial-locational sense, as the result of motion towards a place, is only one part of the task which has been set by this chapter. Application of this sense to Luke 18:35 must also be made. Those who have noted Luke's description of Jesus' determination to enter Jerusalem appear to be on the right track at this point. Luke is arranging his material to enhance the picture of Jesus heading towards his destiny. For whatever reason, Luke also wants to include the story of Zacchaeus, probably already associated with Jericho in the tradition. In Mark, Luke also finds the story of the healing of the blind man which occurred on the way out of Jericho. Luke must make two major decisions. The first is where to place these pericopes in relation to each other. The second is how to deal with the sense of direction in Mark which does not help convey the sense of Jesus always pushing towards Jerusalem. Luke's solutions are two as well. To begin, he puts the healing pericope before the story of Zacchaeus, since the Zacchaeus episode is climactic for his purposes. Zacchaeus is arguably more pointed morally than either of the two preceding stories—those of the rich ruler (Luke 18:18–30) and the healing of the blind beggar—both of which Luke has apparently drawn from his Markan source. The Zacchaeus story illustrates that a rich man, in fact a chief sinner among rich men, can receive salvation. This is a salvation that results in tangible and demonstrable repentance. The thematic order, according to Goulder, is "faithless rich man, faithful poor man, penitent rich man."[44] Schweizer goes further and suggests that Luke sees in Zacchaeus an "outstanding example" of discipleship.[45] To answer the second question, regarding the sense of direction, Luke seems clearly to have redacted the directional words from the Markan account, by substituting phrasing that is typically his own. But the phrasing that he utilizes, as has been established above, is not phrasing that makes ἐγγίζειν into a verb of motion meaning either "after he came out from Jericho" or "as he was approaching Jericho." And it is not phrasing that brings Luke's account into contradiction with Mark and Matthew. Instead, Luke uses what is for him a verb of location, which leaves the directional sense unspecified. Consequently, the clause can be rendered: "when he was in the vicinity of Jericho." This allows Luke to place it before the Zacchaeus episode.

---

44 Goulder, *Luke*, 2.678; also 2.675–78. See Marshall, *Gospel of Luke*, 694–95; Haenchen, *Der Weg Jesu*, 370: "Lukas will die Zacchäusgeschichte erzählen, die in Jericho ihren Schauplatz hat und damit endet, dass Jesus einen Tag in Jericho bleibt und hier, im Hause des Zacchäus, die Parabel von den Minen erzählt. Sie steht in innerem Zusammenhang mit der Erzählung von Zacchäus—jedenfalls wenn man diese so versteht und berichtet, wie Lukas, und sie bereitet (19,11!) den Einzug in Jerusalem vor."

45 E. Schweizer, *The Good News according to Luke* (Atlanta: John Knox, 1984) 288.

An apparent problem might be found in Luke 19:1, however. The verse begins: καὶ εἰσελθὼν διήρχετο τὴν Ἰεριχώ. Luke 18:35 might speak of Jesus' entrance into Jericho, with Luke 19:1 picking up with the healing outside of the city and completing Jesus' entry into the city. This is not the only interpretation of the relation between Luke 18:35 and 19:1, however. There are other explanations as well. A first possible explanation is that Luke has simply taken over his source, which began with the words of motion. Luke then redacts Mark for placement of the healing pericope before the Zacchaeus episode, leaving the Zacchaeus pericope as he found it. A second possible explanation is that Luke uses the verb of direction "towards" to pick up the thread of Jesus' destined trip to Jerusalem. Perhaps realizing that this redaction of the healing pericope requires him to change the Markan directional sense to a neutral one, and not wanting to introduce a factual contradiction (i.e. to say that the healing occurred on the way into Jericho when he knew that it had not), Luke now reiterates the sense of purpose in Jesus' travelling through Jericho on his way to Jerusalem. A third possible explanation is that the grammatical structure may give some indication of what Luke is doing. He uses the aorist participle preceding the finite verb.[46] The preceding participle often refers to antecedent action, but the time-frame in which this action occurs is not specified. Luke uses the aorist participle before the finite verb in the sense of "having at some time entered," followed by indication that Jesus then passed through Jericho. The participle is almost required for tight grammatical structure. Luke establishes the chronology of Jesus' passing through the city so that he can have him meet Zacchaeus on the way out. And a fourth possible explanation simply recognizes that the two pericopes are not chronologically ordered but arranged in relation to each other because of their mutual placements at Jericho. To demand harmony at every point of chronological detail may simply be asking too much.

5. *Conclusion*

In conclusion, I argue that the apparent contradiction of Luke 18:35 with Mark 10:46 and Matt 20:29 is caused by failure to appreciate the semantic range of Luke's use of ἐγγίζειν. This may be a verb of motion for Luke, but it seems much more likely that it is primarily a verb of location. Thus Luke 18:35 should be rendered "when he was in the vicinity of Jericho."

---

46 See Porter, *Verbal Aspect*, 377–87.

CHAPTER EIGHT

DID JESUS EVER TEACH IN GREEK? A LOOK AT SCHOLARLY OPINION AND THE EVIDENCE*

1. *Introduction*

Regarding the question of the languages Jesus may have known and used in his itinerant ministry, current scholarly opinion follows the conclusion of G. Dalman, who stated that, though Jesus may have known Hebrew, and probably spoke Greek (N.B.), he certainly taught in Aramaic.[1] With this

---

* This article is reproduced with permission of the Editor-in-Chief, from the *Tyndale Bulletin* 44.2 (1993) 199–235. Some alterations have been made, in the light of my "Jesus and the Use of Greek in Galilee," in *Studying the Historical Jesus: Evaluations of the State of Current Research* (ed. B. Chilton and C.A. Evans; Leiden: Brill, 1994) 123–54.

1 G. Dalman, *Jesus–Jeshua: Studies in the Gospels* (trans. P.P. Levertoff; London: SPCK, 1929) 1–37; see also P. Lapide, "Insights from Qumran into the Languages of Jesus," *RevQ* 8 (1975) 483–86; M. Black, *An Aramaic Approach to the Gospels and Acts* (3rd edn; Oxford: Clarendon Press, 1967) 16 n. 1, cf. 47–49; J. Fitzmyer, "The Languages of Palestine in the First Century A.D.," in S.E. Porter (ed.), *The Language of the New Testament: Classic Essays* (JSNTSup 60; Sheffield: JSOT Press, 1991) 126–62 (the latest corrected version of an article that originally appeared in *CBQ* 32 [1970] 501–31); *idem*, "Did Jesus Speak Greek?" *BARev* 18.5 (1992) 58–77 (a popular form of the above); M. Wise, "Languages of Palestine," in *Dictionary of Jesus and the Gospels* (ed. J.B. Green and S. McKnight; Downers Grove: InterVarsity Press, 1992) 434–44; G. Mussies, "Languages (Greek)," in *ABD* 4 (1992) 195–203; and L.L. Grabbe, *Judaism from Cyrus to Hadrian* (2 vols.; Minneapolis: Fortress Press, 1992) esp. 1.156–58 on language. The following summary and assessment of the evidence for the use of Aramaic, Hebrew and Greek is directly dependent upon S.E. Porter, *Verbal Aspect in the Greek of the New Testament, with Reference to Tense and Mood* (Studies in Biblical Greek 1; New York: Peter Lang, 1989) 111–17 esp. 112–13; and *idem*, "Introduction: The Greek of the New Testament as a Disputed Area of Research," in Porter (ed.), *Language of the New Testament*, 11–38 esp. 22–25 (the latter reprinted in revised form as ch. 5 in this volume, pp. 75–99). See also G.H.R. Horsley, *New Documents Illustrating Early Christianity*. V. *Linguistic Essays* (New South Wales: Macquarie University, 1989) 19–26. Latin is not dealt with here, since it is not seriously considered as a language of Jesus by recent scholars (some earlier scholars do discuss it), although it was used by some Romans resident in Palestine, especially government officials. See John 19:20, where the

conclusion long maintained, it might seem unnecessary to undertake again an investigation of this topic, except for the fact that it is still not commonly recognized just how strong the probability—even likelihood—is that Jesus not only had sufficient linguistic competence to converse with others in Greek but also even to teach in Greek during his ministry.[2] Once the barrier to Jesus' speaking Greek is crossed and the category of Jesus' teaching in Greek is entertained, this has direct implications for exegesis that I will attempt to exploit in this chapter.

2. *The Possible Languages of Jesus: Aramaic, Hebrew and Greek*

Although the evidence is not as strong as some would contend, it has long been agreed by many scholars that Aramaic was the predominant language of the indigenous Jewish population of Palestine and the primary language of Jesus.[3] This Aramaic hypothesis rests securely upon the fact that, though Greek was the *lingua franca* of the Greco-Roman world, in Palestine it never fully replaced Aramaic, an important Semitic language used by the Jewish population in Palestine after the exile. The widespread use of Aramaic is substantiated, according to this hypothesis, not only by the Aramaic portions of the biblical writings of Daniel and Ezra and by noncanonical *1 Enoch*, but by a large amount of inscriptional, ossuary, epistolary, papyrological and literary evidence, especially now from Qumran but also from the other Judean Desert sites (e.g. Murabba'at, Masada and Nahal Hever). Although it was once thought by some scholars that Aramaic had entered a period of decline in the two centuries on either side of Christ's birth,[4] in the last fifty years many important discoveries have confirmed the rightful place of the Aramaic language,[5]

---

titulus is reported as being written in Latin, Greek and Hebrew or Aramaic.

2 A related topic of comparable significance is the nature of the Greek of the New Testament. Many scholars are apparently even less aware of this discussion than they are of the one with which this chapter is concerned. For a summary of the history of discussion, as well as classic statements of the major positions in this century, see ch. 5 in this volume, "The Greek of the New Testament as a Disputed Area of Research," pp. 75–99, and the collected essays in Porter (ed.), *Language of the New Testament*.

3 See F. Büchsel, "Die griechische Sprache der Juden in der Zeit der Septuaginta und des Neuen Testaments," *ZAW* 60 (1944) 133–42.

4 For example, W.F. Albright, *The Archaeology of Palestine* (revised edn; Baltimore: Penguin, 1960) 201–202.

5 For surveys of the evidence, see especially J.A. Fitzmyer and D.J. Harrington, *A Manual of Palestinian Aramaic Texts* (BibOr 34; Rome: Biblical Institute Press, 1978); Fitzmyer, "Languages of Palestine," 147–58; *idem*, "The Contribution of Qumran Aramaic to the Study of the New Testament," *NTS* 20 (1973–74) 383–407; K. Beyer, *Die Aramäische Texte vom Toten Meer* (Göttingen: Vandenhoeck & Ruprecht, 1984); E. Schürer, *The History*

although there is still some debate regarding the dialect of Aramaic that was spoken.[6] While it is likely that Jesus' primary language was Aramaic, this position is argued primarily by logical and historical inference,[7] since Jesus is not recorded as using Aramaic apart from several odd quotations (e.g. Mark 5:41,[8] 7:34, 15:34//Matt 27:46, where he is quoted as uttering complete clauses).[9] Also, the majority of documentary evidence is of a literary quality, some quite late, while the inscriptional evidence, some of which could be Hebrew, is limited mostly to proper names.[10] Nevertheless, this theory has many important supporters and almost assuredly will continue to dominate scholarly discussion.[11]

---

of the Jewish People in the Age of Jesus Christ (3 vols.; rev. G. Vermes, F. Millar and M. Black; Edinburgh: T. & T. Clark, 1973–86) 2.23–26; and E.M. Meyers and J.F. Strange, *Archaeology, the Rabbis and Early Christianity* (London: SCM Press, 1981) 73–78.

6 For the two sides of this debate, see E.Y. Kutscher, "The Language of the Genesis Apocryphon—A Preliminary Study," in *Hebrew and Aramaic Studies* (ed. Z. Ben-Hayyin *et al.*; Jerusalem: Magnes, 1977) esp. 9, 12–16; P. Kahle, "Das palästinische Pentateuchtargum und das zur Zeit Jesu gesprochene Aramäisch," *ZNW* 49 (1958) 100–15; *idem*, *The Cairo Geniza* (2nd edn; Oxford: Blackwell, 1959) esp. 191–208. For assessment and evaluation, as well as bibliography, see Fitzmyer, "Languages of Palestine," 153–56. On method in Aramaic studies, see L.D. Hurst, "The Neglected Role of Semantics in the Search for the Aramaic Words of Jesus," *JSNT* 28 (1986) 63–80.

7 Some may be surprised that I refer to the "inference" that Jesus spoke and taught in Aramaic. The confirmatory "proof" often marshalled that Jesus taught in Aramaic is the several quotations from Aramaic cited in the Gospels. By this reasoning it is more plausible to argue that Jesus did most of his teaching in Greek, since the Gospels are all essentially Greek documents. In fact, on one occasion when Jesus spoke Aramaic (Mark 15:34), he was apparently misunderstood by those standing by, possibly implying that they did not understand Aramaic or may not have been used to hearing it. And this occurred in Jerusalem, the supposed centre of Semitic language Judaism.

8 This Aramaic phrase may be attested in a Jewish epitaph in Greek from Tiberias, unfortunately undated. See *NewDocs* 1 (1976) 72.

9 J. Jeremias (*New Testament Theology: The Proclamation of Jesus* [trans. J. Bowden; NTL; London: SCM Press, 1971] 4–6) counts 26 Aramaic words in all in the Gospels.

10 As Fitzmyer recognizes ("Languages of Palestine," 149).

11 Only a relatively small number of those who have entered into this discussion can be cited here. Besides those noted above, see W. Sanday, "The Language Spoken in Palestine at the Time of our Lord," *Expositor*, First Series, 7 (1878) 81–99; *idem*, "Did Christ Speak Greek?—A Rejoinder," *Expositor*, First Series, 7 (1878) 368–88 (to A. Roberts; see n. 17 below); A. Meyer, *Jesu Muttersprache: Das galiläische Aramäisch in seiner Bedeutung für die Erklärung der Reden Jesu und der Evangelien überhaupt* (Freiburg: Mohr–Siebeck, 1896); J. Wellhausen, *Einleitung in die drei ersten Evangelien* (Berlin: Reimer, 1905), although compare the second edition of 1911; E. Nestle, *Philologica Sacra: Bemerkungen über die Urgestalt der Evangelien und Apostelgeschichte* (Berlin: Reuther und Reichard, 1896); G. Dalman, *The Words of Jesus: Considered in the Light of Post-Biblical Jewish Writings and the Aramaic Language* (trans. D.M. Kay; Edinburgh: T. & T. Clark, 1902);

A small group of scholars has maintained, however, that some form of Hebrew, whether biblical or Mishnaic, had a far greater importance in first-century Palestine than has been fully appreciated. Segal proposed that Mishnaic Hebrew, rightly considered by him to be the linguistic evolutionary offspring of biblical Hebrew, and much in evidence in the Rabbinic writings as independent of Aramaic (which was thought by Birkeland to be reserved for the upper classes, while Hebrew was predominant at the lower social levels), was a prominent Jewish vernacular at all social levels from approximately 400 B.C. to A.D. 150.[12] The Hebrew Judean Desert documents, including those from

---

C.C. Torrey, "The Translations Made from the Original Aramaic Gospels," in *Studies in the History of Religions* (Festschrift C.H. Toy; ed. D.G. Lyon and G.F. Moore; New York: Macmillan, 1912) 269–317; *idem, Our Translated Gospels: Some of the Evidence* (London: Hodder & Stoughton, 1936); *idem*, "The Aramaic of the Gospels," in Porter (ed.), *Language of the New Testament*, 98–111 (originally published in *JBL* 61 [1942] 71–85); *idem*, "Studies in the Aramaic of the First Century A.D.," *ZAW* 65 (1953) 228–47, along with a number of other works (see ch. 5 of this volume); C.F. Burney, *The Poetry of Our Lord* (Oxford: Clarendon Press, 1925); P. Joüon, "Quelques aramaïsmes: Sous-jacent au grec des Évangiles," *RSR* 17 (1927) 210–29; R.O.P. Taylor, "Did Jesus Speak Aramaic?" *ExpTim* 56 (1944–45) 95–97; *idem, The Groundwork of the Gospels with Some Collected Papers* (Oxford: Blackwell, 1946); G. Bardy, *La question des langues dans l'église ancienne* (vol. 1; Paris: Beauchesne, 1948); H.M. Draper, "Did Jesus Speak Greek?" *ExpTim* 67 (1955–56) 317; R.McL. Wilson, "Did Jesus Speak Greek?" *ExpTim* 68 (1956–57) 121–22; M. Black, "The Recovery of the Language of Jesus," *NTS* 3 (1956–57) 305–13; *idem*, "Second Thoughts—IX. The Semitic Element in the New Testament," *ExpTim* 77 (1965–66) 20–23; *idem*, "Aramaic Studies and the Language of Jesus," in Porter (ed.), *Language of the New Testament*, 112–25 (originally published in *In Memoriam Paul Kahle* [ed. M. Black and G. Fohrer; BZAW 103; Berlin: Töpelmann, 1968] 17–28), among other works (see ch. 5 in this volume); J.A. Emerton, "Did Jesus Speak Hebrew?" *JTS* NS 12 (1961) 189–202; J. Barr, "Which Language Did Jesus Speak?—Some Remarks of a Semitist," *BJRL* 53 (1970) 9–29; F. Zimmermann, *The Aramaic Origin of the Four Gospels* (New York: Ktav, 1979) esp. 3–23; M. Wilcox, "Semitisms in the New Testament," *ANRW* II.25.2 (Berlin: de Gruyter, 1984) 979–86; *idem*, "The Aramaic Background of the New Testament," in *The Aramaic Bible: Targums in their Historical Context* (ed. D.R.G. Beattie and M.J. McNamara; JSOTSup 166; Sheffield: Sheffield Academic Press, 1994) 362–78; L.H. Feldman, "How Much Hellenism in Jewish Palestine?" *HUCA* 57 (1986) 83–111; G. Schwarz, *"Und Jesu Sprach": Untersuchungen zur aramäischen Urgestalt der Worte Jesu* (2nd edn; Stuttgart: Kohlhammer, 1987); J.P. Meier, *A Marginal Jew: Rethinking the Historical Jesus*. I. *The Roots of the Problem and the Person* (New York: Doubleday, 1991) esp. 255–68. See also H. Ott, "Um die Muttersprache Jesu: Forschungen seit G. Dalman," *NovT* 9 (1967) 1–25.

12 M.H. Segal, "Mishnaic Hebrew and its Relation to Biblical Hebrew and to Aramaic," *JQR* 20 (1908) 670–700, 734–37; *idem, A Grammar of Mishnaic Hebrew* (Oxford: Clarendon Press, 1927) 5–19, followed in his major theories by H. Birkeland, *The Language of Jesus* (Oslo: Dybwad, 1954). See also E.Y. Kutscher, "Hebrew Language: Mishnaic," in *EncJud* (vol. 16; Jerusalem: Encyclopaedia Judaica, 1972) cols. 1592–93; *idem, A History of the Hebrew Language* (ed. R. Kutscher; Leiden: Brill, 1982) 115–20.

Qumran (which apparently outnumber those in Aramaic), but especially the Hebrew Bar Kokhba letters,[13] have given further credence to the theory of vernacular Hebrew.[14] There is some ossuary, numismatic and literary (e.g. Ben Sira) evidence for Hebrew as well. Although there is still disagreement over the exact nature of this Hebrew and its extent of use, a number of scholars still consider Mishnaic Hebrew to be a probable language of the first century and a possible if not a probable language of Jesus.[15] Although Jesus may have known sufficient Hebrew to read from Isaiah as recorded in Luke 4:16–30, and Hebrew was probably used in Palestine in some capacity, perhaps by the Jewish leaders or in certain religious rituals, "evidence for colloquial Hebrew is not abundant,"[16] with a surprisingly small number of Hebrew inscriptions in Palestine.

Finally, a third group of scholars has argued for the predominant role of Greek in first-century A.D. Palestine and, consequently, for the strong possibility of its use by Jesus. The arguments for this position rest firmly on the role of Greek as the *lingua franca* of the Roman Empire, the linguistic and cultural character of lower Galilee during the first century, the linguistic fact that the New Testament has been transmitted in Greek from its earliest documents, a diversity of epigraphic evidence, significant literary evidence, and several significant contexts in the Gospels that give plausibility to this hypothesis. Whereas no contemporary scholar would probably argue that Jesus spoke only Greek, a number of scholars have argued in various ways that Greek was in widespread use by upwards of a majority of Jews in the multilingual society of first-century Palestine[17] and, therefore, may well have been a

---

13 For the evidence, see Meyers–Strange, *Archaeology*, 66–73; Fitzmyer, "Languages of Palestine," 158–62.

14 See Barr, "Which Language," 20; cf. R.H. Gundry, "The Language Milieu of First-Century Palestine: Its Bearing on the Authenticity of the Gospel Tradition," *JBL* 83 (1964) 405–407.

15 See, for example, T.W. Manson, *The Teaching of Jesus: Studies of its Form and Content* (2nd edn; Cambridge: Cambridge University Press, 1935); J.M. Grintz, "Hebrew as the Spoken and Written Language in the Last Days of the Second Temple," *JBL* 79 (1960) 32–47; Emerton, "Did Jesus Speak Hebrew?"; *idem*, "The Problem of Vernacular Hebrew in the First Century A.D. and the Language of Jesus," *JTS* NS 24 (1973) 1–23; C. Rabin, "Hebrew and Aramaic in the First Century," in S. Safrai and M. Stern (eds.), *The Jewish People in the First Century* (2 vols.; CRINT 1.2; Assen: Van Gorcum, 1976) 1007-39.

16 Fitzmyer, "Languages of Palestine," 161.

17 Besides those cited above, such as Dalman, Black, Rabin, Barr, Bardy, Birkeland, Emerton, Lapide, Gundry, Meyers and Strange, Fitzmyer, and Meier who mention the possibility of at least a trilingual community, see A. Roberts, *Greek: The Language of Christ and his Apostles* (London: Longmans, Green, 1888) (cf. *idem*, "That Christ Spoke Greek," *Expositor*, First Series, 6 [1877] 81–96, 161–76, 285–99, 307–83; "That Christ Spoke Greek—A Reply," *Expositor*, First Series, 7 [1878] 278–95 [to W. Sanday; see n. 11 above]);

language of Jesus at least on occasion.

In considering the strength of this position in more detail, its several lines of support will be considered in turn, illustrating the strength and integrity of the position on the basis of accumulated evidence. This evidence clearly points to the presumption that Jesus' productive bilingual capacity included the ability to speak and possibly to teach in Greek and, furthermore, that we may have several important contexts in which Jesus spoke Greek.

T.K. Abbott, *Essays, Chiefly on the Original Texts of the Old and New Testaments* (London: Longmans, Green, 1891) esp. 129–82; E.A. Abbott, *Johannine Grammar* (London: A. & C. Black, 1906); S.W. Patterson, "What Language did Jesus Speak?" *The Classical Outlook* 23 (1946) 65–67 (who gives serious consideration to Latin as a language of Jesus); A.W. Argyle, "Did Jesus Speak Greek?" *ExpTim* 67 (1955–56) 92–93, 383; *idem*, "Greek among the Jews of Palestine in New Testament Times," *NTS* 20 (1973–74) 87–89; M. Smith, "Aramaic Studies and the Study of the New Testament," *JBR* 26 (1958) 304–13; N. Turner, "The Language of Jesus and His Disciples," in Porter (ed.), *Language of the New Testament*, 174–90 (originally published in N. Turner, *Grammatical Insights into the New Testament* [Edinburgh: T. & T. Clark, 1965] 174–88); *idem*, "Were the Gospels Written in Greek or Aramaic?" *EvQ* 21 (1949) 42–48; *idem*, "The Unique Character of Biblical Greek," *VT* 5 (1955) 208–13; *idem*, "The Language of the New Testament," in *Peake's Commentary on the Bible* (ed. M. Black and H.H. Rowley; London: Nelson, 1962) 659–62; *idem*, *Syntax*, vol. 3 of *A Grammar of New Testament Greek*, by J.H. Moulton (Edinburgh: T. & T. Clark, 1963) esp. 1–9; *idem*, "The Literary Character of New Testament Greek," *NTS* 20 (1973–74) 107–14; *idem*, "The Quality of the Greek of Luke–Acts," in *Studies in New Testament Language and Text* (Festschrift G.D. Kilpatrick; ed. J.K. Elliott; NovTSup 44; Leiden: Brill, 1976) 387–400; *idem*, "Biblical Greek: The Peculiar Language of a Peculiar People," in *Studia Evangelica*, VII (ed. E.A. Livingstone; Berlin: Akademie Verlag, 1982) 505–12, among other works (see ch. 5 in this volume); S. Lieberman, *Greek in Jewish Palestine: Studies in the Life and Manners of Jewish Palestine in the II–IV Centuries C.E.* (2nd edn; New York: Feldheim, 1965); *idem*, "How Much Greek in Jewish Palestine?" in *Biblical and Other Studies* (ed. A. Altmann; Cambridge, MA: Harvard University Press, 1963) 123–41; K. Treu, "Die Bedeutung des Griechischen für die Juden im römischen Reich," *Kairos* 15 (1973) 123–44; H. Leclercq, "Note sur le grec néo-testamentaire et la position du grec en Palestine au premier siecle," *Les études classiques* 42 (1974) 243–55; P.E. Hughes, "The Language Spoken by Jesus," in *New Dimensions in New Testament Study* (ed. R.N. Longenecker and M.C. Tenney; Grand Rapids: Zondervan, 1974) 127–43; G. Mussies, "Greek in Palestine and the Diaspora," in Safrai and Stern (eds.), *Jewish People in the First Century*, 1040–64; *idem*, "Greek as the Vehicle of Early Christianity," *NTS* 29 (1983) 356–69; M. Hengel, *Judaism and Hellenism: Studies in their Encounter in Palestine during the Early Hellenistic Period* (trans. J. Bowden; London: SCM Press, 1974); *idem*, *Between Jesus and Paul: Studies in the Earliest History of Christianity* (trans. J. Bowden; Philadelphia: Fortress Press, 1983) esp. 1–29; *idem*, *The "Hellenization" of Judaea in the First Century after Christ* (trans. J. Bowden; London: SCM Press, 1989) esp. 7–18; G.R. Selby, *Jesus, Aramaic and Greek* (Doncaster: Brynmill Press, 1989); J.M. Ross, "Jesus's Knowledge of Greek," *IBS* 12 (1990) 41–47; J.W. Voelz, "The Linguistic Milieu of the Early Church," *CTQ* 56.2–3 (1992) 81–97.

3. *Greek as the Lingua Franca of the Greco-Roman World*

That Greek was the *lingua franca* of the Greco-Roman world and the predominant language of the Roman Empire is acknowledged by virtually everyone who has considered this issue, although the full significance of this factor has not been fully appreciated by all New Testament scholars.[18] Some of this is due to failure to understand the development of Greek in the Greco-Roman world. The so-called classical period of Greek developed away from the use of a number of independent regional languages or dialects,[19] which were distinguished by broad phonological, morphological and lexical differences, towards the ascendance of a single dialect, Attic Greek, which formed the basis (along with the regularizing influence of literary or official Ionic) of Hellenistic Greek.[20] During the period of Alexander (educated by Aristotle, who used a pre-Hellenistic form of Greek himself) and the Diadochi, the already ascendant regional variety, Attic, due especially to its cultural and economic superiority

18 Hengel (*Judaism and Hellenism*, 58–64 esp. 61), followed by Meyers–Strange (*Archaeology*, 78), Fitzmyer ("Languages of Palestine," 134) and others, has shown that there were Greek elements in Palestine even before Alexander the Great, such as evidence of Greek pottery, instances of Greek architecture and the use of Greek names. For a list of Greek names used in Palestine around the New Testament period, see Schürer, *History*, 2.73–74. B. Sass ("Arabs and Greeks in Late First Temple Jerusalem," *PEQ* [January–June 1990] 59–61) claims that he may have identified the earliest Palestinian shards with Greek inscriptions, dating to the sixth century B.C. Besides Hengel, for discussion of Hellenistic influence on the Jews, see J.D. Newsome, *Greeks, Romans, Jews: Currents of Culture and Belief in the New Testament World* (Philadelphia: Trinity Press International, 1992), although he fails to make some of the important linguistic distinctions that Hengel does.

19 See J. Lyons, *Introduction to Theoretical Linguistics* (Cambridge: Cambridge University Press, 1968) 33–36; cf. A. Thumb, *Die griechischen Sprache im Zeitalter des Hellenismus: Beiträge zur Geschichte und Beurteilung der KOINH* (Strassburg: Trübner, 1901) 162–63. On the changing fortunes of the dialects, see C.D. Buck, *The Greek Dialects: Grammar, Selected Inscriptions, Glossary* (Chicago: University of Chicago Press, 1955) 141–72; P.W. Costas, *An Outline of the History of the Greek Language, with Particular Emphasis on the Koine and the Subsequent Periods* (Chicago: Ukrainian Society of Sciences of America; repr. Chicago: Ares, 1979) 32–40; and V. Bubenik, *Hellenistic and Roman Greece as a Sociolinguistic Area* (Amsterdam: Benjamins, 1989) esp. 1–72.

20 On the history of Hellenistic Greek, see E. Schwyzer, *Griechische Grammatik* (2 vols.; Munich: Beck, 1939, 1950) 1.116–31; A. Meillet, *Aperçu d'une histoire de la langue grecque* (3rd edn; Paris: Hachette, 1930) 245–54; Costas, *Outline*, 27–71 esp. 41–57; R. Browning, *Medieval and Modern Greek* (2nd edn; Cambridge: Cambridge University Press, 1983) 19–52; J. Humbert, *Histoire de la langue grecque* (Paris: Universitaires, 1972) 115–26; A. López Eire, "Del ático a la *koiné*," *Emerita* 49 (1981) 377–92; L.R. Palmer, *The Greek Language* (London: Faber and Faber, 1980) 189–90, refuting P. Kretschmer, *Einleitung in die Geschichte der griechischen Sprache* (Göttingen: Vandenhoeck & Ruprecht, 1896) 410–17.

initiated under Philip II of Macedon, began a process of regularization and systematization on the basis of the interplay of linguistic innovation and tradition.[21] As the various propagators (soldiers, merchants, etc.) of Greek moved further from their language bases and mingled with those still using other, regional dialects, the result was a standardization of Greek varieties into a "common dialect." As this prestige language spread, startling consequences of foreigners speaking Greek could have been expected, but these appear to have been "reasonably slight,"[22] virtually confined to enrichment of the lexicon and local variances in pronunciation.[23] Hellenistic Greek then held sway as a single essentially sub-dialectless variety until the Byzantine and modern periods, when modern Greek again developed dialectical distinctives.

Despite a reasonable consensus on the development of Hellenistic Greek (in conjunction with the widespread Hellenistic cultural dissemination that took place under the Diadochi and the Herods, as well as the Hasmoneans),[24] there are still a number of linguistic issues that warrant further clarification. For example, often disparaging comments about Hellenistic Greek being bad or sloppy in comparison to classical Greek must be ignored. These kinds of comments seem to derive from those who fail to understand the highly literary

---

21 Meillet, *Histoire*, 24–44, 247–51; Browning, *Greek*, 30–36; Costas, *Outline*, 58–70. The changes to note include: stress over pitch in accentuation, vowel reduction, endings of verbs and nouns regularized, final *nu* used more frequently though often assimilated, prepositions that did not go out of use increasingly used with the accusative case, particles disappearing, *mi* verbs replaced by *omega* forms, sigmatic aorists tending to replace non-sigmatic aorists, optative mood virtually redundant, dual number completely eliminated, middle voice reduced, dative case eventually disappearing, and periphrasis increasing in frequency, among several other developments.

22 Palmer, *Greek Language*, 175.

23 Although Thumb (*Sprache*, 167–69) identifies five different pronunciation areas, he also notes the inflexibility of Hellenistic Greek in relation to other languages. It has been argued that the Greek of the Egyptian papyri was influenced by various Semitic languages and therefore does not constitute an accurate representation of Hellenistic Greek. See, for example, L.-Th. Lefort, "Pour une grammaire des LXX," *Muséon* 41 (1928) 152–60; J. Vergote, "Grec Biblique," *DBSup3* (ed. L. Pirot; Paris: Librairie Letouzey et Ane, 1938) cols. 1353–60; F. Gignac, *A Grammar of the Greek Papyri of the Roman and Byzantine Periods* (2 vols.; Milan: Istituto Editoriale Cisalpino, 1976, 1981) 1.46–48; *idem*, "The Language of the Non-Literary Greek Papyri," in *Proceedings of the Twelfth International Congress of Papyrology* (ed. D.H. Samuel; Toronto: Hakkert, 1970) 137–52; *idem*, "The Papyri and the Greek Language," *Yale Classical Studies* 28 (1985) 157–58. S.-T. Teodorsson argues against this, claiming that no other kind of Greek has ever been found in Egypt, thus there is no evidence of a previous "pure" Greek, no evidence of the creolization process that is implied, and no evidence of this Greek being considered to depart from the acceptable norms of Hellenistic Greek (*The Phonology of Ptolemaic Koine* [Studia Graeca et Latina Gothoburgensia 36; Gothenburg: Acta Universitatis Gothoburgensis, 1977] 25–35).

24 Hengel, *"Hellenization,"* 8 and *passim*.

nature of the classical Greek texts used for comparison, even in such a popular author as Aristophanes;[25] the lack of direct access to the language used in everyday speech by the Attic population;[26] and the relatively value-free natural development of languages, in which they must be evaluated according to their own linguistic systems.[27] A second issue requiring further exploration is that of what is called linguistic register, in which a given linguistic code or system may be utilized by speakers or writers in various contexts to accomplish a variety of purposes.[28] Hellenistic Greek had its own register system, in which the often vulgar language of papyri texts must be distinguished from literary texts such as those of Josephus and the Atticistic texts of Plutarch.[29] A final issue to consider is the role of prestige languages within a multilingual environment.[30] Prestige

25 K.J. Dover, "The Colloquial Stratum in Classical Attic Prose," in *Classical Contributions: Studies in Honour of M.F. McGregor* (ed. G.S. Shrimpton and D.J. McCargar; Locust Valley, NY: Augustin, 1981) esp. 16.

26 S.-T. Teodorsson, "Phonological Variation in Classical Attic and the Development of Koine," *Glotta* 57 (1979) esp. 68–71.

27 See A. Thumb, "On the Value of Modern Greek for the Study of Ancient Greek," *Classical Quarterly* 8 (1914) 182. As F. Blass says, "the Hellenistic language as a whole is in its own way not less subject to rules nor less systematic than Attic" (*Grammar of New Testament Greek* [trans. H.St.J. Thackeray; 2nd edn; London: Macmillan, 1911] 3; see also H.St.J. Thackeray, *A Grammar of the Old Testament in Greek according to the Septuagint* [vol. 1; Cambridge: Cambridge University Press, 1909] 21). Cf. R. Hudson, *Sociolinguistics* (Cambridge Textbooks in Linguistics; Cambridge: Cambridge University Press, 1980) 30–48, on language and dialect.

28 M. Gregory and S. Carroll, *Language and Situation: Language Varieties and their Social Contexts* (Language and Society; London: Routledge and Kegan Paul, 1978) 75–85; M.A.K. Halliday, "Register Variation," in Halliday and R. Hasan, "Text and Context: Aspects of Language in a Social-Semiotic Perspective," *Sophia Linguistica* 6 (1980) 60–75; cf. Hudson, *Sociolinguistics*, 48–53.

29 See Porter, *Verbal Aspect*, esp. 152–54; B.G. Mandilaras, *The Verb in the Greek Non-Literary Papyri* (Athens: Hellenic Ministry of Culture and Sciences, 1973) 45–46; L. Rydbeck, "On the Question of Linguistic Levels and the Place of the New Testament in the Contemporary Language Milieu," in Porter (ed.), *Language of the New Testament*, 191–204 (originally published in L. Rydbeck, *Fachprosa, vermeintliche Volkssprache und Neues Testament: Zur Beurteilung der sprachlichen Niveauunterschiede im nachklassischen Griechisch* [Uppsala: University of Uppsala; Stockholm: Almqvist & Wiksell, 1967] 186–99, although more of the book is of value as well).

30 M. Silva, "Bilingualism and the Character of Palestinian Greek," in Porter (ed.), *Language of the New Testament*, 206–10 (originally published in *Bib* 61 [1980] 198–219); J.H. Moulton, *Prolegomena*, vol. 1 of *A Grammar of New Testament Greek* (3rd edn; Edinburgh: T. & T. Clark, 1908) 6–8; Vergote, "Grec," cols. 1360–67 esp. 1366–67; Horsley, *New Documents Illustrating Early Christianity*, 5.23–25. On bilingualism in general, as well as prestige languages, see E. Haugen, "Problems of Bilingualism," *Lingua* 2 (1950) 278; U. Weinreich, *Languages in Contact: Findings and Problems* (Publications of the Linguistic Circle of New York 1; New York: n.p., 1953); E. Oksaar, "Bilingualism," *Current Trends in*

languages are those languages that dominate the political, educational and economic forces at play in a language milieu. In Palestine, the prestige language was Greek, even if Greek was not the first language for a significant number of its speakers. This means that there would have been cultural, social and especially linguistic pressure to learn Greek in order to communicate broadly within the social structure. My contention in this chapter is that the evidence supports the idea that, besides there being a sizable number of first-language Greek speakers, there were a large and significant number of bilingual Palestinians, especially in Galilee, who had productive (not merely passive) competence in Greek and may even on occasion have preferred their acquired language, Greek, to their first language, Aramaic. The evidence is that Jesus was one of those people, and that he used Greek even in some of his teaching.

It is in the Greek language that the Gospels are written, although it has frequently been debated whether the Gospels were originally written in Greek and how Semitic the Greek is in which they are written.[31] It is well beyond the scope of this chapter to raise the question of whether the Gospels were originally written in a language other than Greek, although it is fair to say that the clear scholarly consensus is that whether or not Jesus originally spoke in Aramaic (as most scholars believe that he did), the Gospels themselves are not literalistic translations, even where they purport to record Jesus' words. As Black admits regarding the Greek of the Gospels, the "'translation' is not literal but literary; in other words, it is doubtful if it can be justly described as translation at all in some cases... The Evangelists, that is to say, are for the most part writing Greek Gospels, even where they are dependent upon sources."[32] The history of this debate over the nature of the Greek of the Gospels is not necessary to pursue here, except to note that it is in this language, Greek, that the New Testament has been preserved and transmitted.

4. *The Influence of Greek in Lower Galilee and Palestine*

A. *Geography*

Regarding the influence of Greek in lower Galilee[33] evidence is increasing that

Linguistics 9 (1972) 476–511; H. Baetens Beardsmore, *Bilingualism: Basic Principles* (2nd edn; Clevedon, England: Multilingual Matters, 1987) esp. 152–78. This point is not considered by many who discuss the question, and its importance is misunderstood by Meier, *Marginal Jew*, 291 n. 21, 294 n. 39.

31 Against the idea that there existed a Jewish-Greek dialect, see Porter, *Verbal Aspect*, 113–17, 141–56; Horsley, *New Documents Illustrating Early Christianity*, 5.5–40.

32 Black, *Aramaic Approach*, 274. He cites two exceptions: the parables of the sower (Mark 4:2–9) and of the well-behaved guest (Matt 20:28), although here he depends on D.

33 On defining the boundaries of Galilee, see Josephus, *War* 3.3.1 §§35–40; cf. also

it was the Palestinian area most heavily influenced by Greek language and culture.[34] Referred to as the "Galilee of the Gentiles" in Matt 4:15, lower Galilee was a centre for trade among the Mediterranean, Sea of Galilee and Decapolis regions. Galilee was completely surrounded by Hellenistic culture, with Acco–Ptolemais, Tyre and Sidon in the west and north-west, Panias–Caesarea Philippi, Hippos and Gadara in the north-east, east and south-east, and Scythopolis and Gaba in the south.[35] Besides being connected by a number of

---

Ant. 5.1.18 §63; 5.1.22 §86; 5.1.23 §91; 8.5.3 §142; E.M. Meyers, "Galilean Regionalism as a Factor in Historical Reconstruction," *BASOR* 221 (1976) 93–101; and Meyers–Strange, *Archaeology*, 35–47. A shift may be occurring in opinion regarding how isolated upper Galilee was from Hellenistic influence. See D. Edwards, "First Century Urban/Rural Relations in Lower Galilee: Exploring the Archaeological and Literary Evidence," in D.J. Lull (ed.), *SBLSP* (vol. 27; Atlanta: Scholars Press, 1988) 179–80 and n. 64 with bibliography; *idem*, "The Socio-Economic and Cultural Ethos of the Lower Galilee in the First Century: Implications for the Nascent Jesus Movement," in L.I. Levine (ed.), *The Galilee in Late Antiquity* (New York: Jewish Theological Seminary of America, 1992) esp. 70–71. For a less optimistic perspective on the Hellenistic influences in Galilee, see S. Freyne, *Galilee from Alexander the Great to Hadrian 323 B.C.E. to 135 C.E.: A Study of Second Temple Judaism* (Notre Dame: University of Notre Dame, 1980) *passim* (but cf. p. 139 n. 90), who emphasizes the cultural and economic but not the linguistic factors.

34 The degree of Greek penetration of rural Palestine is discussed in A.H.M. Jones, *The Greek City: From Alexander to Justinian* (Oxford: Clarendon Press, 1940) 289–95; T. Rajak, *Josephus: The Historian and his Society* (London: Duckworth, 1983) 46–64; T. Tcherikover, *Hellenistic Civilization and the Jews* (Philadelphia: Jewish Publication Society of America, 1959) 114–16; and Hengel, *Judaism and Hellenism*, 58–106, who corrects Tcherikover. As one indication of the pervasive influence of Greek, in Acts 6:1 (cf. 9:29) a distinction is made between Ἑλληνισταί and Ἑβραῖοι, probably a linguistic distinction made between Jews who spoke mainly Greek and those who spoke mainly Aramaic or who also spoke Aramaic. Before the third century A.D. these terms were virtually exclusively linguistic terms referring to language competence. To distinguish those outside Palestine as Greek speakers would not have been necessary (it would have been assumed), but apparently there was a significant part of the population that spoke mostly Greek, even of those resident in Jerusalem. For the evidence of this, see Hengel, *Judaism and Hellenism*, 2 with notes, 58; *idem*, *Between Jesus and Paul*, 8–9 with notes; *idem*, *"Hellenization,"* 7–8 with notes; and *idem*, *The Pre-Christian Paul*, with R. Deines (trans. J. Bowden; London: SCM Press, 1991) 54–55, who estimates that 10–15% of the inhabitants of Jerusalem spoke Greek as their native language. He follows C.F.D. Moule, "Once More, Who were the Hellenists?" *ExpTim* 70 (1958–59) 100–102; Fitzmyer, "Languages of Palestine," 144. This is further confirmed by C.C. Hill, *Hellenists and Hebrews: Reappraising Division within the Earliest Church* (Minneapolis: Fortress Press, 1992) 22–24; and now A. Brehm, "The Meaning of Ἑλληνιστής in Acts in Light of a Diachronic Analysis of ἑλληνίζειν," in *Discourse Analysis and Other Topics in Biblical Greek* (ed. S.E. Porter and D.A. Carson; JSNTSup 113; Sheffield: Sheffield Academic Press, 1995) 180–99. The seven men appointed in Acts 6:5 to serve the Greek-speaking constituency all have Greek names.

35 Hengel, *"Hellenization,"* 14–15; see also Fitzmyer, "Languages of Palestine," 134–35; J.N. Sevenster, *Do You Know Greek? How Much Greek Could the First Jewish*

waterways, there was a road system that utilized a series of valleys to interconnect the Galilean region,[36] tying together such important cities as Sepphoris and Tiberias, as well as tying the area to its surrounding regions. As a result, Galilee was a centre for import and export as well as general trade, resulting in a genuinely cosmopolitan flavour.[37]

Jesus was from Nazareth, and spent a sizable portion of his career in lower Galilee around the cities of Nazareth, Nain, Cana and Capernaum. Although Nazareth was a small village of only 1600 to 2000 in population, and it relied upon agriculture for its economic base (see John 1:46, which might well be supported by what we know of the physical remains), it is not legitimate to think of Jesus as growing up in linguistic and cultural isolation. Nazareth was situated along a branch of and had a position overlooking one of the busiest trade routes in ancient Palestine, the Via Maris, which stretched from Damascus to the Mediterranean. In fact this branch became more significant as Sepphoris grew in importance during Roman times.[38] Capernaum, the village in which Jesus may have had a house (Mark 2:1, although the phrase may refer to Simon's house; in either case it bears witness to Jesus' feeling "at home" in Capernaum), though not a walled city according to the latest archaeological evidence, served as an important entrance to Gaulanitis (Golan Heights), with the means necessary for imposition of taxes and tolls (Mark 2:14). With an estimated population of 12,000 to 15,000,[39] the village was part of a region that may have been one of the most densely populated in the Roman world.[40] The evidence from first-century construction witnesses to "a community which very likely possessed greater financial means that [sic] is often associated with Capernaum."[41] It was a fishing village, with fishing apparently constituting its major source of economic gain. Nearby was Tiberias, a city built by Herod Antipas, where there was a population that was probably even more bilingual than Jerusalem (see Acts 6:1).

All of these factors are consistent with what we know of Jesus' own life and that of his followers. Matthew (Matt 9:9; Luke 5:27–28) or Levi (Mark 2:13–14), the tax collector in Capernaum, would probably have known Greek in order

Christians Have Known? (NovTSup 19; Leiden: Brill, 1968) 96–97; Tcherikover, *Hellenistic Civilization*, 90–116.

36 See Edwards, "First Century Urban/Rural Relations," 171.

37 See J.A. Overman, "Who were the First Urban Christians? Urbanization in Galilee in the First Century," in Lull (ed.), *SBLSP* 27 (1988) 161.

38 See Meyers–Strange, *Archaeology*, 43, 56–57.

39 Meyers–Strange, *Archaeology*, 58.

40 M. Broshi, "The Population of Western Palestine in the Roman-Byzantine Period," *BASOR* 236 (1979) 3, 5.

41 Overman, "First Urban Christians," 162, citing from J.F. Strange, "Review Article: The Capernaum and Herodium Publications," *BASOR* 226 (1977) 65–73.

to conduct his duties with the local taxpayers and the tetrarch Herod Antipas's officials.[42] Many of Jesus' disciples were fishermen who worked the Sea of Galilee, including Simon Peter, Andrew, James and John. They almost assuredly would have needed to conduct in Greek much of their business of selling fish.[43] It is also worth noting that, of his disciples, Andrew and Philip had purely Greek names, and the names of Simon, Bartholomew and Thaddaeus may well have derived from Greek or gone easily into Greek.[44] This information helps to make sense of the scene in John's Gospel at 12:20–22, where Greeks asked Philip, who was from Bethsaida (in Gaulanitis, across from Galilee), to be able to see Jesus. He immediately went to Andrew, who was also reportedly from Bethsaida (John 1:44). Jesus' being a carpenter or craftsman (Mark 6:3), economically a middle level vocation, is consistent with the economic and cultural climate of the region, in which reciprocal trade was widespread.[45] As Kee concludes, "This means that for Jesus to have conversed with inhabitants of cities in the Galilee, and especially of cities of the Decapolis and the Phoenician region, he would have had to have known Greek, certainly at the conversational level."[46]

B. *Epigraphic and Literary Evidence*

More impressive than what is known even of Galilee for establishing the probability that Jesus spoke Greek is the epigraphic and literary evidence for the widespread knowledge of Greek throughout Palestine including Galilee. It is not possible to discuss all of this evidence, and certainly not in the detail that it warrants, but it is useful to cite significant findings as a means of establishing a plausible linguistic milieu for Jesus' possible use of Greek. The evidence can be usefully catalogued in terms of coins, papyri and literary texts, and inscriptions, including in the last especially funerary inscriptions.[47]

---

42 Schürer, *History*, 1.374.

43 See J.A.L. Lee, "Some Features of the Speech of Jesus in Mark's Gospel," *NovT* 27 (1985) 1–36 esp. 6.

44 Hengel, *"Hellenization,"* 16–17; *Pre-Christian Paul*, 55–56. There is some dispute about Simon's name, since John's Gospel says that Jesus gave him the name Cephas (1:42), whereas Mark (3:16) and Luke (6:14) say that he was given the Greek name Peter, a masculine form of the word πέτρα. See ch. 6 in this volume, pp. 103–24.

45 See Edwards, "First Century Urban/Rural Relations," 172–76; Meier, *Marginal Jew*, 278–85.

46 H.C. Kee, "Early Christianity in the Galilee: Reassessing the Evidence from the Gospels," in Levine (ed.), *Galilee in Late Antiquity*, 21.

47 Loan words from Greek found themselves quite frequently incorporated into various Jewish documents, and Greek personal names were quite often found in Jewish writings. Apart from a literary context, it is difficult to know how much use of Greek these factors suggest. For a summary of some of the evidence, see Schürer, *History*, 2.53–54, 73–74; Lieberman, *Greek in Jewish Palestine*. It is noteworthy that this evidence is heaviest in the

Excluding several cities of the Decapolis, where they were minted much earlier, coins with Greek inscriptions were minted by the first century A.D. in the Galilean city of Tiberias. In Palestine, the minting of coins in Greek had begun under the Hasmonean ruler Alexander Jannaeus (103–76 B.C.), who issued bilingual coins with Greek and Hebrew, as did Mattathias Antigonus, the last Hasmonean king, in 40–37 B.C. Under Herodian rule coins were minted exclusively in Greek, or in Greek and Latin under Agrippa II (A.D. 50–100). This includes those minted by Herod Antipas (4 B.C.–A.D. 39), who ruled Galilee during Jesus' lifetime. That these inscriptions were noticed and not strictly routine is made evident by the fact that during the two Jewish revolts (A.D. 66–70 and A.D. 132–35) Greek was not used on coins minted by the rebels. Nevertheless, as the evidence from the Greek Bar Kokhba letters indicates (see below), this does not mean that the rebels were not able to or did not use Greek.[48] To the contrary, their use of Hebrew on the coins indicates that they were attempting to make a political statement that the populace would understand, not abandoning their linguistic ties to Greek.

Papyri and literary texts further establish the widespread use of Greek in Palestine. There have been a number of papyrus texts (including a number of fragments) found in Palestine written in Greek by Jews.[49] The papyri of the Judean Desert include a wide range and variety of artifacts, such as commercial transactions, fiduciary notes, contracts of marriage, and fragments of philosophical and literary texts, among others.[50] Two Greek letters sent among Bar Kokhba and his commanders have been found among these.[51] In one of

third and fourth centuries A.D.

48 See Hengel, *"Hellenization,"* 8 and notes; Sevenster, *Do You Know Greek?* 122–26.

49 For literary texts written in Greek in Palestine but not by Jews, see Hengel, *Judaism and Hellenism*, 83–88. On the Zenon papyri as evidence of correspondence in Greek between Egypt and Palestine, see Hengel, *Judaism and Hellenism*, 7–12 and *passim*; Grabbe, *Judaism*, 1.172.

50 See, for example, P. Benoit, J.T. Milik and R. de Vaux (eds.), *Les grottes de Murabba'ât* (DJD 2; Oxford: Clarendon Press, 1961) nos. 89–107 (pp. 212–33), 108–12 (pp. 224–38), 113 (239–40), 114–17 (pp. 240–58), 118–55 (pp. 258–67), 164 (pp. 275–77); Y. Yadin, "The Expedition to the Judaean Desert, 1960: Expedition D," *IEJ* 11 (1961) 40–50; B. Lifshitz, "The Greek Documents from Nahal Seelim and Nahal Mishmar," *EIJ* 11 (1961) 543–62; N. Lewis, *The Documents from the Bar Kokhba Period in the Cave of Letters: Greek Papyri* (Jerusalem: Israel Exploration Society, 1989); and Y. Yadin, *Bar-Kokhba: The Rediscovery of the Legendary Hero of the Last Jewish Revolt against Imperial Rome* (London: Weidenfeld and Nicolson, 1971) 124–39, 172–83. See Schürer, *History*, 2.78–79; Fitzmyer, "Languages of Palestine," 141; and F. Millar, "Appendix B: Documents from the Bar Kochba War," in *The Roman Near East 31 B.C.–A.D. 337* (Cambridge, MA: Harvard University Press, 1993) 545–52, for a complete listing of documents.

51 See B. Lifshitz, "Papyrus grecs du désert de Juda," *Aeg* 42 (1962) 240–56, now published as SB VIII 9843, 9844.

these letters (both dated to the early second century A.D.), a Simon (?) Bar Kokhba, quite possibly the leader of the rebellion himself, writes to a Jonathan and a Masabala, stating that ἐγράφη / δ[ὲ] Ἑληνιστὶ διὰ / τ[ὸ ὁρ]μὰν μὴ εὑρη/θ[ῆ]ναι Ἑβραεστὶ / γ[ρά]ψασθαι ("[the letter] was written in Greek because the desire [?] was not found to write in 'Hebrew'"[52]).[53] Even though these texts date to the early second century A.D., they are still useful for indicating the general linguistic climate of Palestine, witnessed to further by the discovery of a letter in Greek to a Judas at Masada, one of the last survivors of the first revolt, about the mundane topic of the supply of vegetables.[54] As Fitzmyer states, "at a time when the nationalist fever of the Jews must have been running high the leader of the revolt—or someone close to him, if Soumaios is not Simeon bar Kosibah—frankly prefers to write in Greek, or at least has to write in Greek. He does not find the ὁρμά, 'impulse, desire', to compose the letter ἑβραϊστί."[55] The assumption is that the letter's recipients would have been able to read Greek to engage in the menial supply tasks asked of them.[56]

So far as Jewish literature is concerned, there is also significant evidence of composition being done in Greek in Palestine by Jews for Jewish audiences.[57] For example, the book of Daniel, besides using Greek names to refer in 3:5 to three musical instruments (lyre, harp and pipes [NIV]), and being composed in Hebrew and Aramaic, in its deuterocanonical form includes additional sections

---

52 On whether this refers to Aramaic or Hebrew, see Schürer, *History*, 2.28 n. 118.

53 The original transcription by Lifshitz is followed by Fitzmyer, "Languages of Palestine," 142, with questions noted on p. 143 n. 1 (in a text full of misspellings, the problem with the *alpha* rather than the *eta* in ὁρμά may not be that serious); Sevenster, *Do You Know Greek?* 172; and Hengel, *"Hellenization,"* 73 n. 82. The major difficulty is interpreting τ[ὸ ὁρ]μάν. G. Howard and J.C. Shelton ("The Bar-Kokhba Letters and Palestinian Greek," *IEJ* 23 [1973] 101–102) have suggested restoring this as Ἑρμᾶν, but do not give a clear idea of whether the neuter article is still to be read. Their understanding is that there were a limited number in Bar Kokhba's ranks who wrote Greek. Yadin has a plausible translation (he disputes that this letter is from the rebel leader), but it is difficult to see how he construes the Greek (*Bar-Kokhba*, 130, 132, cf. 132–33); similar in translation is Wise, "Languages," 440: "because no one was found to write it in 'Hebrew.'"

54 See Mussies, "Greek in Palestine," 1058, citing the letter from Y. Yadin, "The Excavation of Masada—1963/64: Preliminary Report," *IEJ* 15 (1965) 110. For a summary of the significant use of Greek at Masada, see H.M. Cotton and J. Geiger, *The Latin and Greek Documents*, vol. 2 of *Masada, The Y. Yadin Excavations 1963–65, Final Reports* (Jerusalem: Israel Exploration Society, 1989) esp. 9–10, cited in Hengel, *Pre-Christian Paul*, 136 n. 259.

55 Fitzmyer, "Languages of Palestine," 143.

56 See E.M. Smallwood, *The Jews under Roman Rule: From Pompey to Diocletian* (SJLA 20; Leiden: Brill, 1976) 452–53.

57 See Hengel, *"Hellenization,"* 23–27; *idem*, *Judaism and Hellenism*, 83–102; and Schürer, *History*, 3.370–704 for literature composed in Greek, but not all of it composed in Palestine; and 3.705–808 for literature where the language of composition is ambiguous.

composed in Greek (Prayer of Azariah and the Song of the Three Children, Susanna, and Bel and the Dragon).[58] Similarly, the six additions (107 verses) to Esther were composed in Greek and interposed in the Septuagintal version of the text.[59] Furthermore, two apocryphal books, 1 Esdras and 2 Maccabees, are thought likely to have been composed in Greek in Palestine. Worth noting as well is the fact that, although 2 Esdras and Judith were written in Hebrew, they survive virtually entirely or at least in significant part in Greek versions, quite possibly reflecting Jewish linguistic priorities for preservation of religious texts. Other writings worth mentioning for their probable Greek and Palestinian origins are the *Testaments of the Twelve Patriarchs*, especially the *Testament of Judah* and *Testament of Levi*.[60] A number of the books of the Septuagint were probably translated into Greek in Palestine as well, including 1 Maccabees, Esther (by one Lysimachus son of Ptolemaeus in 114 B.C.; probably in conjunction with the additions made in Greek), Chronicles, 2 Esdras (Ezra–Nehemiah), Song of Songs, Lamentations and Qoheleth, not to mention the continuing translation work of Theodotion and Aquila.[61] Even though Jubilees was written in Hebrew it appears to have made extensive use of Greek geographical literature, requiring advanced knowledge of Greek by its author.[62] Perhaps most striking of all is the finding of the Greek Minor Prophets Scroll at Nahal Hever (8HevXIIgr), probably dating from the late first century B.C. or possibly the first century A.D.[63]

There are a number of other Jewish literary figures known to have written in Greek, although it is difficult to determine how many of them wrote in Palestine. Two of the most significant for whom there is information are Justus of Tiberias and Flavius Josephus. Justus, the author of a history of the Jewish wars against Vespasian, is known only through what is said about him by Josephus, his rival, who respected his knowledge of Greek, acquired in the Greek educational system in Tiberias (*Life* 9 §§34–42; 65 §§336–360; cf. also 12 §65; 17 §88; 35 §§175–178; 37 §186; 54 §279; 70 §§390–393; 74 §410).

58 See C.A. Evans, *Noncanonical Writings and New Testament Interpretation* (Peabody: Hendrickson, 1992) 14–15.

59 Evans, *Noncanonical Writings*, 12.

60 See on this H.D. Slingerland, *The Testaments of the Twelve Patriarchs: A Critical History of Research* (SBLMS 21; Missoula, MT: Scholars Press, 1975).

61 Hengel, *Judaism and Hellenism*, 101–102; *"Hellenization,"* 24–25.

62 Wise, "Languages," 439.

63 See B. Lifshitz, "The Greek Documents from the Cave of Horror," *IEJ* 12 (1962) 201–207, which includes discussion of a non-biblical Greek papyrus fragment; and now E. Tov (ed.), *The Greek Minor Prophets Scroll from Nahal Hever (8HevXIIgr)* (DJD 8; Oxford: Clarendon Press, 1990). A number of Greek documents have been found at Qumran as well, presumably written in Palestine, including a fragment of the apocryphal Letter of Jeremiah and a paraphrase of Exodus (7Q1LXXEx, 4QLXXLev[a], 4QLXXNum, 4QLXXDeut, and 7Q2EpistJer) (see Hengel, *Pre-Christian Paul*, 61 and 136 n. 257).

Although there is some difference of opinion regarding Josephus's ability in Greek, from his own statements it seems that, although his pronunciation may not have been as good as he would have liked even after living in Rome, his grammatical ability was more than sufficient, certainly for day to day conversation, if not for highly literary purposes. The simple fact is that all of his publications have survived in Greek.[64] Despite Josephus's statements deprecating his oral linguistic skills, he also claims to have acted as interpreter for the Roman general Titus (*War* 5.9.2 §§360–361). Titus apparently spoke in Greek that was not sufficiently well understood by his listeners. Although the ability of Titus in Greek is attested by Suetonius (*Divus Titus* 3), it is not known whether the deficiency in this situation was with his listeners or with Titus. The urgency on Titus's part to make sure that the Jews understood exactly what he was saying may have influenced his desire to have Josephus, their kinsman, represent his position to them, especially those in Jerusalem.[65]

Other Palestinian and/or Jewish authors worth mentioning are the anonymous Samaritan historiographer (Pseudo-Eupolemus) (Eusebius, *Praep. Ev.* 9.17 and 9.18.2) and the Jewish historian Eupolemus (Eusebius, *Praep. Ev.* 9.26; 9.30–34; 9.39; cf. Clement of Alexandria, *Strom.* 1.21),[66] and Jason of Cyrene, summarized in 2 Maccabees. The Samaritan historiographer probably wrote in Palestine sometime between 200 and 165 B.C., Eupolemus sometime after 158/157 B.C., and Jason anywhere from soon after the death of Judas Maccabeus to significantly later.[67] Although the evidence is not strong, Hengel

64 There is debate about the sense in which Josephus's *Antiquities* and *Jewish War* are translations or original compositions in Greek. He claims that they are translations (*Ant.* 1.1.1 §5; 10.10.6 §218; *War* 1.1.1 §3; see also *Apion* 1.9 §50). Fitzmyer ("Languages of Palestine," 139) downplays the significance of this evidence for Josephus as a Palestinian historian, because he composed his writings in Rome. However, Rajak (*Josephus*, 51; followed by Wise, "Languages," 440) concludes that Josephus's statements about his use of assistants indicates that he had never studied Greek formally while in Palestine, and consequently had never thought of it as much of an achievement. It must be kept in mind that there is a difference between the kind of Greek competence necessary to compose the *Jewish War* and that necessary to carry on conversation or transact business. It seems indisputable that Josephus had the latter competence while resident in Palestine. On Josephus and the New Testament, see S. Mason, *Josephus and the New Testament* (Peabody: Hendrickson, 1992).

65 See Meier, *Marginal Jew*, 261 and notes; Fitzmyer, "Languages of Palestine," 138; and Sevenster, *Do You Know Greek?* 62–65. Sevenster takes note of the varying Greek linguistic abilities of the Roman emperors, including the excellent Greek of Claudius and the halting Greek of Augustus (Suetonius, *Divus Claudius* 42, *Divus Augustus* 89), although he does not mention Titus's ability referred to by Suetonius.

66 See Schürer, *History*, 3.517–21, 528–31; J.H. Charlesworth, *The Old Testament Pseudepigrapha* (2 vols.; Garden City, NY: Doubleday, 1985) 2.861–82. The anonymous Samaritan historiographer (Pseudo-Eupolemus) is, according to most recent scholarship, miscited by Eusebius as Eupolemus.

67 See Hengel, *Judaism and Hellenism*, 83–96 esp. 88 and 92 with notes. Hengel also

and others entertain the possibility that several writers or works usually identified with Alexandria may well have had their origins in Palestine, including the epic poet Philo, the poet Theodotus, Demetrius the Chronographer, the Tobiad Romance (Josephus, *Ant.* 12.4.1 §154–12.4.11 §236), and perhaps above all the grandson of Ben Sira, who translated his grandfather's work from Hebrew into Greek. Hengel concludes from these kinds of examples that "it is not so simple to distinguish between the 'Jewish-Hellenistic' literature of the Diaspora and the 'genuine Jewish' literature of Palestine... there were connections in all directions, and a constant and lively interchange."[68] That Greek was used not only in the Diaspora but also in Palestine, even for composition by Jews of distinctly Jewish literature including much religious literature, indicates that Greek was an important and widely used language by a sizable portion of the Palestinian Jewish population.

The inscriptional evidence points in the same direction, although the quantity of material is simply too large to refer to in anything close to comprehensive terms.[69] Nevertheless, there are a number of crucial texts that do point to the early and sustained, widespread use of Greek in Palestine and in particular in Galilee. The reasonable assumption is that if these inscriptions were written in Greek they could be read or understood by a significant portion of the population, with their wide dissemination and various functions indicating that Greek was a primary language of communication for widespread and diverse segments of the populace. Several texts are fairly early, giving evidence of a longstanding and pervasive influence of Greek.

It is perhaps wise, in order to appreciate fully the nature of the evidence, to give a brief recounting of it. Included are several public documents, including an inscription from Joppa, one of the oldest Palestinian cities but thoroughly Hellenistic since the Ptolemies, in honour of Ptolemy IV Philopator after his victory over Antiochus III of Seleucia (217 B.C.),[70] an inscription from Hefzibah (Beth Shean–Scythopolis, the largest city of the Decapolis, according to Josephus, *War* 3.9.7 §446) with two memoranda, one from Antiochus III (223–187 B.C.) and one from Seleucus IV Philopator (187–175 B.C.),[71] an

---

notes that the Greek Peripatetic Nicolaus of Damascus wrote his 144 books of universal history in Jerusalem while at the court of Herod.

68 Hengel, *"Hellenization,"* 26.

69 For convenient reference to the variety of material, see Hengel, *"Hellenization,"* 64; Fitzmyer, "Languages of Palestine," 135–36 and *passim*; Meyers–Strange, *Archaeology*, 79–84; and Sevenster, *Do You Know Greek?* 115–38. The present chapter corrects a number of references in the secondary treatments, and adds several references to newer evidence.

70 Printed in Sevenster, *Do You Know Greek?* 100. See also J. Kaplan, "Jaffa's History Revealed by the Spade," *Archaeology* 17 (1964) 270–76.

71 Y.H. Landau, "A Greek Inscription Found Near Hefzibah," *IEJ* 16 (1966) 54–70. See also Meyers–Strange, *Archaeology*, 80 (their bibliographical citation is incorrect).

inscription from Jamnia-on-the-Sea with a petition to Antiochus V of Seleucia and his response regarding their service and taxation (163–162 B.C.),[72] and an inscription from Acco–Ptolemais (130 B.C.) honouring Antiochus VII Sidetes (138–129 B.C.) and his consort Cleopatra Thea.[73] Several religious inscriptions, bearing witness to the presence of Greek religious practices and to widespread use of Greek language in their performance, include not only the Acco–Ptolemais inscription dedicated to Zeus-Soter (see above) but also a votive inscription celebrating Hadad and Atargatis (130 B.C.),[74] in Samaria a dedicatory inscription to Serapis and Isis (201 B.C.)[75] and a list of priests of Zeus Olympius (2nd century B.C.),[76] a bilingual (Greek and Aramaic) votive inscription from Tell Dan to "the god in Dan" (late 3rd or early 2nd century B.C.),[77] a statue from Bashan dedicated to Herod the Great (23 B.C.),[78] pagan temple inscriptions from Mt. Hermon (1st or 2nd century A.D.),[79] and several major examples of Greek graffiti.[80] In all, these inscriptions bear significant testimony to the widespread use of Greek in a variety of civil and religious practices.

The most important inscriptions, however, include the following erected in conjunction with Jewish religious practices. The first, with two physical examples plus reference in Josephus (*War* 5.5.2 §§193–194; 6.2.4 §§124–125; *Ant.* 15.11.5 §417), is the inscription forbidding non-Jews to enter the inner courts of the temple in Jerusalem.[81] Perhaps it is not surprising that this

---

72 B. Isaac, "A Seleucid Inscription from Jamnia-on-the-Sea: Antiochus V Eupator and the Sidonians," *IEJ* 41 (1991) 132–44.

73 SEG 19.904, cf. 20.413; Y.H. Landau, "A Greek Inscription from Acre," *IEJ* 11 (1961) 118–26; cf. J. Schwartz, "Note complémentaire (à propos d'une inscription grecque de St. Jean d'Acre)," *IEJ* 12 (1962) 135–36. See also Meyers–Strange, *Archaeology*, 80.

74 SEG 18.622.

75 SEG 8.95.

76 SEG 8.96.

77 *NewDocs* 1 (1976) 67.

78 OGIS 1.415. There are other inscriptions in this collection that refer to Herod the Great, or one of the Herods. See OGIS 1.414, 416, 417, 418, 419, 421, 422, 423, 424, 425, 426, 427.

79 S. Dar and N. Kokkinos, "The Greek Inscriptions from Senaim on Mount Hermon," *PEQ* (January–June 1992) 9–25. Several Semitic names have recently been deciphered on an inscription in a Roman temple (second century A.D.): A. Lajtar, "Two Greek Inscriptions from Tell Kadesh (Upper Galilee)," *ZPE* 89 (1991) 155–57.

80 See, for example, SEG 8.247–251, cf. 8.252–260 for names in tombs; CIJ 2.1184; P. Benoit, "L'inscription grecque du tombeau de Jason," *IEJ* 17 (1967) 112–13. Cf. also L.J. Rahmani, "Jason's Tomb," *IEJ* 17 (1967) 61–100; M. Avi-Yonah (ed.), *Encyclopedia of Archaeological Excavations in the Holy Land* (Englewood Cliffs, NJ: Prentice-Hall, 1976) 2.630–31; Meyers–Strange, *Archaeology*, 80–81; Fitzmyer, "Languages of Palestine," 135–36.

81 OGIS 2.598; SEG 8.169; CIJ 2.1400. Reprinted many times, this inscription is

inscription is in Greek, since Jews are attempting to warn off non-Jews from entering the sacred precinct, although Kee notes that "when the synagogue movement began to flourish and to take on architectural forms in the second century C.E., the inscriptions were in Greek, even in Jerusalem."[82] It is just as likely, therefore, that Greek was one of the major languages of Jewish life, even in its religious institutions, as the two following inscriptions also bear witness. The second inscription is one honouring a man named Paris who paid for a stone pavement on or around the temple. This inscription probably dates to the time of Herod the Great.[83] That the donor was from Rhodes may have influenced the choice of Greek for the inscription, although the nature of the inscription would indicate that its erection was for the benefit of those in Jerusalem who could read it or have it read to them at least as much as for the benefactor. Third is the so-called Theodotus inscription, found outside of Jerusalem. It probably dates to the first century, before A.D. 70.[84] The significance of this Greek inscription is that it bears witness to one Theodotus, son of Bettenos, a priest and head of the synagogue, who was the son and grandson of the head of the synagogue, and who himself built a synagogue for the reading of the law and study of the commandments. This thoroughly Jewish man is highly commemorated in Greek. A fourth inscription is a unilingual Greek decree of a Caesar forbidding the violation of sepulchres. This inscription most likely dates to the first century A.D., although this is not agreed upon by all, and it may well have been erected in Galilee (Nazareth), although there is dispute about this also. Although perhaps not a formal decree but a response by a Caesar to a question regarding these sepulchral violations, it can be reasonably assumed that it would only have had significance if those who read it (or had it read to them) were able to understand Greek.[85] The last example is a

---

conveniently found in A. Deissmann, *Light from the Ancient East* (trans. L.R.M. Strachan; London: Hodder & Stoughton, 1927; repr. Grand Rapids: Eerdmans, 1978) 80; J. Finegan, *The Archaeology of the New Testament: The Life of Jesus and the Beginning of the Early Church* (Princeton: Princeton University Press, 1969) 119–20, who prints both versions; Schürer, *History*, 2.222 n. 85; and now P. Segal, "The Penalty of the Warning Inscription from the Temple of Jerusalem," *IEJ* 39 (1989) 79–84. Fully 40% of the inscriptions found in Jerusalem are in Greek. It was not uncommon for inscriptions to be bilingual with Greek and Latin used outside of Palestine during the Roman period. Although Josephus cites a Latin version of this temple inscription, the Latin inscription itself has not been found.

82 Kee, "Early Christianity in the Galilee," 20.

83 B. Isaac, "A Donation for Herod's Temple in Jerusalem," *IEJ* 33 (1983) 86–92. See Hengel, *"Hellenization,"* 66 n. 34.

84 SEG 8.170; CIJ 2.1404. See Hengel, *Between Jesus and Paul*, 148 n. 119; Sevenster, *Do You Know Greek?* 131–32. Most synagogue inscriptions date to the second and third centuries A.D. and consequently do not add anything to what has already been said here.

85 SEG 8.13. See Sevenster, *Do You Know Greek?* 117–21; F.F. Bruce, *New Testament History* (Garden City, NY: Doubleday, 1971) 300–303. The Greek may at several points

first or second century A.D. dedicatory inscription upon a column from Capernaum.[86] In all, this inscriptional evidence confirms the significant and widespread use of Greek throughout Palestine, even in conjunction with Jewish religious practices.

Concerning inscriptional evidence from burial sites, Leon has said that the best indicator of the language of the common people is the sepulchral inscriptions,[87] and the evidence certainly indicates a widespread and constant use of Greek in Palestine, including especially Galilee. To put the evidence from funerary inscriptions into its proper context,[88] it is worth noting that, according to the latest statistics on published inscriptions, 68% of *all* of the ancient Jewish inscriptions from the Mediterranean world are in Greek (70% if one counts as Greek bilingual inscriptions with Greek as one of the languages). As van der Horst observes, "The first impression one gains from these data is that Greek was the language of the great majority among the Jews in the Imperial period, probably of more than two-thirds of them."[89] In Palestine in particular, the situation is similar. For example, at the city of Beth She'arim, in western Galilee, a set of catacombs and tombs were used as burial sites from the

---

indicate that it is a translation from Latin. Contra Meier, *Marginal Jew*, 256, with reference to the Pilate inscription.

86 SEG 8.4, cf. 17.774. See Fitzmyer, "Languages of Palestine," 140.

87 H.J. Leon, *The Jews of Ancient Rome* (Philadelphia: Jewish Publication Society of America, 1960) 75–76, at the beginning of his discussion of language. Most recent analysts of the funerary inscriptions would endorse this position; contra Meier, *Marginal Jew*, 289 n. 10. Speculation whether the language used was actually that of the deceased, his or her relatives or the stone mason is futile and largely beside the point, since the use of Greek by Jews in such a context indicates its significance in Palestine.

88 For convenient reference to the funerary inscriptions, see P.W. van der Horst, *Ancient Jewish Epitaphs: An Introductory Survey of a Millennium of Jewish Funerary Epigraphy (300 BCE–700 CE)* (Kampen: Kok Pharos, 1991), who analyses the linguistic character of the Greek; "Das Neue Testament und die jüdischen Grabinschriften aus hellenistisch-römischer Zeit," *BZ* 36 (1992) 161–78; "Jewish Funerary Inscriptions—Most are in Greek," *BARev* 18.5 (1992) 46–57, a summary of his work.

89 Van der Horst, *Ancient Jewish Epitaphs*, 22, cf. 129–32. Regional variation confirms this opinion, in van der Horst's mind. For example, of the Jewish funerary inscriptions from Rome, 78% are in Greek but only 1% are in Hebrew or Aramaic (21% are in Latin). "This is surprising, the more so in view of the fact that in the vast majority of Roman tomb-inscriptions Latin is the predominant language in those of other orientals, especially the numerous Syrians in Rome" (p. 22). From this evidence, he concludes that "One should not assume that they used Greek only on their tombstones as a kind of sacred language (comparable to the use of Latin in later Christian funerary epigraphy in the West), for their sacred language remained Hebrew, as is witnessed by the many Greek and Latin inscriptions ending in the single Hebrew word *shalom*, or the expressions *shalom 'al mishkavo* or *shalom 'al Yisra'el*" (p. 23). The Hebrew is often transliterated into Greek: e.g. CIJ 2.1034, 1036 and 1037, 1038, 1113.

first to the sixth centuries A.D. At this Jewish site, where many significant Jewish religious figures, including rabbis, are buried, the earliest catacombs (first to second centuries A.D.) are *all* in Greek. In all, up to 80% of the Beth She'arim catacombs are in Greek, some of it quite colloquial and reflecting aphoristic Greek thinking.[90] Even in Jerusalem, probably the most linguistically Semitic of the Jewish cities, the number of epitaphs in Greek is approximately equal to the number in Semitic languages.[91] Taking all of the Palestinian funerary inscriptions into account, it is estimated that 55% to 60% of all of them are in Greek. These data are not to be underestimated. Since Hebrew may well still have been the predominant Jewish religious language, at least of the devout, it is easy to account for the Semitic inscriptions. But it is less easy to account for the Greek ones unless Greek was simply a commonly used language by many Jews. The logical conclusion is that the statistics for Greek may well be a conservative estimate of the percentage of people who spoke Greek in the Jewish population of Galilee and even of Palestine. At the most private and final moments when a loved one was finally to be laid to rest, in the majority of instances, Jews chose Greek as the language in which to memorialize their deceased. Greek was apparently that dominant, that in the majority of instances it took precedence over the Jewish sacred language, even at a moment of highly personal and religious significance. As van der Horst concludes, "If even rabbis and their families phrased their epitaphs in Greek, there is only one natural explanation for that phenomenon: Greek was the language of their daily life."[92]

5. *Jesus' Use of Greek and the New Testament Evidence*

In the light of this accumulated Greek evidence, which is overwhelming when compared to the equivalent Aramaic evidence, it is surprising that many scholars have not given more consideration to the hypothesis that Jesus spoke and even possibly taught in Greek, and furthermore that there is a possibility if

---

90 Meyers–Strange, *Archaeology*, 86, 101. See Sevenster, *Do You Know Greek?* 138–42, who concludes, "If Greek is used on the majority of the tombstones and ossuaries, this is a strong indication that Greek was mainly spoken in that region and that consequently the Semitic language had become the secondary one for many people, though still used as a sacred language in the funerary inscriptions."

91 See Avi-Yonah (ed.), *Encyclopedia of Archaeological Excavation*, 2.629–41; N. Avigad, "A Depository of Inscribed Ossuaries in the Kidron Valley," *IEJ* 12 (1962) 1–12. In nearby Jericho, the tomb of the "Goliath" family has over half of its epitaphs in Greek, much of it in better-formed letters than the Aramaic. See R. Hachlili, "The Goliath Family in Jericho: Funerary Inscriptions from a First Century A.D. Jewish Monumental Tomb," *BASOR* 235 (1979) 31–65.

92 Van der Horst, *Ancient Jewish Epitaphs*, 24.

not a likelihood that we have some of the actual words of Jesus recorded in the Gospels.[93] In fact, it is almost as if there is an inherent resistance to this hypothesis. It is found in several forms. For example, some scholars attempt to trivialize the claim by differentiating between the ordinary spoken words of Jesus and his teaching.[94] The point being argued for here is that, when the evidence is laid out, there is a presumption in favour of the hypothesis that at the least Jesus knew and in fact spoke Greek (he had productive linguistic competence), whether or not he could carry on extensive discourse.[95] To some extent this makes it unnecessary to differentiate between ordinary speaking and teaching. To be able to speak in Greek would imply at least the possibility of teaching in Greek but it would not necessarily require it on account of circumstances, such as his level of competence, the composition of his audience, the subject matter, or the particular context. It must be recognized, of course, that the very nature of the compositional process of the Gospels makes it extremely difficult to know which passages may reflect the words of Jesus. For instance, since the Gospels are in Greek, one must devise a means to differentiate the Greek words of Jesus from the Greek wording of the author. Lee has made us aware of the fact that the Greek used by Jesus in Mark's Gospel at points conforms to a higher register than the Greek of the narrative itself. One could speculate that this captures the actual language of Jesus, but it may also simply reflect an attempt by the author to ensure that due respect and reverence are given to Jesus even in the language that he uses.[96]

Nevertheless, I believe that, first, it can be firmly established that Jesus did speak Greek and that we do indeed have some of his actual words. This will be established by examining several passages where Jesus would have had the highest likelihood of using Greek. When these passages are examined in conjunction with the cultural-linguistic context established above regarding the widespread use of Greek in Palestine, it becomes clear that there is a strong likelihood that Jesus spoke Greek, and that in at least one of these passages we may have his actual words. Once this has been established, then it can be seen that there may be at least one passage where the teaching of Jesus in Greek is recorded, in particular the scene at Caesarea Philippi, when Jesus endorses

---

93 See Argyle, "Did Jesus Speak Greek?" 93; Gundry, "Language Milieu," 408.

94 Fitzmyer, "Did Jesus Speak Greek?" 62. But cf. Sevenster, *Do You Know Greek?* 27.

95 It is outside the parameters of this chapter to raise the question of whether Jesus could read or write Greek. It is difficult to define what exactly constitutes literacy, but it has been estimated that in the Hellenistic world 20% to 30% of males were literate, or could read and write (W.V. Harris, *Ancient Literacy* [Cambridge, MA: Harvard University Press, 1989] 16–46 esp. 41). Meier (*Marginal Jew*, 268–78) thinks that Jesus was literate in Semitic languages. See Porter, "Introduction," 36–37, and ch. 5 in this volume, pp. 75–99.

96 Lee, "Some Features of the Speech of Jesus," 1–8.

Peter's confession that he is the Christ.[97] The contexts to be considered below include several where Jesus is recorded as speaking to others who plausibly did not speak a Semitic language, and where no translator or interpreter is indicated (see also Matt 8:28–34; Mark 5:1–20; Luke 8:26–39). Interpreters or translators are specified by other writers during this period (e.g. Josephus, *Apion* 1.9 §§50–51; *War* 5.9.2 §361; 6.2.1 §96; 6.2.5 §129; 6.6.2 §327; all of these in Jerusalem).[98] Whereas the Gospel writers may have failed to do so, this is not consistent with how the Gospels often treat similar linguistic situations, for example where ὅ ἐστιν μεθερμηνευόμενον or similar phrases are used when Aramaic is cited and a translation in Greek is included (e.g. Matt 1:23; Mark 5:41; 15:22, 34; John 1:38, 41, 42; 9:7; cf. also Acts 4:36; 9:36; Heb 7:2).

A. *Mark 15:2–5//Matthew 27:11–14//Luke 23:2–5//John 18:29–38*
The first and most important example, and the one that sets the tenor for the subsequent treatment of passages, is Jesus' trial before Pilate (Mark 15:2–5; Matt 27:11–14; Luke 23:2–5; John 18:29–38; cf. 1 Tim 6:13). It is highly unlikely that Pilate, the prefect assigned to this remote posting in the Roman empire, would have known any Semitic language. No translator or interpreter is mentioned for the conversation that occurs between Jesus and Pilate, making it unlikely that Latin or Aramaic was used. In fact, the pace of the narrative, in which conversation is held between not only Pilate and Jesus but Pilate and the Jewish leaders, Pilate and the crowd, and the Jewish leaders and the crowd, argues against an interpreter intervening.[99] It is most likely, therefore, that Jesus spoke to Pilate in Greek.[100] In fact, there is the probability that all of the conversation, including that of Pilate with the Jewish leaders and the crowd (and possibly that of the Jewish leaders and the crowd?), took place in Greek. But do we have the actual words spoken? I believe that we may well have at least some of these words, confirmed by forms of the criteria of multiple attestation and dissimilarity (from redactional tendencies).[101] There are

97 But see Meier, *Marginal Jew*, 294–95 and n. 40; and Fitzmyer, "Did Jesus Speak Greek?" 60–61, among others, who question these contexts. Other instances where Jesus may have spoken Greek have been suggested, including the Sermon on the Mount (Matt 5–7; cf. also Luke 6), and Jesus' conversations with the Samaritan woman (John 4) and with Mary Magdalene (John 20) (Roberts, *Greek*, 145–57), the use of ἐπιούσιος in the Lord's Prayer and ὁ υἱὸς τοῦ ἀνθρώπου (Ross, "Jesus's Knowledge of Greek," 43–46), and ὑποκριτής in Matt 6:2, 15, 16 (A.W. Argyle, "'Hypocrites' and the Aramaic Theory," *ExpTim* 75 [1963–64] 113–14; *idem*, "Greek among the Jews," 89).

98 Problems with translation and interpretation were recognized by the ancients. See J. Behm, ἑρμηνεύω, *TDNT*, 2.661–66 *passim* for the evidence.

99 Roberts, *Greek*, 161–62.

100 As Dalman himself recognizes (*Jesus–Jeshua*, 5).

101 For a recent statement on authenticity criteria, see C.A. Evans, *Jesus and his Contemporaries: Comparative Studies* (AGJU 25; Leiden: Brill, 1995) 13–24 esp. 15–18.

apparently two separate accounts of Jesus' trial in the Synoptic Gospels and John.[102] There is little overlap in detail or wording, except at two places: John 18:33–34 and 37, and Mark 15:2, Matt 27:11, and Luke 23:3, and only in a few words spoken by Pilate and Jesus. The narrative surrounding these few select words is clearly dependent upon Mark in Matthew and Luke, but this same narrative shares virtually no wording between the Synoptic accounts and John's Gospel except in the question posed by Pilate and in Jesus' response. Pilate asks Jesus, σὺ εἶ ὁ βασιλεὺς τῶν Ἰουδαίων;[103] and Jesus replies σὺ λέγεις. Although the Synoptic Gospels allow this reluctant, affirmative answer to stand as Jesus' only words of response, in Jesus' extended and delayed reply John embellishes the account, wrapping around these two words a complex answer that explicates Jesus' kingship. The words σὺ λέγεις appear nowhere else in the Synoptic Gospels, revealing that they are not a part of any of the Gospels' redactional tendency. The same two words do appear in John 8:33, 52, 9:17 and 14:9,[104] but in these Johannine instances they are used not in a statement but only in a question, and all of these but 14:9 not on the lips of Jesus. The infrequency of this wording in the Synoptic Gospels (criterion of dissimilarity), as well as the way in which it is used in John's apparently independent account (criterion of multiple attestation), indicates that not only is there a likelihood that we have the Greek wording of Pilate's question to Jesus,[105] but in these two words we may well have Jesus' actual response.[106]

---

102 So most commentators, including R.E. Brown (*The Gospel according to John* [2 vols.; AB 29, 29A; Garden City, NY: Doubleday, 1966, 1970] 2.861) and R. Schnackenburg (*The Gospel according to St. John* [3 vols.; New York: Crossroad, 1982] 3.247–48); contra C.K. Barrett, *The Gospel according to St. John* (2nd edn; Philadelphia: Westminster Press, 1978) 536, who thinks it is an expansion of Mark.

103 These same words are found in the *titulus* placed above the cross (see Matt 27:37; Mark 15:26; Luke 23:38; John 19:19). C.E.B. Cranfield (*The Gospel according to St. Mark* [CGTC; Cambridge: Cambridge University Press, 1972] 457) notes that, whereas Pilate uses the word Ἰουδαίων in his question, the chief priests and scribes use the more proper Ἰσραήλ (Mark 15:32; Matt 27:42; but cf. Luke 23:37). See Josephus, *Ant.* 15.10.5 §373, 16.10.2 §311 for the title "king of the Jews" (cf. 14.3.1 §36, for similar language on a Latin or Greek inscription), showing the currency of this title in Palestine of that time (see J. Fitzmyer, *The Gospel according to Luke X–XXIV* [AB 28A; Garden City, NY: Doubleday, 1985] 1475).

104 These eight are the only instances in the entire New Testament. The plural ὑμεῖς λέγετε is used in Luke 22:70, its only use in the Synoptic Gospels. σὺ εἶπας appears only at Matt 26:25, 64.

105 A.H. McNeile (*The Gospel according to St. Matthew* [1915; repr. Grand Rapids: Baker, 1980] 409) contends that Pilate's question is unexpected, except in Luke's Gospel, with no foundation for its being asked. This supports the hypothesis of the words being authentic. See also Barrett, *John*, 536.

106 See also Birkeland, *Language of Jesus*, 17. For the similarities of Pilate's interrogation of Jesus with what might have been expected from a Roman official at the time, see A.N. Sherwin-White, *Roman Society and Roman Law in the New Testament* (Sarum

B. *Mark 7:25–30*

Firmly establishing the high probability that Jesus spoke Greek and that we have his very words opens up the possibility that other passages may also record Jesus' words. Of these instances, an example of a passage in which Jesus may well have spoken Greek is Mark 7:25–30, when Jesus travels to the area of Tyre.[107] A woman with a daughter possessed by an evil spirit hears of his presence there and begs for Jesus' help. The woman is called in Mark's Gospel a Ἑλληνίς, a Συροφοινίκισσα by birth, that is, a gentile (7:26).[108] Even though the indigenous language of the area was Semitic, this area had long been under Hellenistic influence (and antagonistic to the Jews; see Josephus, *Apion* 1.13 §§69–72) and evidenced widespread use of Greek, as has been noted above. The description of the woman in the Gospel makes sure that the reader knows that the woman was a Greek-speaker despite her birth. Otherwise the reference is gratuitous or perhaps even potentially misleading. There is no indication of an interpreter being present. Although there is not sufficient corroborative evidence to know whether Jesus' words here are his own, the context clearly indicates the likelihood that Jesus spoke in Greek to the gentile woman, and that his discussion may record his actual words, even if he is bested by her in their battle of wits.[109]

C. *John 12:20–28*

A further incident is John 12:20–28 (or –36), already mentioned above. Ἕλληνές τινες came to Philip, who went to Andrew, both of whom have Greek names, and who both went to Jesus. The use of Ἕλληνες here almost certainly refers to Greek-speaking gentiles (cf. Mark 7:26 above), whether or

---

Lectures, 1960–61; Oxford: Clarendon Press, 1963; repr. Grand Rapids: Eerdmans, 1978) 24–47.

107 Many good early manuscripts read "Tyre and Sidon" (א A B *f*1, 13 Majority text *pc*), but this is probably assimilation to Mark 7:31 and Matt 15:21. *UBSGNT*3 gives the reading "Tyre" an A rating.

108 See R.H. Gundry, *Mark: A Commentary on his Apology for the Cross* (Grand Rapids: Eerdmans, 1993) 379–80. The Syrophoenicians (as distinguished from other Phoenician groups) can probably be identified with what are traditionally called the Canaanites. This indicates that the parallel in Matt 15:21–28 probably reflects the same incident. It is in keeping with Matthew's character as a more Jewish Gospel that he does not emphasize the gentile and Greek characteristics of the woman. See H.B. Swete, *The Gospel according to Mark* (London: Macmillan, 1898) 148; C.S. Mann, *Mark* (AB 27; Garden City, NY: Doubleday, 1986) 320; R. Guelich, *Mark 1:1–8:26* (WBC 34A; Dallas: Word, 1989) 385; G. Schwarz, "ΣΥΡΟΦΟΙΝΙΚΙΣΣΑ—ΧΑΝΑΝΑΙΑ (Markus 7.26/Matthäus 15.22)," *NTS* 30 (1984) 626–28.

109 See esp. Gundry, *Mark*, 375; G. Theissen, "Lokal- und Sozialkolorit in der Geschichte von der syrophönischen Frau (Mk 7:24–30)," *ZNW* 75 (1984) 202–25 esp. 206–13; F. Dufton, "The Syrophoenician Woman and her Dogs," *ExpTim* 100 (1988–89) 417.

not they came from Greece (as they almost assuredly did not), and does not mean Greek-speaking Jews, as the comparative terminology of Acts 6:1 indicates.[110] These people would probably have been gentiles from one of the Greek-speaking areas, quite possibly of northern Palestine in the area of Galilee or the Decapolis, since Philip and Andrew (and Peter; cf. John 1:44) were reportedly from Bethsaida.[111] Dalman was of the opinion that the Greek-speakers went to the disciples because Jesus was not identified with the Greek-speaking Jews.[112] The narrative does not prove this point, however, since there could have been a variety of reasons why they would have not wanted to approach Jesus directly, including perhaps Jesus' perceived status. Jesus' response gives no indication that he could not communicate with them.[113] If the incident is historical[114] then there is the presumption that Jesus could well have addressed at least some of his words to them in Greek.[115]

D. *Matthew 8:5–13//Luke 7:2–10*

The next example is Jesus' meeting in Capernaum with the centurion (Matt 8:5–13; Luke 7:2–10; he is probably referred to in John 4:46–53 as a βασιλικός, perhaps a commander of a troop of soldiers serving under Herod Antipas).[116] This Q passage has been independently redacted by Matthew and Luke, with Luke including Jewish emissaries to represent the centurion's cause to Jesus, which would possibly exclude this example if Luke's version is original (commentators are divided on which version depicts what actually happened, although the tendency is to see Matthew's as primary).[117] Nevertheless, several common points emerge from the accounts. They both retain Jesus' commendation of the ἑκατόνταρχος as a man demonstrating faith not found in Israel, the presumption being that he is seen by Matthew and Luke as a gentile

---

110 Barrett, *John*, 421.

111 Bethsaida, in Gaulanitis and not technically in Galilee, was quite possibly referred to as being in Galilee, especially after A.D. 66–70. Andrew and Philip may have had Greek names, even if they were Jews. See Barrett, *John*, 183; cf. D.A. Carson, *The Gospel according to John* (Grand Rapids: Eerdmans, 1991) 436.

112 Dalman, *Jesus–Jeshua*, 5.

113 See Sevenster, *Do You Know Greek?* 25–26.

114 For a summary of the issues, see J. Beutler, "Greeks Come to See Jesus (John 12,20f)," *Bib* 71 (1990) 333–35.

115 See John 7:35–36, where the Jews' response indicates that they thought that Jesus could go into the Diaspora, that is, to a Greek or gentile populated area, presumably with the ability to teach them in Greek.

116 See R.H. Gundry, *Matthew: A Commentary on His Literary and Theological Art* (Grand Rapids: Eerdmans, 1982) 141; J.A.G. Haslam, "The Centurion at Capernaum: Luke 7:1–10," *ExpTim* 96 (1984–85) 109–10.

117 See M.D. Goulder, *Luke: A New Paradigm* (2 vols.; JSNTSup 20; Sheffield: JSOT Press, 1989) 1.379–80.

centurion, and presumably a Greek speaker. Even though we probably have both the Q version and the Johannine version of this incident,[118] there is no common dialogue to compare for authentication, even though there is the likelihood that Jesus would have spoken to the centurion in Greek, if he spoke directly to him.

E. *Matthew 16:13–20//Mark 8:27–30//Luke 9:18–21*

The final example for consideration is Jesus' discussion with his disciples at Caesarea Philippi (Matt 16:13–20; Mark 8:27–30; Luke 9:18–21), although the teaching material attributed to Jesus in this incident is found only in Matthew's Gospel. Although the certainty of the incident itself or of the very words being those of Jesus is not as great as with the incidents recorded above, a number of features of the language in its Matthean version[119] point to this being material formulated early on in Greek. It might at first seem strange that Jesus and his followers would speak Greek and not Aramaic in this private conversation, unless the full force of the evidence above is taken into consideration. In conjunction with what we know of Jesus' linguistic ability and the location to the south of Galilee in which the incident occurred, there is a reasonable likelihood—if not probability—that this pericope records the Greek words of Jesus.

The first line of support comes from the location itself. The incident occurred in the region (Matthew) or villages (Mark) of Caesarea Philippi. Caesarea Philippi, located in Gaulanitis in the far north of Palestine, was a gentile city long before its Hellenistic refounding by Herod the Great, who built a temple in honour of Caesar Augustus, and its rebuilding and renaming from Panias (so-called after its grotto to Pan) by Herod Philip.[120] It is as likely a location for the use of Greek language as almost any other in Palestine. Of course, this likelihood does not determine that Jesus must have spoken in Greek, but it does not make the use of Greek foreign to one who had such capability, as shown above.

A second factor is with regards to Synoptic priorities. Although the majority of scholars usually endorse Markan priority in recounting this incident, this is not entirely certain, even though many would recognize the essential historicity

---

[118] See W.D. Davies and D.C. Allison, *A Critical and Exegetical Commentary on the Gospel according to Saint Matthew* (3 vols.; ICC; Edinburgh: T. & T. Clark, 1988–) 2.17–18.

[119] For more detailed discussion, especially of the grammatical issues, see S.E. Porter, "Vague Verbs, Periphrastics, and Matthew 16:19," *FN* 1.2 (1988) 155–73, reprinted as ch. 6 in this volume, pp. 103–24.

[120] On the history of Caesarea Philippi, including some of its Hellenistic elements, see G. Dalman, *Sacred Sites and Ways: Studies in the Topography of the Gospels* (trans. P.P. Levertoff; London: SPCK, 1935) 195–207.

of the event.[121] Discussion of the major features of the Matthean account will serve to suggest if not Matthean priority at least Matthean independence, and the probability that these words were early on formulated in Greek, quite possibly by Jesus himself.

One of the most important features of Jesus' words to Peter after his confession of Jesus as the Christ, the Son of the living God (only Matthew has the entire title), is Jesus' word-play revolving around Peter's name. Although there is debate about the meanings of כיפא (Aramaic *kepha'*; Greek κηφᾶς) and πέτρος,[122] the major issue revolves around whether the apparent word-play in the biblical text works in Aramaic or in Greek alone.[123] In Aramaic, Jesus would apparently have said, "You are כיפא (rock) and upon this כיפא (rock) I intend to build my church." It cannot be determined whether this was the first time Jesus addressed the issue of Peter's name, an issue raised elsewhere in the New Testament (e.g. John 1:42; cf. 1 Cor 1:12; 3:22; 9:5; 15:5; Gal 1:18; 2:9, 11, 14). While some scholars would argue that the word-play does not work well in Greek because two different Greek words are used rather than simply citing the statement on the basis of an Aramaic original, the use of cognate forms (possibly indicating paronomasia) points to the importance of the Greek formulation. According to this reasoning, πέτρος, a masculine noun, and the name given to Simon (Mark 3:16; Luke 6:14), is frequently in Greek literature

121 For those who dispute the historical veracity of the account, among others see R. Bultmann, *The History of the Synoptic Tradition* (trans. J. Marsh; revised edn; Oxford: Blackwell, 1968) 138–40, 258–59, who tries to argue that the place-reference belongs to the previous pericope; T.W. Manson, *The Sayings of Jesus* (London: SCM Press, 1947) 201–205; R.E. Brown *et al.*, *Peter in the New Testament* (Minneapolis: Augsburg, 1973) 83–101; B.P. Robinson, "Peter and his Successors: Tradition and Redaction in Matthew 16.17–19," *JSNT* 21 (1984) 86–87; J. Lambrecht, "'Du bist Petrus'—Mt 16,16–19 und das Papsttum," *SNTU* 11 (1987) 5–32; cf. also M. Wilcox, "Peter and the Rock: A Fresh Look at Matt 16:17–19," *NTS* 22 (1976) 73–74. Significant defenses of the authenticity of the passage are found in O. Cullmann, *Peter: Disciple, Apostle, Martyr: A Historical and Theological Study* [trans. F.V. Filson; 2nd edn; London: SCM Press, 1962) 176–217 esp. 190–91; B.F. Meyer, *The Aims of Jesus* (London: SCM Press, 1979) 185–97. See the appendix to ch. 6 in this volume, pp. 103–24.

122 See J.A. Fitzmyer, "Aramaic Kepha' and Peter's Name in the New Testament," in *Text and Interpretation: Studies in the New Testament Presented to M. Black* (ed. E. Best and R.McL. Wilson; Cambridge: Cambridge University Press, 1979) 121–32.

123 Cullmann (*Peter*, 191–93; πέτρος, *TDNT*, 6.106; πέτρα, *TDNT*, 6.98–99) claims that the pun cannot work in Greek, while P. Lampe ("Das Spiel mit dem Petrus-Namen—Matt. xvi.18," *NTS* 25 [1979] 227–45) and Hughes ("Language Spoken by Jesus," 141), followed by Gundry (*Matthew*, 333–34), claim that the pun works only in Greek. B.D. Chilton (*Targumic Approaches to the Gospels: Essays in the Mutual Definition of Judaism and Christianity* [Lanham, MD: University Press of America, 1986] 80 n. 31) claims that "*Ptr*, however, is an Aramaic term borrowed from Greek which appears in Aramaic with the meaning 'foundation.'"

understood to mean a simple "stone" (Sophocles, *O.C.* 1595; Euripides, *Her.* 1002).[124] πέτρα, a feminine noun and inappropriate as a man's name, often is used to refer to a mass of rock (Euripides, *Ion* 936). Jesus thus says, "You are πέτρος (a name for an individual male and a single stone) and upon this πέτρα (firm foundation of stone) I intend to build my church." This accounts well for the alternation in Greek words, unnecessary if it merely translates the same Aramaic word, and it accommodates general Greek usage of the two words as well.[125] It might be objected that this word-play is to be attributed to the Matthean redactor. The fact that there are no similar scenes in Matthew, in which there is a play on a disciple's name, indicates that it is not part of Matthew's redactional tendency, and therefore could well be attributed to earlier tradition, quite possibly even to Jesus himself.

Virtually every discussion of Matt 16:17–19 seems to mention sooner or later the periphrastic constructions in v. 19, found elsewhere in the New Testament only in Matt 18:18 and Heb 2:13. Debate over this future perfect passive periphrastic has not disputed its Greek origin or formulation,[126] but has disputed its meaning and translation. Rather than as the equivalent of an English future perfect passive (where a future event is the result of a first event occurring before the time of speaking or writing, that is, "shall have been bound/loosed"),[127] or as a statement of once for all action,[128] or as a nonperiphrastic use of the adjectival participle,[129] a more accurate understanding of the periphrastic construction appreciates the stative rather than temporal verbal aspect of the perfect participle, and temporal reference based on the discourse structure rather than the simple use of the future form of the

---

124 See H.G. Liddell and R. Scott, *A Greek–English Lexicon* (ed. H.S. Jones with R. McKenzie, and E.A. Barber; 9th edn; Oxford: Clarendon Press, 1968) s.v.

125 Cf. Lampe, "Das Spiel mit dem Petrus-Namen," 242–45, who concludes similarly, although on the basis of a folk etymology by early Christians. The question regarding whether Jesus intends to found his church upon Peter himself is outside the bounds of this chapter. On the issue, see now C.C. Caragounis, *Peter and the Rock* (BZNW 58; Berlin: de Gruyter, 1990) 88–113, but who argues for two differing underlying Aramaic words.

126 See Porter, *Verbal Aspect*, 471 n. 35, 473–74, for extra-biblical Greek parallels.

127 J.R. Mantey, "The Mistranslation of the Perfect Tense in John 20:23, Mt 16:19, and Mt 18:18," *JBL* 58 (1939) 243–49; "Evidence that the Perfect Tense in John 20:23 and Matthew 16:19 is Mistranslated," *JETS* 16 (1973) 129–38.

128 H.J. Cadbury, "The Meaning of John 20:23, Matthew 16:19, and Matthew 18:18," *JBL* 58 (1939) 251–54.

129 N. Turner, *Grammatical Insights into the New Testament* (Edinburgh: T. & T. Clark, 1965) 80–82; *idem, Syntax*, 81–82; K.L. McKay, "On the Perfect and Other Aspects in the Greek Non-Literary Papyri," *Bulletin of the Institute of Classical Studies* 27 (1980) 23–49; C.F.D. Moule, *An Idiom Book of New Testament Greek* (2nd edn; Cambridge: Cambridge University Press, 1959) 18.

auxiliary verb.[130] (A translational gloss: "whatever you might bind upon the earth [if such a binding event were to occur], this is expected to be in a state of boundness in heaven; and whatever you might loose upon the earth, this is expected to be in a state of loosedness in heaven.") Again it might be argued that this complex conditional-like periphrastic might be the work of the Matthean redactor. As mentioned above, however, apart from Matt 18:18, found in a similar context, there is no other use of this structure in Matthew's Gospel or in any of the other Gospels, denying this as a Matthean redactional tendency. The closest conceptual parallel is John 20:23, which does not use the periphrastic construction but the simplex verb form. This provides further evidence that this passage was formulated early on in Greek, quite possibly by Jesus himself.

The third and final major textual feature to discuss is the use of the word ἐκκλησία. The use in Matt 16:18 of ἐκκλησία, found in the Gospels only here and at Matt 18:17, has often been cited as clear indication either of a later formulation of this passage by the early church,[131] or of a translation of some Hebrew or Aramaic word originally used by Jesus.[132] There are several responses that might be made to these assertions. The first is the recognition that there are several conceptually parallel phrases in the Gospels, indicating that even though the word ἐκκλησία may not occur elsewhere similar concepts are present.[133] The second response is that the objection to Jesus using the word ἐκκλησία seems to neglect several important linguistic factors. The use of the word ἐκκλησία is quite frequent in the earliest documents of the New Testament, namely Paul's letters, as well as Acts. It is plausible that use of ἐκκλησία was adopted because of the use of this word by Jesus himself here in Matt 16:18 and 18:17, the use of a common Greek word to refer to a group of people gathered for a purpose. In 16:18 the word seems to denote an idealized assembly or gathering of Jesus' followers (i.e. the universal church), whereas in 18:17 a specific body of followers seems to be indicated, perhaps as an instantiation of the idealized group. Both uses are found in pre-New Testament Greek literature. Whereas in Herodotus ἐκκλησία is used simply of a meeting or gathering of people, during the Attic period it could be used of the authoritative Athenian political body (see Plato, *Gorg*. 452E, 456B; Thucydides 2.22.1; and numerous inscriptions), or it could refer to other assemblies gathered for various purposes (see Euripides, *Rhes*. 139; Xenophon, *Anab*. 1.3.2). The more general meaning seems to have been constricted through a process of lexical conservatism to refer to early Christian gatherings and then was applied to the

130 Besides Porter, *Verbal Aspect*, 251–60, see J.P. Louw, "Die Semantiese Waarde van die Perfektum in Hellenistiese Grieks," *Acta Classica* 10 (1967) 23–32.

131 See Gundry, *Matthew*, 335; Robinson, "Peter and his Successors," esp. 90–91.

132 See K.L. Schmidt, ἐκκλησία, *TDNT*, 3.524–25.

133 See Schmidt, ἐκκλησία, *TDNT*, 3.520.

whole church, although the general usage also persisted (e.g. Acts 19:39).[134] Thus, assuming that Jesus spoke Greek, as seems clearly to be the case as has been shown above, there is no linguistic restriction on his using the term ἐκκλησία here to specify his gathered followers. In fact, since this vocabulary is not a part of Matthew's redactional tendency, or any of the Gospels' for that matter, it appears possible if not likely that these words go back to Jesus himself.

Other issues could be mentioned in this passage in support of the hypothesis that Jesus delivered these words in Greek. Those who might argue that the use of οὐρανός in the plural is a distinctively Semitic phenomenon must take note first that the plural is used in a number of extra-biblical Greek authors, including Aristotle, and secondly that Matthew himself uses both the singular and the plural (Matt 5:34–35, 6:10, 19–20, as well as 18:18, use the singular), making it difficult to establish clear patterns of usage that point to an Aramaic substratum.[135] There is also the use of the phrasing regarding Hades. Although there are numerous parallels to this phrasing in Old Testament literature (e.g. Job 17:16; 38:17; Pss 9:13; 107–118; Isa 38:10) and noncanonical literature (Wis 16:13; *3 Macc* 5:51; *Pss. Sol.* 16:2), there are also of course numerous parallels in secular Greek literature, since the depiction of Hades is a traditional classical image (e.g. Homer, *Il.* 9.312; *Od.* 11.277; Aeschylus, *Ag.* 1291; Euripides, *Hec.* 1).[136] And lastly, regarding the concepts of binding and loosing, whereas there are several proposals that rely on Semitic thought (not necessarily excluded even if Jesus delivered the words in Greek!), the most likely proposal relies upon a literary parallel from Josephus (*War* 1.5.2 §111), where he refers to the Pharisees as ingratiating themselves to the empress Alexandra so that they might "loose and bind" (λύειν τε καὶ δεσμεῖν). In all, this evidence seems to point to Matthew recording a tradition that is related to Mark and Luke but independent of theirs and formulated early in Greek. The tenor of the discussion in Matthew's Gospel, in which Peter is depicted independently of Mark's account as the representative disciple,[137] and in which Peter's confession is

---

134 See A. Hilhorst, "Termes chrétiens issus du vocabulaire de la démocratie athénienne," *FN* 1.1 (1988) 29; J.Y. Campbell, "The Origin and Meaning of the Christian Use of the Word ΕΚΚΛΗΣΙΑ," *JTS* 49 (1948) 130–42; M. Silva, *Biblical Words and their Meaning: An Introduction to Lexical Semantics* (2nd edn; Grand Rapids: Zondervan, 1994 [1983]) 26, 79.

135 W.G. Thompson (*Matthew's Advice to a Divided Community: Mt. 17,22–18,35* [AnBib 44; Rome: Pontifical Biblical Institute, 1970] 189) notes that the compound phrase "heaven and earth" (e.g. Matt 5:18; 11:25; 24:35; 28:18) signifies a totality. The words are probably used in terms of spheres of existence.

136 D.A. Carson, "Matthew," in *The Expositor's Bible Commentary* (11 vols.; ed. F.E. Gaebelein; Grand Rapids: Zondervan, 1984) 8.370.

137 J.D. Kingsbury, "The Figure of Peter in Matthew's Gospel as a Theological Problem," *JBL* 98 (1979) esp. 72–73.

followed by Peter's rebuke, points towards Jesus having delivered these words in Greek very similar to that found here in the canonical text.

6. *Conclusion*

In conclusion, it seems to me that the evidence regarding what is known about the use of Greek in ancient Palestine, including the cosmopolitan Hellenistic character of lower Galilee, the epigraphic and literary evidence, including coins, papyri, literary writers, inscriptions and funerary texts, but most of all several significant contexts in the Gospels, all points in one direction: whereas it is not always known how much and on which occasions Jesus spoke Greek, it is virtually certain that he used Greek at various times in his itinerant ministry. It is probable that we have his actual words in Mark 15:2 and parallels, and may well have a passage of his teaching originally delivered in Greek recorded in Matt 16:17–19. This says nothing about the overall linguistic competence of Jesus, nor do we know the frequency with which he used the languages at his disposal. But this conclusion at least opens up the possibility of further exploration of this topic, since it must be recognized that this conclusion has a solid foundation and cannot be ruled out on the basis of presupposition alone.

CHAPTER NINE

THUCYDIDES 1.22.1 AND SPEECHES IN ACTS: IS THERE A THUCYDIDEAN VIEW?*

1. *Introduction*

Over the last approximately eighty-five years, there have been two major positions regarding the speeches in Acts.[1] The first position, perhaps best summarized by its most well-known proponent, F.F. Bruce, is that "Taken all in all, each speech suits the speaker, the audience, and the circumstances of delivery," and thus "gives good ground, in my judgment, for believing these speeches to be, not inventions of the historian, but condensed accounts of speeches actually made, and therefore valuable and independent sources for the history and theology of the primitive Church." This is the conclusion Bruce arrived at in his 1942 monograph, reasserted several times since, including most recently in 1985.[2] He was anticipated by several significant scholars and has been widely followed. What is interesting to note, however, is his assumption in all of his works on the subject that there is such a thing as a "Thucydidean view" of speeches followed by ancient historians. In his 1942 lecture he accepts

* This essay is reprinted with the permission of E.J. Brill Publishers, from *Novum Testamentum* 32 (1990) 121–42. Slight changes have been made to the footnotes.

1 For a history of research into the book of Acts, including the issue of the speeches, see W.W. Gasque, *A History of the Criticism of the Acts of the Apostles* (BGBE 17; Tübingen: Mohr–Siebeck; Grand Rapids: Eerdmans, 1975); F.F. Bruce, "The Acts of the Apostles: Historical Record or Theological Reflection?" *ANRW* II.25.2 (Berlin: de Gruyter, 1985) 2569–2603; and C.K. Barrett, *Luke the Historian in Recent Study* (London: Epworth Press, 1961) esp. 21–41. I do not attempt to cite all of the relevant literature, but single out works by significant figures, especially those who refer to Thucydides 1.22.1.

2 F.F. Bruce, *The Speeches in the Acts of the Apostles* (London: Tyndale, 1942) 27; "The Speeches in Acts—Thirty Years After," in *Reconciliation and Hope: New Testament Essays on Atonement and Eschatology* (Festschrift L.L. Morris; ed. R. Banks; Grand Rapids: Eerdmans, 1974) 53–68; "Acts," 2582–88. This position is also reflected in his commentaries, most particularly on the Greek text: *The Acts of the Apostles: The Greek Text with Introduction and Commentary* (2nd edn; London: Tyndale, 1952 [3rd edn; Grand Rapids: Eerdmans, 1990]) 18–21.

what he believes is the clear interpretation of Thucydides as reflected in Crawley's translation.[3] In his 1951 commentary he says

> It is well known that the speeches which classical historians put into the mouths of their characters were admittedly not intended to be a verbatim account of what was actually said. The fashion in this respect was set by Thucydides... The speeches of Thucydides are thus not merely rhetorical exercises, but may be regarded as giving a general impression of the sort of thing said on certain occasions.[4]

In his 1974 article, he asks, "If one valid perspective on Acts is to view it as a historical work in the tradition of Thucydides, the question immediately arises: Are the speeches Thucydidean? The answer, I think, must be Yes. But it is good to remind ourselves what 'Thucydidean' speeches really are." Then he cites Jowett's translation and says "This last clause is the expression of Thucydides's historical conscience. Close attention has been paid to the probable meaning of his phrase 'the general purport of what was actually said'; it seems clear, however, that while he disclaims anything in the nature of precise verbatim reproduction, he does claim to express the sense and intention of the speaker's words on each occasion."[5] In his last assessment, he is again brief, referring to a Thucydidean view in which it is not a verbatim reproduction but suited to "the speaker, the audience and the occasion."[6] Bruce has commanded quite a following, which he claims reflects the sentiments of a number of classicists whose opinions he knows on this issue.[7]

---

3 Bruce, *Speeches*, 6, citing R. Crawley (*The History of the Peloponnesian War* [London: Longman, Green, 1874] 41): "With reference to the speeches in this history, some were delivered before the war began, others while it was going on; some I heard myself, others I got from various quarters; it was in all cases difficult to carry them word for word in one's memory, so my habit has been to make the speakers say what was in my opinion demanded of them by the various occasions, of course adhering as closely as possible to the general sense of what they really said."

4 Bruce, *Acts*, 18, apparently citing his own translation of Thucydides 1.22.1: "As for the speeches made by various persons either on the eve of the war or during its actual course, it was difficult for me to remember exactly the words which I myself heard, as also for those who reported other speeches to me. But I have recorded them in accordance with my opinion of what the various speakers would have had to say in view of the circumstances at the time, keeping as closely as possible to the general gist of what was really said."

5 Bruce, "Speeches," 54. The following is B. Jowett's translation (*Thucydides* [2 vols.; Oxford: Clarendon Press, 1900] 1.16): "As to the speeches which were made either before or during the war, it was hard for me, and for others who reported them to me, to recollect the exact words. I have therefore put into the mouth of each speaker the sentiments proper to the occasion, expressed as I thought he would be likely to express them, while at the same time I endeavoured, as nearly as I could, to give the general purport of what was actually said."

6 Bruce, "Acts," 2582.

7 Other representatives of this position include T.E. Page, *The Acts of the Apostles*

The second position holds that "The safest way is to regard as Luke's work the speeches in Acts: since, for reasons concerning the history of tradition, they can hardly have been handed down and, considered from the literary angle, they have their parallels in the historians and, as regards content, they often enough express a later standpoint."[8] This position is perhaps best represented by Martin Dibelius, especially in his essay, "Die Reden der Apostelgeschichte und die antike Geschichtsschreibung."[9] In this essay, Dibelius discusses Thucydides 1.22.1, where, after recognizing the possible difficulties with how it should be interpreted, he argues that ξύμπασα γνώμη refers not to the general content of

(London: Macmillan, 1886) xxxvi, citing Thucydides: "And as regards speeches, it was hard to record the exact words spoken, both in cases where I was myself present, and where I used the reports of others. But I have used language in accordance with what I thought the speakers in each case would have been most likely to say...adhering as closely as possible to the general sense of what was actually spoken"; T.F. Glasson, "The Speeches in Acts and Thucydides," *ExpTim* 76 (1964–65) 165, apparently following Page's translation; A.W. Mosley, "Historical Reporting in the Ancient World," *NTS* 12 (1965–66) esp. 12–14; W.W. Gasque, "The Speeches of Acts: Dibelius Reconsidered," in *New Directions in New Testament Study* (ed. R.N. Longenecker and M.C. Tenney; Grand Rapids: Zondervan, 1974) 232–50; *idem*, *History*, esp. chs. 9 and 10 *passim*; *idem*, "The Book of Acts and History," in *Unity and Diversity in New Testament Theology* (Festschrift G.E. Ladd; ed. R.A. Guelich; Grand Rapids: Eerdmans, 1978) 54–72; C.J. Hemer, "Luke the Historian," *BJRL* 60 (1977) esp. 29–34; *idem*, *The Book of Acts in the Setting of Hellenistic History* (ed. C.H. Gempf; WUNT 49; Tübingen: Mohr–Siebeck, 1989) esp. ch. 3; I.H. Marshall, *The Acts of the Apostles* (TNTC; Grand Rapids: Eerdmans, 1980) 39–42; and now C. Gempf, "Public Speaking and Published Accounts," in *The Book of Acts in its First Century Setting*. I. *The Book of Acts in its Ancient Literary Setting* (ed. B.W. Winter and A.D. Clarke; Grand Rapids: Eerdmans, 1993) 266–70.

8 M. Dibelius, "Style Criticism of the Book of Acts," in *Studies in the Acts of the Apostles* (ed. H. Greeven; London: SCM Press, 1956) 3 = "Stilistisches zur Apostelgeschichte [1923]," in *Aufsätze zur Apostelgeschichte* (FRLANT, NF 42; 5th edn; Göttingen: Vandenhoeck & Ruprecht, 1968) 10.

9 M. Dibelius, "The Speeches in Acts and Ancient Historiography," in *Studies*, 138–85 esp. 183: "Thus by comparing the speeches in Acts with those of the historians we observe an important ambiguity. Luke indeed uses the historical technique and does set himself certain historical aims; this becomes clear enough when we give up trying to measure him by our ideas of historiography and historians. In the last analysis, however, he is not an historian but a preacher; we must not allow our attempts to prove the authenticity of the speeches to cloud our perception of their kerygmatic nature" = "Die Reden der Apostelgeschichte und die antike Geschichtsschreibung," in *Aufsätze*, 120–58 esp. 157. Other important essays in *Studies* are "Paul on the Areopagus" (pp. 26–77), "The Acts of the Apostles as an Historical Source" (pp. 102–108), "The Acts of the Apostles in the Setting of the History of Early Christian Literature" (pp. 192–206). Whereas Gasque criticizes Dibelius in his assessment of Acts, A.D. Nock ("The Book of Acts," in *Essays on Religion and the Ancient World* [2 vols.; ed. Z. Stewart; Cambridge, MA: Harvard University Press, 1972] esp. 2.822) in his 1953 review gives Dibelius high marks.

authentic speeches but to the reconstructed intention of a speech in its context.[10] Dibelius uses Thucydides as only one part of his reconstruction of ancient historiography regarding the speeches in Acts. Whereas Dibelius might legitimately be criticized for being overly pessimistic in the viewpoint he adopts, at least he does attempt to come to grips with the difficulties in understanding Thucydides with regard to speeches. Dibelius has also been followed by a number of other scholars.[11]

Recently a third position has been argued for. In one form it argues that the book of Acts is not meant to be seen as a historical document, but primarily as an example of the ancient novel.[12] R.I. Pervo is correct in pointing out the entertainment value of historical literature in the ancient world,[13] but as Aune indicates, in the eyes of the ancients this did not necessarily put it at odds with a serious historical purpose as well, including the kinds of episodes and events included in Acts.[14]

---

10 Dibelius, "Speeches," 141–42 = "Die Reden," 122.

11 Other representatives of this position include H.J. Cadbury *et al.*, "The Greek and Jewish Traditions of Writing History," in *The Beginnings of Christianity*, Part I: *The Acts of the Apostles*. II. Prolegomena II, Criticism (ed. F.J. Foakes Jackson and K. Lake; London: Macmillan, 1922) 7–29; Cadbury, "The Speeches in Acts", in *The Beginnings of Christianity*, Part I: *The Acts of the Apostles*. V. Additional Notes to the Commentary (ed. F.J. Foakes Jackson and K. Lake; London: Macmillan, 1933) 402–27; B. Gärtner, *The Areopagus Speech and Natural Revelation* (ASNU 21; Uppsala: Gleerup, 1955) 7–36 esp. 13–14, where he cites a translation of Thucydides 1.22.1: "As to the speeches that were made by different men, either when they were about to begin the war or when they were already engaged therein, it has been difficult to recall with strict accuracy the words actually spoken, both for me as regards that which I myself heard, and for those who from various other sources have brought me reports. Therefore the speeches are given in the language in which, as it seemed to me, the several speakers would express, on the subjects under consideration, the sentiments most befitting the occasion, though at the same time I have adhered as closely as possible to the general sense of what was actually said," but claims that Thucydides did not always adhere to his own principles, and neither certainly did Luke; E. Schweizer, "Concerning the Speeches in Acts," and H. Conzelmann, "The Address of Paul on the Areopagus," in *Studies in Luke–Acts* (ed. L.E. Keck and J.L. Martyn; Philadelphia: Fortress Press, 1980) 208–16, 217–30 respectively (cf. H. Conzelmann, *Die Apostelgeschichte* [HNT 7; 2nd edn; Tübingen: Mohr–Siebeck, 1972] 9–10); U. Wilckens, *Die Missionsreden der Apostelgeschichte: Form- und Traditionsgeschichtliche Untersuchungen* (WMANT; Neukirchen: Neukirchener Verlag, 1961) 7–31 esp. 13–16; E. Haenchen, *The Acts of the Apostles* (Philadelphia: Westminster Press, 1971 [1965]) 90–112; and G. Schneider, *Die Apostelgeschichte*, I (HTKNT; Freiburg: Herder, 1980) esp. 97.

12 R.I. Pervo, *Profit with Delight: The Literary Genre of the Acts of the Apostles* (Philadelphia: Fortress Press, 1987).

13 See, for example, B.L. Ullman, "History and Tragedy," *TAPA* 73 (1942) 250–53; F.W. Walbank, "History and Tragedy," *Historia* 9 (1960) 216–34.

14 D.E. Aune, *The New Testament in its Literary Environment* (Philadelphia: Westminster Press, 1987) 80; cf. also S.E. Porter, "The 'We' Passages," in *The Book of Acts*

In conjunction with this view, it has recently been argued that Luke–Acts, not a history in the classical mode but not unconcerned with historical material, is best described as representative of *Fachprosa*, to use L. Rydbeck's term, and this conclusion has been asserted after analysis of the prefaces.[15] This position has been argued most fully to date by L.C.A. Alexander.[16] It is not appropriate to enter into a full analysis of this position, since it is not central to the argument of this chapter, but several criticisms of this position are warranted in light of its tangential importance. First, there is the status of the *Fachprosa* itself. The most extensive analysis of *Fachprosa* has concerned itself with syntactic or linguistic (narrowly defined) factors, and has neglected such considerations as art, style, situation, and subject matter.[17] Alexander must admit that although the prefaces in Luke–Acts share many characteristics with the prefaces of scientific prose (e.g. address in second person), there are also several differences, for example, some scientific prefaces are much longer than Luke's (one of Archimedes's letters has an eight page preface; some scientific works have no preface),[18] suggesting that a continuum rather than a simple opposition between literary and scientific prose is necessary. But there are also significant Lukan similarities with literary prose (e.g. periodic style).

Secondly, in describing the author's intention Alexander seems further to confuse several issues. In her effort to distance Luke from literary writing, she states that she approaches Luke's style as a matter of "unconscious" or "fairly instinctive" choice.[19] But then she refers to "Luke's choice of style" as drawing

in its First Century Setting. II. *The Book of Acts in its Graeco-Roman Setting* (ed. D.J.W. Gill and C. Gempf; Grand Rapids: Eerdmans, 1993) 548–54.

15 H.J. Cadbury, "Commentary on the Preface of Luke," in *Beginnings of Christianity*, I.2.489–510; cf. *idem*, "The Knowledge Claimed in Luke's Preface," *Expositor*, Eighth Series, 24 (1922) 401–20; *idem*, "'We' and 'I' Passages in Luke–Acts," *NTS* 3 (1956–57) 128–32. Cadbury was the major proponent of the view that the prefaces of Luke–Acts conformed to established Hellenistic historiographic conventions. See also L. Rydbeck, *Fachprosa, vermeintliche Volkssprache und Neues Testament: Zur Beurteilung der sprachlichen Niveauunterschiede im nachklassischen Griechisch* (Uppsala: University of Uppsala; Stockholm: Almqvist & Wiksell, 1967).

16 L.C.A. Alexander, "Luke's Preface in the Context of Greek Preface-Writing," *NovT* 28 (1986) 48–74; *The Preface to Luke's Gospel: Literary Convention and Social Context in Luke 1.1–4 and Acts 1.1* (SNTSMS 78; Cambridge: Cambridge University Press, 1993).

17 E. Pax, "Probleme des neutestamentlichen Griechisch," *Bib* 53 (1972) 560–62, who questions the very concept of *Fachprosa*; cf. H. Kurzová, "Das Griechische im Zeitalter des Hellenismus," in *Soziale Probleme im Hellenismus und im römischen Reich* (ed. P. Oliva and J. Burian; Prague: n.p., 1973) 218–24, who disputes Rydbeck's denial that through the popular documents one can know the *Vulgärsprache* spoken during the Hellenistic period.

18 Alexander, *Preface to Luke's Gospel*, 102–106; "Preface," 59–60.

19 Alexander, "Preface," 65. The above quotation is from D. Crystal, *Linguistics* (Harmondsworth: Penguin, 1971) 29, who, however, refers to scientific writers as consciously following rules to get their articles accepted, with reference to "unconscious

on the "only style he knows which is at all appropriate to the occasion."[20] It is true that one cannot be sure of Luke's full range of literary styles, but as Alexander admits, at least two are evidenced in the Gospel alone. Alexander has apparently confused the issue of dialect with register.[21] Dialect refers to the language system one knows, one's code or competence, while register refers to the specific use on the basis of need and context, one's text or performance. She is trying unnaturally to limit Luke's registers by equating them with a particular dialect. But she acknowledges that Luke had enough competence to know that one shifts registers when changing from the personal address of the preface to the body of a literary writing.

A third and final difficulty is related to content. Alexander must admit that the content of descriptive scientific prose is quite different from Luke's narrative biography, and her appeal to the Gospel as a functional school text recording the distilled teaching of a tradition is forced; in fact, she admits that the body of Luke–Acts is not written in the style of the scientific treatise and that it is difficult to see it as anything other than a historical work.[22] This leads Gempf to propose the following corrective to Alexander:

> Perhaps that adoption [by Luke] of form and vocabulary had nothing to do with the scientific tradition, but merely to the sociological group, level of training etc. In other words, it is possible that at least some of the features that Alexander notes in the works of Luke and the scientific writers concern their social standing *and not specifically* their vocation... What seems likely is not that Luke was writing in the scientific tradition, but that he was simply not as skilled as some authors.[23] Both his work and that of some of the scientists survived despite their formal short-comings because of the value of their content to the community. Inferior works by historians stood less chance of survival. The scientists are thus of interest primarily as possible socio-economic peers of Luke, rather than as his fellow tradesmen. In this way, his choice of the word διήγησις and use of the narrative style remain understandable.[24]

Much more work needs to be done on the issue of the relationship of Luke–Acts to the historians and scientific writers of the Hellenistic period. Although the issue of dialect and register has been raised above, there is still much more

awareness of 'how scientific writers write.'"

20 Alexander, "Preface," 65.

21 See M. Gregory and S. Carroll, *Language and Situation: Language Varieties and their Social Contexts* (Language and Society; London: Routledge and Kegan Paul, 1978) esp. 75–85. But see Alexander, *Preface to Luke's Gospel*, 173–74.

22 Alexander, "Preface," 69; cf. *Preface to Luke's Gospel*, 168–86.

23 Gempf does not delimit the authors for comparison, but considering the texts of the New Testament Gempf's point is easier *prima facie* to demonstrate with almost any other New Testament author than with Luke.

24 C.H. Gempf, *Historical and Literary Appropriateness in the Mission Speeches in Acts* (Ph.D. thesis, University of Aberdeen, 1988) ch. 1 sec. D.5.

work that needs to be done on matters of sociolinguistics and the Greek of the Hellenistic period, including that of the New Testament. In the light of the uncertainty of the findings thus far, it is still legitimate to investigate the programmatic statement of Thucydides as a necessary preface to discussing the speeches in Acts, especially if, as has recently been argued, Thucydides's language lies behind the *Volkssprache*.[25]

2. *Analysis of Thucydides 1.22.1*

Having determined that Luke–Acts must be evaluated as historical literature, however, does not decide what standards of historiography are at play in the work, and what models were employed by the ancient authors. As seen above, there is the assumption among a number of New Testament scholars that there is a so-called Thucydidean view of speech-writing among ancient historiographers. It must not be supposed that this view is unique to New Testament scholars. Classicists too have assumed that there is a so-called Thucydidean view. C.W. Fornara, for example, asserts that "Thucydides' methodological rule proved authoritative."[26] And D. Kagan cites several examples of scholars who assume that there is a Thucydidean view.[27] But the statement by Thucydides is highly and persistently problematic. In this chapter, I wish to analyse several varied interpretations of Thucydides's statement about speech-writing, to illustrate that there can be no unchallenged Thucydidean view and that any view of the speeches in Acts which assumes such a position does fatal harm to its argument. This chapter does not set out to decide the issue of the speeches in Acts, but to go behind such discussion to clear the ground for further work in this area.

Fornara contends that the meaning of Thucydides 1.22.1 is straightforward, but that the major problem is whether Thucydides and subsequent historians

25 A. López Eire, "Del ático a la koiné," *Emerita* 49 (1981) 379, 387–88. It is worth noting that D. Earl ("Prologue-Form in Ancient Historiography," *ANRW* I.2 [Berlin: de Gruyter, 1972] 842–43) cites only the first sentence of Thucydides's history as the prologue (contra Alexander, *Preface to Luke's Gospel*, 30, who opts for the first fourteen pages), noting that what took Thucydides only a sentence to do took later historians much longer. This might constitute a further point of correlation between the prefaces of Luke and Acts and ancient historiography.

26 C.W. Fornara, *The Nature of History in Ancient Greece and Rome* (Berkeley: University of California Press, 1983) 145.

27 D. Kagan, "The Speeches in Thucydides and the Mytilene Debate," *Yale Classical Studies* 24 (1975) 71–72. See more recently M. Cogan, *The Human Thing: The Speeches and Principles of Thucydides' History* (Chicago: University of Chicago Press, 1981) esp. x–xiii; and the older but still standard J.B. Bury, *The Ancient Greek Historians* (London: Macmillan, 1909; repr. New York: Dover, 1958) 81–82, 99–100, 109.

were faithful to the programme established. An examination of this crucial passage from Thucydides, however, reveals that it is anything but straightforward. At least the following problematic areas in Thucydides's statement regarding speeches merit renewed attention: (a) χαλεπόν; (b) τὴν ἀκρίβειαν αὐτὴν τῶν λεχθέντων; (c) ὡς ἂν ἐδόκουν μοι...εἰπεῖν; (d) τὰ δέοντα; (e) ὅτι ἐγγύτατα; (f) τῆς ξυμπάσης γνώμης; (g) τῶν ἀληθῶς λεχθέντων (cf. Thucydides 1.22.2 for the contrast of word and deed).

A. *Χαλεπόν*

The word χαλεπόν has several potential difficulties, but the major one revolves around the precise sense of the word here relative to the probability of accomplishment. χαλεπόν is usually understood along the lines of "difficult, but within the realm of possibility,"[28] especially as an antonym of ῥᾴδιον, implying that an action undertaken is "easy" as opposed to difficult (cf. Demosthenes 37.47; 41.15). As Plato, *Prot.* 341D says: ὃ ἂν μὴ ῥᾴδιον ᾖ ἀλλὰ διὰ πολλῶν πραγμάτων γίγνηται. For example, Aristotle in his *Rhet.* 1363A27 exploits the opposition of χαλεπόν and ῥᾴδιον. Examples of this usage are abundant and will not be documented further. If this understanding is correct for Thucydides 1.22.1,[29] it implies that the rest of Thucydides's statement is addressed to how he set about accomplishing a grantedly difficult but still possible task (cf. Demosthenes 27.2, with reference to the difficulty of making a defense). This has special bearing on problem c (see below) and the subjective element implied by ὡς ἂν ἐδόκουν μοι...εἰπεῖν. But in some contexts χαλεπόν, though still appropriately translated "difficult," does not imply the difficulty of an accomplishable task, but the difficulty of something which cannot readily be accomplished, perhaps under any circumstances (the sense is close to that of ἀδύνατον). For example, in Xenophon, *Mem.* 2.1.23, two women approach Heracles and promise τῶν...χαλεπὸν ἄπειρος διαβιώσῃ, referring apparently to any insurmountable difficulties being removed from his life. And Demosthenes closes his funeral speech (60.35): ἔστι μὲν οὖν ἴσως χαλεπὸν τὰς παρούσας συμφορὰς λόγῳ κουφίσαι, although it is still necessary to turn to more pleasant thoughts, and for good to be seen (καλὸν...ὁρᾶσθαι) ending affliction (cf. Demosthenes 60.24, where he says that, if the sun were removed, life would be χαλεπός [fourth class conditional]). The implications of this understanding result in a different reading of Thucydides 1.22.1, this one being particularly

28 See P. Huart, *Le vocabulaire de l'analyse psychologique dans l'oeuvre de Thucydide* (Études et commentaires 69; Paris: Klincksieck, 1968) 95–97.

29 In support of this position, A. Andrewes ("The Mytilene Debate: Thucydides 3.36–49," *Phoenix* 16 [1962] 65–66) says that "it is of basic importance that Thucydides should bring the speeches actually delivered into the question at all and suggest that they might be of concern to his readers," although this reveals Andrewes presupposition regarding the words and ends up begging the question.

skeptical of the basis for the speeches in actual events. Instead, emphasis is placed directly on the subjective process involved in arriving at the speeches, since access to first-hand sources cannot be secured through either memory or report.[30] A third option also presents itself. In Xenophon, *Mem.* 2.9.1, Criton complains to Socrates that χαλεπὸν ὁ βίος Ἀθήνησιν εἴη ἀνδρὶ βουλομένῳ τὰ ἑαυτοῦ πράττειν. This could be construed according to the second category above, with Criton lamenting the fact that life in Athens has become so litigious that unaffected life is stringently difficult if not impossible. It is not likely that Criton is referring to difficulties which are surmountable, since his complaint appears to have been made in desperation. But Socrates's response is instructive. He tells Criton that he can in fact avoid being overcome by trouble if he hires someone to act as his representative. Thucydides 2.35.2 says χαλεπὸν γὰρ τὸ μετρίως εἰπεῖν ἐν ᾧ μόλις καὶ ἡ δόκησις τῆς ἀληθείας βεβαιοῦται. Pericles then describes the paradox of the difficulty, but concludes that he must do his best to satisfy his audience's expectations. In these last two instances, the meaning of χαλεπόν appears to have an intermediate sense, that is, what is impossible can be made possible, but only by some intervening action or circumstance. This understanding implies that Thucydides is saying that whereas reconstructing the speeches was virtually impossible, he was able to render a close approximation if he applied a particular method.

B. *Τὴν ἀκρίβειαν αὐτὴν τῶν λεχθέντων*

The second difficulty with Thucydides's statement arises from the phrase τὴν ἀκρίβειαν αὐτὴν τῶν λεχθέντων. Again there is a range of serious options. Most interpreters understand this to mean "the exact words,"[31] taking the participle to refer to the specific individual utterances themselves. This sense is widely evidenced in the use of λέγω, where a speaker is called upon to produce exact words since he himself is the originator of the words (e.g. Thucydides 2.48.2; 5.86; Plato, *Pol.* 268E; *Phlb.* 12B). But Thucydides, in the light of the possibility that he found it overwhelmingly difficult to remember what he needed in order to produce the exact words, may mean something slightly different by using the participle. He may be referring to the accuracy of the statements taken as a whole (plenary sense). This sense also is widely attested for λέγω, especially in contexts of discussion where one speaker is called upon to address comments to an issue (e.g. Plato, *Crat.* 404A; *Apol.* 30B, 24E; *Gorg.*

30 See, for example, D. Rokeah, "Τὰ δέοντα περὶ τῶν αἰεὶ παρόντων: Speeches in Thucydides: Factual Reporting or Creative Writing?" *Athenaeum* 60 (1988) 386, who suggests "difficult or in fact impossible" as the understanding of χαλεπόν.

31 K.J. Dover, *Thucydides* (*Greece & Rome*, New Surveys in the Classics 7; Oxford: Clarendon Press, 1973) 21. Cf. also J.H. Finley, Jr., *Thucydides* (Cambridge, MA: Harvard University Press, 1942; repr. Ann Arbor: University of Michigan Press, 1963) 95; Huart, *Vocabulaire*, 222 esp. n. 2.

447B; *Prot.* 310B; cf. Xenophon, *Mem.* 3.3.4; 3.6.8), where the intention of the comment or its general sense rather than exact words is at issue (e.g. Plato, *Apol.* 24E; *Gorg.* 480B; *Phaedr.* 265C; *Theaet.* 181C), or where second-hand information is being reported or recounted, that is, as some say (Xenophon, *Mem.* 1.2.30; esp. Homer, *Il.* 2.435; 13.275; *Od.* 12.165; 14.197; 23.308). There is even the slight possibility that use of the passive participle of λέγω is to be interpreted as referring to a process of counting or reckoning regarding the exactness of Thucydides's investigation (e.g. Homer, *Il.* 3.188). This second set of renderings of the participle casts a different slant upon Thucydides's programmatic statement. Instead of Thucydides lamenting that the accuracy of the statements delivered cannot be recovered, implying that the accuracy of more general accounts may still be possible, these renderings mean that Thucydides is lamenting that the preciseness cannot be recovered of even the general meaning or intention of the original words, implying that what he does recount is that much further from any actual speech.[32] Each of these positions is particularly crucial to understanding the sixth difficulty (f) with reference to ἡ γνώμη, as well as the seventh difficulty (g), the meaning of the phrase τῶν ἀληθῶς λεχθέντων.

The discussion above has not yet taken into account the meaning of ἀκρίβειαν and its implications for precision or exactness. Is it possible that exactness with respect to memory of words can be spoken of in the same way as exactness with respect to reporting accomplished acts (e.g. Antiphon 4.3.1: τὴν ἀκρίβειαν τῶν πραχθέντων, where the discussion is regarding determination of a man's behaviour; cf. Thucydides 1.22.2: τὰ...ἔργα τῶν πραχθέντων)? Thucydides himself introduces this contrast in 1.22.2, where he refers to ὅσον δυνατὸν ἀκριβείᾳ περὶ ἑκάστου ἐπεξελθών.[33] A.W. Gomme treats the phrases in Thucydides 1.22.1 and 1.22.2 as instructive parallels on the basis of the similar language, where, although he recognizes a difference in Thucydides's method, with 1.22.1 appearing skeptical and 1.22.2 more optimistic regarding "accuracy," he states that the "difference is not an exact contrary."[34] Even though there are verbal parallels here, Connor is less optimistic about Thucydides's accuracy regarding speeches, contending that "Thucydides has used different methods for reconstructing speeches and events. The second has a smaller degree of guesswork. In reconstructing the speeches it would not pay

---

32 It has been suggested that one interpretation of Thucydides's statement is that he combined two or three speeches into what he presents as one speech (A. Grosskinsky, *Das Programm des Thukydides* [Neue Deutsche Forschungen, Abt. Klass. Philologie; Berlin, 1936] 38–41), although that would be difficult to prove from the wording itself (see Finley, *Thucydides*, 95, from whom Grosskinsky is cited).

33 A.W. Gomme, *A Historical Commentary on Thucydides* (vol. 1; Oxford: Clarendon Press, 1959) 142–43, where he discusses understanding of the participle ἐπεξελθών.

34 Gomme, *Historical Commentary*, 140.

him to cross-examine witnesses about the detailed arguments and exact wording. But for a battle or the like Thucydides could check each informant's report point by point..."[35] It appears that "accuracy" must be determined by the nature of the action spoken about, with accuracy not being an absolute but a relative term (cf. Thucydides 7.87.4: ἀκριβείᾳ...χαλεπὸν ἐξειπεῖν, where he then posits a numerical figure regarding prisoners).

C. *Ὡς ἂν ἐδόκουν μοι...εἰπεῖν*

The third difficulty is introduced by the clause ὡς ἂν ἐδόκουν μοι...εἰπεῖν. Thucydides 1.22.2 has a similar phrase, οὐδ' ὡς ἐμοὶ ἐδόκει, which introduces a necessary comparison with the phrase in 1.22.1. Gomme, on the basis of what he sees as Thucydides's parallel method for treating speeches and actions (see above), argues that these two phrases cannot be fully contrastive, that is, Thucydides does not mean in the second that "I did not write the account of a battle as I imagine it ought to have taken place" but in the first that "I did compose the speeches as I imagined they ought to have been spoken."[36] The single most important fact about these words, however, is that they introduce an acknowledgment by Thucydides himself of a subjective element in his method, or as Kagan says regarding the phrase in 1.22.1, it "plainly calls for some imagination and special perception on the part of Thucydides."[37] Even Gomme admits that there is substance to the argument that the speeches are fabrications by Thucydides on the basis of this phrase,[38] but rather than dispute this interpretation of it, he solves it by appealing to other statements in 1.22.1.[39] Kagan supports the conservative estimation by stating the following:

> The clause ὡς δ' ἂν ἐδόκουν ἐμοὶ ἕκαστοι περὶ τῶν αἰεὶ παρόντων τὰ δέοντα μάλιστ' εἰπεῖν presents little difficulty for the view that Thucydides tries to report actual speeches accurately. The subjective and imaginative faculties come into play in two ways. Without recording devices or shorthand stenographers memory alone

35 W.R. Connor, *Thucydides* (Princeton: Princeton University Press, 1984) 27–28 n. 22. Cf. A.M. Parry, *Logos and Ergon in Thucydides* (New York: Arno, 1981) 103, however, who argues that the "implication [of Thucydides 1.22.2 regarding the accounts of the actions] is that whatever is known about an event is largely a creation of language."

36 Gomme, *Historical Commentary*, 140. His translation with "ought" is problematic.

37 Kagan, "Speeches," 73. Cf. also Huart, *Vocabulaire*, 252–53, citing Thucydides 1.3.2; 1.9.1–2.

38 A.W. Gomme, "The Speeches in Thucydides," in *Essays in Greek History and Literature* (Oxford: Blackwell, 1937) 159, in responding to E. Schwartz's review of Taeger's *Thukydides*, in *Gnomon* 2 (1926) 65–82 esp. 79–80. Cf. E. Schwartz, *Das Geschichtswerk des Thukydides* (3rd edn, 1929; repr. Hildesheim: Olms, 1960) esp. 25–26, for a summary of his position, which is skeptical about authenticity of the speeches.

39 Rokeah ("Τὰ δέοντα," 387) is correct that Gomme "has no answer" for this interpretation as formulated by Schwartz.

could not hope to achieve an accurate record, and Thucydides acknowledges the need to reconstruct rather than record. Thus the statement may be taken to refer to the form rather than the content of the speeches. It is also likely that Thucydides received reports of some speeches that were less complete than others. He may have been told of the general line of argument and given a few quotations and details and supplied the rest of the speech from what seemed to him τὰ δέοντα. That, however, is as far as his words permit us to go.[40]

Kagan's analysis begs several questions, however, and it appears that a strong case regarding ὡς ἂν ἐδόκουν μοι...εἰπεῖν and γράφειν οὐδ' ὡς ἐμοὶ ἐδόκει can in fact be made for the contrastive usage which Gomme disputes: "the speeches are given as I thought, the events are not, but by a strict canon of accuracy."[41] First, quite clearly the first phrase is not negated while the second is. Secondly, there appears to be a conscious contrast between use of the imperfect and infinitive with ἂν and the imperfect and infinitive without ἂν in the light of the two similar phrases appearing in close proximity. And third is appreciation of use of ἂν as the conditional particle. If as is generally conceded there is even a slight difference between Thucydides's method for recounting speeches and actions, as even Gomme acknowledges, the non-negated subjectively-oriented construction with the particle ἂν would be entirely consistent with a subjective interpretation (on possible implications of the meaning of εἰπεῖν, see above on λέγω). The conditional particle results in what is in effect an unstated protasis, so that the phrase might be understood as stating: "as they [the speakers] seemed to me as they would have spoken (if they could have been heard)" with the indication that a second class or an unreal (contra-factual) conditional is implied with the infinitive.[42] There are several other occasions where Thucydides refers to a subjective element in his interpretation of actions, using the non-negated phrase: e.g. 7.87.5; 8.64.5. The second potential problem with this phrase is that it seems to run contrary to the next major clause (see difficulties e, f and g below).

40 Kagan, "Speeches," 74–75. Cf. Andrewes, "Mytilene Debate," 66.

41 Gomme, "Speeches," 159.

42 See W.W. Goodwin, *Syntax of the Moods and Tenses of the Greek Verb* (1889; repr. London: Macmillan, 1966) §§192, 243–44, 778; H.W. Smyth, *Greek Grammar* (rev. G.M. Messing; Cambridge, MA: Harvard University Press, 1956) §§1786–89. This interpretation takes ἂν with the infinitive (cf. Thucydides 4.80.3; see Goodwin, §220), although taking it with the finite verb is also possible (cf. Thucydides 2.48.3; 6.2.4; is this Gomme's understanding, *Historical Commentary*, 140?), and would make this point just as forcefully, with ἂν with the imperfect also equivalent to a second class or an unreal (contra-factual) conditional: "if I had been able (but was not)..." On conditional statements, including the second class conditional, see S.E. Porter, *Verbal Aspect in the Greek of the New Testament, with Reference to Tense and Mood* (Studies in Biblical Greek 1; New York: Peter Lang, 1989) 291–320 esp. 304–306.

Further disagreement is to be found in understanding μάλιστα, especially whether it modifies τὰ δέοντα, as R.C. Jebb and later K.J. Dover posit, or whether it modifies εἰπεῖν, as Gomme, followed by, for example, D. Rokeah, believes.[43] The syntax is susceptible to either interpretation. But before the difference can be elucidated, it must be decided how μάλιστα is to be interpreted. Gomme renders it "roughly," Dover "more than anything," and Rokeah "certainly," "precisely," and "especially." Virtually no argumentation is provided for any of these renderings, although the first certainly demands explanation in this context (a survey of Thucydidean usage reveals few convincing examples). But the difference such interpretation makes can readily be seen. If μάλιστα is taken with τὰ δέοντα it could be referring to anything from "what was roughly required" (if this is a possible understanding) to "what was especially or precisely required," quite a significant range of requirement. If μάλιστα is taken with εἰπεῖν, the emphasis is significantly shifted from the degree of precision attached to the required material to the degree of precision attached to the speeches themselves, ranging from "to speak roughly" to "to speak precisely." Whereas μάλιστα may be used with numerals with the sense of "roughly" or "approximately" (see Thucydides 3.29.2; 3.92.6; cf. 1.118; among many), its regular adverbial sense is clearly "certainly" or the like, although its placement between two verbal forms does not clarify its syntactical function.[44] It is even possible that it is serving as an adverb modifying the entire clause, in which case it could be translated "to speak the things that are required, as certainly as possible," perhaps closest to Dover's sense (although cf. Thucydides 2.35.2).

D. *Τὰ δέοντα*

The fourth major difficulty revolves around use of the phrase τὰ δέοντα, along with the preceding modifying phrase περὶ τῶν αἰεὶ παρόντων, which Kagan relies upon in his support of a conservative position. Dover is possibly correct in rendering the phrase τὰ δέοντα μάλιστα as "what was necessary, more than anything,"[45] but that leaves open the question of necessary for what or for whom. Dover says that Thucydides "cannot mean 'what I, Thucydides, perceive the situation to have required,' because on some occasions two speakers disagree. He must therefore mean the arguments which the speaker needed for

43 See, for example, R.C. Jebb, "The Speeches of Thucydides," in *Hellenica: A Collection of Essays on Greek Poetry, Philosophy, History and Religion* (ed. E. Abbott; London: Longmans, Green, 1898) 252; Dover, *Thucydides*, 22; Gomme, *Historical Commentary*, 140; Rokeah, "Τὰ δέοντα," 390.

44 Instances of μάλιστα modifying either the infinitive or another verbal form in the same clause are widely attested: e.g. Thucydides 2.48.3; 3.38.6; 3.53.1; 4.4.2; 4.12.3; 4.79.2; 5.36.1; 6.15.2; 8.91.3.

45 Dover, *Thucydides*, 22.

the purpose of persuading his hearers, given his (and their) situation, interests, and intentions."[46] Dover might be correct that this phrase could refer to an individual speaker's requirements, but this is not satisfactory in the light of the previous discussion. It has already been noted that there is a tension between Thucydides's method regarding speeches and actions, so it is entirely possible that use of multiple speeches simply further reflects indecision on Thucydides's part regarding what was in fact necessary.

Rokeah has thoroughly studied the phrase. In Thucydides, he says, τὰ δέοντα appears four times elsewhere (1.70.8; 1.138.3; 2.43.1; 2.60.5), whereas τὸ δέον appears twice, meaning the thing needed, necessary or requiring execution (4.17.2; 5.66.3); εἰς δέον once, in the sense of right or proper time (8.94.2); and δέον adverbially once, meaning "needed" or "necessary" (7.15.1).[47] On the basis of its fourfold usage, and the preceding phrase meaning "about the matters which are always current," Rokeah argues that the intended sense is "the things which are required for the benefit of the city" (see Thucydides 1.70.8: τὸ τὰ δέοντα πρᾶξαι). Thus he concludes that the phrase means that "Thucydides' aim was to present material which would further his description of the Peloponnesian War, and because of this he censored those parts of the speeches which were not useful for the understanding of matters on his agenda."[48] This is a possible solution, although there are several mitigating factors to this interpretation. First, interpreting "the necessary things" as a process of limitation rather than inclusion may be questioned, especially in the light of Rokeah's own estimation of the verb to mean that which is "useful."[49] Secondly, Rokeah may put too much emphasis upon the preceding modifying phrase referring to things "always present," when the adverb αἰεί may give the phrase a more specific reference to current affairs (see Herodotus 2.98; Demosthenes 21.223). Thirdly, whereas it is possible that Thucydidean usage of τὰ δέοντα relates to usefulness to the city (several of Rokeah's examples are worth re-examination), it is questionable whether Rokeah has argued sufficiently for the kind of usefulness Thucydides's selective process would demand. For example, Jebb says that the phrase "can mean only 'what the occasion required'—not necessarily what was most suitable to the character of the speaker."[50] The "necessary things" could refer to what was necessary for a variety of contexts, dependent upon how other phrases are understood, especially the following one. Perhaps Thucydides is referring to what was necessary in the light of the narrative development of his history. In other words, if it is granted (although it need not be) that Thucydides was trying to

46 Dover, *Thucydides*, 22.

47 Rokeah, "Τὰ δέοντα," 391.

48 Rokeah, "Τὰ δέοντα," 392.

49 Rokeah, "Τὰ δέοντα," 396.

50 Jebb, "Speeches," 253.

stick with the facts of the events as he knew them, he could be arguing here for speeches to fill in this development with necessary statements reflecting the various factors which he thought would have been relevant at that time. Perhaps Thucydides was trying to fulfil a historical and prophetic function. Finley sees the necessary things neither exclusively reflecting Thucydides's view nor being simply limited to the words of the actual speakers, but fulfilling a rhetorical function in the light of Thucydides's reference to his own setting forth the nature of coming events (1.22.4). τὰ δέοντα are "the instruments of conveying the tendencies of society and human nature on which alone foresight can be based."[51] Perhaps Thucydides is referring solely to his own political or historiographic interests, in which case "what is necessary" might refer to the furtherance of this *Tendenz*, a credit he may be giving to Themistocles regarding his own speeches (1.138.3: κράτιστος...οὗτος αὐτοσχεδιάζειν τὰ δέοντα) and Pericles (2.60.5: γνῶναι...τὰ δέοντα καὶ ἑρμηνεῦσαι ταῦτα; cf. 8.68.1). In the light of the grantedly subjective element in Thucydides's reporting and the syntax at this point, the "necessary things" must refer at least in part to something necessary for Thucydides. Although this does not necessarily lessen the historical character of the speech material he draws upon, it emphasizes at the least the selective process he has undertaken, as he himself admits.

The next several difficulties are found in the next major clause. Before discussing the particular difficulties, it is necessary to look at the possible relationships between the clauses. Many have seen a tension between the previous clause, ὡς...εἰπεῖν and the following one, ἐχομένῳ...λεχθέντων, since the first one seems clearly to imply a subjective element and the second has been construed as implying "accurate reporting."[52] As Finley says, "For [Thucydides] goes on to say that, though he has kept as close as possible to the general import of what was said (the clause, it should be noted, has a purely secondary, limiting force), he has caused his speakers to say primarily what he himself thought called for at each stage of events."[53] Kagan and Andrewes have reacted to this limitation placed upon the participial clause by saying that its limiting force does not imply a secondary purpose, and that the best explanation will weigh each clause without emphasizing one over the other.[54] A second means of handling this tension is to reinterpret the second clause as not in fact dealing with accurate reporting but only referring to the general intentions of

---

51 Finley, *Thucydides*, 98, cf. 95–98. Cf. F.W. Walbank, "Speeches in Greek Historians," in *Selected Papers: Studies in Greek and Roman History and Historiography* (Cambridge: Cambridge University Press, 1985) 244.

52 Kagan, "Speeches," 73.

53 Finley, *Thucydides*, 95.

54 Kagan, "Speeches," 73; Andrewes, "Mytilene Debate," 66.

various speakers,[55] a view which Gomme dismisses with more sarcasm than argument.[56] A third position is to leave the contradiction intact. As Walbank says,

> There is a contradiction between the two ideas of recording what was actually said and recording what the historian thought the speakers would have said...on the various occasions... In the ambiguous formulation of 1.22.1[57] Thucydides calls for truth and then confuses it with something quite other. Thus his theory contains a residual contradiction, never fully surmounted and an unfortunate legacy to his successors.[58]

An examination of several of the individual elements of the second clause is warranted.

E. *Ὅτι ἐγγύτατα*

The fifth difficulty centres around use of the phrase ὅτι ἐγγύτατα. This phrase also is open to several different interpretations, revolving around the degree of precision which can be implied by use of the word ἐγγύς. Thucydides uses the word in several instances which prove instructive: 1.13.2: πρῶτοι...Κορίνθιοι λέγονται ἐγγύτατα τοῦ νῦν τρόπου μεταχειρίσαι; and 7.86.5: ὅτι ἐγγύτατα τούτων. In the first, reference is made to the subjective judgment that in their naval and military affairs the Corinthians are said to have come nearest to the modern methods (cf. Thucydides 1.143.5 regarding trying to formulate as near as possible an image of oneself), and in the second, reference is made to an accusation against Nicias, or a reason very near to this. In both instances there is an implied approximation (cf. Thucydides 6.4.4, 6.5.3 with numerical approximation). How this applies to Thucydides 1.22.1 is even more complex, although it is clear that absolute exactitude cannot be the meaning of ἐγγύτατα. If continuity between the ὡς...εἰπεῖν and the ἐχομένῳ...λεχθέντων clauses is seen, Thucydides may be referring to keeping as close as possible to the general sense of what he himself sees as necessary (see above), or he may be referring

---

55 Schwartz, Review, 79–80, cited in Gomme, *Historical Commentary*, 157: "Und dann die entscheidenden Worte ἐχομένῳ ὅτι ἐγγύτατα τῆς ξυμπάσης γνώμης τῶν ἀληθῶς λεχθέντων: ἡ ξύμπασα γνώμη heisst nicht 'der Gesamtsinn,' sondern 'die Willensrichtung im ganzen,' der praktische Zweck der Rede, und τὰ ἀληθῶς λεχθέντα meint nicht den authentischen Wortlaut, sondern dass die Redner nur in solchen Situationen auftreten sollten, in denen sie wirklich gesprochen hatten."

56 Gomme, "Speeches," 158.

57 Walbank actually refers to 1.22.2, but he clearly means 1.22.1, since the entire section of his essay discusses this section of Thucydides.

58 Walbank, "Speeches," 245. Rokeah ("Τὰ δέοντα," 387) believes that "it is wholly illogical to assume that Thucydides would have formulated a contradiction in terms in one and the same sentence." But is it?

to keeping as close as possible to the general sense of what is said in the light of what is necessary for whatever reason. If discontinuity between the two clauses is seen, Thucydides may be referring to keeping as close as possible to the genuine sense of what was said (cf. Thucydides 5.74.1, where he refers to a description of a battle as ὅτι ἐγγύτατα τούτων), even though this runs contrary to what is required, whether this is with reference to his own standard or another one.

F. *Τῆς ξυμπάσης γνώμης*

The sixth difficulty is with the phrase τῆς ξυμπάσης γνώμης. The widely accepted understanding of this phrase has been "general sense,"[59] although there has been little sustained argumentation for this position. The various senses of γνώμη have been surveyed by P. Huart, who classifies them as: état d'esprit, sentiments; réflexion, jugement; idée, avis, opinion, motion; dessein, intention, résolution.[60] Huart illustrates the great flexibility during this period—and even within Thucydides himself—of this word's meaning. He argues that in 1.22.1, Thucydides, "parlant des discours, et notant la difficulté d'en reproduire les termes avec exactitude, dit qu'il s'est tenu le plus près possible des paroles qui furent réellement prononcées, faisant comprendre que l'essentiel était de rester fidèle à 'la pensée générale,' τῆς ξυμπάσης γνώμης: γνώμη suggère ici l'esprit plus que la lettre des discours," arguing under the third sense above for a meaning similar to the standard one.[61] But this analysis has recently been criticized by I. Plant, for two reasons. First, he contends that "γνώμη is not attested elsewhere as having this particular meaning ['general sense']," and secondly, "this interpretation leads to illogical conflict in the phrase 'ὅτι λεχθέντων' between the stress on precise accuracy in 'ὅτι ἐγγύτατα τῶν ἀληθῶς λεχθέντων,' and the vagueness of the phrase '...τῆς ξυμπάσης γνώμης...' What can Thucydides mean by '...keeping *as close as possible* to the *general sense* of what was actually said'?"[62] The first criticism is not entirely convincing, since Huart illustrates what he sees as related uses (e.g. Thucydides 1.54.2). Although he does not suggest these meanings for Thucydides 1.22.1, Huart does state that the idea of thought suggests intention,

[59] See Gomme, "Speeches," 160; Walbank, "Speeches," 244; Kagan, "Speeches," 74, who goes further and says that "if it does not mean 'the general sense' or even 'the general intention' of a speech really given it means nothing."

[60] P. Huart, *Γνώμη chez Thucydide et ses contemporains (Sophocle - Euripide - Antiphon - Andocide - Aristophane) (Contribution à l'histoire des idées à Athènes dans la seconde moitié du Ve siècle av. J.-C.)* (Études et commentaires 81; Paris: Klincksieck, 1973).

[61] Huart, *Γνώμη*, 118–19; cf. *Vocabulaire*, 308.

[62] I. Plant, "A Note on Thucydides 1.22.1: ἡ ξύμπασα γνώμη = General Sense?" *Athenaeum* 66 (1988) 201, citing Gomme, "Speeches," 160, in the final quotation, with his own italics added.

as in 3.31.2: τὸ πλεῖστον τῆς γνώμης (cf. Thucydides 2.20.1; 5.73.3; 4.32.4).[63] Huart also suggests a series of meanings concerning thought related to the "idea" about a situation, which readily lends itself to the translation "opinion" (e.g. Thucydides 7.15.1: τὴν γνώμην ἔχετε). Plant and Dover endorse this translation, although for different reasons and with different results.[64] Plant argues that "opinion as a whole," "the general opinion," or the freer sense of "the consensus view"[65] is most convincing, on the basis of, for example, Thucydides 7.8.2, where Nicias wrote in order for the Athenians to know τὴν αὑτοῦ γνώμην. He concludes that Thucydides is saying that he is "keeping as close as possible to the consensus view of what was actually said,"[66] emphasizing Thucydides's critical use of sources. But one might legitimately wonder how Plant's solution proves more satisfactory than another, when although he wishes to stress Thucydides's critical evaluation of sources he simply supports Thucydides's acceptance of a consensus of which he may or may not find himself a part (see below on the final phrase, rendered by Plant as "of what was actually said"). This view does not establish how far-ranging a consensus is being considered. Dover argues slightly differently. On the basis of Thucydides 7.80.2 (ἡ ξύμπασα ὁδός), which he says refers to "a journey with reference to its ultimate destination, as distinct from the separate parts of it," there are two legitimate interpretations of ἡ ξύμπασα γνώμη.[67] The first is a simple recounting of the gist of the message, but for Dover keeping as close as possible to this would "be a curious thing to say; one could hardly do less" in reporting a speech. The second is that Thucydides's technique occupies a middle ground between the bare message and the total sequence of the argument, that is, "the line taken by the speaker." "Thucydides is telling us not to expect verbal fidelity, but at the same time promising that he has not invented anything incompatible with that amount of the argument known to him."[68] This interpretation is dependent upon a fairly conservative reading of the following phrase (see below), as well as several presuppositions about the context in which the phrase is found. But if these presuppositions are not true, and the following phrase is not understood conservatively, this understanding says little if anything about the specificity of Thucydides's reference (perhaps Thucydides's knowledge of the argument was very limited). Even if these presuppositions are true, and the following phrase is understood conservatively,

---

63 Huart, *Γνώμη*, 119–20. Schwartz apparently held that the sense was "aim" or "intention," according to Gomme, "Speeches," 159, although he dismisses this.

64 See also Fornara, *History*, 144–45.

65 Cf. Thucydides 4.39.1: χρόνος ὁ ξύμπας; 5.26.1; 3.62.4; 6.23.4; 6.41.2; 7.42.4; 7.75.5, where ξύμπας supports this understanding.

66 Plant, "Note," 202.

67 Cf. Thucydides 8.26.3: τὰ ξύμπαντα πράγματα; 8.72.1.

68 Dover, *Thucydides*, 22.

Dover's interpretation says little more than that Thucydides is attempting to create harmony, not necessarily an accurate report.

G. *Τῶν ἀληθῶς λεχθέντων*

The seventh and final phrase of dispute is τῶν ἀληθῶς λεχθέντων. Use of λέγω has been treated above. The major issue with this phrase is how to interpret the adverb and how to understand its modification of the participle. Even though Walbank sees an inherent contradiction in Thucydides's programmatic statement, he argues that this phrase, modifying τῆς ξυμπάσης γνώμης, makes it "surely hard to reconcile these three words with any theory which envisages that Thucydides simply composed his speeches without reference to the original words."[69] But it has in fact been argued otherwise. Schwartz says, "τὰ ἀληθῶς λεχθέντα meint nicht den authentischen Wortlaut, sondern dass die Redner nur in solchen Situationen auftreten sollten, in denen sie wirklich gesprochen hatten."[70] The difference then is between the sense usually argued for by interpreters, that is, "spoken truthfully," and Schwartz's sense of "truly spoken," with reference to the act and not the content. There is substance to Schwartz's analysis, since ἀληθῶς may refer to the actuality of an event or action, as apparently in Thucydides 5.89: τὰ δυνατὰ δ' ἐξ ὧν ἑκάτεροι ἀληθῶς φρονοῦμεν διαπράσσεσθαι (cf. Liddell–Scott, where Thucydides 1.22.1 is cited for comparison under the definition "actually, in reality").

3. *Conclusion*

Virtually every scholar, from the conservative Gomme to the more progressive Walbank and especially to the skeptical Schwartz, recognizes that in his programmatic statement Thucydides warns his readers. As F.E. Adcock states, "his readers have been warned that the speeches are not, and could not be…, the ipsissima verba of the speakers."[71] The varied interpretations above have shown that, on the basis of his programmatic statement, the degree of credibility Thucydides himself gives to his statements is open to serious question. The result is that Thucydides's statement can be interpreted as saying something from the fairly conservative, "it has been difficult (but I have done it) to remember with accuracy the things which were stated, but the speeches are given as they were required on the basis of the events, possessing an accuracy of the specific words which were spoken truthfully," to the more skeptical, "it

69 Walbank, "Speeches," 245.

70 Quoted in Gomme, "Speeches," 157.

71 F.E. Adcock, *Thucydides and his History* (Cambridge: Cambridge University Press, 1963) 27.

has been impossible to remember with any accuracy the things which were stated, so the speeches are given as seemed required for my purposes, possessing an accuracy equivalent to a consensus view of the things said by those who would have really spoken."

Rather than despair of this assessment for evaluation of Thucydidean and New Testament speeches, however, several important points can be made as a result. First, this presentation of several of the major issues is not designed to establish a single interpretation of Thucydides's statement but to recognize and illustrate its problematic nature. Secondly, any invocation of the Thucydidean view of speeches must argue for and defend a position rather than assume one. The attempt to formulate a position may prove profitable, although it may prove to be perpetually frustrating. Thirdly, future work with the Thucydidean view of speeches needs to rely less upon a troublesome programmatic statement than what Thucydides appears to be doing within the speeches themselves. The same applies to examination of the speeches in Acts. This raises the possibility that there is a fourth and most important point to be introduced by setting Thucydides's statement in a larger context. As Cogan says,

> There is no way for us to question Thucydides' guarantee in the one instance and not in all the others. If we claim that Thucydides has tampered with the facts of the historical circumstances in the case of the speeches, we must also be prepared to admit that he has tampered with the facts on other occasions as well... To question the veracity of the speeches has the ultimate consequence of undermining—if not utterly destroying—the credibility of all of Thucydides' history.
>
> Such a nihilistic position is unacceptable. It is not merely practically unacceptable..., there is no evidence to support it. Not only can we find no objective evidence to make us doubt Thucydides' essential reliability, every internal indication reinforces our belief in the fundamental veracity of his account...
>
> Throughout this chapter [1.22] Thucydides attempts to convince us of the trustworthiness of his account by demonstrating the difficulties he has overcome in dealing with both sorts of material [speeches and events]. On the one hand, he says, it is hard to recollect speeches exactly. On the other, even first-hand reports of events are incomplete or biased. In both cases the historian's responsibilities do not end with the collection of raw data, but begin there. The historian must sift the data, scrutinize it to purge it of error or bias, and then analyze it to fill lacunae and to discover significance.
>
> ...Thucydides' display of concern here is our proof that he intends us to accept the factuality and accuracy of his reports of the speeches in the history.[72]

I have quoted Cogan at length to illustrate one of the bedeviling problems of understanding the programmatic statement in Thucydides. This problem is the failure, first, to interpret the statement both in terms of the author's historical

---

72 Cogan, *Human Thing*, x–xiii *passim*.

programme and in terms of what the writing of his text implies for its interpretation, and secondly, to appreciate the internal coherence of the text, even or especially where outside corroboration cannot be substantiated. Interpretation requires an interpretative act of faith to begin.

CHAPTER TEN

ΚΑΤΑΛΛΑΣΣΩ IN ANCIENT GREEK LITERATURE AND ROMANS 5: A STUDY OF PAULINE USAGE*

1. *Introduction*

Scholars have long recognized the importance of "reconciliation" language in Pauline thought, some even seeing it as the centre of his theology.[1] This conclusion is reached despite the fact that the verb καταλλάσσω is only used with theological significance in two places in the main Pauline epistles, Romans 5 and 2 Corinthians 5 (it is also used in a prefixed form in Colossians 1 and Ephesians 2, and in a non-theological way in 1 Cor 7:11). 2 Corinthians 5:18–21 is often viewed by commentators as a more important passage, since Paul apparently uses the active voice form of the verb to refer to God, the angered party, reconciling humankind to himself, a sense apparently unattested in antecedent Greek literature.[2] However, there are reasons for seeing the usage

* This essay uses material with the permission of Ediciones El Almendro de Córdoba, Spain, and the editor of their monograph series, Estudios de Filología Neotestamentaria, Professor Jesús Peláez, from my *Καταλλάσσω in Ancient Greek Literature, with Reference to the Pauline Writings* (Estudios de Filología Neotestamentaria 5; Córdoba, Spain: Ediciones El Almendro, 1994), especially the "Introduction to Categories of Usage," 13–19, and ch. 7, "Καταλλάσσω in Romans 5:8–11," 145–62.

1 Most recently, this has been argued by R.P. Martin, *Reconciliation: A Study of Paul's Theology* (Atlanta: John Knox, 1981); *idem*, "Center of Paul's Theology," in *Dictionary of Paul and his Letters* (ed. G.F. Hawthorne, R.P. Martin and D.G. Reid; Downers Grove, IL: InterVarsity Press, 1993) 92–95. See also C. Breytenbach, *Versöhnung: Eine Studie zur paulinischen Soteriologie* (WMANT 60; Neukirchen–Vluyn: Neukirchener Verlag, 1989); *idem*, "Versöhnung, Stellvertretung und Sühne: Semantische und Traditionsgeschichtliche Bemerkungen am Beispiel der Paulinischen Briefe," *NTS* 39 (1993) 59–79. Contra the by now well-known statement by E. Käsemann that the theme of reconciliation does not have "any significant meaning for Pauline theology as a whole," in "Some Thoughts on the Theme 'The Doctrine of Reconciliation in the New Testament,'" in *The Future of our Religious Past* (Festschrift R. Bultmann; ed. J.M. Robinson; London: SCM Press, 1971) 51.

2 For a summary of the data, see S.E. Porter, "Reconciliation and 2 Cor 5,18–21," in

in Romans 5 as just as important to the Pauline material, and this is for at least two reasons. First, the Romans 5 passage is more self-defining than the 2 Corinthians 5 passage, through the use of a number of parallel statements both in the immediate and in the wider contexts. Secondly, the means by which reconciliation is effected is more directly stated in Romans 5 than in any other Pauline text. This is not to deny the importance of the use of καταλλάσσω in 2 Cor 5:18, 19, since the pattern of usage as noted above (with the active voice verb) is apparently the first recorded instance of this pattern in extant Greek literature. But it establishes that examination of Romans 5 in terms of use of καταλλάσσω also merits serious attention. It is beyond the purview of this chapter to discuss all of the major exegetical issues involved in this passage. Instead the focus will fall upon those directly related to use of καταλλάσσω (with secondary comments on καταλλαγή). In fact, in Rom 5:8–11 the verb appears twice (both in v. 10) and the noun appears once (v. 11). This study will touch upon the following issues related to Romans 5 and Paul's use of καταλλάσσω: use of καταλλάσσω in the light of previous (and subsequent) use of the word in ancient Greek literature; Romans 5 in the argument of the book of Romans, especially chs. 1–8; and an exegetical analysis of usage of the verb (and noun) forms in the context of Romans 5. Many of the exegetical issues related to use of "reconciliation" language in Romans 5 are not easily solved, and thus warrant further discussion.

2. *Καταλλάσσω in the Light of Previous Use in Ancient Greek Literature*

Paul's use of καταλλάσσω must first be seen in terms of previous (and subsequent) use of the word. Despite the numerous studies of Romans 5, it is noteworthy that thorough and complete study of the use of καταλλάσσω has only recently been done.[3] In most studies of the word, which are usually more

The Corinthian Letters: Papers from the 1994 Leuven Biblical Colloquium (ed. R. Bieringer; BETL; Leuven: Leuven University Press/Peeters, 1995). For more detailed treatment, see S.E. Porter, *Καταλλάσσω in Ancient Greek Literature, with Reference to the Pauline Writings* (Estudios de Filología Neotestamentaria 5; Córdoba, Spain: Ediciones El Almendro, 1994) esp. 125–43.

3 Besides my monograph mentioned above, which has utilized the Thesaurus Linguae Graecae data-base, see I.H. Marshall, "The Meaning of 'Reconciliation,'" in *Unity and Diversity in New Testament Theology* (Festschrift G.E. Ladd; ed. R.A. Guelich; Grand Rapids: Eerdmans, 1978) 117–32, repr. in *idem*, *Jesus the Saviour: Studies in New Testament Theology* (Downers Grove, IL: InterVarsity Press, 1990) 258–74, whose study introduces a useful means of classification of usage of καταλλάσσω; C. Spîcq, *Theological Lexicon of the New Testament* (3 vols.; trans. J.D. Ernest; Peabody: Hendrickson, 1994 [1978, 1982]) 2.262–66; and Breytenbach, *Versöhnung*, utilized in *idem*, "Versöhnung, Stellvertretung und Sühne," but who relies upon previously published sources and his own manual searching.

theologically than linguistically centred, there is some reference to significant usage especially in the Church Fathers,[4] but there is little reference to extra-Christian usage, apart from Sophocles, *Ajax* 743–744, OGIS 1.218.104–106 (3rd century B.C.), and 2 Maccabees. The first two references are found in Liddell–Scott[5] and subject to much misinterpretation. It is not uncommon to find these referred to as "religious" uses by some commentators. A closer examination does not support a strong assertion of their religious usage, however, at least to the degree that they would be useful for aiding exegesis of Romans 5.

The example from Sophocles, *Ajax* 743–744 reads as follows: ἀλλ' οἴχεταί τοι πρὸς τὸ κέρδιστον τραπεὶς / γνώμης, θεοῖσιν ὡς καταλλαχθῇ χόλου. Ajax has discovered the folly of his actions in killing the Greek sheep and cattle, and since he cannot be comforted by his wife or son, he leaves the stage, vowing to purge his sin (lines 654–656), and claiming to have learned too late the lesson that an enemy can become a friend (lines 678–682). Nowhere in this soliloquy before his departure does Ajax use a word from the ἀλλάσσω word-group. It is the chorus which uses καταλλάσσω for the first and only time. This passage has fostered discussion on two levels. First is grammatical discussion. It has been understood by some as a pregnant construction, implying that the anger of the gods is pacified.[6] Since Ajax is the grammatical subject of the aorist passive verb, and hence the apparent recipient of the reconciling action, there is no grammatically stated means for his act of reconciliation, although the fact that it is directed towards the gods is clear (using the dative case). The grammatical issue raises the second, conceptual issue, regarding the theological implications of this passage. Storr (LCL) and Jebb take the passage as theologically significant: "Well, he is gone...to make his peace with the gods."[7] This explanation certainly seems to be the best understanding in the light of the larger context, but it leaves several issues unresolved. First is the orientation of this series of events. It is apparently Ajax, the man betrayed by the gods (Athena in particular), who, feeling the guilt-laden burden for his actions,

While his treatment refers to a number of previous uses, it is far from complete in its coverage (and includes other words than the one I study), especially since his study is not designed to be primarily linguistic but linguistic and theological, concentrating on the semantic field of "reconciliation" words.

4 See, for example, J. Michl, "Die 'Versöhnung' (Kol. 1:20)," *TQ* 128 (1948) 442–62.

5 H.G. Liddell and R. Scott, *A Greek–English Lexicon* (rev. H.S. Jones with R. McKenzie, and E.A. Barber; 9th edn; Oxford: Clarendon Press, 1968) s.v., but neither as religious usage.

6 See J.C. Kamerbeek, *The Plays of Sophocles*. I. *The Ajax* (trans. H. Schrender; rev. A. Parker; 2nd edn; Leiden: Brill, 1963) 156.

7 R.C. Jebb, *Sophocles*. VII. *The Ajax* (Cambridge: Cambridge University Press, 1896) 117.

undertakes to exonerate himself and rid himself of his guilt. He approaches the gods to make amends. Dupont makes much of this, specifying that Ajax is going to reconcile himself to the gods through purification rituals.[8] This is less likely than simply that Ajax, the guilty party, offers himself to the gods as a suitable sacrifice.[9]

The religious sense, however, is even less likely in the inscription, OGIS 1.218.104–106 (3rd century B.C.), which is a Seleucid (Ilium) judicial text, describing capital crimes and their punishments. The text reads: φόνον / δὲ ἐπιγαμία(ι)ς μὴ καταλλάσ[σεσ]θαι μηδὲ χρή/μασιν. Although Dunn in his comments on Rom 5:10 contends that the inscription gives support for a religious use of καταλλάσσω not being unnatural in Paul,[10] at most this text supports the use of this word to speak of atonement being made for capital crimes for those who violate the law. This section of the text speaks of the vote of death and then forfeiture of citizenship for heirs of anyone who would flee to avoid justice, with one being unable to be reconciled by means of marital relations or possessions.[11]

One of the most prominent sets of examples of use of καταλλάσσω is found in the Septuagint. This is the clearest and most sustained theological usage to precede that of the New Testament and Church Fathers.[12] Three passages in particular are worth noting. The first is 2 Macc 1:5: ἐπακούσαι ὑμῶν τῶν δεήσεων καὶ καταλλαγείη ὑμῖν καὶ μὴ ὑμᾶς ἐγκαταλίποι ἐν καιρῷ πονηρῷ. The rendering of Bartlett captures the sense: "May he...answer your prayers, and be reconciled to you and not forsake you in an evil hour."[13] In this example, the aorist passive optative form, parallel with a similar clause, refers to God responding to the prayers of the Jews and putting his anger aside to be reconciled to his people (using the dative case for the goal or direction of reconciliation), and not abandoning them even when their evil angers him. The second is 2 Macc 7:33: πάλιν καταλλαγήσεται τοῖς ἑαυτοῦ δούλοις. In 2 Maccabees 7 is found the story of Antiochus's martyrdom of the seven brothers for their loyalty to Judaism. The brothers viewed their suffering both as

8 J. Dupont, *La réconciliation dans la théologie de St. Paul* (Paris: Brouwer, 1953) 13.

9 See J.A. Fitzmyer, "Reconciliation in Pauline Theology," in *No Famine in the Land* (Festschrift J.L. McKenzie; ed. J.W. Flanagan and A.W. Robinson; Missoula, MT: Scholars Press, 1975) 173 n. 20.

10 J.D.G. Dunn, *Romans* (2 vols.; WBC 38A, B; Dallas: Word, 1988) 1.259. He also cites Sophocles, *Ajax* 744.

11 See Spîcq, *Theological Lexicon*, 2.262–63 n. 3, who notes discussion regarding marriage as a means of reconciliation.

12 See Marshall, "Meaning of 'Reconciliation,'" 120–21; Porter, *Καταλλάσσω in Ancient Greek Literature*, 60–62.

13 J.R. Bartlett, *The First and Second Books of the Maccabees* (Cambridge: Cambridge University Press, 1973) 220.

divine punishment for their sins (7:18) and as a means of inducing God to forgive their nation for its apostasy and sin. Verse 33 is translated by Goldstein as "He will again become reconciled with His servants."[14] The translator notes reference to God's anger in this verse and v. 38, where the seventh brother beseeches God to be merciful towards the nation so that through trials and afflictions it may confess that he alone is God, and that in him and his brothers the wrath (ὀργή) of God brought upon the nation may cease. Using the unusual future passive form, the angry party, God, gives up its anger against another. The dative case indicates the goal or direction of his reconciliation, not the instrument. The third example is 2 Macc 8:29: κοινὴν ἱκετείαν ποιησάμενοι τὸν ἐλεήμονα κύριον ἠξίουν εἰς τέλος καταλλαγῆναι τοῖς αὑτοῦ δούλοις. Regarding Judas Maccabeus and his men after their first military victory over Nicanor's men, by making a common supplication they were attempting to make themselves worthy of their merciful Lord for the purpose that "he would be completely reconciled with His servants."[15] This is an example in which God is called upon so that he will put his anger aside, again with the goal or direction of reconciliation in the dative case.

In the light of this brief discussion of significant usage, an accurate assessment of the extra-Christian evidence (though one formulated without the data-base now available) is found in Büchsel's summary in his *TDNT* article: "καταλλάττω and καταλλάττεσθαι play no essential part in even the expiatory rites...of Greek and Hellenistic pagan religion."[16] καταλλάσσω and its derived cognates are only used a relatively few times by classical and Hellenistic writers before 2 Maccabees and Paul. For example, there are the one instance in Sophocles and one in Euripides, six instances in Herodotus, two in Thucydides and one in Xenophon, a number of instances in the orators, and several instances in the philosophers Plato and Aristotle.[17] Among Hellenistic writers up to the first century A.D., the historians of Alexander the Great, Polybius,

---

14 J.A. Goldstein, *II Maccabees* (Garden City, NY: Doubleday, 1983) 291, 316.

15 Goldstein, *II Maccabees*, 320, 338. Cf. SPCK *Commentary on the Old Testament: The Apocryphal Books* (London: SPCK, 1880) loc. cit.: "they besought the merciful Lord to be reconciled with his servants for ever."

16 F. Büchsel, ἀλλάσσω, *TDNT*, 1.254.

17 Besides Sophocles, *Ajax* 743–744, see Euripides, *Iph. Aul.* 1157–1158; Herodotus 1.61.2; 5.29.1; 6.108.5; 5.95.2; 7.154.3; 7.145.1; Thucydides 4.59.4; 6.89.2; Xenophon, *Anab.* 1.6.1; Isocrates 5.135; 6.109; Demosthenes 19.114; 39.23; 40.29; Lycurgus, *Against Leocrates* 88; Aeschines, *Against Ctesiphon* 92; Demades Fr. 83.1 (= P.Oxy. II 216.2–4); Dinarchus 1.2; 3.21; 1.14; 3.17; Plato, *Phaedo* 69AB; *Ep. 7* 350E; *Rep.* 8.566E; Aristotle, *Nic. Eth.* 1117B20; 1157A; 1158B3; *Econ.* 1348B; *Pol.* 1257A; *Rhet.* 1367A; 1372A; 1373A; 1416A; 1418B; *Mag. Mor.* 1.15.2; 1.17.3; 1.33.10; 1.33.12; 1.33.28; 2.11.33; *Part. Anim.* 645A. Aristotle is the most frequent user of this word in the pre-Christian era. See Porter, *Καταλλάσσω in Ancient Greek Literature*, 23–38.

Diodorus Siculus and Dionysius of Halicarnassus each have a few instances.[18] There are a couple of instances in the papyri and three in the inscriptions.[19] In none of these is it clear that there is a religious use, with only the instance in Sophocles coming close to such a usage. Thus, religious usage of this word only becomes significant first in 2 Maccabees (1:5; 7:33; 8:29), and then in the Pauline writings.

After that, καταλλάσσω and its cognates appear in relatively larger numbers in the later Hellenistic writers, the papyri, and especially the Church Fathers, most notably John Chrysostom, who accounts for fully one-fifth of all ancient usage.[20] Although it is difficult to account for the increase in usage among the non-Christian writers, the large number of biblically motivated passages, in the form of quotations and allusions, in the Church Fathers is a direct reflection of the influence of the Pauline writings. This is clear.

In few treatments of usage of καταλλάσσω is there any attention paid to differentiating much more than the two major senses of the word, with much of the history and development of the word beyond concern. With regard to these two senses, καταλλάσσω, a prefixed form of ἀλλάσσω, a word for changing shape, colour or appearance or for exchange, seems to have been used by Greek writers to describe the exchange of goods or things, and to describe the process by which hostility between parties is eliminated and friendship is created. In other words, the basic sense of the word can be metaphorically extended to include the exchange of relationships, such as the exchange of enmity for friendship, between persons or larger political entities.[21] Thus the term fits comfortably within the larger semantic spheres of legal and personal relations, as recognized by the UBS lexicon.[22] Although this kind of scheme provides a means of describing the two major kinds of contexts in which this word might be used—material and personal or legal—it is clear that a more refined scheme would be helpful if one wished to distinguish more precise usage. Such a scheme was introduced by Marshall,[23] and has now been applied to all of the

---

18 Historia Alexandria Magni Recension λ 50.12; Codex Marcianus 408.3213–14; Polybius 2.42.6; 15.20.5; Diodorus Siculus 1.2.4; 8.2.1; 10.21.5; Fr. 22.8.4; Dionysius Halicarnassus 4.34.1; 12.1.7. See Porter, *Καταλλάσσω in Ancient Greek Literature,* 39–41.

19 Besides OGIS 1.218.104–106 (3rd century B.C.), see P.Paris 63.vi.189–91 (165 B.C.); P.Mil. Congr. XVII (page 21 text 1, ll. 13–15) (142/141 B.C.); IGV[2] 3.1–2 (390 B.C.); SEG 28.732.2–4 (3rd century B.C.). See Porter, *Καταλλάσσω in Ancient Greek Literature,* 66, 74–76. The data are almost certainly incomplete in this area.

20 The references are simply too numerous to list. See Porter, *Καταλλάσσω in Ancient Greek Literature,* 41–60, 66–74, 78–116.

21 See Porter, *Καταλλάσσω in Ancient Greek Literature,* 13–14.

22 J.P. Louw and E.A. Nida, *Greek–English Lexicon of the New Testament based on Semantic Domains* (2 vols.; New York: United Bible Societies, 1988) 1.502–503; cf. Breytenbach, "Versöhnung, Stellvertretung und Sühne," 59–61.

23 Marshall, "The Meaning of 'Reconciliation,'" 117–32.

known instances of καταλλάσσω in ancient Greek literature. Six categories of usage allow for refinement of discussion of the usage of this word. The scheme is as follows:

A1: The subject (or agent) effects the exchange of goods between parties (active, middle or passive voice forms). This is the first sense mentioned above, that of the exchange of goods or things. For example, Plato speaks of the simple change or exchange of emotions as if they were coins to be traded (*Phaedo* 69AB).

The following five categories make finer distinctions regarding the second sense mentioned above, that of exchanging enmity for friendship.

A2: The subject (or agent) effects reconciliation between mutually antagonistic parties (active, middle or passive voice forms). For example, in Herodotus 6.108.5 it is said that the Corinthians reconciled the mutually hostile Thebans and Plataeans.

B: The subject effects reconciliation by persuading a hostile party to give up its anger against the subject (active voice form). Usage B is relatively rare throughout the course of ancient Greek usage. This may well be the sense in Col 1:20 but with ἀποκαταλλάσσω, when God (it is implied) is said to reconcile all things to Christ.[24] If this is not the best description of the usage (in which case usage E would probably describe the usage best), then the first clear instance of usage B (and in any case with καταλλάσσω) may occur in Dio Cassius 54.12.1. This category of usage remains the least frequent, although it does appear with some frequency in Pseudo-Macarius and John Chrysostom.[25]

C: The subject is reconciled (or effects reconciliation) by persuading a hostile party to give up its anger, usually against the subject (middle and/or passive voice forms). In Sophocles, *Ajax* 744, Ajax expresses his wish to be reconciled to the gods, with the passive voice form.

D: The subject effects reconciliation by giving up its own anger against another party (passive voice form). In Euripides, *Iph. Aul.* 1157, Tyndareus speaks of Clytemnestra being reconciled to Agamemnon, in fact a vain hope. Usage D is also to be found in OGIS 1.218.104–106 (3rd century B.C.), and 2 Macc 1:5, 7:33, and 8:29.

E: The subject effects reconciliation by giving up its own anger against another party (active voice form). Usage E is found for the first time in the extant ancient Greek literature in 2 Cor 5:18 and 19.[26] The first instance is

---

24 In Porter, *Καταλλάσσω in Ancient Greek Literature*, 183 (cf. p. 180 on the object of reconciliation), I debate whether usage B or E is in effect. I am now inclined to think that usage B is more likely.

25 See Porter, *Καταλλάσσω in Ancient Greek Literature*, 91–93 and 93–116.

26 See Porter, *Καταλλάσσω in Ancient Greek Literature*, 143. Breytenbach ("Versöhnung, Stellvertretung und Sühne," 64) recognizes the distinctive of Pauline usage, although he only mentions 2 Cor 5:19.

found in v. 18, where the active voice form of the participle, καταλλάξαντος, modifies the noun θεοῦ in attributive structure, parallel with a second participle, δόντος.[27] In this instance, the main or head term, "God," has the actions of "reconciler" and "giver" attributed to it. In v. 19, Paul apparently restates and expands upon his previous statements regarding God's reconciling actions (ὡς ὅτι).[28] The second instance of usage E is found in v. 19, a far more complex grammatical construction. Numerous solutions have been proposed along grammatical, conceptual and theological lines.[29] The best understanding is to take the construction as periphrastic, with the auxiliary verb and the participle forming a single verbal unit: "through Christ God was reconciling the world to himself." God functions as the grammatical subject of the clause and, therefore, of the active voice participle, and thus as the agent of the reconciling action.[30]

The usage of the verb in Rom 5:10 is not so clear, since the verb appears in both instances in the aorist passive form and hence could be categorized under several of the above categories. This is discussed in the conclusion, in the light of the exegetical evidence.

3. *Romans 5 in the Argument of the Book of Romans*

The placement of Romans 5, especially vv. 1–11, in the argument of Romans has been notoriously difficult, although the conclusions have direct implications for understanding the use of καταλλάσσω, a fact often overlooked in discussion of "reconciliation" language. Several of the difficult issues include lexical and conceptual similarities of ch. 5 with chs. 1–4 and chs. 6–8, and the use of both justification and reconciliation language in parallel in 5:1–11, among others.[31]

---

27 On attributive structure, see S.E. Porter, *Idioms of the Greek New Testament* (Biblical Languages: Greek 2; 2nd edn; Sheffield: JSOT Press, 1994) 116–17.

28 See R. Bieringer, "2 Kor 5,19a und die Versöhnung der Welt," *ETL* 63 (1987) 296–304. The three major options for the conjunctive phrase are: comparative emphasizing the use of ὡς, causal emphasizing the ὅτι, and epexegetic or explicative introducing content. See V.P. Furnish, *II Corinthians* (AB 32A; Garden City, NY: Doubleday, 1984) 317–18.

29 See A. Plummer, *A Critical and Exegetical Commentary on the Second Epistle of St Paul to the Corinthians* (ICC; Edinburgh: T. & T. Clark, n.d.) 183; J.-F. Collange, *Énigmes de la deuxième épître de Paul aux Corinthiens: Étude exegetique de 2 Cor 2,14–7,4* (SNTSMS 18; Cambridge: Cambridge University Press, 1972) 270–72; and Furnish, *II Corinthians*, 318.

30 I find it useful to distinguish between grammatical roles (e.g. agent, patient, beneficiary, means) and grammatical relations (e.g. subject, direct object, indirect object, instrument), although a formal–functional relationship must be seen to exist between them.

31 On these issues, see Porter, *Καταλλάσσω in Ancient Greek Literature*, esp. 145–47. See now also S.E. Porter, "A Newer Perspective on Paul: Romans 1–8 through the Eyes of Literary Analysis," in *The Bible in Human Society: Essays in Honour of John Rogerson* (ed.

These difficulties are especially significant in view of the fact that ch. 5 has been at the heart of discussion about the argument of Romans,[32] although the tendency has been to marginalize the significance of the chapter by forcing it to the extremes.

Within the book of Romans, it is reasonable to accept with most commentators that it is composed around several general themes, among them God's judgment (1:18–3:20), God's righteousness (3:21–4:25), and God's eschatological work through the Spirit (8:1–39) (at least these three are significant for the discussion below).[33] But where does Romans 5 and its discussion of reconciliation fit within this framework? Those who argue for placing ch. 5 with chs. 1–4 often cite lexical usage of especially δικ-, καυχ- and πιστ- words,[34] seeing the righteousness of God as excluding human boasting and effecting atonement for humankind through faith in Jesus Christ as the theme of Rom 3:21–5:21.[35] Those who argue that chs. 1–4 and 5–8 belong together often appeal to a perceived pattern of development in chs. 5–8, in which the first section in each chapter is a basic statement about the life promised to the justified person and the second section clarifies what is said in the first.[36] Dahl goes so far as to argue that Rom 5:1–11 is expanded upon in greater detail in ch. 8.[37] In all, Romans 5 is seen either as the conclusion to the first section of the book but inevitably not quite as important as some of the material presented in chs. 3 and 4, or as an introductory chapter, although again not as important as later chapters, such as ch. 8.[38]

D.J.A. Clines, P.R. Davies and M.D. Carroll R.; JSOTSup 200; Sheffield: Sheffield Academic Press, 1995).

32 See J. Dupont, "Le problème de la structure littéraire de l'épître aux Romains," *RB* 62 (1955) 368.

33 See, for example, N.A. Dahl, *Studies in Paul: Theology for the Early Christian Mission* (Minneapolis: Augsburg, 1977) 81; W.G. Kümmel, *Introduction to the New Testament* (trans. H.C. Kee; Nashville: Abingdon Press, 1975) 306; Dunn, *Romans, passim*; and J.A. Fitzmyer, *Romans* (AB 33; New York: Doubleday, 1993) *passim*.

34 C.E.B. Cranfield, *A Critical and Exegetical Commentary on the Epistle to the Romans* (2 vols.; ICC; Edinburgh: T. & T. Clark, 1975, 1977) 1.253; F.J. Leenhardt, *The Epistle to the Romans: A Commentary* (New York: World, 1961) 131–32; A. Feuillet, "Le plan salvifique de Dieu d'après l'épître aux Romains," *RB* 57 (1950) 356 n. 1; but cf. H. Schlier, *Der Römerbrief* (HTKNT; 2nd edn; Freiburg: Herder, 1979) 138.

35 W. Manson, "The Argument of the Epistles [?] to the Romans (Chaps. 1–8)," in *Jesus and the Christian* (Grand Rapids: Eerdmans, 1967) 140–44.

36 See Cranfield, *Romans*, 1.254.

37 N.A. Dahl, "Two Notes on Romans 5," *ST* 5 (1951) 37–42 esp. 37–38; *idem*, *Studies in Paul*, 88–89. See also P. Rolland, "L'antithèse de Rm 5–8," *Bib* 69 (1988) 396–97, who sees significant lexical parallels between Rom 5–7 and ch. 8. The position that argues for a split between vv. 11 and 12 of Rom 5 has much less to commend it and will not be discussed here.

38 This view is perhaps most disappointingly represented of late by W. Schmithals, *Der*

Kaye has shown, however, that Romans 5 seems to be a point of convergence for many of the themes in the book, especially as these are represented through particular vocabulary items. As Kaye states, "Those words which are not used after Rom. 5 are often found in Rom. 5 in conjunction with words which are used subsequently but have not been used significantly, or at all, before Rom. 5."[39] But there is more to Romans 5 than simply vocabulary convergence: there are plausible conceptual and structural reasons for seeing unity of the chapter and its occupation of a significant place in the argument of Romans, making it appropriate that καταλλάσσω appears just here (and reciprocally this reinforces the importance of the use of καταλλάσσω). On the basis of the kinds of evidence presented by those concerned to decide where Romans 5 fits within the argument of the book as a whole, "reconciliation" language, it seems to me, serves as a crucial lexical and conceptual fulcrum between chs. 1–4 and 6–8, although the significance of this has not been fully developed.[40] On the one hand, Rom 5:1, with reference to justification by faith, the enjoyment of peace with God and the means of effecting this justification "through our Lord Jesus Christ" is echoed in 5:9 with reference to justification by Christ's blood. The phrasing of 5:9 (as well as 5:1) is very similar to that of 5:10, with reference to being reconciled to God by means of the death of his son. In vv. 9 and 10 justification and reconciliation are said to result in salvation. It is noteworthy that the language of three major concepts in Romans is found within Rom 5:1–11 (in particular in vv. 9–10, besides v. 1): justification, reconciliation and salvation, all said to be by means of the work of Christ. These three concepts correlate with several of the major themes of the book of Romans, as noted above.

4. *Exegetical Analysis of Usage of Καταλλάσσω in Romans 5*

Paul uses forms of the verb καταλλάσσω twice in Rom 5:10, and the noun form καταλλαγή once in v. 11. Several important grammatical and conceptual parallels revolve around the usage of these words, especially the verb. Six of the issues are discussed below, before attempting to categorize the usage of καταλλάσσω in Romans 5 according to the scheme presented above.

Römerbrief: Ein Kommentar (Gütersloh: Mohn, 1988) 149–65.

39 B.N. Kaye, *The Thought Structure of Romans with Special Reference to Chapter 6* (Austin: Schola, 1979) 7, 150.

40 On the unity of Rom 1–8, see Porter, "Newer Perspective on Paul"; on the unity of Rom 5, in the light of the use of diatribe throughout the entire book, see S.E. Porter, "The Argument of Romans 5: Can a Rhetorical Question Make a Difference?" *JBL* 110 (1991) 655–77, reprinted as ch. 11 in this volume, pp. 213–38.

A. *Peace with God and Reconciliation*
Having peace with God (Rom 5:1) and reconciliation (Rom 5:10a) are apparently equated by Paul, with both ἔχωμεν[41] of v. 1 and κατηλλάγημεν of v. 10 the main verbs of complex sentences modified by adverbial participles and directing their action towards God (πρὸς τὸν θεόν, τῷ θεῷ). This conforms to the subdomain outlined in the UBS lexicon, in which words for peace (εἰρηνοποιέω, εἰρηνοποιός) are placed within the same domain as καταλλάσσω and its cognates.[42] Although many scholars believe that the conceptual background to use of εἰρήνη depends upon a theological sense of this lexical item in the Septuagint,[43] another proposal seems more likely. The classical sense of a state or time of peace without war seems to be implied on the basis of v. 10. εἰρήνη thus functions in the wider realm of relational words, in which a state of well-being, leading to harmonious relations between people or nations, is spoken of; a spiritual sense is only secondary.[44] This fully conforms to use of καταλλάσσω to denote the establishment of peace between hostile parties. In both Rom 5:1 and 10a, the acts of pacification are addressed towards God. ἔχωμεν is modified by the following prepositional phrase πρὸς τὸν θεόν,[45] whereas κατηλλάγημεν has the usual dative, τῷ θεῷ, associated with use of καταλλάσσω in the New Testament (see 2 Cor 5:18, 19).

B. *Δικαιόω and Καταλλάσσω*
In Romans 5 Paul apparently wants to describe God's work using two lexical items with overlapping semantic ranges, δικαιόω[46] and καταλλάσσω. This

---

41 The textual evidence clearly indicates the subjunctive reading in Rom 5:1. See B.M. Metzger, *A Textual Commentary on the Greek New Testament* (corrected edn; London: United Bible Societies, 1975) 511. The internal reasons point in this direction as well. See Porter, "Argument of Romans 5," 657–60 and ch. 11 in this volume; contra M. Wolter, *Rechtfertigung und zukünftiges Heil: Untersuchungen zu Röm 5,1–11* (BZNW 43; Berlin: de Gruyter, 1978) 91–94.

42 Louw–Nida, *Greek–English Lexicon,* subdomain 40.1; cf. also Breytenbach, "Versöhnung, Stellvertretung und Sühne," 60–61.

43 See E. Dinkler, *EIRENE: Der urchristliche Friedensgedanke* (SHAW; Heidelberg: Winter, 1973) 15, 34–35; U. Wilckens, *Der Brief an die Römer* (3 vols.; Zürich: Benziger, 1987) 1.288.

44 W. Foerster, G. von Rad, εἰρήνη, *TDNT,* 2.400–406.

45 The preposition πρός here conveys the sense of close relation, one directed towards God. See N. Turner, *Syntax,* vol. 3 of *A Grammar of New Testament Greek,* by J.H. Moulton (Edinburgh: T. & T. Clark, 1963) 274; F. Blass and A. Debrunner, *A Greek Grammar of the New Testament and Other Early Christian Literature* (trans. R.W Funk; Chicago: University of Chicago Press, 1961) §239(5); Porter, *Idioms of the Greek New Testament,* 172–73.

46 On justification as a forensic term in Paul and in particular in Romans, see M.A. Seifrid, *Justification by Faith: The Origin and Development of a Central Pauline Theme* (NovTSup 68; Leiden: Brill, 1992) esp. 182–249.

semantic analysis is consistent with the findings of the UBS lexicon as well. The overlap of these two lexical items is seen in two ways. In vv. 1 and 9 δικαιωθέντες is used adverbially, and in v. 10b καταλλαγέντες is used adverbially; in vv. 9 and 10 the verb forms enter into similar syntactical relations with the same main verb, σωθησόμεθα. But it is not entirely clear how to understand this parallelism of forms, in the light of the first parallel mentioned in the paragraph above between the phrase εἰρήνην ἔχωμεν and κατηλλάγημεν. Perhaps Paul is not concerned with the exact precision of his terminology, but is speaking in metaphorical terms of the transforming power of the work of Christ, in which two separate and distinct metaphors are used.[47] This is unlikely in the light of the clear structure of this chapter, in which Paul posits the conditions of justification and peace, raises an objection to his conceptions in vv. 6–7,[48] and then proceeds to restate and clarify his position, all using a number of grammatically and conceptually parallel statements. Perhaps the event denoted by καταλλάσσω is a more wide-ranging and encompassing action, in which justification and the resultant peace are both included.[49] This proposal has merit in its appreciation of the various salvific metaphors upon which Paul draws, including also access, boasting, etc., although it neglects the clear parallelism in vv. 1, 9 and 10. Perhaps justification and reconciliation or enjoying peace are to be seen as overlapping metaphors, even verging on equation but each suggesting a different perspective on God's one work through Christ.[50] As seen above, the parallelism of vv. 1 and 10a, with God as the common object, illustrates that the securing of peace (εἰρήνην

---

47 Cf. E.P. Sanders, *Paul and Palestinian Judaism: A Comparison of Patterns of Religion* (Philadelphia: Fortress Press, 1977) 502.

48 I follow J.H. Michael ("A Phenomenon in the Text of Romans," *JTS* 39 [1938] 152), followed also by M. Black (*Romans* [NCB; Grand Rapids: Eerdmans, 1973] 83), who suggests εἰς τί γὰρ...ἔτι for the textual variants in v. 6, so that the verse becomes a question posed by Paul's hypothetical interlocutor in his diatribe. See Porter, "Argument of Romans 5," 655–77 *passim* (and ch. 11 in this volume), for detailed argumentation regarding the diatribal character of Rom 5.

49 See, for example, J. Calvin, *Commentaries on the Epistle of Paul the Apostle to the Romans* (repr. Grand Rapids: Eerdmans, 1947) 187; C. Hodge, *Commentary on the Epistle to the Romans* (1886 rev. edn; repr. Grand Rapids: Eerdmans, 1953) 131.

50 See, for example, C.K. Barrett, *A Commentary on the Epistle to the Romans* (BNTC; London: A. & C. Black, 1957) 108; Cranfield, *Romans*, 1.258; Black, *Romans*, 82; O. Michel, *Der Brief an die Römer* (MeyerK 4; 14th edn; Göttingen: Vandenhoeck & Ruprecht, 1978) 130; Dunn, *Romans*, 1.259; W. Sanday and A.C. Headlam, *A Critical and Exegetical Commentary on the Epistle to the Romans* (ICC; 5th edn; Edinburgh: T. & T. Clark, 1902) 129; Martin, *Reconciliation*, 134; Schlier, *Römerbrief*, 156; H.A.W. Meyer, *Critical and Exegetical Hand-Book to the Romans* (New York: Funk & Wagnalls, 1884) 180; E. Gaugler, *Der Römerbrief* (2 vols.; Zürich: Zwingli, 1958) 1.112–13; and Fitzmyer, *Romans*, 401, cf. 116–20; among others.

ἔχωμεν πρὸς τὸν θεόν) is contextually synonymous with what is meant by reconciliation (καταλλαγέντες).

In this context the exhortation to enjoy peace (v. 1), using the hortatory subjunctive, is not to be seen as exhorting movement to a subsequent stage, but as exhorting appropriation of circumstances attendant with justification. Therefore, the juridical and the personal language of the two metaphors is inseparably linked, making an obvious and immediate association between justification and peace. After the interruption of Paul's argument by his hypothetical interlocutor in vv. 6–7 concerning how it is possible to think of Christ dying for the ungodly, Paul goes back to pick up the same concepts, although this time he uses forms of δικαιόω and καταλλάσσω as overlapping in sense. This is confirmed by the structure of vv. 9 and 10. In v. 9 Paul states that πολλῷ...μᾶλλον δικαιωθέντες...σωθησόμεθα, and in v. 10 he states πολλῷ μᾶλλον καταλλαγέντες σωθησόμεθα, with salvation being the expected consequence of both justification and reconciliation. As these several sets of parallel statements illustrate, καταλλάσσω is used to denote the same event which is described by Paul on the one hand as an initiatory juridical event, justification, treated at some length in chs. 3 and 4,[51] and on the other hand as the appropriation of attendant peaceful status with God, developed further in subsequent chapters in the letter. This analysis overcomes the possible objection that nowhere does Paul link δικαιόω with εἰρήνη. Formally they are not linked, since each functions within its own particular metaphorical sphere, but conceptually there is a large semantic overlap. Although Barrett perhaps goes too far in minimizing their distinctives, he is probably correct that "Justification and reconciliation are different metaphors describing the same fact. The meaning of the verb 'to reconcile' is determined by the noun 'enemies'; it puts an end to enmity, just as 'to justify' puts an end to legal contention."[52]

C. *The Means of Reconciliation*

The means for these actions of reconciliation and justification are stated as well. Interestingly, δικαιωθέντες in v. 1 is modified by ἐκ πίστεως, a relatively common Pauline collocation,[53] and then by ἐν τῷ αἵματι αὐτοῦ in v. 9. How to understand use of πίστις in Romans is not easy,[54] but it apparently describes the necessary belief by which justification is accomplished (with instrumental

51 See Seifrid, *Justification by Faith*, 210–26.

52 Barrett, *Romans*, 108; see also P. Althaus, *Der Brief an die Römer* (NTD; Göttingen: Vandenhoeck & Ruprecht, 1970) 52 (but without his apparent equation of the tense forms with when these events supposedly occurred).

53 For example, Rom 1:17; 3:26, 30; 9:30; 10:6; Gal 2:16; 3:8, 11, 24.

54 See Dunn, *Romans*, 1.43, 166–67, 246, and related bibliography (although Dunn overplays use of the aorist tense to extrapolate that 5:1 refers to "the particular act in which that faith was first exercised, the initial act of commitment," p. 246).

or causal ἐκ).[55] The ἐν phrase with reference to "his blood" probably denotes an act sacrificial in nature,[56] describing the death of Christ as an act by which justification was effected.[57] καταλλαγέντες in v. 10b is not syntactically linked to any instrumental phrase, although it can be assumed that the phrase from v. 10a, διὰ τοῦ θανάτου τοῦ υἱοῦ αὐτοῦ, is understood. The significance of the death of Christ for effecting reconciliation is confirmed by the parallelism of v. 8b and v. 10a, where it is stated in v. 8 that Χριστὸς ὑπὲρ ἡμῶν ἀπέθανεν, in response to the objection in vv. 6–7. The phrase διὰ τοῦ κυρίου ἡμῶν Ἰησοῦ Χριστοῦ is also used in v. 1 to modify ἔχωμεν, drawing the connections between these statements even closer.

Whereas 2 Cor 5:18–21 only mentions the means of effecting reconciliation twice (vv. 18, 19), every verse in this section of Romans 5—vv. 8, 9, 10 and 11, as well as v. 1—mentions it explicitly. Moreover, v. 10 also refers to "the death of his son" (as does v. 21). As Hengel says, "Kyrios became the current title in worship and in the individual life of the believer, while the form 'Son of God,' with its more complicated language, was kept for exceptional usage, at the climax of certain theological statements."[58] Martin looks to Paul's reference to the love of God in vv. 5 and 8 as the heart of the passage and the basis of reconciliation.[59] Whereas this may make sense as a theological analysis of reconciliation, this kind of phrase only occurs a few times in Paul (Rom 8:39; 2 Cor 13:13), and the text here does not make that correlation explicit. In fact the text constructs the correlation only in an indirect way. Verse 8 states that God proved or demonstrated his love to humankind because Christ died, but it does not say that the love of God is the basis or source of reconciliation. Instead, as Keck argues in his assessment of references to "Jesus" (or Christ) in Romans, especially in Paul's significant and virtually synonymous phrases of means, ἐν Χριστῷ and διὰ Χριστοῦ, "although Romans is a theocentric book, everything about Paul that matters and everything that Christians are and hope for pivot on this figure 'in' whom and 'through' whom God effects salvation.

---

55 On the instrumental use of ἐκ, see Porter, *Idioms of the Greek New Testament*, 155–56; Turner, *Syntax*, 170; C.F.D. Moule, *Idiom Book of New Testament Greek* (2nd edn; Cambridge: Cambridge University Press, 1959) 72–73.

56 Martin, *Reconciliation*, 147; Dunn, *Romans*, 1.257; contra Fitzmyer, "Reconciliation in Pauline Theology," 162; *idem*, *Romans*, 401.

57 On the instrumental and hence probably similar use of the ἐν phrase with the διά phrase, see Cranfield, *Romans*, 1.266; Dunn, *Romans*, 1.257; cf. Moule, *Idiom Book*, 77; Turner, *Syntax*, 253; BDF, §213(3); Porter, *Idioms of the Greek New Testament*, 149–50.

58 M. Hengel, *The Son of God: The Origin of Christology and the History of Jewish-Hellenistic Religion* (trans. J. Bowden; Philadelphia: Fortress Press, 1976) 14.

59 Martin, *Reconciliation*, 145–47; see also *idem*, "Center of Paul's Theology," 94. The genitive is subjective, not objective (so most commentators: Dunn, *Romans*, 1.252; Cranfield, *Romans*, 1.262).

That is, Paul refers to him 'adverbially'—to specify and qualify God's act."[60]

D. *Being an Enemy of God*

Paul apparently equates being a sinner with being an enemy of God. This is seen in the parallel use of ἔτι ἁμαρτωλῶν ὄντων ἡμῶν, a genitive absolute, in v. 8, and εἰ...ἐχθροὶ ὄντες, an adverbial use of the participle, in v. 10a. There has been well-known controversy over the nature of wrath in Paul, in particular the book of Romans, ever since Dodd argued for wrath as an "objective principle and process in the moral order."[61] This is not the place to rehearse arguments for or against this position, but suffice it to say that the idea of wrath as God's personal indignation displayed either in the present age and/or at the final judgment against evil has commended itself to many subsequent commentators.[62] This view is reinforced by the logic of Rom 5:8–11, where the wrath from which one is saved is related to being a sinner and an enemy of God. The reader of Romans is prepared for reference to humans being sinners on the basis of 1:18–3:20, where all humankind, including the Jew, is indicted. But the explicit terminology of being an enemy is perhaps unexpected (this is the first reference; see also Rom 11:28; 12:20 [Prov 25:21]), and probably has both active and passive senses. Romans states that humans constitute themselves as God's enemies not only by their sin but also in their disdain for godly things (see Rom 1:18–32), and ἐχθροί logically summarizes the human's status as both cut off in relation to God and as contentious with God. Human sin therefore precipitates God's wrath and hostility, thereby severing his relationship with humanity. As Michel says, "die Feindschaft des Menschen gegen Gott wird zur Feindschaft Gottes gegen den Menschen..."[63]

E. *Final Salvation*

In Romans 5, Paul sees the expectation of final salvation as the result of this common act—called either justification or reconciliation—in his parallel use of the future passive form, σωθησόμεθα, in vv. 9b and 10b. The first instance of use of the verb is modified by the phrase δι' αὐτοῦ, and the second by ἐν τῇ

60 L. Keck, "'Jesus' in Romans," *JBL* 108 (1989) 449.

61 C.H. Dodd, *The Epistle of Paul to the Romans* (MNTC; London: Hodder & Stoughton, 1932) 77, but esp. 20–24. See also A.T. Hanson, *The Wrath of the Lamb* (London: SPCK, 1957) esp. 68–111; G.H.C. Macgregor, "The Concept of the Wrath of God in the New Testament," *NTS* 7 (1960–61) 101–109; D.E.H. Whiteley, *The Theology of St Paul* (2nd edn; Oxford: Blackwell, 1974) 61–72.

62 See, for example, Cranfield, *Romans*, 1.108–10; Dunn, *Romans*, 1.54–55; A. Nygren, *Commentary on Romans* (Philadelphia: Muhlenberg, 1949) 202–206; Fitzmyer, *Romans*, 400–401; L. Morris, *The Apostolic Preaching of the Cross* (3rd edn; Grand Rapids: Eerdmans, 1965) 147–54.

63 Michel, *Römer*, 136.

ζωῇ αὐτοῦ. These are probably synonymous instrumental statements,[64] both referring to the work of Christ. Although a few scholars take αὐτοῦ in v. 9b as referring to the blood mentioned in the previous phrase, or even to "his life" in v. 10,[65] the most logical explanation is the same referent as αὐτοῦ in v. 9 regarding the blood, that is, of Jesus Christ. It might appear strange that reference is made in v. 10 to the life of Christ, when there is so much emphasis on his death, blood, etc. Based upon Rom 4:25, as well as the parallel nature of the statements in vv. 9 and 10, it is unlikely that Paul intended any distinction between the accomplishments of Christ's death and life. The two are inseparably connected, the one necessitating and confirming the other.[66] This understanding is further supported by the loose chiasmic structure in the instrumental statements in vv. 9 and 10.

That the future form verbs are part of an eschatological statement is confirmed by reference in v. 9 to salvation from the wrath of God; the same is probably to be understood in v. 10. Wrath has a similar eschatological sense in Rom 2:5 and 8, and salvation is characteristically spoken of by Paul in Romans using the future tense (9:27; 10:9, 13; 11:26; but cf. 8:24). As Cranfield says, however, it is not entirely clear the exact connection between forensic justification (and reconciliation, it might be added) and eschatological salvation, but for Paul "since God has already done the really difficult thing, that is, justified impious sinners, we may be absolutely confident that He will do what is by comparison very easy, namely save from His wrath at the last those who are already righteous in his sight."[67]

F. *Καταλλαγή*

The noun, καταλλαγή, is used once in Romans 5, in v. 11, which closes off the section. Paul says that not only are his readers to understand that "we" can expect to be saved (vv. 9, 10) but "we" are to boast because of what God has accomplished through our Lord Jesus Christ. The syntax of v. 11 has been variously interpreted. It appears that the participle, καυχώμενοι, is independent,

---

64 See Cranfield, *Romans*, 1.266; Schlier, *Römerbrief*, 154–55; Wilckens, *Römer*, 299.

65 See, for example, R. Bultmann, ζάω, *TDNT*, 2.865 on the former; Sanday–Headlam, *Romans*, 129; Michel, *Römer*, 135; Meyer, *Romans*, 191; and Cranfield, *Romans*, 1.266 on the latter.

66 See F. Godet, *Commentary on St. Paul's Epistle to the Romans* (New York: Funk & Wagnalls, 1883) 197; Keck, "'Jesus,'" esp. 449.

67 Cranfield, *Romans*, 1.266. Cranfield well captures the sense of expectation (not absolute future reference) grammaticalized by the future tense form: see S.E. Porter, *Verbal Aspect in the Greek of the New Testament, with Reference to Tense and Mood* (Studies in Biblical Greek 1; New York: Peter Lang, 1989) 409–16. Contra many commentators, such as Fitzmyer, *Romans*, 401.

functioning as the main verb of its clause.[68] The sense of boasting is the same as in vv. 2 and 3, that "we" jubilantly exult through our Lord Jesus Christ, our mediator (διά), in what God has done: reconciliation (v. 11b). The repetition of the διὰ...Χριστοῦ, δι' οὗ phrases ties the verses concerning reconciliation together, with the reminder that it is Christ who serves as the means (using instrumental phrases) for this work. As Cranfield says, "It is through Christ...through whom we have already received the gift of reconciliation with God, that we exult; for this gift which we have received through him is ground enough for ceaseless exultation."[69] καταλλαγήν collects these various strands and motifs "under the catchword of the reconciliation that exists in the eschatological present,"[70] as a culmination of the past and a hope for the future.

5. *Conclusion*

In conclusion, there remains the difficult question of determining usage of καταλλάσσω in Rom 5:10, according to the patterns of usage presented in section 2 above. There have been two possible interpretations of the category of usage. The first is that humans persuade God to give up his anger against them, a deponent or middle use of the passive form (usage C). That this does not seem to be the best understanding of the use of καταλλάσσω in Rom 5:10 is clear for at least four reasons. (a) The other verbs that refer to redemptive activity, including δικαιωθέντες (v. 1), are true passives. (b) The deponent sense would ruin the continuity of development, that is, "we have been justified" (v. 9) and "we shall be saved" (vv. 10, 11) cannot rightly be interpreted by "we have reconciled God." (c) The other passive verbs, rightly in terms of the context of Rom 5:1–11, concentrate upon God through Christ as the agent of the action (divine passives), although this is never stated explicitly. To reach the climax in Rom 5:10 (κατηλλάγημεν) and say that "we" have done this makes the Pauline logic rather confused. (d) To make all the passive verbs deponent would verge on both grammatical and conceptual nonsense. As Denney says, "To represent κατηλλάγημεν by an active form [he means function]...is to miss the point of the whole passage." He emphatically states, "κατηλλάγημεν is a real passive."[71]

---

68 Cranfield, *Romans*, 1.268 n. 5; Moule, *Idiom Book*, 179; cf. Porter, *Verbal Aspect*, 370–77.

69 Cranfield, *Romans*, 1.268–69.

70 E. Käsemann, *Commentary on Romans* (trans. G.W. Bromiley; Grand Rapids: Eerdmans, 1980) 139. Michel (*Römer*, 136) draws attention to the double νῦν in vv. 9, 11. See Porter, *Verbal Aspect*, 228, where I argue against the past use of the aorist here.

71 J. Denney, *St. Paul's Epistle to the Romans* (5 vols.; Expositor's; repr. Grand Rapids: Eerdmans, n.d.) 2.626.

The second proposal is to understand the verb as passive in form and sense, an example of usage C in which humanity persuades God to give up his anger.[72] The passive form is used so that the means (the work of Christ) might be specified, as well as to show that the action was effected outside of the action of humans, even though they are the grammatical focus. The dative, τῷ θεῷ, is included to specify clearly the goal (or beneficiary) of reconciliation.[73] This analysis maintains the Pauline distinction that καταλλάσσω in the active voice is used only of God and in the passive only of humanity as the grammatical subjects, even though God stands behind these events as their initiator and agent.[74]

Is there a possibility that usage D may be implied? In the light of the analysis above regarding the anger of God over sin, not to be minimized in the book of Romans, usage C cannot be easily dismissed. But there may well be a sense in which humankind as God's enemy, in the process of reconciliation, gives up its own anger against him (usage D). Thus usage in Rom 5:8–11 would be bipartite, but in a slightly different sense than Marshall suggests. God does put "away the wrath which he has toward men and women on account of their sins so that there is no longer any barrier on his side to fellowship with them."[75] But we would then require a sense in which humanity puts away its own wrath and hostility so that there is no longer any barrier on its side to fellowship with God. This is more difficult to establish in the context of Romans 5. As was stated at the outset of this chapter, however, this usage of καταλλάσσω is perhaps the most interesting example because it is the most suggestive.

---

72 Contra Marshall, "Meaning of 'Reconciliation,'" 125, who maintains that there are two senses of καταλλάσσω in Rom 5, one in v. 10a of "God reconciling men to himself (passive, of men), and second in verse 10b of men who have actually entered into the state of reconciliation." This draws unwarranted temporal and theological distinctions that the parallelism and verbal usage do not support.

73 Schlier, *Römerbrief*, 155.

74 Contra V. Taylor, *Forgiveness and Reconciliation: A Study in New Testament Theology* (London: Macmillan, 1948) 74, who says that all forms of the expression in Rom 5:10–11 show that reconciliation is the work of God and that humanity is its object. Conceptually, God is both the agent and one of the beneficiaries of reconciliation, and humanity is the beneficiary exclusively.

75 Marshall, "Meaning of 'Reconciliation,'" 128.

CHAPTER ELEVEN

THE ARGUMENT OF ROMANS 5: CAN A RHETORICAL QUESTION MAKE A DIFFERENCE?*

1. *Introduction*

There has been widespread disagreement about the place of Romans 5 in the argument of Romans, much of the disagreement focusing on isolated factors such as vocabulary items.[1] I wish to approach the question from a different angle, in the light of recent work in Pauline rhetoric.[2] It has been well established by a number of scholars that Romans exemplifies features of the diatribe at significant junctures, in particular 2:1–5, 17–29, 3:1–9, 3:27–4:25, 6:1–16, 9:19–21, 11:17–24, and 14:4–10,[3] but to my knowledge it has not been

* This essay is reprinted with the permission of the Society of Biblical Literature, from the *Journal of Biblical Literature* 110 (1991) 655–77. Footnotes have been updated in places.

1 See, for example, A. Feuillet, "Le plan salvifique de Dieu d'après l'épître aux Romains," *RB* 57 (1950) esp. 344–63; N.A. Dahl, "Two Notes on Romans 5," *ST* 5 (1951) 37–42 esp. 37–38; C.E.B. Cranfield, *A Critical and Exegetical Commentary on the Epistle to the Romans* (2 vols.; ICC; Edinburgh: T. & T. Clark, 1975, 1977) esp. 1.252–54; B.N. Kaye, *The Thought Structure of Romans with Special Reference to Chapter 6* (Austin: Schola, 1979) esp. 14–23; J.D.G. Dunn, *Romans* (2 vols.; WBC 38A, B; Dallas: Word, 1988) 1.242–44. See also ch. 10 in this volume, pp. 195–212, for discussion of καταλλάσσω.

2 Articles utilizing this approach are growing in number. See, for example, W. Wuellner, "Paul's Rhetoric of Argumentation in Romans: An Alternative to the Donfried–Karris Debate over Romans," *CBQ* 38 (1976) 330–51; and more recently S.E. Porter, "The Theoretical Justification for Application of Rhetorical Categories to Pauline Epistolary Literature," in *Rhetoric and the New Testament: Essays from the 1992 Heidelberg Conference* (JSNTSup 90; Sheffield: JSOT Press, 1993) 100–22; and D.F. Watson and A.J. Hauser, *Rhetorical Criticism of the Bible: A Comprehensive Bibliography with Notes on History and Method* (Biblical Interpretation Series 4; Leiden: Brill, 1994) 178–201.

3 See S.K. Stowers, *The Diatribe and Paul's Letter to the Romans* (SBLDS 57; Chico, CA: Scholars Press, 1981) esp. 85–115; *idem*, "Paul's Dialogue with a Fellow Jew in Rom 3:1–9," *CBQ* 46 (1984) 707–22; cf. Dunn, *Romans*, 1.lxii and loc. cit.; H.-J. Findeis, *Versöhnung—Apostolat—Kirche: Eine exegetisch-theologische und rezeptionsgeschichtliche Studie zu den Versöhnungsaussagen des Neuen Testaments (2 Kor, Röm, Kol, Eph)* (FB; Würzburg: Echter, 1983) 253–54, who recognizes a rhetorical pattern of question and answer

argued that Romans 5 evidences sustained or concentrated use of the diatribe.[4] I wish to argue, first, that there was a genre called "diatribe" in Hellenistic rhetoric; secondly, that Romans 5 exemplifies several important features of diatribe; and, thirdly, that recognition of these diatribal features helps to understand how the chapter furthers Paul's argument. In his dialogue with a hypothetical interlocutor Paul makes precise statements about the work of Christ in justification and especially reconciliation, using the Adam/Christ typology as a poignant example of this process. Paul establishes the chapter's diatribal unity through use of rhetorical questions, connectives and phrases common to diatribe and other dialogical rhetorical styles.

2. *Greco-Roman Diatribe*

Revival of interest in the rhetorical world of the first century has fostered research once more into the question of Greco-Roman diatribe. Discussion of Greco-Roman diatribe has gone through various stages, which Stowers and Schmeller have chronicled.[5] The earliest reference to diatribe, reportedly by Usener in his *Epicurea*, was soon followed by studies advocating "diatribe" as a particular literary form or genre.[6] Bultmann accepted these conclusions.[7] Soon

in chs. 3, 4, 6, 7, 9, 11; and T. Schmeller, *Paulus und die "Diatribe": Eine vergleichende Stilinterpretation* (Münster: Aschendorff, 1987) 70–71, who cites secondary literature recognizing perceived elements of the diatribe in every chapter from 1–15 (perceptively reviewed by S. K. Stowers in *JBL* 108 [1989] 538–42).

4 Individual commentators have recognized select features in ch. 5 (e.g. H. Schlier, *Der Römerbrief* [HTKNT; 2nd edn; Freiburg: Herder, 1979] 139 regarding the application of Abraham to "us" in Rom 5:1), and several scholars have focused upon vv. 12–14: e.g. G. Bouwman, "'Zonde wordt niet aangerekend, wanneer er geen wet is,'" *Tijdschrift voor Theologie* 17 (1977) 131–44; B. Englezakis, "Rom 5:12–15 and the Pauline Teaching on the Lord's Death: Some Observations," *Bib* 58 (1977) 231–36; M. Black, *Romans* (NCB; Grand Rapids: Eerdmans, 1973) 89.

5 Stowers, *Diatribe*, 7–48; *idem*, "The Diatribe," in *Greco-Roman Literature and the New Testament* (ed. D.E. Aune; SBLSBS 21; Atlanta: Scholars Press, 1988) 71–74; Schmeller, *Paulus*, 1–54. See these sources for further bibliography.

6 H. Usener, *Epicurea* (Leipzig, 1887; repr. Rome: "L'Erma," 1963) lxix; R. Hirzel, *Der Dialog: Ein Literarhistorischer Versuch* (vol. 1; 1895; repr. Hildesheim: Olms, 1963) 369–70 esp. n. 2; E. Norden, *Die Antike Kunstprosa vom VI. Jahrhundert v. Chr. bis in die Zeit der Renaissance* (2 vols.; 1898; repr. Darmstadt: Wissenschaftliche Buchgesellschaft, 1958) 1.128–31, 2.556–58, who includes diatribe as "ein in die Form der Deklamation umgewandelter Dialog"; P. Wendland, *Die hellenistisch-römische Kultur in ihren Beziehungen zu Judentum und Christentum* (HNT 2; 1907; repr. Tübingen: Mohr–Siebeck, 1972) 75–81, who traces what he perceives as a decline in the vitality of the genre.

7 R. Bultmann, *Der Stil der paulinischen Predigt und die kynisch-stoische Diatribe* (1910; FRLANT; repr. Göttingen: Vandenhoeck & Ruprecht, 1984).

afterwards the climate changed, however. Scholars began critically to evaluate diatribe as a literary genre, and many, though by no means all,[8] abandoned this characterization.[9] After World War II a consensus emerged when a number of scholars took the position that diatribe was not a distinct genre but a literary style or set of techniques, often found in other rhetorical philosophical prose.[10] It is often said that New Testament scholarship in this area has not been cognizant of research in classical studies[11] but has relied on Bultmann, while classical research long ago dismissed diatribe as a genre.[12] This statement is overly bold. There are good reasons for arguing for the genre "diatribe," and

8 Those who retained diatribe as a literary genre include W. von Christ, *Geschichte der griechischen Literatur* (ed. O. Stählin and W. Schmid; Munich: Beck, 1920) II.1.55–56 esp. n. 3, in Wendland's sense; A.D. Nock, "Diatribe Form in the Hermetica," in *Essays on Religion and the Ancient World* (2 vols.; ed. Z. Stewart; Cambridge, MA: Harvard University Press, 1972) 1.26–32 (originally published as "A New Edition of the Hermetic Writings," *JEA* 11 [1925] 126–37); *idem* (ed.), *Sallustius, Concerning the Gods and the Universe* (Cambridge: Cambridge University Press, 1926) xxvii–xxxii.

9 Those who abandoned diatribe as a genre include O. Halbauer, *De Diatribis Epicteti* (Diss. Leipzig, 1911) 3–18 [which I have not seen]; and A. Bonhöffer, *Epiktet und das Neuen Testament* (Religionsgeschichtliche Versuche und Vorarbeiten; Giessen: Töpelmann, 1911) esp. 179 n. 1, who does not consider Epictetus's diatribes characteristic (see below), and whose own definition of diatribe is problematic (cf. Stowers, *Diatribe*, 26–28). See also M. Pohlenz, *Die Stoa: Geschichte einer geistigen Bewegung* (2 vols.; Göttingen: Vandenhoeck & Ruprecht, 1948, 1949), who conspicuously lacks reference to diatribe apart from a footnote to Usener (2.137).

10 For example, G. Schmidt, "Diatribai," in *Der Kleine Pauly* (vol. 2; ed. K. Ziegler and W. Sontheimer; Stuttgart: Druckenmüller, 1967) Nachträge 1577–78; H. Rahn, *Morphologie der antiken Literatur: Eine Einführung* (Die Altertumswissenschaft; Darmstadt: Wissenschaftliche Buchgesellschaft, 1969) 153–56; K.P. Donfried, "False Presuppositions in the Study of Romans," in *The Romans Debate* (ed. K.P. Donfried; 2nd edn; Peabody: Hendrickson, 1991 [1977]) 112–21 (originally published in *CBQ* 36 [1974] 332–55); Stowers, *Diatribe*, 49; A.J. Malherbe, *Moral Exhortation: A Greco-Roman Sourcebook* (Library of Early Christianity; Philadelphia: Westminster Press, 1986) 129–34; *idem*, *Paul and the Popular Philosophers* (Philadelphia: Fortress Press, 1989) esp. 1–9; Schmeller, *Paulus*, 1–54 esp. 33–54.

11 Cf. W. Capelle and H.I. Marrou, "Diatribe," in *RAC* (Stuttgart: Hiersemann, 1952) 3.990–1010; D.E. Aune, "De Esu Carnium Orationes I and II (Moralia 993A–999B)," in *Plutarch's Theological Writings and Early Christian Literature* (ed. H.D. Betz; SCHNT; Leiden: Brill, 1975) 303–305; *idem*, *The New Testament in its Literary Environment* (Library of Early Christianity; Philadelphia: Westminster Press, 1987) 200–202.

12 See especially E.A. Judge, "St. Paul and Classical Society," *JAC* 15 (1972) 33; endorsed by A.J. Malherbe, *Social Aspects of Early Christianity* (Baton Rouge: Louisiana State University Press, 1977 [2nd edn; Philadelphia: Fortress Press, 1983]) 50 n. 55; also H.D. Jocelyn, "Diatribes and Sermons," *Liverpool Classical Monthly* 7 (1982) 3; Stowers, *Diatribe*, 45–46; *idem*, "Diatribe," 71; Donfried, "Presuppositions," 118–19.

many of these are made by classical scholars.[13]

If a concept of genre is established by word usage, it cannot be denied that διατριβή and its cognates most often refer not to a clear literary form but to discussion, philosophical discourse, or the passing of time.[14] But a fundamental principle of determining genre is to compare and contrast literary works to find suitable descriptive categories.[15] Whether a piece of literature belongs in a particular generic category can only be answered in terms of what other categories are available. And here the strongest evidence for a genre of diatribe emerges.[16]

---

13 Besides Nock above, see for example A. Lesky, *Geschichte der griechischen Literatur* (2nd edn; Bern: Francke, 1963 [1957/58]) 719: "Die folgenreichste literarische Leistung der Kynischen Popularphilosophie ist jedoch die Augestaltung der Diatribe, der mit scharfen Witz und angriffslustiger Satire vorgetragenen und durch Polemik in fingierten Dialogen belebten Werberede"; H.B. Gottschalk, "Diatribe Again," *Liverpool Classical Monthly* 7 (1982) 91–92; *idem*, "More on DIATRIBAI," *Liverpool Classical Monthly* 8 (1983) 91–92, who uses arguments also made by Hirzel (Gottschalk responds to Jocelyn, "Diatribes and Sermons," 3–7; *idem*, "'Diatribe' and the Greek Book-Title Διατριβαί," *Liverpool Classical Monthly* 8 [1983] 89–91).

14 This point was made when I searched the Thesaurus Linguae Graecae data-base for all uses of διατριβή. After generating twenty-five pages of examples for authors beginning with A, I gave up.

15 The complex question of genre is one which many biblical scholars have failed to address satisfactorily. Stowers (*Diatribe*, 49; contra "Diatribe," 73), for example, acknowledges the problem, but only cites E.D. Hirsch, Jr., *Validity in Interpretation* (New Haven: Yale University Press, 1967). There is often confusion when discussing genre whether a generic category is to be one formulated by modern interpreters or recognized by the ancients. Ancient categories often appear anachronistic when discussed centuries later, and comparison with other bodies of literature from various times or by various other groups is often difficult. On the other hand, modern categories often overlook distinctions important to the ancients. (Schmeller [*Paulus*, esp. 13–21] recognizes a difference between "diatribe" as an ancient category—equating it with "dialexis"—and what modern interpreters call "diatribe.") In any case, a genre should only be spoken of comparatively, whether in comparison with categories in the ancient or modern worlds. See C.H. Holman, *A Handbook to Literature* (3rd edn; Indianapolis: Bobbs-Merrill, 1974) s.v.; H. Dubrow, *Genre* (Critical Idiom; London: Methuen, 1982); and the still valuable R. Wellek and A. Warren, *Theory of Literature* (3rd edn; New York: Harcourt, Brace and World, 1956) 226–37.

16 Many scholars refer to the small size of the potential corpus (e.g. Donfried, "Presuppositions," 113; cf. Stowers, *Diatribe*, 48–75; Schmeller, *Paulus*, 5–13). They often fail to realize that only a small and highly unrepresentative portion survives of the literary works of the Hellenistic period. For example, over one hundred tragedians are known by name, but only 403 lines of their work are extant, less than about one-third of one complete play. But there is an unrepresentatively high proportion of poetry and literature revealing Atticistic tendencies. It is only within the last approximately 140 years, with the discovery of the Egyptian papyri, that a more realistic estimation of the literary character of the Hellenistic world has been formulated. The diatribe, as representative of popular philosophy, probably

The word διατριβή, usually plural, occurs in several formulations as the title of Hellenistic literary works.[17] For example, in Diogenes Laertius (DL) 2.83–84, 85, 7.34, 36, 163, 174–175, 178, διατριβαί is used of works by Aristippus, Zeno, Persaeus, Ariston, Cleanthes, Sphaerus, and other Stoics.[18] Dio Chrysostom's *Or.* 27 is entitled: Διατριβὴ περὶ τῶν ἐν συμποσίῳ.[19] Archytas's selection 4 is entitled: Διατριβαί (cf. Stobaeus 1 pr. 4: Ἐκ τῶν Ἀρχύτου διατριβῶν). And Athenaeus (11.508F) tells of Εὐαίων δ' ὁ Λαμψακηνός, ὥς φησιν Εὐρύπυλος καὶ Δικαιοκλῆς ὁ Κνίδιος ἐνενηκοστῷ (ἐν εἰκοστῷ Musurus) καὶ πρώτῳ διατριβῶν. Three features of the contexts in which διατριβή appears strengthen the argument that diatribe is a recognizable genre. First, in DL διατριβαί is used as distinct from other terms for literary forms,[20] and hence distinguishes diatribe from other apparent genres. Secondly, in some contexts διατριβαί, like other generic titles in these lists, is modified not by reference to the author or originator[21] but by a word or phrase that identifies its

was not considered worth preserving by those responsible for such things, such as the Alexandrian librarians. At the least, there is little evidence that popular philosophical authors were preserved as well as some of their literary counterparts. For example, only four of a reported eight books of Epictetus's writings survive, which is much better than Epicurus, whose 300 volumes have vanished apart from quotation by others. Cynic philosophy was skeptical towards established conventions, and this would have run contrary to the educational and political structures of the Hellenistic world. See K.J. Dover *et al.*, *Ancient Greek Literature* (Oxford: Oxford University Press, 1980) 134–76 esp. 134–36; C.G. Starr, *A History of the Ancient World* (3rd edn; New York: Oxford University Press, 1983) 413–34.

17 This discussion analyses Gottschalk's and Jocelyn's work (cf. Hirzel, *Dialog*, 369 n. 2), examining evidence not appreciated by Schmeller (*Paulus*, 5–6).

18 Stobaeus refers in 3.13.37 (cf. 3.13.38), 4.8.27 to Ἐκ τῶν Διογένους διατριβῶν. Jocelyn ("Diatribes and Sermons," 5) points out that DL at 6.80 does not refer to αἱ Διογένους διατριβαί, positing that the references above are to λόγοι of Diogenes. This he purports is the source of Arrian's titles for the words of Epictetus (see n. 23). Cf. Humenias of Apamea (Eusebius, *Praep. Ev.* 14.6.6), who refers to αἱ ἐπιγραφόμεναι διατριβαί of a Diocles as the source for a story.

19 It is beyond the scope of this chapter to discuss which of these titles was applied by the author and which by an editor (see discussion regarding Epictetus in n. 23). In either case the evidence witnesses to an ancient conception of the genre of diatribe.

20 For example, σχολή (7.163), ἀπομνημόνευμα (7.36, 163), διάλογος (2.83; 7.163, 178), ἱστορία (2.83), ἐπιστολή (2.84; 7.163, 178), τέχνη (7.34, 174?, 178), ὑπόμνημα (7.163), χρεία (2.84, 85; 7.36, 163, 175?), πολιτεία (7.34, 36, 178?), προτρεπτικός? (2.85; 7.36, 163, 175), ἐρώτησις? (2.84). DL at 2.77 refers to ὥς φασιν οἱ περὶ τὸν Βίωνα ἐν ταῖς διατριβαῖς (cf. 4.47, where DL refers to Bion's work using ὑπομνήματα and ἀποφθέγματα). Jocelyn ("'Diatribes'...Διατριβαί," 90) takes this to mean "Bion and his associates," disputing singular authorship, rather than the "periphrastic" sense endorsed by Gottschalk.

21 Jocelyn ("Diatribes and Sermons," 4–5) asserts that many of the accounts may have been reports of the philosopher's activities or may have titles attached by librarians. But Gottschalk ("Diatribe," 91; "More on DIATRIBAI," 91) dismisses this argument: the

number, subject or content.[22] Thirdly, the ancients themselves occasionally refer to the writing of diatribes. For example, DL 7.34 says, Ζήνων...ἐν ταῖς διατριβαῖς τὰ παραπλησία γράφει, where DL refers to works written by Zeno, distinguishing them from other writings, such as ἡ Ἐρωτικὴ τέχνη (7.34) and ἡ Πολιτεία (7.34). Sextus Empiricus (*Adv. Math.* 11.190–194) quotes Zeno's diatribes (ἐν ταῖς διατριβαῖς) (190) in the same way that he quotes ἡ Πολιτεία (192) and περὶ δικαιοσύνης (193), and περὶ τοῦ καθήκοντος (194) of Chrysippus. These factors indicate that the title "diatribe" may well refer to a genre of literary work attributed to the author or originator of its ideas.[23]

Even Jocelyn admits that διατριβή refers to a kind of writing in Athenaeus 11.508CD: κατὰ τῆς Πλάτωνος διατριβῆς by Isocrates's pupil Theopompus of Chios, where Athenaeus continues with reference to other diatribes.[24] Jocelyn,

---

contexts in DL do not indicate such difficulty and it is unlikely that every Stoic philosopher had a scribe.

22 For example, DL 2.85: διατριβῶν ἕξ; 7.163: Περὶ σοφίας διατριβῶν ζ' and Ἐρωτικαὶ διατριβαί; 7.175: διατριβῶν δύο; 7.178: Περὶ Ἡρακλείτου πέντε διατριβῶν; contra Jocelyn ("'Diatribes'...Διατριβαί," 90), who interpreting τέχνης διαλεκτικῆς δύο as "two books about the τέχνη διαλεκτική" takes reference to diatribes as "a book about διατριβαί."

23 There is dispute over the formal title of the books of Epictetus. The correct title appears to be Ἀρριανοῦ τῶν Ἐπικτήτου διατριβῶν ΑΒΓ, as opposed to αἱ Ἐπικτήτου διατριβαί. This could possibly, though not necessarily, contradict the above analysis, since Arrian is the author of this work, containing the ideas of Epictetus. The title is perhaps best explained by Photius: ὁ Ἀρριανὸς φιλόσοφος...ἔγραψε δὲ βιβλία καὶ ἕτερα, τῶν μὲν Διατριβῶν Ἐπικτήτου τοῦ διδασκάλου ὅσα ἴσμεν βιβλία ὀκτώ (Bibl. cod. 58, p. 17b 17–19; testim. VI Schenkl; cf. Simplicius in testim. III Schenkl: περὶ μὲν τοῦ βίου τοῦ Ἐπικτήτου καὶ τῆς αὐτοῦ τελευτῆς Ἀρριανὸς ἔγραψεν, ὁ τὰς Ἐπικτήτου Διατριβὰς ἐν πολυστίχοις συντάξας βιβλίοις... τὸ δὲ βιβλίον τοῦτο τὸ Ἐπικτήτου Ἐγχειρίδιον ἐπιγεγραμμένον καὶ τοῦτο αὐτὸ συνέταξεν ὁ Ἀρριανός. Photius [Bibl. cod. 241, p. 339a 17–18; in testim. XLII Schenkl] refers to a Theosebius who ἔλεγε...τὰ πολλὰ ἀπὸ τῶν Ἐπικτήτου σχολῶν). In his preface Arrian refers to τοὺς Ἐπικτήτου λόγους, and says that the process required that he write down ὑπομνήματα. For Jocelyn this provides evidence that diatribe is not a technical generic distinction, although he does recognize that αἱ Ἐπικτήτου ὁμιλίαι by Arrian referred to in Photius (Bibl. cod. 58, p. 17b 11ff.) must report "more formal types of discourse" (Photius refers to Arrian as εἷς τῶν ὁμιλητῶν Ἐπικτήτου) ("Diatribes and Sermons," 5; contra Gottschalk, "Diatribe," 91, who equates ὁμιλίαι and διατριβαί). The lack of numerous references to διατριβή in Epictetus's work perhaps indicates that the title refers formally to a kind of work (Epictetus 2.16.29; 3.24.5, 6, 40, 68, 72, 75, 99, 109; *Enchiridion* 20.1; 41.1; 52.2). But the title itself, with double attribution, is worth considering. It may serve as a means of establishing that, whereas written conveyance was by Arrian, the form itself or at least its content had its origin with Epictetus. The fact that the books were so labeled, as Gottschalk notes, points to distinguishing features of the discourses, and diatribe as a category of literary work (Hirzel [*Dialog*, 370 n. 2] argues that this pattern is the norm. See also Bion, recorded in Teles).

24 τοὺς πολλούς...τῶν διαλόγων αὐτοῦ ἀχρείους καὶ ψευδεῖς ἄν τις εὕροι·

however, dismisses this by saying that from it nothing is learned about the "mode and structure of the true Socrates' discourse."[25] This may be, but his admission is significant. His inclusion of this example leaves the opportunity open for positive assessment of other ancient formulations (such as above), where although they may not refer to a type of writing familiar to the modern interpreter, they may well refer to a genre familiar to the ancient. DL 3.8 states: ὁ δ' οὖν φιλόσοφος καὶ Ἰσοκράτει φίλος ἦν. καὶ αὐτῶν Πραξιφάνης ἀνέγραψε διατριβήν τινα περὶ ποιητῶν γενομένην ἐν ἀγρῷ παρὰ Πλάτωνι ἐπιξενωθέντος τοῦ Ἰσοκράτους. Jocelyn acknowledges the singular usage in the sense of "philosophical discourse," but argues that DL "used this word rather than διάλογος because σχολαστικοί...rather than men of the world were involved."[26] The written record of philosophers engaged in debate sounds very much like diatribe. As Stowers has shown, there is a logical development from philosophical activity to philosophical literary form.[27] Thus Gottschalk concludes:

> This is enough to establish...that διατριβαί denotes a literary *genre*. What kind of *genre* is a more difficult question. We have to ask first how precisely the word was used... In that case all we can say is that it must have denoted a body of literature sufficiently homogenous and substantial to deserve a separate name...and sufficiently different from the other recognized categories to be kept distinct. If we want to know more, all we can do is to look at the few specimens of διατριβαί which have come down to us, entire or in fragments.[28]

Lists of the literary features of the diatribe have been compiled by many scholars (documentation of particular features will be noted as they are discussed).[29] Few if any of the features are unique to diatribe as opposed to other rhetorical and especially dialogical literary types. Thus Stowers states, "there is no typical structure to a diatribe."[30] The diatribe does, however, seem

---

ἀλλοτρίους δὲ τοὺς πλείους, ὄντας ἐκ τῶν Ἀριστίππου διατριβῶν, ἐνίους δὲ κἀκ τῶν Ἀντισθένους, πόλλους δὲ κἀκ τῶν Βρύσωνος τοῦ Ἡρακλεώτου. Contra Hirzel, *Dialog*, 369 n. 2, who claims that this refers to a school; cf. DL 10.1, 2.

25 Jocelyn, "Diatribes and Sermons," 6.

26 Jocelyn, "Diatribes and Sermons," 4. Whether Plato or Isocrates would have monopolized debate, as Jocelyn fears, is completely beside the point.

27 Stowers, "Diatribe," 74–75; cf. *Diatribe*, 77–78.

28 Gottschalk, "More on DIATRIBAI," 91.

29 Features applicable to study of the New Testament are discussed in Stowers, *Diatribe*, 79–154 esp. 85–100; *idem*, "Diatribe," 74–76; *idem*, "Dialogue," 710–14; Aune, "Orationes," 304–305; Norden, *Kunstprosa*, 1.129 n. 1; A.J. Malherbe, "ΜΗ ΓΕΝΟΙΤΟ in the Diatribe and Paul," *HTR* 73 (1980) 231–40; *idem*, "The Beasts at Ephesus," *JBL* 87 (1968) 72–73; K. Berger, "Hellenistische Gattungen im Neuen Testament," *ANRW* II.25.2 (Berlin: de Gruyter, 1984) 1130–32; Bultmann, *Stil*.

30 Stowers, "Diatribe," 75.

to evidence certain features more frequently than do other rhetorical strategies. The basic orientation of the genre is dialogical,[31] and this dialogical framework entails several features that are relevant to a discussion of Romans 5. These include the introduction of questions or objections by a hypothetical interlocutor speaking as an opponent, as a helper, or even for the author.[32] These statements are often written in the third person apart from direct dialogical exchanges, where imperatives (second person) and hortatory subjunctives (first person) are frequently used.

3. *Diatribe in Romans 5*

In Romans, Paul conducts a recognizable dialogue with an interlocutor off and on from 1:18 to ch. 14.[33] Occasionally, though not always, the questions or objections are introduced by stylistic features, such as the adversative particle ἀλλά (e.g. 10:8, 18, 19; 11:4). Other connectives also occur relatively frequently: οὐ μόνον δέ, ὥστε...οὕτως, εἰ as if the speaker poses a hypothetical scenario (e.g. 3:5, 7; 11:15), and γάρ. Many questions or objections, however, are not introduced by any formulaic phrase. Furthermore, the diatribe style relies on short, crisp sentences connected paratactically (e.g. 2:21–24; 12:8; 14:6), using parallelism and antithesis (e.g. 1:23–28; 3:4–6; 6:1–10; 12:4–15; 14:7–9), with statements occasionally contrasted by οὐ μόνον δέ. In support of an argument Paul occasionally turns to a historical or mythological figure. For example, in Rom 3:25–4:25 Paul utilizes a dialogical exchange (3:27–4:2) followed by an exemplum using the figure of Abraham (4:2–25; cf. Jas 2:21–26),[34] an instructive and helpful parallel to the argument in Romans 5. Paul also may invoke a catalogue of vices or hardships which the wise person must face

---

31 For example, of Teles's eight dialogues, four (1, 3, 4A, 7) actually quote the interlocutor, while the other four, in a style reminiscent of Paul, have the single speaker formulating his interlocutor's responses. Stowers sees all of Rom 1–11 as dialogical (*Diatribe*, 179; *idem*, "Diatribe," 75; cf. *idem*, "Dialogue," 710–11; Norden, *Kunstprosa*, 1.556), raising questions regarding the status of Paul's interlocutor. Whereas Donfried ("Presuppositions," 112, 113–25) believes that the diatribe entails less than a concrete situation, R.J. Karris ("The Occasion of Romans: A Response to Professor Donfried," in *Romans Debate*, 125–27) shows that this does not follow.

32 It is not always clear which function the interlocutor plays. It is not always necessary to decide, however, since the author in responding to the questions or objections moves the argument along. Stowers, "Dialogue," 714.

33 This is seen most obviously in 2:3–4, 21; 3:1–9; 4:1–3, 9–10; 6:1–3, 15; 7:1, 7, 13; 9:14, 19–23; 10:6–8, 14–18; 11:1–7, 11, 15; 14:4, often answered by μὴ γένοιτο: e.g. Rom 3:4, 6, 31; 6:2, 15; 7:7, 13; 9:14; 11:1, 11.

34 Stowers, *Diatribe*, 155–74, rightly noting (p. 238 n. 24) that Bultmann gives no serious attention to the exemplum; cf. Bultmann, *Stil*, 62–63.

(2:8, 21–23). Many other features could be cited, but the above bear directly upon discussion of Romans 5.

At first appearance Romans 5 does not follow the dialogical pattern of question and response so obviously followed in the earlier and later chapters of the book. It seems strange that Paul would use the diatribe in chs. 2–4 and resume use of it in chs. 6–14, while making no use of this literary form in ch. 5. This alone makes it worth looking at ch. 5 in more detail. In fact, there are several significant features in Romans 5 that do point to diatribe.

The first significant diatribal feature is Paul's use of subjunctives in 5:1–3, especially ἔχωμεν in 5:1. Whereas most diatribes proceed in third person, it is not unknown for the first person plural to be used to introduce an interlocutor.[35] Romans 5:1 begins with several points of connection with what has preceded in the epistle. First, the use of δικαιωθέντες draws verbal connections with the previous material and establishes that what follows is grounded in justification.[36] Secondly, the connective οὖν reinforces the point of correlation and establishes that what follows is to build on the argument as a logical consequence.[37] The argument probably builds from 3:21 to 4:25, although 1:18 to 4:25 is also a possibility.[38] Then, having already discussed the language of faith as the means of justification, Paul says, εἰρήνην ἔχομεν/ἔχωμεν πρὸς τὸν θεὸν διὰ τοῦ κυρίου ἡμῶν Ἰησοῦ Χριστοῦ. Although several of the older commentators argue for the subjunctive, most recent scholars argue that the correct reading is the indicative, ἔχομεν (C rating in the *UBSGNT*[3] text).[39] The

---

35 See Stowers, "Diatribe," 714, citing Dio Chrysostom, *Or.* 61.2, 3; Musonius Rufus 8.64, 35; and Aune, "Orationes," 304, citing Plutarch, *Moralia* 997F. See also Teles 2.195 (19H) quoting Socrates; cf. 3.78 (21H) with λέγηται (O'Neil's edition, with Hense's pages included).

36 Cranfield (*Romans*, 1.253) and Schlier (*Römerbrief*, 138) cite statistics on δικ- and πιστ- words in chs. 1–4 and 6–8. On justification and faith in Paul, see Dunn, *Romans*, esp. 1.36–49, 161–83, 246; J. Ziesler, *The Meaning of Righteousness in Paul: A Linguistic and Theological Enquiry* (SNTSMS 20; Cambridge: Cambridge University Press, 1972) 82–162; and M.A. Seifrid, *Justification by Faith: The Origin and Development of a Central Pauline Theme* (NovTSup 68; Leiden: Brill, 1992).

37 F. Blass and A. Debrunner, *A Greek Grammar of the New Testament and Other Early Christian Literature* (trans. R.W. Funk; Chicago: University of Chicago Press, 1961) §421. οὖν is often used as a logical connective in diatribe, often in an objection: e.g. Teles 1.5 (3H); 3.33 (23H), 67 (24H), 91 (25H), 97 (26H); 4A.63 (37H), 165 (43H); 5.37 (51H); 6.3 (52H); 7.4 (55H); cf. Rom 3:31; 7:13; 1 Cor 6:15; Gal 3:21. See Malherbe, "ΜΗ ΓΕΝΟΙΤΟ," 233–34 for further examples.

38 H.A.W. Meyer, *Critical and Exegetical Hand-Book to the Epistle to the Romans* (New York: Funk & Wagnalls, 1884) 180; Cranfield, *Romans*, 1.257.

39 Subjunctive: e.g. Lightfoot, Dodd, Kuss, Sanday and Headlam, Tasker, Jewett, and R.P. Martin, *Reconciliation: A Study of Paul's Theology* (Atlanta: John Knox, 1981) 135, 148; indicative: e.g. Cranfield, Dunn, Schlier, Fitzmyer.

better external evidence clearly rests with the subjunctive (א* A B* C D K L 33 63 81 1175 it$^{d, g}$ vg syr$^{p, pal}$ cop^{bo} arm eth Marcion *al*) rather than the indicative (א^{a} B^{3} F G^{gr} P Ψ 0220^{vid} 88 104 326 330 451 629 1241 1739 1881 2495 *Byz Lect* it$^{61vid?}$ syr^{h} cop^{sa} *al*).[40] The subjunctive reading is distributed among the major families and geographical areas, from a variety of time periods, including the original hands of א and B and several versions.

The major arguments against the subjunctive, therefore, are internal. First, the subjunctive is said to yield an entirely unsuitable sense because Paul is entering a doctrinal section (using indicative verbs) in which exhortation is out of place.[41] Secondly, if ἔχωμεν and καυχώμεθα are both subjunctives, they are inconsistent with οὐ μόνον δέ (instead of μή) and a general awkwardness results.[42] Thirdly, the indicative is required for parallelism with the indicative, ἐσχήκαμεν, in v. 2.[43] Finally, the linkage of διὰ τοῦ κυρίου ἡμῶν Ἰησοῦ Χριστοῦ with the subjunctive is inconsistent with Paul's linkage of similar phrases elsewhere and calls into question the effectiveness of the work of Christ.[44]

Before arguments for the subjunctive are presented, the reasons against it, cited above, warrant response. First, if it is accepted that in places Romans 1–14 utilizes the diatribe, and more particularly that chs. 3–4 and 6–14 evidence numerous specific features of diatribe, the first objection evaporates. The exhortative stance surely fits well within Paul's persuasive rhetorical mode. Paul has just completed his exemplum using Abraham and, developing his argument further, uses justification as groundwork for reconciliation. Then the response in 6:1 by his hypothetical interlocutor receives the curt μὴ γένοιτο in v. 2. This short exchange continues the exhortative style. Secondly, the use of οὐ μόνον δέ is not a pressing difficulty. This elliptical contrastive construction, reinforced here with ἀλλὰ καί to focus upon the consequence,[45] is used to refer

---

40 B.M. Metzger, *A Textual Commentary on the Greek New Testament* (corrected edn; London: United Bible Societies, 1975) 511.

41 Meyer, *Romans*, 179; Dunn, *Romans*, 1.245.

42 J. Denney, *St. Paul's Epistle to the Romans* (5 vols.; Expositor's; repr. Grand Rapids: Eerdmans, n.d.) 2.623. But J.B. Lightfoot (*Notes on the Epistles of Saint Paul: 1 and 2 Thessalonians, 1 Corinthians, Romans 1–7, Ephesians 1:1–14* [London: Macmillan, 1895] 284) argues for the subjunctive ἔχωμεν and the indicative of καυχώμεθα in v. 2, as well as the textual variant καυχώμενοι in v. 3 (B C Origen).

43 U. Wilckens, *Der Brief an die Römer (Röm 1–5)* (EKK; 2nd edn; Zürich: Benziger, 1987) 288. Schlier (*Römerbrief*, 140) includes καυχώμεθα in 5:2 and καυχώμενοι in v. 11 as parallel as well.

44 M. Wolter, *Rechtfertigung und zukünftiges Heil: Untersuchungen zu Röm 5,1–11* (BZNW 43; Berlin: de Gruyter, 1978) 91–94.

45 See G.B. Winer, *A Treatise on the Grammar of New Testament Greek* (trans. W.F. Moulton; 3rd edn; Edinburgh: T. & T. Clark, 1882) 729–30; cf. BDF, §479(1). Malherbe ("ΜΗ ΓΕΝΟΙΤΟ," 237) notes that ἀλλά is used in diatribe to introduce supporting

to something which immediately precedes. In this case, the use of the finite verb is apparently not referred to, since the same verb, καυχώμεθα, follows. Rather, the phrase ἐπ' ἐλπίδι τῆς δόξης τοῦ θεοῦ is contrasted with ἐν ταῖς θλίψεσιν by means of οὐ μόνον δέ. οὐ μόνον δέ also occurs in v. 11, where there is apparent elision of the participle, καταλλαγέντες, which contrasts with the following participle.[46] Thirdly, the perfect, ἐσχήκαμεν, is not parallel to ἔχωμεν or ἔχομεν, being in a subordinate relative clause. The actual parallel to ἔχωμεν (or ἔχομεν) is καυχώμεθα in v. 2b, repeated in v. 3. Finally, Wolter confuses the issue of verbal attitude.[47] This use of the hortatory subjunctive exhorts the reader or interlocutor to possess what is; it does not call into question what is. Conversely, use of the indicative would not make the effectiveness of the work of Jesus Christ any more certain. It would only indicate the author or speaker's attitude towards the event.

The arguments in favour of the subjunctive reading are more substantial than credit is often given. First, Paul in other places is able to include exhortation in his argument (e.g. 6:1, 12, 15; 8:12).[48] This is sometimes accomplished with the subjunctive but also with the future and other rhetorical forms.[49] Secondly, the context of previous enmity and present peace allows for Paul to say that Christians should no longer fight against God but now cultivate their privilege. This leads to the exhortation to boast despite one's circumstances.[50] Thirdly, if it does not demand it, use of diatribe in chs. 3 and 4 at least encourages the exhortative subjunctive, urging the reader to accept what Paul has already asserted. Use of the subjunctive in 5:1 is mirrored in 6:1 with ἐπιμένωμεν, just before Paul turns his argument again towards a possible objection. The result of

---

affirmations. οὐ μόνον ἀλλὰ καί appears, for example, in Teles at 6.23 (53H); 7.130–131 (61H).

46 W. Sanday and A.C. Headlam, *A Critical and Exegetical Commentary on the Epistle to the Romans* (ICC; 5th edn; Edinburgh: T. & T. Clark, 1902) 129. There is some textual uncertainty in 5:11, with the participle found in ℵ B C D F G Majority lat syr, but καυχωμεθα/μεν in F G L 104 365 *al*. Winer takes the entire phrase, καταλλαγέντες σωθησόμεθα, as the elided phrase in v. 11 (*Grammar*, 729; contra Cranfield, *Romans*, 1.268 n. 5). The future form may well be understood (Wolter, *Rechtfertigung*, 196–97; although two participles dependent upon the same governing verb is common enough without repetition of the verb), but the change in participle seems to be Paul's emphasis (Meyer, *Romans*, 192). Findeis calls vv. 3 and 11 formal analogies (*Versöhnung*, 254).

47 S.E. Porter, *Verbal Aspect in the Greek of the New Testament, with Reference to Tense and Mood* (Studies in Biblical Greek 1; New York: Peter Lang, 1989) 163–78 and 321–35.

48 Sanday–Headlam, *Romans*, 120. Significantly, these examples follow Rom 5:1, illustrating that Paul is not yet finished with exhortation.

49 See Malherbe, "ΜΗ ΓΕΝΟΙΤΟ," 233–34.

50 Lightfoot, *Notes*, 284; cf. F.F. Bruce, *Romans* (TNTC; Grand Rapids: Eerdmans, 1963) 122–23.

this analysis is parallel uses of the subjunctive καυχώμεθα in vv. 2 and 3 as well, with Paul continuing to exhort his audience.[51]

A red herring is often dragged across this argument for the subjunctive. It is suggested that a scribe misheard the *omega* for the *omicron* in 5:1.[52] But this claim cuts both ways; it is just as possible that the scribe misheard *omicron* for *omega*. Both internal and external criteria indicate that the subjunctive is the better reading. Thus when diatribe is considered, the "more difficult" reading, the subjunctive, becomes the more plausible reading. In 5:1–3, the hypothetical interlocutor is addressed again in the first person plural or "we" style of 3:28–4:1 (although the person has been present since 1:18 and appears elsewhere sporadically). The effect is to suggest to the interlocutor that justification provides the groundwork for enjoying a new relationship of peace with God.[53] Paul bases this relationship on Jesus Christ, who provides access to God;[54] this relationship allows boasting despite ill fortune which may also be experienced.

This boasting introduces in vv. 3–5 the transitional Pauline chain progression: from tribulation to endurance to provenness,[55] culminating in hope.[56] These could refer to the physical hardships and sufferings that Paul regards as the inevitable lot of the Christian or as the important signifiers of

---

51 Minor punctuation should separate ἑστήκαμεν from καυχώμεθα in v. 2.

52 See, for example, Dunn, *Romans*, 1.245. J.A.T. Robinson speculates that the original MS was in error (with the subjunctive) and that the scribal correction of ἔχομεν is correct (*Wrestling with Romans* [Philadelphia: Westminster Press, 1979] 57). He cites 1 Cor 15:49; cf. Gal 6:10.

53 On "peace," see E. Dinkler, *EIRENE: Der urchristliche Friedensgedanke* (SHAW; Heidelberg: Winter, 1973) esp. 23–35.

54 This access is variously interpreted as: cultic (O. Michel, *Der Brief an die Römer* [MeyerK 4; 14th edn; Göttingen: Vandenhoeck & Ruprecht, 1978] 130)); regal (Bruce, *Romans*, 123; Wolter, *Rechtfertigung*, 107–20); military (F. Godet, *Commentary on St. Paul's Epistle to the Romans* [New York: Funk & Wagnalls, 1883] 187–88; Sanday–Headlam, *Romans*, 121); or nautical (Black, *Romans*, 82). In any case, the access is grounded in a state of grace.

55 Scholars differ on whether this progression is Rabbinic or Greek. Perhaps this is a false disjunction: see E. Käsemann, *Commentary on Romans* (trans. G.W. Bromiley; Grand Rapids: Eerdmans, 1980) 134; H.L. Strack and P. Billerbeck, *Kommentar zum Neuen Testament aus Talmud und Midrasch* (6 vols.; Munich: Beck, 1961–65) 3.222; R. Scroggs, "Paul as Rhetorician: Two Homilies in Romans 1–11," in *Jews, Greeks and Christians: Religious Cultures in Late Antiquity* (Festschrift W.D. Davies; ed. R. Hamerton-Kelly and R. Scroggs; Leiden: Brill, 1976) 285. Schlier hypothesizes that Paul follows parenetic tradition (*Römerbrief*, 131).

56 Cf. Jas 1:3 for the reverse movement. On "hope," see J.P. Heil, *Romans—Paul's Letter of Hope* (AnBib 112; Rome: Biblical Institute Press, 1987) esp. 35–40. For the dominant eschatological perspective, see G. Nebe, *"Hoffnung" bei Paulus: Elpis und ihre Synonyme im Zusammenhang der Eschatologie* (SUNT 16; Göttingen: Vandenhoeck & Ruprecht, 1983) 122–36.

redemption through the work of Christ.[57] The progression culminates in an eschatological hope that does not disappoint.[58] This list appears to be a Pauline version of the catalogue of vices or hardships that a wise person faces to show character.[59]

Appeal to use of diatribe in ch. 5 also makes understandable vv. 6–7. The traditional points of dispute in these verses include a textual variant, what the verses purport to say about human nature, and how they seem to intrude into the argument of the chapter.[60] Keck analyses what many scholars before him have noted: the argument of Rom 5:1–11 seems to remain intact even if vv. 6–7 are deleted, although v. 6 seems to anticipate v. 8.[61] This has resulted in several proposals, most of which focus upon the set of textual variants in v. 6a regarding connectives. Most scholars prefer the widely and well attested ἔτι γάρ...ἔτι (ℵ A C D^{gr*} 81 104 365 1241 1506 syr^h Marcion),[62] which only warrants a D rating from the *UBSGNT*^{3}. A significant number prefer εἴ γε...ἔτι (B 945 syr^p cop^{sa}).[63] A variant reading of ἔτι γάρ omits the second ἔτι (D^c K P Ψ 33 minuscules arm eth Origen lat).

A noticeable but not fully appreciated factor in trying to solve this textual dilemma is the repetition of ἔτι. Michael calls this a "faulty repetition," and supports εἰς τί γάρ...ἔτι (D^b F G it vg $Iren^{lat}$ Pelagius).[64] Several of the

57 See, for example, Sanday–Headlam, *Romans*, 125; versus H. Lietzmann, *Einführung in die Textgeschichte der Paulusbriefe an die Römer* (HNT 8; 5th edn; Tübingen: Mohr-Siebeck, 1971) 59. Some see a strictly eschatological interpretation of the tribulations: for example, Käsemann, *Romans*, 134–35; H. Schlier, θλῖψις, *TDNT*, 3.143–46; *idem*, *Römerbrief*, 146–47.

58 καταισχύνει is probably a present indicative, not a future, in form. Establishing temporal reference is difficult, but it is probably timeless. See Michel, *Römer*, 133 n. 3; Schlier, *Römerbrief*, 149.

59 Cf. Epictetus 1.24.1; 4.9.5–6. See Michel, *Römer*, 131 n. 3, on εἰδότες as a Pauline formula conveying certain knowledge; cf. G. Bertram, κατεργάζομαι, *TDNT*, 3.635.

60 See G. Bornkamm, *Das Ende des Gesetzes: Paulusstudien* (BEvT; Munich: Kaiser, 1952) 78–80, who labels it a "Pauline anacoluthon," solved by seeing vv. 6–8 unified around each clause ending with a form of ἀποθνῄσκω. A few scholars see no difficulties here: e.g. C.H. Dodd, *The Epistle of Paul to the Romans* (MNTC; London: Hodder & Stoughton, 1932) 74–75; D.A. Black, *Paul, Apostle of Weakness: Astheneia and its Cognates in the Pauline Literature* (American University Studies 7.3; New York: Peter Lang, 1984) 182–84 esp. n. 18.

61 L.E. Keck, "The Post-Pauline Interpretation of Jesus' Death in Rom 5:6–7," in *Theologia Crucis—Signum Crucis* (Festschrift E. Dinkler; ed. C. Andresen and G. Klein; Tübingen: Mohr–Siebeck, 1979) 237–48.

62 For example, Lietzmann, Bornkamm, Cranfield, Käsemann, Kuss, Schlier, Wilckens, and Dunn.

63 For example, Sanday and Headlam, Thrall, Sahlin.

64 J.H. Michael, "A Phenomenon in the Text of Romans," *JTS* 39 (1938) 152. Cranfield (*Romans*, 1.263 n. 5) speculates that the first ἔτι "was intended to carry some such sense as

readings make understandable sense in context, including especially εἴ γε and εἰς τί γάρ, but much less likely ἔτι γάρ...ἔτι. More important in this instance is deciding which reading accounts most plausibly for the others. It is possible that εἰς τί γάρ resulted from a conscious attempt to alleviate the double ἔτι. Since there is no pressing theological significance to call forth textual changes, however, a more likely explanation is one that illustrates scribal tendencies in the course of normal textual transmission. In that case it is not clear how εἰς τί γάρ would have occurred through normal textual transmission in the light of the variants attested. But the reading εἰς τί γάρ would clearly explain the readings with εἰ through deletion, as well as avoid the serious difficulty of the repetition of ἔτι. The first ἔτι in all likelihood was not expanded from εἴ γε but resulted from deletion from εἰς τί γάρ.[65] The reading with εἰς τί γάρ would then be translated, following Black, as a dialogical question: "For to what purpose did Christ, while we were yet helpless, die at the right time [or "then"][66] for the ungodly?"[67]

In introducing a hypothetical question to clarify Paul's argument, this solution recognizes and solves the awkward transition from v. 5 to v. 6. This hypothetical objection is not introduced by one of the more common rhetorical formulas, but as Stowers rightly notes, "Objections and false conclusions without formulae of saying are even more frequent" than those with formulas.[68] And Rom 5:6 does at least resemble several other formulas for objections.[69] Although v. 7 linked by γάρ may be Paul's answer to the hypothetical question, it is more likely that this verse is part of the question raised by the hypothetical speaker. This is supported by Wisse's argument for the weakness of Paul's apparent response.[70] The sentiments expressed are very much in keeping with

---

'actually' (see LSJ, s.v. II), and only the second the sense 'still.'"

65 Contra M. Thrall, *Greek Particles in the New Testament: Linguistic and Exegetical Studies* (NTTS 3; Leiden: Brill, 1962) 88–90; Lightfoot, *Notes*, 285, who cites Gal 5:11, where there is apparent repetition of ἔτι (note that some texts [D* F G 6 1739 1883 vg^{mss} Ambst among others] omit the first ἔτι).

66 Käsemann, *Romans*, 127; BAGD, s.v.; Godet, *Romans*, 191; J.C. O'Neill, *Paul's Letter to the Romans* (Pelican; Harmondsworth: Penguin, 1975) 94; contra many other commentators, including Dunn, *Romans*, 1.254–55, who reads eschatological overtones into καιρός. See rightly J. Barr, *Biblical Words for Time* (SBT 33; 2nd edn; London: SCM Press, 1969) esp. 21–67.

67 Black, *Romans*, 83. Sanday–Headlam recognize this reading as early (*Romans*, 126). Cf. Acts 19:3; Mark 15:34.

68 Stowers, *Diatribe*, 126. See his list in n. 58 (p. 228).

69 For example, Plutarch, *Moralia* 605A; Teles 4A.175 (44H); 5.1 (49H), 12 (50H) with εἰ δέ; Teles 3.163 (29H) with τί γάρ, among many examples with εἰ and τί.

70 See F. Wisse, "The Righteous Man and the Good Man in Rom 5:7," *NTS* 19 (1972–73) 91–93; cf. M. Zerwick, *Biblical Greek* (trans. J. Smith; Rome: Pontifical Biblical Institute Press, 1963) 159.

reflection on the virtuous person in Hellenistic thought, and the passage is similar to one in Teles regarding Socrates.[71]

This proposal also solves the perceived theological difficulty of v. 6 and possibly v. 7. Keck, in arguing for later interpolation, claims that v. 6 says that Christ died on behalf of the ungodly, a statement Paul does not make any other place (except possibly in 2 Cor 5:14 for rhetorical reasons!).[72] Keck goes much too far, however. Paul does at least allude to Christ dying for the ungodly in other places, even in Romans, for example 4:5, where he speaks of the one who justifies the ungodly (τὸν δικαιοῦντα τὸν ἀσεβῆ).[73] The statement of v. 6 is better understood as Pauline, but not as Paul pursuing a straight line of argument. As he does elsewhere in the book (e.g. 3:27–4:2; 6:1–3), he posits a possible question that might be raised in the mind of his audience, as if it were posed by an interlocutor. The question is related to both the phenomenal fact that one would die for the ungodly[74] and the possible purpose of this death. This solution not only vindicates the text's integrity (i.e. solutions that require multiple authorship or textual excision are unnecessary[75]), but brings cohesion to the chapter's line of argument. Paul now responds in v. 8: "But (δέ) God established his love towards us in this way, that while we were yet sinners, Christ died for us."[76] The syntax of v. 8b, which clearly reiterates v. 6, is

---

71 Teles 2.179–182 (18H): ἡμεῖς δέ, κἂν ἄλλον <θανατῶντ'> ἴδωμεν, πεφρίκαμεν. καὶ μέλλων ἀποθνῄσκειν, ἐκάθευδε βαθέως, ὥστε μόλις διεγεῖραι τινά. ταχύ γ' ἂν καὶ ἡμῶν τις ἂν κοιμηθείη… See also Michel, *Römer*, 181 n. 20, who cites Philostratus, *Life Apoll.* 7.12; Epictetus 2.7, among others, including a roll from Herculaneum (no. 1044): [ὑπὲρ?] τοῦ μάλιστ' ἀγαπωμένου τῶν ἀναγκαίων ἢ τῶν φίλων παραβάλοι ἂν ἑτοίμως τὸν τράχηλον (see A. Deissmann, *Light from the Ancient East* [trans. L.R.M. Strachan; London: Hodder & Stoughton, 1927; repr. Grand Rapids: Baker, 1978] 118); cf. Aune, "Orationes," 305. Bultmann sees it as typical of Rabbinic argumentation (*Stil*, 102). Cf. A.D. Clarke, "The Good and the Just in Rom 5:7," *TynBul* 41.1 (1990) 128–42.

72 Keck, "Post-Pauline Interpretation," 245. If what I am arguing is correct, 2 Cor 5:14 becomes pertinent evidence for vv. 6–7 being Pauline.

73 Cf. C.T. Rhyne, *Faith Establishes the Law* (SBLDS 55; Missoula, MT: Scholars Press, 1981) 80.

74 See Porter, *Verbal Aspect*, esp. 76–83 on timeless statements, which are found in v. 7; contra E.D.W. Burton, *Syntax of the Moods and Tenses in New Testament Greek* (3rd edn; Chicago: University of Chicago Press, 1900; repr. Grand Rapids: Kregel, 1976) 36; BDF, §349(1), who argue for gnomic usage; cf. §385(1), where Blass–Debrunner say that τάχα with the indicative verb is equivalent to the potential optative or future indicative, so that the two sentences in Rom 5:7 are functionally equivalent.

75 For example, O'Neill, *Romans*, 93–94; H. Sahlin, "Einige Textemendationen zum Römerbrief," *TZ* 9 (1953) 96–97; C.K. Barrett, *A Commentary on the Epistle to the Romans* (BNTC; London: A. & C. Black, 1957) 105; Lietzmann, *Einführung*, 59.

76 The ὑπέρ clause, though left ambiguous, seems to warrant a substitutionary sense: A.T. Robertson, "The Use of ΥΠΕΡ in Business Documents in the Papyri," *Expositor*, Eighth Series, 18 (1919) 321–27; E.H. Blakeney, "ὑπέρ with Genitive in N.T.," *ExpTim* 55 (1943–

explained by this analysis. The genitive absolute introduced by ἔτι and the ὑπέρ phrase placed after the emphatically positioned main clause, all connected to v. 8a by an explanatory ὅτι,[77] establish continuity between the rhetorical question in v. 6 and its answer.

Having responded to an objection—that it is inconceivable that Christ would die for sinners, since there is no suitable example in the human realm—Paul draws two further contrasts. He does this by restating and yet expanding what he has established concerning justification and peace at the beginning of the chapter (before the objection is raised). This fittingly leads to discussion of reconciliation and the example of Christ and Adam. Paul builds this crescendo using the phrase πολλῷ...μᾶλλον (which occurs four times in this chapter: vv. 9, 10, 15, 17, linking parallel statements). Whereas some consider the phrase distinctly Rabbinic,[78] μᾶλλον is common in diatribe when elements are compared in order to draw a striking conclusion.[79] In v. 9 the first use of this transition occurs. Rather than state the opposition as "not this but this," Paul uses "this much, how much more." The heightened comparison echoes v. 1 with δικαιωθέντες ἐκ πίστεως, but here leads to salvation from God's wrath. Paul uses a similar apodosis in v. 10, saying that "being reconciled, we shall be saved in his life."

Paul now introduces the word καταλλάσσω, which governs the major metaphor of the chapter: reconciliation.[80] The first use of the verb is linked with

---

44) 306; cf. L. Keck, "'Jesus' in Romans," *JBL* 108 (1989) 457–58. The sacrificial nature of Christ's death is widely accepted: see, for example, R. Bultmann, *Theology of the New Testament* (New York: Scribners, 1951, 1955) 1.295–97; contra J.A. Fitzmyer, *Romans* (AB 33; New York: Doubleday, 1993) 401.

77 BDF, §394.

78 For example, Dahl, "Two Notes," 44–45, esp. regarding v. 15; Dunn, *Romans*, 1.257.

79 For example, Teles 1.14–28 (3H); 2.124 (14H); cf. 4B.55 (48H) with πολὺ μᾶλλον used similarly to Paul. See N. Turner, *Syntax*, vol. 3 of *A Grammar of New Testament Greek*, by J.H. Moulton (Edinburgh: T. & T. Clark, 1963) 29; BDF, §246; cf. Berger, "Gattungen," 1130; Godet, *Romans*, 194; Dodd, *Romans*, 77. This heightened comparative is found in other dialogical styles as well: e.g. Demosthenes 39.23; 40.29; Isocrates 6.109.

80 R.P. Martin sees reconciliation as the heart of Pauline theology. See his *Reconciliation*, and "Center of Paul's Theology," in *Dictionary of Paul and his Letters* (ed. G.F. Hawthorne, R.P. Martin and D.G. Reid; Downers Grove, IL: InterVarsity Press, 1993) 92–95. Few have followed him: e.g. E. Käsemann, "Some Thoughts on the Theme 'The Doctrine of Reconciliation in the New Testament,'" in *The Future of our Religious Past* (Festschrift R. Bultmann; ed. J.M. Robinson; London: SCM Press, 1971) 51. Recent treatments of καταλλάσσω include I.H. Marshall, "The Meaning of 'Reconciliation,'" in *Unity and Diversity in New Testament Theology* (Festschrift G.E. Ladd; ed. R.A. Guelich; Grand Rapids: Eerdmans, 1978) 117–32, repr. in *idem*, *Jesus the Saviour: Studies in New Testament Theology* (Downers Grove, IL: InterVarsity Press, 1990) 258–74; C. Breytenbach, *Versöhnung: Eine Studie zur paulinischen Soteriologie* (WMANT 60; Neukirchen-Vluyn: Neukirchener Verlag, 1989); *idem*, "Versöhnung, Stellvertretung und Sühne: Semantische

being an enemy of God (cf. 5:1);[81] the second treats reconciliation as the presupposition for those who are to be saved by Christ's life (cf. 5:9, where justification is referred to as leading to the same result).[82] Paul uses καταλλάσσω in Romans 5 as a means of conveying his unique perspective on the work of Jesus Christ. There are several sets of parallel statements worth noting: 5:1: δικαιωθέντες οὖν ἐκ πίστεως (cf. 4:25 with διὰ τὴν δικαίωσιν ἡμῶν; also 3:21–26; 4:1–5) and 5:9: δικαιωθέντες νῦν ἐν τῷ αἵματι αὐτοῦ with 5:10b: καταλλαγέντες; 5:1: εἰρήνην ἔχωμεν πρὸς τὸν θεόν with 5:10a: κατηλλάγημεν τῷ θεῷ; and 5:1: διὰ τοῦ κυρίου ἡμῶν Ἰησοῦ Χριστοῦ with 5:10: διὰ τοῦ θανάτου τοῦ υἱοῦ αὐτοῦ. Parallelism of balanced cola, as noted above, is characteristic of the diatribe.[83] But it serves more than a simple rhetorical purpose. The first two sets emphasize the transformation which has occurred, and the third set emphasizes the means of this transformation. Several of these parallels, especially the equation of vv. 9 and 10 in the light of v. 1, have been recognized by others, although none as characteristics of diatribe.[84] For example, Barrett comments on the close parallel between justification and reconciliation in vv. 9 and 10 (cf. v. 1, where "let us have peace" is apparently synonymous with reconciliation), such that each is achieved through the death of Christ and results in salvation. Barrett states, "Justification and reconciliation are different metaphors describing the same fact. The meaning of the verb 'to reconcile' is determined by the noun 'enemies' [here Paul's usage is very much in line with other Greek authors]; it puts an end to enmity, just as 'to justify'

---

und Traditionsgeschichtliche Bemerkungen am Beispiel der Paulinischen Briefe," *NTS* 39 (1993) 59–79; and now S.E. Porter, *Καταλλάσσω in Ancient Greek Literature, with Reference to the Pauline Writings* (Estudios de Filología Neotestamentaria 5; Córdoba, Spain: Ediciones El Almendro, 1994) esp. 145–62; and ch. 10 in this volume, pp. 195–212.

81 See Rom 1:18–3:20; cf. Dunn, *Romans*, 1.258, although God's active (versus his passive) animosity seems in keeping with the context of Romans (see M.-J. Lagrange, *Saint Paul: Épître aux Romains* [EBib; Paris: Gabalda, 1950] 104; Wolter, *Rechtfertigung*, 86).

82 P. Althaus (*Der Brief an die Römer* [NTD; Göttingen: Vandenhoeck & Ruprecht, 1970] 52) claims it is a greater accomplishment to change humans from enmity to reconciliation than from reconciliation to final salvation.

83 Examples abound: e.g. Teles 1.1–3 (3H): κρεῖττον...ἐστιν; uses parallel wording of entire clauses; Teles 1.6, 7, 9, 10 (cf. 11), 12, 13 (3H) use a catch phrase διὰ τὸ εἶναι; Teles 1.14–28 (3H) uses parallel syntax in a chain progression. See also Teles 3.9–26 (22H), with a variety of parallel constructions.

84 For example, L. Goppelt, "Versöhnung durch Christus," in *Christologie und Ethik: Aufsätze zum Neuen Testament* (Göttingen: Vandenhoeck & Ruprecht, 1968) 153, cf. 156–57; Findeis, *Versöhnung*, 254; Wolter, *Rechtfertigung*, 35, cf. 177–80, 193–95, where he sees a progression *a minori ad maius*; as well as many commentators (e.g. Cranfield, Althaus, Dunn, and esp. Barrett; contra Schlier, *Römerbrief*, 156, who argues that after one is removed from being an enemy and made at peace with God, then one is justified).

puts an end to legal contention."[85] Paul's usage here prepares for his exemplum in 5:12–21.

In the second part of the chapter, by using several features of diatribe, Paul gives a poignant illustration of the significance of God's initiating reconciliation through the death of his son. In 5:12–21 an exemplum, which in diatribe often singles out a mythical or ancient hero to exemplify particular moral qualities or attributes, confirms and establishes what Paul has said in vv. 1–11.[86] It fits very much into the same pattern as Stowers has described for use of the example of Abraham. There is the added rhetorical feature, however, that an extended comparison between Adam and Christ is developed through a number of balanced cola.[87] As Cranfield says, "Verses 12–21 indicate the conclusion to be drawn from the previous sub-section. The fact that there are those who, being justified by faith, are also now God's friends means that something has been accomplished by Christ which does not just concern believers but is as universal in its effect as was the sin of Adam."[88]

Four issues relevant to diatribe require special attention in Rom 5:12–21. First is whether the connective διὰ τοῦτο in 5:12 refers forward or backward, that is, cataphorically forecasting something not yet introduced, or anaphorically citing something that has preceded. Cranfield notes that there are about sixty appearances of διὰ τοῦτο in the New Testament, and Pauline usage is similar to that of the rest of the New Testament, with the connective referring

85 Barrett, *Romans*, 108. The question of the exact relation between justification, peace and reconciliation—which occupies many commentators—cannot be discussed here.

86 Exempla are discussed in Stowers, *Diatribe*, 168–71 and nn., including, for example, in Epictetus, Maximus Tyrinus, Dio Chrysostom, Plutarch, Teles, and Philo. Cf. N.A. Dahl, *Studies in Paul: Theology for the Early Christian Mission* (Minneapolis: Augsburg, 1977) 82.

87 Besides the major commentaries, see E. Brandenburger, *Adam und Christus: Exegetisch-Religionsgeschichtliche Untersuchung zu Röm 5:12–21 (1 Kor 15)* (Neukirchen: Neukirchener Verlag, 1962) 158–205, 219–55; S.-H. Quek, "Adam and Christ according to Paul," in *Pauline Studies* (Festschrift F.F. Bruce; ed. D.A. Hagner and M.J. Harris; Grand Rapids: Eerdmans, 1980) esp. 67 nn. 7, 8, 9; L. Goppelt, *Typos: Die Typologische Deutung des Alten Testaments im Neuen* (Darmstadt: Wissenschaftliche Buchgesellschaft, 1966) 155–56.

88 Cranfield, *Romans*, 1.269; cf. also Bornkamm, *Ende*, 81, even though he sees sections of 5:12–21 as Pauline anacolutha. On Adam/Christ typology, see C.K. Barrett, *From First Adam to Last: A Study in Pauline Theology* (London: A. & C. Black, 1962) 68–91; R. Scroggs, *The Last Adam: A Study in Pauline Anthropology* (Oxford: Blackwell, 1966) 76–82; J.D.G. Dunn, *Christology in the Making: A New Testament Inquiry into the Origins of the Doctrine of the Incarnation* (Philadelphia: Westminster Press, 1980) 98–128; N.T. Wright, "Adam in Pauline Christology," in *SBLSP* (vol. 22; ed. K.H. Richards; Chico, CA: Scholars Press, 1983) esp. 370–73; and J.R. Levison, *Portraits of Adam in Early Judaism: From Sirach to 2 Baruch* (JSP 1; Sheffield: JSOT Press, 1988) esp. 13–31.

back in a ratio of two to one.[89] A useful contrastive instance for 5:12 is found in 4:16. Firmly into his discussion of Abraham, Paul uses διὰ τοῦτο followed by a ἵνα clause. The following purpose or causal clause is the distinguishing mark of cataphoric use.[90] Like 1:26, a true parallel, however, 5:12 has no following purpose or causal clause,[91] unless it is the ὥσπερ clause, which would be highly unnatural. In addition, anaphoric reference makes most sense of the passage. It unifies the example with the previous discursive material, rather than leaving an abrupt, unconnected introduction to the comparison. The same pattern of argumentation is followed in chs. 3 and 4 (widely recognized as diatribal). In these chapters, Paul discusses the issues of law, sin and grace, and then exemplifies this discussion by citing Abraham as an illustrious individual who apart from law had his faith counted as righteousness. Within the first part of ch. 5 itself (v. 7), the instance of one dying for a good person is cited by Paul's hypothetical interlocutor as being a rare act. Paul expands this analogy in citing the highly contrastive example of Adam and Christ.[92] As Sanday and Headlam indicate, whether the exact reference of διὰ τοῦτο is v. 11, vv. 9–11, 5:1–11, or 1:17 and following is difficult to determine exactly, but "it seems natural to include at least as much as contains a brief outline of [the work of Christ and Adam], i.e. as far as vv. 1–11."[93] Thus διὰ τοῦτο unites the theological metaphor regarding the work of Christ on behalf of sinners (i.e. reconciliation) with the exemplum of vv. 12–21 and its specific, contrastive reference to the actions of two men, Adam and Christ.

In v. 12 Paul uses a chiasmic structure with four separate, balanced elements (the short, crisp sentences are typical of diatribe):[94] through one man sin entered into the world, which reminds the reader that it was for sinners that Christ died; sin led to death, death passed through to all humans, and the cause of sin is laid

89 C.E.B. Cranfield, "On Some of the Problems in the Interpretation of Rom 5:12," *SJT* 22 (1969) esp. 324–26.

90 Contra Rhyne, *Faith*, 85 n. 117, following Käsemann, *Romans*, 146. Cf. Teles 2.202 (19H), where διὰ τοῦτο is picked up by a following ὅτι clause.

91 Barrett (*Romans*, 110) mentions cataphoric reference, adopted by, for example, Michel, *Römer*, 138; Wolter, *Rechtfertigung*, 214; Brandenburger, *Adam*, 258–59; cf. Lagrange, *Romains*, 105, who calls it a literary transition.

92 Bultmann claims that the translation of the formulaic connective, διὰ τοῦτο, occurring regularly in Epictetus (cf. Teles 2.201 [19H]), is "so zum Beispiel," before the actual citation (*Stil*, 54).

93 Sanday–Headlam, *Romans*, 131; followed by Wilckens, Michel, and Lietzmann; contra Dunn, *Romans*, 1.271–72; Schlier, *Römerbrief*, 159.

94 For example, Teles 1.1–14 (3H) averages seven words in each of its ten sentences, all asyndetic. Similar repartee is found throughout Teles, as well as other diatribe, even in extended discourse. On the balanced cola, see Brandenburger, *Adam*, 175 n. 1; Englezakis, "Rom 5:12–15," 231–32; cf. Bornkamm, *Ende*, 80–82; Brandenburger, *Adam*, 180–205, 219–31; Schlier, *Römerbrief*, 169–71, for problems with vv. 13–17.

squarely at the feet of humans. While there has been much debate about the meaning of ἐφ' ᾧ in 5:12, it is pretty well agreed that it should be rendered "because" or serves as a causal connective, that is, there is a causal relation between Adam's sin and the sin of all humans.[95] Paul, perhaps sensing the importance and complexity of the analogy, breaks off his initial ὥσπερ construction in order to clarify several points raised in v. 12.

Paul never returns to the exact grammatical construction, however. This raises the second issue of this section, the structure of vv. 13–16.[96] In vv. 13 and 14 Paul argues for the existence and relation of sin and death stemming from Adam, who is the type of the coming one, Christ.[97] Both Barrett as a traditional commentator and Louw as a discourse analyst see the importance of the phrase, "the type of the coming one": it introduces in the same sentence the agent who is to undo the other's action. This parallel opposition is typical of much diatribe and found throughout Romans 5 in the chapter's opposition of death and life.[98] As Louw further notes, reference to Adam being the type of the one to come returns the section to the agent of v. 12a.[99] At this point, Paul is again interrupted by his hypothetical interlocutor. He does not return to the argument directly until he restates the protasis in v. 19 and then completes his thought by moving straight to the issues of justification and law, with a final summary in v. 21.[100]

In dealing with the possible confusion of vv. 12–15, Englezakis has made an intriguing proposal. In the light of Paul's statement in Rom 4:15b, that where

---

95 For summaries of the many issues involved here, see Cranfield, *Romans*, 1.274–81; *idem*, "Some of the Problems," 330–40; contra now J.A. Fitzmyer, "The Consecutive Meaning of ἐφ' ᾧ in Romans 5.12," *NTS* 39 (1993) 321–39; *idem*, *Romans*, 413–17. I am not convinced by Fitzmyer's vigorous attempt to prove the consecutive sense.

96 Cranfield, *Romans*, 1.272 n. 5, with most commentators; contra Barrett, *Romans*, 109–10; J.T. Kirby, "The Syntax of Rom 5:12: A Rhetorical Approach," *NTS* 33 (1987) 283–86; Scroggs, *Adam*, 79–80 n. 13; Englezakis, "Rom 5:12–15," 232.

97 So Dunn, *Romans*, 1.277; Käsemann, *Romans*, 151–52; Goppelt, *Typos*, 155–56; contra those who argue for, for example, Moses (e.g. Scroggs, *Adam*, 80–81).

98 For example, Teles juxtaposes seeing and being in dialogue 1; poverty and wealth in dialogues 4A and 4B. Within these and other dialogues many lesser oppositions are also found, often with similar parallel syntax: e.g. Teles 1.15–28 (3–4H); 2.106–119 (13H). Cf. J. Cambier, "Péchés des hommes et péché d'Adam en Rom 5:12," *NTS* 11 (1964–65) 218, cf. 223–28.

99 J.P. Louw, "Discourse Analysis and the Greek New Testament," *BT* 24 (1973) 109, 111; Barrett, *Romans*, 112; cf. G. Segalla, "La struttura circolare di Romani 5,12–21 e il suo significato teologico," *Studia Patavina* 28 (1981) esp. 378, who finds a chiasmic structure in 5:12–21.

100 Cranfield (*Romans*, 1.288–91) hints at this understanding; cf. M.C. de Boer, *The Defeat of Death: Apocalyptic Eschatology in 1 Corinthians 15 and Romans 5* (JSNTSup 22; Sheffield: JSOT Press, 1988) 162–63.

there is no law there is no transgression, Paul's hypothetical interlocutor in 5:13b, Englezakis believes, raises an objection to Paul's statements about sin in vv. 12–13a: "Sin though [δέ] cannot be imputed in the absence of law!" Paul then answers the objection in v. 14 with the strong adversative ἀλλά: "Yet death reigned from Adam to Moses..."[101] This requires an unusually strong adversative sense of δέ. Moreover, in much diatribe the objection by the hypothetical interlocutor, not the statement by the speaker, is introduced by ἀλλά.[102] In the light of vv. 15 and 16 (see below), Cranfield's analysis is more plausible: ἀλλά links two statements which consequentially explain how it is that all sinned, including those who sinned when there was no law.[103]

More convincing in the light of Paul's use of diatribe is Caragounis's suggestion that, after referring to the coming one (v. 14), Paul is interrupted regarding the issue of transgressions. This coordinates well with the idea that the exemplum primarily focuses upon the sinful behaviour of Adam. Caragounis proposes a reinterpretation of vv. 15a and 16a, both of which are problematic.[104] The first problem concerns the several uses of οὕτως in vv. 12, 15, 18 and 19. Paul introduces the protasis of his argument in v. 12 with ὥσπερ, a common introductory formula in diatribe,[105] but he apparently leaves the formal structure to pursue a different line of argument in vv. 13 and 14. Cranfield correctly points out that the καὶ οὕτως of v. 12 is not the same as οὕτως καί (see below).[106] But v. 15a has οὕτως καί, raising the question whether v. 15 is the completion of v. 12. But the completion is reserved for vv. 18 or 19 (this depends upon one's reading: Caragounis, following Cranfield, Käsemann, Bruce and others, believes that the argument picks up with v. 18). The result in v. 15, if it is taken as a statement, is a very badly balanced sentence on account of the negative and connectives in the first part. This suggests to Caragounis that v. 15 requires further analysis. The second problem

---

101 Englezakis, "Rom 5:12–15," 233. Bouwman ("'Zonde wordt,'" 138–44) argues that Paul, interrupted in v. 12 by an imaginary opponent, must reassert his thesis in vv. 13a, 14. Bouwman agrees that v. 13b contains another objection by an opponent, but the supposition that v. 12d requires completion is unnecessary.

102 See, for example, Teles 1.29 (4H); 2.124 (14H); 3.52 (23H), 69 (24H), 105 (26H), 116, 130 (27H), 146 (29H); 7.121 (61H); but cf. 3.14, 17, 22 (22H); Aune ("Orationes," 304) cites Plutarch, *Moralia* 993A, 994F.

103 Cranfield, *Romans*, 1.282–83. He treats δέ in v. 13 as coordinate.

104 C.C. Caragounis, "Rom 5:15–16 in the Context of 5:12–21: Contrast or Comparison?" *NTS* 31 (1985) 142–48; also H. Sahlin, "Adam-Christologie im Neuen Testament," *ST* 41 (1987) 32 n. 18; in the light of questions raised, for example, by Dahl, "Two Notes," 44–47.

105 For example, Teles 2.1 (5H), 56 (9H), 156, 158, 162 (16H); 3.80 (25H), 160, 161 (29H), 168 (30H); 4A.5 (33H), 13, 17 (34H); 6.28 (53H), 30 (54H); 7.12, 17 (55H), cf. 2.148 (15H), often with οὕτω or οὕτως following.

106 Cranfield, "Some of the Problems," 327; cf. Dunn, *Romans*, 1.271.

is conceptual. When Paul resumes his argument in v. 18 or v. 19, he essentially reasserts in dogmatic fashion what he has already posited in v. 12. This indicates to Caragounis that something important occurs in the intervening verses which requires that Paul restate the foundation of his argument. The pattern of repetition is similar to the one that Paul uses with regard to vv. 6–7 and 8 in the first part of the chapter.

To alleviate these two problems Caragounis suggests that vv. 15a and 16a, with οὐ, are meant to introduce rhetorical questions expecting affirmative answers. Thus he renders them: "But does not the free gift operate just like the trespass did?… And is not the free gift transmitted in the same way as sin was transmitted by the one who sinned?" The answer required to each question is "yes." Dunn resists Caragounis's repunctuation here, although there is a parallel that Dunn does endorse in Rom 2:21–22, a section that Dunn and others recognize as diatribe. Noting that the sentences in ch. 2 could be either statements or questions, Dunn argues that the rhetorical style "suggests" that they are questions.[107] The only apparent syntactical indicator is asyndeton (except for the first, connected with οὖν), less evidence by far than Caragounis cites for repunctuating vv. 15a and 16a. There is further evidence for vv. 15 and 16 to be taken as questions, however. Caragounis does not note this, but the introductory ἀλλά with the question posed by the hypothetical interlocutor, including the negated form, ἀλλ' οὐ, is a common feature of diatribe, seen regularly in Teles.[108] The resumption of Paul's argument with the explanatory use of γάρ is well exemplified in diatribe as well. γάρ connects the speaker's answer directly to his interlocutor's question,[109] formulating a response in the language of the question. Paul carries forward the interlocutor's suggested contrast between the trespass and free gift by means of a conditional statement. The protasis constitutes the common starting point (with γάρ best translated "in fact" or "indeed") from which Paul goes on to assert, in a heightened comparison, the ascendance of the work of Christ over the work of Adam (πολλῷ μᾶλλον, vv. 15b, 16b). In his analysis, Kaye discerns several of these elements of diatribe, although he claims that ch. 5 contains no rhetorical questions.[110] By the analysis proposed above, however, ch. 5, with three rhetorical questions linking the theoretical discussion with a pertinent example, can clearly be seen as a unity very much in the diatribe style.[111]

---

107 Dunn, *Romans*, 1.113.

108 For example, Teles 2.39 (8H), 207 (19H); 3.84 (25H), 108, 115 (26H); cf. 3.160 (29H); 7.110 (60H), and n. 103 above. See Aune, *Literary Environment*, 201.

109 For example, Teles 1.34 (4H); 3.54, 71 (24H); 5.6 (49H) with μὲν γάρ; 7.122, 123, 126, 127, 130 (61H). See Zerwick, *Biblical Greek*, 159–60; Winer, *Grammar*, 558.

110 Kaye, *Structure*, 14–20.

111 This assessment is similar to one proposed by Jeremias. He argued that Rom 1–11 is based upon a question and answer technique, whereby Paul brings up his own objections to

The third issue of Rom 5:12–21 is Paul's use of parallelism, typical of diatribe, in developing the exemplum with Adam and Christ. In 5:15–18, Paul draws the disproportionate comparison of Adam and Christ, explaining that Christ is the coming one who overcomes the work of Adam. As bad as the effect of Adam's sin was, it has been overcome by Christ. Paul, as Caragounis argues, begins v. 15 with a rhetorical question. This is followed by Paul's first conditional statement, which pivots around the phrase discussed above, "much more" (πολλῷ μᾶλλον), emphasizing the work of Christ. This same pattern of argument is repeated in vv. 16–17, and concludes with v. 18: "therefore" (ἄρα οὖν) the result of one man's sin is judgment on all, and because of the righteousness of one man righteousness for all.[112] Verse 19 resumes the ὥσπερ clause of v. 12, although Paul alters the protasis to make the statement a summary of his entire previous discussion (vv. 12–18). In typical diatribe fashion, vv. 19–21 utilize a balanced comparison between the work of Adam and Christ, this time focusing upon obedience and disobedience. The comparison concludes in v. 21 with the phrase, "through Jesus Christ our Lord."

Surprisingly, Bultmann, though he notes balanced cola as typical of diatribe style,[113] never draws serious attention to Rom 5:12–21, in particular vv. 15, 16, 17, 18, 19, 21. Brandenburger has noted the several significant statements about Adam's work, but he does not see connections to the diatribe either.[114] The hypothetical interlocutor raises the question of sin and the free gift in vv. 15a

---

his teaching and then answers these queries. Romans 5 can now be placed within the group in which Paul responds to questions (3:1–9; 3:31–4:25; chs. 6–7; and chs. 9–11). J. Jeremias, "Zur Gedankenführung in den Paulinischen Briefer," in *Studia Paulina* (Festschrift J. de Zwaan; ed. J.N. Sevenster and W.C. van Unnik; Haarlem: Bohn, 1953) 146–49.

112 I find unconvincing in the light of v. 17 M.E. Boring's suggestion ("The Language of Universal Salvation in Paul," *JBL* 105 [1986] 283–88) that this passage is clearly universalistic. See E.P. Sanders, *Paul and Palestinian Judaism: A Comparison of Patterns of Religion* (Philadelphia: Fortress Press, 1977) 473; *idem*, *Paul, the Law and the Jewish People* (Philadelphia: Fortress Press, 1983) 57 n. 64; Bultmann, *Theology*, 1.302–303; Dunn, *Romans*, 1.285.

113 Bultmann, *Stil*, 20–31, 74–96.

114 Brandenburger, *Adam*, 158, 219–55, esp. 240, 247, for further parallels; Lietzmann, *Einführung*, 63–65; Michel, *Römer*, 185–86; Lagrange, *Romains*, 113: "Toute cette péricope est donc une suite d'antithèses. Deux acteurs, Adam et le Christ. Le péché actuel d'Adam, τὸ παράπτωμα, et le don de la grace, τὸ χάρισμα (v. 15), le jugement de condamnation conduisant au chatiment, le don de la grace conduisant à la justification (v. 16). Le péché d'Adam amène le règne de la mort, le don de la justice amène le regne de ceux qui l'ont reçue (v. 17). Un péché actuel d'un seul procure le chatiment, l'acte méritoire d'un seul procure la justification (v. 18). La désobéissance constitue des pécheurs, l'obéissance fait des justes (v. 19). Le péché, grandi par les péchés actuels, règne et tue; la grace par la justice règne et prépare la vie éternelle (20. 21)." Cf. N. Schneider, *Die rhetorische Eigenart der Paulinischen Antithese* (HUT 11; Tübingen: Mohr–Siebeck, 1970) *passim*, but who concludes that Paul's antitheses derive from a Jewish context.

and 16a, and this provides impetus for the unequal comparison between the work of the two men, Adam and Christ.[115] Sentences that refer to Adam (vv. 15b, 16b, 17a, 18a, 19a, 21a) are opposed by sentences devoted to Christ (vv. 15c, 16c, 17b, 18b, 19b, 21b). Verses 15b and c and vv. 17a and b are linked by the familiar connective, πολλῷ μᾶλλον, and focus upon the significant grace brought by Christ overcoming the sin or transgression of Adam which affected the many.[116] Both sets are introduced by εἰ (with γάρ, see above), a first class conditional which posits the sinful condition of humanity in the protasis and then answers this accusation with the surpassing work of Christ in the apodosis. Verse 18 uses ἄρα οὖν[117] to introduce its comparison regarding the transgression of one being surpassed by righteousness for many. This is highlighted by the common diatribal connective οὕτως καί.[118] Verse 19, as noted above, restates the now expanded protasis of 5:12a and completes the argument, using ὥσπερ...οὕτως καί. This pattern is utilized again in v. 21, referring to the many who are established through sinful disobedience being overcome by obedience which establishes many as righteous. Verse 21 is grammatically dependent (ἵνα) upon v. 20, the two verses forming a chiasm revolving around use of πλεονάζω. The bold claims Paul makes in vv. 20–21 for the law as multiplier of sin so that grace may also multiply, and the reign of sin passing to the rule of grace, encapsulate what Paul is saying by his use of the exemplum. The language of these claims serves as another example of striking Pauline prose that solicits a legitimate objection from the hypothetical interlocutor in 6:1 and is used to push the argument further along.[119]

The fourth issue regarding 5:12–21 and the diatribe—and one that potentially threatens the unity posited above—is the shift in person from the first person in 5:1–11 to the third person in vv. 12–21. For some scholars this has been a crucial factor in calling for separation of the chapter between vv. 11 and 12.[120] Two factors are worth noting, however. First is that the shift from

---

115 Lagrange, *Romains*, 108; Dahl, "Two Studies," 42–48, although he focuses primarily on the issue of law.

116 Michel, *Römer*, 188. Lagrange calls the connective in v. 17 "Un enchainement mathematique" (*Romains*, 110).

117 Cf. BDF, §451(2b); K.W. Clark, "The Meaning of APA," in *Festschrift to Honor F.W. Gingrich* (ed. C.H. Barth and R.E. Cocroft; Leiden: Brill, 1972) 79; Brandenburger, *Adam*, 232.

118 For example, Teles 2.3 (5H), 59 (9H), 82 (11H), 121 (13H), 157, 160 (16H); 3.78 (25H); 7.2, 9–10, 13 (55H), 20 (56H), 146 (62H); cf. 2.148 (15H); 3.5 (21H), 81 (25H), 121, 123 (27H), 192 (32H); 4A.10 (34H), 24 (35H), 72 (38H); 6.32 (54H); 7.110 (60H) without καί.

119 See Stowers, *Diatribe*, 150. These verses may reflect an *ad hominem* argument (Malherbe, "Beasts," 73), although Lagrange (*Romains*, 112) treats them as an appendix, and Wolter (*Rechtfertigung*, 215) sees a new theme introduced.

120 For example, Schlier, *Römerbrief*, 138. Leenhardt, Zahn, Feuillet and Luz also divide

first to third person conforms to a previous intense section of diatribe in this letter, 3:27–4:25. In 3:28–4:1 Paul uses first person, although he switches to third person for the exemplum of Abraham.[121] Use of the third person for this exemplum and the exemplum in 5:12–21 conforms well to diatribe style, although exempla are not obligated to be presented using third person, as Stowers illustrates.[122] A second factor to consider, however, is a number of unifying phrases Paul has woven through ch. 5. First and foremost is the διά + genitive phrase "through our Lord Jesus Christ," or variants. It appears in vv. 1, 11, and 21 (note the slight change in word order). This phrase also appears in similar forms at 1:8, 2:16, 6:23 (with ἐν), 7:25, 8:39 (with ἐν), 15:30 (cf. 5:17), unifying the entire epistle.[123] But it is only within ch. 5 that this phrase occurs three times. At the beginning it introduces the discussion by stating the means for peace on the basis of justification; in the middle it is used in conjunction with the boasting that results from the awareness of reconciliation that leads to salvation; and at the end it refers to grace that reigns forever. This unifying phrase has other parallels within the chapter which also serve to establish internal coherence. For example, in 5:21 the διά + genitive phrase διὰ δικαιοσύνης is parallel to "through Jesus Christ our Lord."[124] The second important phrase, πολλῷ μᾶλλον, used four times (5:9, 10, 15, 17—Paul uses the phrase nine times in all), serves a similar unifying function in this chapter, as noted above. This common diatribal phrase, as opposed to a contrastive connective, fashions the argument so that it progresses forward by building each piece of information upon a previous one.

4. *Conclusion*

In conclusion, it has been noted by many commentators that there are elements of the diatribe in the book of Romans. Yet few have seen any significant and concentrated use of these elements to unify the argument of ch. 5. Elements of the diatribe in Romans 5 become apparent in the light of two important textual variants (vv. 1 and 6), the repunctuation of several verses (vv. 6, 15 and 16), and careful attention to the development of the argument, in which a theoretical discussion of reconciliation is followed by the Adam/Christ exemplum. All of

the chapter between vv. 11 and 12.

121 Rhyne illustrates the unity of 4:1–25, although he does not link it directly to diatribe (*Faith*, 75–89).

122 Stowers, *Diatribe*, 168.

123 See O. Kuss, *Der Römer Brief* (3 vols.; 2nd edn; Regensburg: Pustet, 1957) 1.213–18.

124 Keck emphasizes the significance of διὰ τῆς ὑπακοῆς τοῦ ἑνός in v. 19 ("'Jesus,'" 457).

these elements, noted individually by others, combine to point to Romans 5 as reflecting the rhetorical conventions of diatribe. But this is not rhetoric simply for its own sake. Paul develops this argument to convey the significance of what it means to be reconciled to God, that is, to overcome the alienation of Adam, through the death of Jesus Christ.

CHAPTER TWELVE

WITTGENSTEIN'S CLASSES OF UTTERANCES AND PAULINE ETHICAL TEXTS: A STUDY OF GALATIANS 3:28–29 IN CONTEXT*

1. *Introduction*

It has long been recognized that there are numerous pressing problems in formulating an adequate Christian ethic. Several of these are the problems that pertain to any ethical theory: (1) whether an ethical theory should be teleological (concerned with the goals of actions) or deontological (concerned with what one ought to do regardless of its ends); (2) the relation between meta-ethical and normative ethical statements; (3) the number and nature and kind of absolutes, if the ethical theory holds that there are absolutes; (4) the method by which absolutes are formulated, whether through reason, nature, or intuition, if a subjectivist position is not advocated; and (5) for those ethical theories that maintain a minimum of two or more ethical absolutes, how one makes ethical decisions when these absolutes come into conflict (although some ethical positions advocate that at no time do ethical absolutes ever come into conflict).

Biblical ethics, however, has a pressing problem not present in other ethical formulations: determining the role of the Bible not only in formulating the set of ethical absolutes and regulating ethical decisions when these norms run into conflict but also in determining the meaning of biblical passages and using these statements as an interpretative control on ethical decision-making.

Christians seem to want to recognize that the Bible stands as a functional control or authority over Christian ethical behaviour and consequently that it ought to be included in some way in formulating a Christian ethic, that it provides a normative standard unlike any other standard accessible to the Christian, and that biblical claims establish the degree of "Christianness" of any

---

* This essay is reprinted with the permission of the Editor-in-Chief, from the *Journal of the Evangelical Theological Society* 32 (1989) 85–97. Slight changes have been made to the format.

ethical formulation.[1] Or at least this is the theory.

Exploration of the issues, however, reveals several difficulties. For example, Edward Lory, in his survey of Christian ethics, states that there is a recognizable difference between "Love your neighbor as yourself" and "Give a cup of coffee to everyone who knocks on your door." The difference is that the first "sets forth a principle; the second specifies a type of expected behavior; the first invites deliberation about the means necessary to express love for the neighbor; the second states how the neighbor is to be treated."[2] But this comparison is unfair, since the first example is from the Bible but the second is not. Can the same opposition be made between "Love your neighbour as yourself" and Paul's closing exhortation in 1 Cor 16:20, 2 Cor 13:12, and 1 Thess 5:26 to greet each other (or the brothers) with a holy kiss?

Some biblical scholars are becoming increasingly aware of many of the hermeneutical and linguistic issues involved in interpreting the biblical text, though this has not always been the case in formulating a so-called Christian ethic. Hence Paul Lehmann criticizes several treatments such as that by Ramsey for ignoring the hermeneutical problems and consequently disregarding the basic question of what Christian ethics really is—in other words, what its relation is to the Bible, the basic document for Christianity.[3]

More recently, several ethicists have taken seriously the hermeneutical task in ethics and realized that any simple equation between text and ethical formulation is not possible. Paul Simmons singles out several of the areas where this discrepancy can be noted.[4] First is the nature of biblical teaching. All the biblical documents are context-bound, mostly concerned—in the New Testament at least—with early response to the coming of Jesus Christ into the world. Secondly, the Bible nowhere purports to speak directly to every issue. The nature of the documents dictates that many issues are not directly addressed, if for no other reason than that the issues involved could not be foreseen by their authors. Thirdly, it is recognized that some biblical material is irrelevant to modern ethical concerns. Fourthly, many scholars find difficulty in reconciling what they see as variant perspectives in the Bible on various issues. Perhaps this is most easily seen in differences in the Old Testament and New Testament regarding issues such as the law, obedience, and so forth. Fifthly, scholars have moral objections to some of the biblical practices (for example, Joshua's extermination of an entire family; Joshua 7).

---

1 P.D. Simmons, "The Bible and Christian Ethics," in *Issues in Christian Ethics* (ed. P.D. Simmons; Nashville: Broadman, 1980) 21ff.

2 E.L. Lory, Jr., *A Survey of Christian Ethics* (New York: Oxford University Press, 1967) 73.

3 P.L. Lehmann, *Ethics in a Christian Context* (New York: Harper, 1963) 26–27 n. 1.

4 Simmons, "Bible," 21ff. See also S.C. Mott, "The Use of the New Testament for Social Ethics," *JRE* 15 (1987) 225–60.

Several relatively recent attempts, of which I shall note three, have shown awareness of the importance of the biblical text in formulating a Christian ethical perspective. The first is Norman Geisler's hierarchicalism,[5] which takes seriously the possible conflict of absolutes. But its support is essentially intuitionist, confirmed by several grantedly important biblical texts. Many will not be happy with the use made of intuition in defense of the biblical position, and biblical scholars might be perplexed to know why and how the statements about love are given precedence over other biblical statements that at least *prima facie* are linguistically similar and would appear to command the same sort of attention.

A second position is put forward by David Cook.[6] He states that any ethical formulation must be checked against three broad standards: creation, the Old Testament, and the New Testament. Under creation are the subcategories of natural law, humans being in the image of God, conscience, creation ordinances, and the influence of the fall; under the Old Testament are covenant and law, wisdom literature, and prophets; under the New Testament are redemption, kingdom ethics, Paul's ethics, and pastoral epistles. Cook recognizes the important function of both Testaments and at least acknowledges the hermeneutical issues involved, but he introduces a whole host of new problems regarding individual biblical statements and the possibility of conflict with other criteria.

A third attempt is by Stephen Charles Mott,[7] who rightly sets aside the first several chapters of his book for discussing the role and place of the biblical material in formulating a social ethic. But he lacks an ordering principle for his accumulation of the biblical data. It seems rather that the biblical quotations are designed to support (and support they do) a preconceived notion about the rightness of justifying a biblical social ethic.

The analysis of these three attempts is not so stringent as it might be, since I believe that each has something of value to offer. But I approach the question of biblical ethics from the position of a student of the New Testament. Perhaps if I were to approach it from that of an ethicist I would not experience the same disquietude that I feel when I am told that the Christian thing to do is *a*, not *b*. Even if a broad and general principle were to be established—for example, the love principle is the one inviolable norm—this would only go part of the way in relieving my anxiety, which rests in two major areas: (1) I am not convinced that any biblical ethical model that I have read has fully appreciated the

5 N. Geisler, *Ethics: Alternatives and Issues* (Grand Rapids: Zondervan, 1971) esp. 114–36.

6 D. Cook, *Moral Maze: A Way of Exploring Christian Ethics* (London: SPCK, 1983) esp. 82–85.

7 S.C. Mott, *Biblical Ethics and Social Change* (New York: Oxford University Press, 1982).

hermeneutical issues involved in taking seriously the entire witness of Scripture as primary evidence in formulating a biblical ethic, including especially the full force of the actual language of the New Testament (which includes not only specific passages, but consideration of these passages in their original language, Greek); (2) I have found no convincing method by which to determine how individual statements in the Bible are to be taken in relation to the entire scope of biblical ethics. In other words, why is it that we all would probably agree that loving our neighbour as ourselves is a good thing but that greeting each other with a holy kiss is not such a good thing but, in fact, is an embarrassing thing?

2. *Wittgenstein's Classes of Utterances and the New Testament*

Anthony Thiselton's *The Two Horizons* contains several highly provocative pages on classes of grammatical utterances in his stimulating discussion of Ludwig Wittgenstein.[8] This section has been noted by at least one reviewer as an important area for further discussion and thought.[9] (In a moment I will show why Thiselton has in personal conversation indicated that he has dismissed the central importance of this formulation.) Drawing mostly on Wittgenstein's later work, especially the *Philosophical Investigations*, Thiselton notes how important are grammatical clarifications to Wittgenstein's work. He even holds out the possibility that all of the utterances in the New Testament could be classified according to the following criteria and hence appropriately analysed.

A. *First-Class Utterances*

First-class grammatical utterances are neutral or universal grammatical utterances, similar to the analytical or *a priori* utterances of logical positivism and hence not culturally relative. As Wittgenstein says, they are the kinds of utterances that describe a situation that cannot be described as other than it is.

A.J. Ayer expands on this definition:

> We have already explained how it is that these analytic propositions are necessary and certain. We saw that the reason why they cannot be confuted in experience is that they do not make any assertion about the empirical world. They simply record our determination to use words in a certain fashion. We cannot deny them without infringing the conventions which are presupposed by our very denial, and so falling into self-contradiction. And this is the sole ground of their necessity. As Wittgenstein puts it, our justification for holding that the world could not conceivably disobey the laws of logic is simply that we could not say of an unlogical world how it would look.

---

8 A.C. Thiselton, *The Two Horizons: New Testament Hermeneutics and Philosophical Description* (Grand Rapids: Eerdmans, 1980) 357–85, 386–407.

9 V.S. Poythress in *WTJ* 43 (1981) 179.

> And just as the validity of an analytic proposition is independent of the nature of the external world, so is it independent of the nature of our minds. It is perfectly conceivable that we should have employed different linguistic conventions from those which we actually do employ. But whatever these conventions might be, the tautologies in which we recorded them would always be necessary. For any denial of them would be self-stultifying.[10]

Thiselton gives the following examples from the Pauline writings:[11] "And if by grace, then it is no longer by works; if it were, grace would no longer be grace" (Rom 11:6). This example works by mutual exclusion, Thiselton says. "When a man works, his wages are not credited to him as a gift, but as an obligation" (Rom 4:4). As Thiselton explains: "Just as 'due' is implied in the grammar of the concept 'wages,' so it is excluded from the grammar of 'grace.'"[12] "Hope that is seen is no hope at all. Who hopes for what he already has?" (Rom 8:24). "When perfection comes, the imperfect disappears" (1 Cor 13:10). If "perfection" is seen to mean "totality," the statement may then be seen as analytical. "A mediator does not represent just one party" (Gal 3:20). Thiselton cites E.D.W. Burton, who says that this sentence is "a general statement deduced from the very definition of a mediator."[13] "It is for freedom that Christ has set us free" (Gal 5:1). Objecting to contentions that this is a linguistic pleonasm, Thiselton says, "if this freedom does not entail their release from bondage and subsequent status as free men," then it does not "make sense to speak of having been 'freed' by Christ."[14] "Love does no harm to its neighbour" (Rom 13:10). "If I do not grasp the meaning of what someone is saying, I am a foreigner to the speaker, and he is a foreigner to me" (1 Cor 14:11).

From Thiselton's definition and the examples cited above, especially Rom 13:10, it would appear that ethics should be based upon first-class biblical utterances in that they are necessary and certain—a profitable place from which to begin formulating an ethical stance.

This class of utterance, however, is not free from several trenchant criticisms. At this point it is not necessary to invoke the standard criticism of logical positivism, true as it might be—that is, that the verifiability principle itself is unverified.[15] But several other comments are also worth making.

---

10 A.J. Ayer, *Language, Truth and Logic* (2nd edn; New York: Dover, 1952 [1946]) 84.

11 All translations are based upon the New International Version, unless otherwise noted.

12 Thiselton, *Two Horizons*, 389.

13 Thiselton, *Two Horizons*, 390. See E.D.W. Burton, *A Critical and Exegetical Commentary on the Epistle to the Galatians* (ICC; Edinburgh: T. & T. Clark, 1921) 190.

14 Thiselton, *Two Horizons*, 391.

15 See, for example, W.T. Jones, *A History of Western Philosophy*. V. *The Twentieth Century to Wittgenstein and Sartre* (2nd edn revised; New York: Harcourt Brace Jovanovich,

First, the question must be asked concerning what constitutes a self-evident or tautological statement. To the mathematician 1 + 1 = 2 appears to be self-evident, as does the addition function. But, Ayer's caveats aside,[16] is this the case for the elementary-school child learning how to add? And what of multiplication? 1 x 1 = 1 and 2 x 2 = 4 may be self-evident to the mathematician, but to the child learning the multiplication tables they are not. And is 11 x 12 self-evident to anyone? The same kind of analogy might be drawn in the theological realm. "God is love" is not a self-evident statement to the logical positivist, but there are many Christians who would argue that this is the most self-evident statement of all, a statement for which a contrary situation cannot even be imagined.

Secondly, the functional and descriptive powers of such an analysis are open to serious question if it makes no assertion whatever about the empirical world. This is especially true in the area of ethics, which is supposed to be concerned with determining what is right and how to do it in the world of human experience. But there in fact may be a hidden assumption here. For example, roundness is part of what it means to be a circle. But this is only true in a world where the plane is the area of description. And a straight line is the shortest distance between two points only in a Euclidean world. In a world of doughnut geometry the shortest distance may in fact be a curved line. There must be some relation between the self-evident assertion and the world itself. In fact, if the world were constituted differently, it is conceivable that the rules would be greatly different. Thus tautologies do have a world- and mind-dependent element in their formulation.

Thirdly, most of the examples that Thiselton cites may be questioned according to his own method of classification. For example, in Rom 11:6 does the law of exclusion apply to the grace/works distinction? A similar opposition is often cited between faith and works, an exclusion that James flatly denies: "Even so faith, if it has no works, is dead, *being* by itself. But someone may *well* say, 'You have faith, and I have works; show me your faith without the works, and I will show you my faith by my works.' You believe that God is one. You do well; the demons also believe, and shudder. But are you willing to recognize, you foolish fellow, that faith without works is useless?" (Jas 2:17–20 NASB). Regarding Rom 4:4, virtually anyone who teaches will find it less than self-evident that one's payment is not counted according to grace but according to obligation, especially at a time when wages are being cut for various economic reasons. And is it obvious that one cannot hope for what one "sees" (Rom 8:24)? Or is it more self-evident that often humans do not begin to hope for that for which they have no incentive? It seems to be the case with presents

1975) esp. 220–22, 245–48.

16 Ayer, *Language*, 85–86.

at Christmas time—or why is so much money spent on advertising? Regarding 1 Cor 13:10, does it mean that the perfect in some way fills up what is lacking in the partial, or is it that the partial is eliminated in order to make way for the perfect? Thiselton himself shows that Rom 13:10 ("Love does no harm to its neighbour") is problematic, since there are examples in everyday experience that would seem to undermine this supposedly self-evident statement. The result may well be a vacuous category even if the analysis is correct.

Fourthly, Wittgenstein states that "it is impossible for there to be propositions of ethics. Propositions can express nothing that is higher. It is clear that ethics cannot be put into words. Ethics is transcendental. (Ethics and aesthetics are one and the same.)"[17] It would appear that any attempt to formulate an ethical statement in terms of a first-class utterance is usually only an application of a nonethical proposition. For example, when I say that "it is always right to do the right thing" this is an application of the law of noncontradiction ($a = a$). There is also the subsequent problem, which again Wittgenstein notes, of the relation between "ought" and "is." First-class utterances may depict what self-evidently "is," but the line of connection to "ought" requires a further step that leads beyond the utterance itself and into designation of the world.

B. *Second-Class Utterances*

Second-class utterances are described this way by Thiselton, quoting Wittgenstein but developing the category using his own perspective:

> Wittgenstein considers a special class of statement about which the speaker would, as it were, "like to say: 'If I am wrong about *this*, I have no guarantee that anything I say is true.'"...in this case, he would be *expressing the attitude of a particular tradition.* The opposite would be inconceivable *within* a given cultural or perhaps religious tradition... In Wittgenstein's words, they amount to "hinges" on which other statement [sic] or inquiries turn. They articulate "the scaffolding of our thoughts."
>
> Wittgenstein compares this type of utterance with propositions which have the status or function of the words "It is written..." Within particular communities they have become virtually unquestioned or even unquestionable axioms; they function "as a *foundation* for research and action," but are often simply "isolated from doubt, though not according to any explicit rule." Wittgenstein seems to suggest that in any culture, including our own, "all enquiry...is set so as to exempt certain propositions from doubt... They lie apart from the route travelled by enquiry."... "Now it gives our way of looking at things, and our researches, their form."[18]

---

17 L. Wittgenstein, *Tractatus Logico-Philosophicus* (trans. D.F. Pears and B.F. McGuinness; London: Routledge and Kegan Paul, 1961) 71 §§6.42, 6.421.

18 Thiselton, *Two Horizons*, 392–93 (italics are his), citing L. Wittgenstein in *On Certainty* (Oxford: Blackwell, 1969) §§69, 216, 87, 88, 211.

> ...class-two grammatical utterances regularly occur in the context of an appeal which presupposes a given religious or ethical "common understanding."[19]

Examples that Thiselton cites include Rom 3:4, 5b–6: "Let God be true, and every man a liar... That God is unjust in bringing his wrath upon us? (I am using a human argument.) Certainly not! If that were so, how could God judge the world?" As Thiselton says, "Both for Paul and for most, if not all, of his readers, the justice and truthfulness of God constitutes an unshakable axiom which cannot be questioned without, among other things, calling in question the very tradition of life and thought to which they belong. It has itself become a fixed hinge on which further statements or inquiries turn." Citing C.H. Dodd, who says Paul's statement is not an argument, Thiselton admits that "it would be very difficult to see what might 'count as a test' of the truth-or-falsity of the axiom within the primitive Christian tradition."[20] In Rom 9:14–24, "Paul is drawing on a tradition of thought, familiar in first-century Judaism, within which part of what is entailed in God's being God is that his verdicts cannot be challenged by guilty men."[21] Concerning Rom 8:8, "Those controlled by the sinful nature cannot please God," Thiselton, noting comments by C.K. Barrett, calls use of "cannot" not an empirical limitation but a grammatical one: It is contradictory to say that flesh is obedient to God, since by definition God is excluded from the flesh. "But since this understanding of [flesh] remains relative to a particular theological tradition or frame, this would hardly amount to a topic-neutral grammatical utterance."[22] As for 1 Cor 12:3, "no one can say 'Jesus is Lord,' except by the Holy Spirit," again the grammatical and not empirical sense of "cannot" is used. "Paul is not inviting his readers to imagine that someone tries hard to make such a confession, but fails to bring it off, in the event, without the aid of the Spirit. Paul's concern, rather, is with the grammar of Christian 'spirituality.'"[23]

This classification too is open to question.

First, it is not entirely clear that these examples are best seen as second-class utterances. Thiselton notes that second-class utterances are part of a theological tradition, and several of the examples are concerned with statements about God. Whereas one might question several of the assumptions of Christians regarding the nature of God, can it be said that every view of God qualifies as a second-class utterance—that is, that one's view of God is merely theologically

---

19 Thiselton, *Two Horizons*, 397.

20 Thiselton, *Two Horizons*, 393. See C.H. Dodd, *The Epistle of Paul to the Romans* (MNTC; London: Hodder & Stoughton, 1932) 45.

21 Thiselton, *Two Horizons*, 394.

22 Thiselton, *Two Horizons*, 394, 395. See C.K. Barrett, *A Commentary on the Epistle to the Romans* (BNTC; London: A. & C. Black, 1957) 158.

23 Thiselton, *Two Horizons*, 395.

conditioned and outside the parameters of investigation? This points up possible difficulties in distinguishing the definition of first- and second-class utterances. A plausible case might be made that in every society and culture, or at least in every religious tradition, there is some concept of God, and he would be defined in such a way that a common assumption about his knowledge or power or being would run consistently through these definitions (the way language is used would entail a certain definition of God). Discounting an atheistic view, since it is for the most part self-contradictory, even an agnostic view of God would have some concept that would appear to be surprisingly similar to theism at several points.

Secondly, Thiselton puts this analysis forward in partial reaction to D.E. Nineham's claim that second-class utterances constitute presuppositions behind the outlook of a given culture: "The propositions that express them so take their truth for granted that *within a given tradition* their denial is inconceivable."[24] But if they are so fundamental it is interesting that so many of them have been called into question in this century alone, especially in regard to the nature of God. For example, a process-theological view of God would question the consistent divine nature that is truthful or knowledgeable in comparison to deceptive and limited humanity, since God himself is defined by nature as limited and subject to experience.

Thirdly, Thiselton equates second-class utterances and their contextual appearance with Wittgenstein's language-games. Thus these utterances merely serve a function within a given language-game and have no ability to lead to understanding beyond the confines of the given game. Therefore, their validity shifts as the validity of the language-game shifts. If ethical statements are bound to this class of utterance, then there is no sense in which an ethical statement has any universal value beyond the terms of this particular cultural or theological tradition or language-game. The ethical statement has no power to compel acceptance and has questionable descriptive capabilities, especially in relation to the commonsense view of the world.

C. *Third-Class Utterances*

Third-class utterances are those utterances that challenge the accepted means of thinking and result in a new and provocative view of the structures of thought. This class of utterance contains the new categories by which reality is described, replacing the second-class utterance. According to Thiselton, this entails three aspects:

> [First,] class-three grammatical utterances remain *grammatical* utterances, since they concern the elucidation and the application of certain *concepts*, and are not statements

24 Thiselton, *Two Horizons*, 395 (italics are his).

> about the world. Secondly, class-three grammatical utterances often turn not simply on linguistic convention or habit, but on what John Searle calls "institutional facts."... Thirdly, as Wittgenstein often stressed, how language is used affects how a thing is "seen." How something is pictured often determines its place in our wider system of concepts, and hence also our attitudes towards it.[25]

Thiselton cites the following examples from Paul: "If you belong to Christ, then you are Abraham's seed, and heirs according to the promise" (Gal 3:29), an important and relevant citation in the light of the scope of this chapter; "A man is not a Jew if he is only one outwardly, nor is circumcision merely outward and physical. No, a man is a Jew if he is one inwardly; and circumcision is circumcision of the heart" (Rom 2:28–29); and "For since there is jealousy and quarreling among you, are you not worldly?" (1 Cor 3:3).

In each of these, Paul is making a "linguistic recommendation"—that is, recommending a new way of viewing a state of affairs, whether or not this is based on the institutional facts of the time. Thus Paul is making a linguistic recommendation about who is the true heir of Abraham, who is the true Jew, and what is fleshly and spiritual, in each instance in order to lead to a "reappraisal of the theological situation of the readers."[26] In Wittgenstein's terminology: Whereas one picture had been operative in the Romans', Galatians', or Corinthians' consciousness, Paul substitutes another, different picture.

This class of utterance as well may be criticized.

First, there is the question of what relation these pictures, or new ways of viewing, have to the state of affairs they replace. Is it that no state of affairs has any necessary relation to what is but only is a picture? If so, a picture of what? Is it merely a mental conception? If it is believed that one picture is better in some sense than another, it would seem incumbent upon these pictures to have some relation beyond themselves so that evaluation may be made. With no means of evaluation, one may as well substitute one picture as another or keep the picture the same. By Paul's use of third-class utterances, in his thinking at least, he was not simply painting a new picture or suggesting a new picture only to provoke discussion. He believed that in very important and vital ways the new picture was a more accurate depiction of the state of affairs. This certainly seems to be the case in each of the instances Thiselton cites.

Secondly, distinguishing the relation between third- and second-class utterances requires more contextual knowledge than Thiselton seems to realize. For example, let it be assumed that the Corinthian, Roman or Galatian readers did not have the same picture as Paul did. Is it possible that what for the audience was a third-class utterance was a second-class utterance in Paul's

---

25 Thiselton, *Two Horizons*, 401–402 (italics are his).

26 Thiselton, *Two Horizons*, 403.

mind, such that his theological tradition had already been so altered (possibly on the Damascus road) that these statements did not constitute a linguistic recommendation but an expression of the scaffolding of his thought? How can it be evaluated when such a transition occurs, and is it worth it to attempt such an estimation? It is quite possible that the audience had already been told of such an estimation but had failed to act upon such knowledge. Does a reminder of what (at least from Paul's perspective) already is constitute a third-class utterance?

The above discussion has attempted to indicate several problems with the scheme that Thiselton describes concerning Wittgenstein's classes of utterances. The criticism is not intended to render the scheme entirely useless, but it does indicate several areas of potential difficulty in developing and articulating it. Perhaps a similar scheme can be made more functionally useful with further modification, but as it stands now there appear to be several significant difficulties.

3. *Galatians 3:28–29 in Recent Discussion*

One of the most important and widely-cited Pauline ethical texts in current discussion, especially in relation to the women's issue, is Gal 3:28–29, especially v. 28, although it has other far-reaching implications as well. As Mary Hayter says,

> Galatians 3.28 presents a crux in the consideration of the use of Scripture in the debate about woman's status and ministry in the Church. On the one hand, it is the *locus classicus* of biblical texts for those who believe that, ultimately, Scripture does not discriminate between male and female and that it is therefore wrong for the Church to perpetuate such discrimination in its ordination practice. On the other hand, this text is dismissed as insignificant by those who allege that it does not mean what feminists say it means or that even if it does have a "liberationist' tenor, it is outranked by "subordinationist" passages.[27]

In this section a brief investigation of several approaches to this text is chronicled. What emerges of interest is the various ways in which the passage is treated. Although none of the authors shows awareness of the classes of utterances cited above, all three of the categories are apparently drawn upon, often unknowingly and often without explicit support or reasoning for such classification. This offers significant insight into how this crucial New

27 M. Hayter, *The New Eve in Christ: The Use and Abuse of the Bible in the Debate about Women in the Church* (London: SPCK, 1987) 134.

Testament text is being interpreted and understood.[28]

Richard Longenecker appears to consider Gal 3:28–29 an application of a first-class utterance, although he does not develop his justification at length. In fact he introduces his justification as follows:

> The most forthright statement on social ethics in all the New Testament is found in Galatians 3:28... The statement has been widely heralded as the "Magna Carta of the New Humanity," for it sets forth a relationship "in Christ Jesus" in which believers through baptism not only have been "united with Christ" and "clothed with Christ" (v. 27) but also have entered into a new relationship of oneness with one another.[29]

What he says could classify this statement as a third-class utterance. He also believes that this section could have been an already existent and generally used baptismal liturgy of the early Church,[30] which could classify this statement as a second-class utterance. But specifically concerning the so-called three pairings, Longenecker says that they "cover in embryonic fashion all the essential relationships of humanity."[31] In the light of his statement that the New Testament's teachings are proclamations to be taken as "normative,"[32] he implies that they constitute essential oppositions. And this foundation provides the basis for his subsequent discussion of social ethics. He seems to feel that once this groundwork has been established, there is no need to justify the egalitarian stance he advocates since it is founded upon an unimpeachable standard.

But what application of a context-neutral statement does this verse make? The closest one that comes to mind is the law of noncontradiction, in which the verse would be saying that "if *a*, then not non-*a*." But this is not correct, since the verse seems to say more. Whereas there may have been *a* and *b*, such that one would have to be one or the other, now there is neither *a* nor *b*. This would appear to be an endorsement of androgyny or some form of sexual negation, although most scholars (rightly) distance themselves from this view.[33]

---

28 See, for example, D.R. MacDonald, *There is No Male and Female: The Fate of a Dominical Saying in Paul and Gnosticism* (HDR 20; Philadelphia: Fortress Press, 1987) 2–5, with extensive bibliography. It is noteworthy to observe which books do not spend much time discussing this passage; see, for example, G.W. Knight, III, *The Role Relationship of Men and Women: New Testament Teaching* (2nd edn; Chicago: Moody, 1985); L. Scanzoni and N. Hardesty, *All We're Meant to Be: A Biblical Approach to Women's Liberation* (Waco, TX: Word, 1974).

29 R.N. Longenecker, *New Testament Social Ethics for Today* (Grand Rapids: Eerdmans, 1984) 30.

30 Longenecker, *New Testament Social Ethics,* 31–33.

31 Longenecker, *New Testament Social Ethics*, 34.

32 Longenecker, *New Testament Social Ethics*, 27, cf. 84.

33 An apparent exception is W. Meeks, "The Image of the Androgyne: Some Uses of a

Several scholars endorse a view that sees Gal 3:28–29 as a second-class utterance. For example, Hayter cites many examples from Paul's ministry that she claims show that Paul worked side by side with women throughout his missionary ventures. Paul had already gone far beyond the restrictions of the Judaism of his time. And it is in the light of his Judaism that Paul utters the statement of Gal 3:28–29. It is a statement that constitutes the scaffolding of thinking regarding Paul's view of women in the light of the oppressive Old Testament context. Thus, as Hayter says, "It is, then, male and female as the oppressive custody of the law ordered their relationship which is transcended in Christ."[34]

This view is stated more explicitly by Burton, who says that Paul presents

> an inspiring picture of the world under one universal religion... It is only in the religion of Christ that Paul conceives that men can thus be brought together. That he is speaking of these distinctions from the point of view of religion is evident from the context in general, but especially from his inclusion of the ineradicable distinction of sex.[35]

Those commentators who see Paul's comments dependent upon an earlier baptismal formula accepted by and used in the Christian Church probably view the sentence as a second-class utterance, one that constitutes the scaffolding of their thought. And several more conservative commentators, such as Mary Evans, place the passage in this category as well.[36]

But if these comments are of a purely religious nature, what sort of compelling or normative value do they have apart from the Christian theological tradition? The implication is that Christians have the obligation to ignore or even eliminate distinctions made on the basis of sex, social status, and race, but they have no jurisdiction for imposing such an obligation upon any other theological (or sociological) tradition. These guidelines merely provide a basis for Christian thought. Many would find this ethic very dissatisfying, because it endorses a relativistic ethic that makes Christianity as traditionally conceived in no way significantly different from any other religious tradition, and it eliminates any basis for evangelism or missions, traditionally considered as distinctives of Christian practice. There is also the problem that the second-class utterance appears to endorse the status quo, possibly awaiting a re-adjustment in perspective such as the third-class utterance makes.

And a third group of scholars seems to argue that Gal 3:28–29 constitutes a

Symbol in Earliest Christianity," *HR* 13 (1974) 165–208, and his followers.

34 Hayter, *New Eve*, 138.

35 Burton, *Galatians*, 206.

36 M.J. Evans, *Woman in the Bible: An Overview of All the Crucial Passages on Women's Roles* (Downers Grove, IL: InterVarsity Press, 1983) 62–64.

third-class utterance, one that makes a "linguistic recommendation." For example, F.F. Bruce, who denies that the verses originated in any sort of pre-Pauline context, sees Paul as running contrary to the kind of prayer that a Jewish man would make, thanking God that he was not a Gentile, slave or woman.[37] Or, as Don Williams says, "Here is Paul's radical step beyond the old order."[38]

I believe that this third view is essentially correct, although only a few of the scholars cited give full credence to a number of issues that must be discussed at greater length. These revolve around the specific language of the text in its context. First is the linguistic context itself, as Thiselton has pointed out. Paul's discussion is the "nature of justification or, more specifically, the conditions of full inclusion in the Abrahamic covenant."[39] Several commentators have agreed that this is what accounts for Paul's abbreviated treatment of the first pair on slave and free and the third pair on men and women, since his focus at this point is the relation of Jew and Gentile. Second is the specific contextual feature of being "in Christ Jesus" (ἐν Χριστῷ Ἰησοῦ, cf. v. 26). This factor must be calculated into the analysis, although most authors neglect its important function. This is developed further in a summative way in v. 29 (I follow Thiselton's classification of the verse as a third-class utterance). Being "in Christ" is recapitulated as being "of Christ" (Χριστοῦ) in the verbless protasis of a first class conditional construction, providing the basis for being "seed of Abraham" and "heirs according to promise." Third is the fact that the grammatical structure of the paired items in v. 28 is not identical (οὐκ ἔνι Ἰουδαῖος οὐδὲ Ἕλλην, οὐκ ἔνι δοῦλος οὐδὲ ἐλεύθερος, οὐκ ἔνι ἄρσεν καὶ θῆλυ). The third uses different negation, possibly reflecting the imitated language of the LXX (Gen 2:7) but possibly calling attention to itself because the statement made is so startling. Fourthly, Paul seems to suggest two simple alternatives by his statement that there is neither male nor female. Either he is advocating an androgynous society, or there is some way in which the "in Christ Jesus/of Christ" context disambiguates such an obviously problematic interpretation, both for the ancient and the modern. In the light of the Old Testament, as well as the rest of the New Testament, the latter is surely correct. Paul has stepped into a theological context ripe for discussion of several fundamentals, including what it means to be justified apart from the law or to be

---

37 F.F. Bruce, *Commentary on Galatians* (NIGTC; Grand Rapids: Eerdmans, 1982) 187.

38 D. Williams, *The Apostle Paul and Women in the Church* (Ventura: Gospel Light, 1977) 82. See also P.K. Jewett, *Man as Male and Female* (Grand Rapids: Zondervan, 1975) 144.

39 See, for example, S.B. Clark, *Man and Woman in Christ: An Examination of the Roles of Men and Women in Light of Scripture and the Social Sciences* (Ann Arbor: Servant, 1980) 137–38.

the seed of Abraham. This he attributes to the work of Christ. It is therefore in the "in Christ Jesus/of Christ" context that these statements are made. He is insisting that being "in Christ Jesus" or "of Christ" there is a whole new perspective or "linguistic recommendation," one that in this instance at least has some basis in the world as it is.[40]

4. *Conclusion*

The following conclusions emerge from the above discussion.

1. Classification of utterances is not an easy task, primarily because the categories themselves are problematic. This does not, however, invalidate the legitimacy of further attempts to define, refine and apply similar classificatory schemes. This will need to be done in conjunction with closer attention being paid to the actual language and its linguistic context.

2. It would appear that only class-one utterances can provide the necessary sure basis for formulating an ethical theory, but it does not appear possible to show that any ethical statement can be included within class-one utterances. That is, it is doubted by most scholars that an analytic statement that describes the world can be formulated (similar to Immanuel Kant's synthetic *a priori*, which tells us about the world before experience of it). Even a widespread or nearly universal generalization does not necessarily qualify as analytic.

3. Failing to find this basis, one must realize that the formulation of any ethical theory is an extrapolation, at least some distance removed from analytic statements. Whereas it may be realized that this is a logical necessity, it also must constitute a call to humility concerning the status of one's ethical formulations.

4. There is much confusion among scholars in attempting to formulate an ethical position regarding the "role of women" in church and family, much of it revolving around use of Gal 3:28–29, especially v. 28. Some scholars assume that Gal 3:28–29 is a class-one utterance, others that it is a class-two utterance, and still others that it is a class-three utterance. Once one realizes how the passage is classified, it becomes clear what assumptions are being made and how the passage will influence understanding of the women's issue.

5. Those who argue for a second-class utterance use of Gal 3:28–29 must be content to realize that their view may simply perpetuate the standard and agreed-upon structure of thought. Those who argue for a third-class utterance use of it must realize that they are calling for a radical shift in the approach one

40 In some ways, D.E.H. Whiteley shows the most scholarly integrity, admitting to the meaning of the passage even though he does not agree or find it convincing (*The Theology of St. Paul* [2nd edn; Oxford: Blackwell, 1974] 222–23).

is taking towards an issue, with all of its concomitant risks in relation to other agreed-upon categories of thought.

CHAPTER THIRTEEN

WHAT DOES IT MEAN TO BE "SAVED BY CHILDBIRTH" (1 TIMOTHY 2:15)?*

1. *Introduction*

> σωθήσεται δὲ διὰ τῆς τεκνογονίας ἐὰν μείνωσιν ἐν πίστει καὶ ἀγάπῃ καὶ ἁγιασμῷ μετὰ σωφροσύνης (1 Tim 2:15)

1 Timothy 2:15, like few other passages in the New Testament, is almost embarrassing in the attention it draws to itself. It is one of those passages that makes discussion of "Pauline theology," in particular the debate over "Paul" and women, so difficult. Although the passage raises a number of interesting exegetical issues (examined in more detail below), the nature and kind of reaction it prompts is out of all proportion to its exegetical significance. Nevertheless, the passage refuses to go away as an item of debate, consistently garnering an entry or two each year in the standard bibliographies. What is disappointing in many of these discussions, however, is that they assume far too many "self-evident" interpretations of many of the text's lexical and grammatical phenomena. But many of the interpretations are anything but self-evident, despite many self-assured comments. What the text seems to be saying to many of its interpreters is apparently formulated more on the basis of ideology than critical exegesis. This ideological criticism has been of two kinds. The first simply dismisses or marginalizes the verse, and the second tends to over-theologize various elements of its interpretation. Such reductionism has made the text more problematic than it need be. This has resulted in a facile handling of the text, and in a failure to give due weight and consideration to its linguistic context. In the light of this, the linguistic issues must be systematically considered once more. The major lexical and grammatical questions raised in this single verse include determining (a) the subject of the

---

* This essay is reprinted with the permission of Sheffield Academic Press, from the *Journal for the Study of the New Testament* 49 (1993) 87–102. Slight changes have been made to the format and presentation.

verb σωθήσεται with respect to "the woman" of v. 14, (b) the sense of the verb σῴζω, (c) the denotation of the term τεκνογονία, (d) the function of the preposition διά with the genitive case, (e) the shift in number of the verbs from singular to plural, and (f) the use of the third class conditional construction. In themselves, each of these issues may not be particularly complex, but their composite understanding is necessary to avoid irresponsible interpretation.

2. *A Survey of Previous Interpretation of 1 Timothy 2:15*

Before offering a re-examination of the primary lexical and grammatical issues, several examples of ideologically based criticism that dismisses the force of the passage warrant mention. An obvious solution to interpretative difficulties is simply to dismiss them, a solution made possible for this passage because it appears in one of the so-called deutero-Pauline epistles, and in an unpopular section at that (1 Tim 2:8–15). The author or authors of 1 Timothy may in some loose way have been connected to the original, authentic Paul (for example, the progressive and enlightened Paul of the *Hauptbriefe*, best exemplified in such a strongly egalitarian passage as Gal 3:28–29).[1] But this passage, so this theory goes, links the woman with the fall of humankind and equates her redemption with giving birth to children; this reflects a later, reactionary attempt to control the enthusiasm of the early Christian movement.[2] This solution is both instructive and questionable. On the one hand, it recognizes a clear sense to the meaning of the passage. But the meaning is seen to be offensive. It is offensive morally, for it relies upon traditional oppressive sexual stereotypes, including a distorted interpretation of the fall, or it reflects a primitive mythology that links woman as tempter with evil. On the other hand, this view manages to skirt around the all too clear implications of this passage, relegating not only the passage itself but the book in which it is found into a marginalized position, beyond the consideration given to other "authentic" material. This attempt is ultimately less than satisfactory. I am not fully convinced that 1 Timothy can be so easily or clearly distanced from authentic Pauline material, either because the rise of early Catholicism is not so well proven, or because it is difficult to conceive of an early Pauline church that would so easily enshrine undifferentiatedly both the progressive and the reactionary Paul in its established canon.

A second dismissive solution is one that posits that the author of the epistle

1 For examples of how Gal 3:28–29 has been interpreted, see S.E. Porter, "Wittgenstein's Classes of Utterances and Pauline Ethical Texts," *JETS* 32 (1989) 85–97, reprinted as ch. 12 in this volume, pp. 239–54.

2 See, for example, M. Hayter, *The New Eve in Christ: The Use and Abuse of the Bible in the Debate about Women in the Church* (London: SPCK, 1987) 133–39 and 131–33.

is quoting 1 Cor 14:34–35 at 1 Tim 2:11–14.[3] The Corinthian passage says, "Let the women keep silent in the churches; for they are not permitted to speak, but let them subject themselves, just as the law also says. And if they desire to learn anything, let them ask their own husbands at home; for it is improper for a woman to speak in the church." The author of 1 Timothy, so this theory says, quotes this passage but without Paul's further negative assessment of this statement attributed to his Corinthian antagonists. By doing a little exegetical legerdemain, an interpreter who holds to this solution has not really explained anything. First, there is the matter of the significant changes in wording between the two passages. Someone who took over the wording so clumsily as to miss the important Pauline commentary (and dismissal) might have had some difficulty in re-writing the passage so thoroughly to begin with. Secondly, this explanation does not treat v. 15 at all. Verse 15 would have to be a further comment by the author, but recognizing that fact does not explain its meaning. If anything, it adds to the difficulty.

A third solution is simply to posit that this passage is a later interpolation within 1 Timothy.[4] Alonso Diaz recognizes difficulties with this view, related first to when the interpolation may have occurred (he suggests during the Montanist controversy), and secondly to how the verses are to be understood (the verses oppose Montanism and attempt to bring practice into conformity with other Pauline teaching). This view is not exegetically or historically sound, and should not be perpetuated as a satisfactory explanation of any of the passage's difficulties. According to the most thorough analysis of the textual tradition, there are no major texts that delete this verse,[5] and such a solution has to be viewed with great suspicion as pure conjecture meant to deal dismissively with admittedly difficult verses.

Other scholars reflect their ideological bias by the tendency to over-theologize various elements of interpretation of 1 Tim 2:15. These proposals, in common with the ideologically based dismissals of it, fail to give due weight to the linguistic considerations. These proposals will be evaluated within the larger context of considering anew the individual lexical and grammatical elements that compose this verse.

---

3 See D.W. Odell-Scott, "In Defense of an Egalitarian Interpretation of 1 Cor. 14.34–36: A Reply to Murphy-O'Connor's Critique," *BTB* 17 (1987) 100–103. He is responding to J. Murphy-O'Connor, "Interpolation in 1 Corinthians," *CBQ* 48 (1986) 90–92.

4 J. Alonso Diaz, "Restricción en algunos textos paulinos de las reivindicaciones de la mujer en la Iglesia," *Estudios Eclesiásticos* 50 (1975) 77–93; cf. O. Michel, "Grundfragen der Pastoralbriefe," in *Auf dem Grunde der Apostel und Propheten* (Festschrift T. Wurm; Stuttgart: Kohlhammer, 1948) 93.

5 See J.K. Elliott, *The Greek Text of the Epistles to Timothy and Titus* (Studies and Documents 36; Salt Lake City: University of Utah Press, 1968) 45.

3. *An Interpretation of 1 Timothy 2:15*

There are at least six important exegetical issues to consider in analysis of 1 Tim 2:15. These will be treated in logical order, citing the variety of scholarly opinion on each issue, before drawing conclusions regarding interpretation of the verse in the context of the entire book.

A. *The Subject of the Verb Σωθήσεται*

The first issue considers the subject of the future passive verb, σωθήσεται, found in v. 15. Since no explicit subject of the verb is designated, it makes best exegetical sense in the grammatical context to begin from the assumption that the subject of the verb corresponds in some way with the last mentioned possible antecedent, "the woman" (ἡ γυνή) of v. 14. But who exactly is this woman? The solutions here have been at least five.[6] In the light of mention of Adam and Eve in v. 13 and Adam again in v. 14, it has been proposed that ἡ γυνή in v. 14b is still Eve, "*the* woman."[7] A second solution is that this is the consummate or ideal woman, Mary, the mother of Jesus.[8] Several interpreters have combined the first two proposals in a grand theological synthesis, concluding that the passage is stating that Eve will find her ultimate redemption or salvation in the birth of Christ. Thus "the childbirth" (see below) refers to the *protoevangelium* of Gen 3:15 and the overcoming of the consequences of the fall.[9] A third solution is that ἡ γυνή is any woman, or woman in general.[10] A

---

6 See C. Spîcq, *Les épîtres pastorales* (2 vols.; EBib; 4th edn; Paris: Gabalda, 1969 [1947]) 1.382–83; J. Roloff, *Der erste Brief an Timotheus* (EKK; Zürich: Benziger Verlag, 1988) 140–41, for a survey of the views.

7 See, for example, E.K. Simpson, *The Pastoral Epistles* (Grand Rapids: Eerdmans, 1954) 48; Roloff, *Erste Brief*, 139–40.

8 This is perhaps the most popular view in the light of church history. It appears to be the view of Ignatius in *Eph.* 19; Irenaeus in *Haer.* 3.22; 5.19; and *Praedic. in Apostolica* 33; Justin in *Dial.* 100; and Tertullian in *de Carne* 17. Among modern commentators it has been widely supported as well: e.g. W. Lock, *A Critical and Exegetical Commentary on the Pastoral Epistles* (ICC; Edinburgh: T. & T. Clark, 1924) 32–33; P.B. Payne, "Libertarian Women in Ephesus: A Response to Douglas J. Moo's Article, '1 Timothy 2:11–15: Meaning and Significance,'" *Trinity Journal* 2 (1981) 177–78 (giving the above evidence); and T.C. Oden, *First and Second Timothy and Titus* (Louisville: John Knox, 1989) 101. It is attested in the RV, Berkeley, Amplified Bibles (and at least suggested in the margins of RSV, NEB, ASV, and Weymouth).

9 See, for example, A.D.B. Spencer, "Eve at Ephesus (Should Women be Ordained as Pastor according to the First Letter to Timothy 2:11–15?)," *JETS* 17 (1974) 215–22; M.D. Roberts, "Woman Shall be Saved: A Clearer Look at 1 Timothy 2:15," *TSF Bulletin* 5.2 (November–December 1981) 6; Payne, "Libertarian Women," 177–81; Oden, *First and Second Timothy and Titus*, 101–102; and A. Padget, "Wealthy Women at Ephesus: I Timothy 2:8–15 in Social Context," *Int* 41 (1987) 28.

10 See, for example, J.N.D. Kelly, *A Commentary on the Pastoral Epistles* (BNTC;

fourth proposal is that "the woman" is the representative woman of Ephesus, the city to which the letter is purportedly addressed.[11] And a fifth solution is that she is the representative Christian woman.[12] These proposals run a gamut from the general to the specific, and from the exalted to the mundane, along the way raising issues warranting closer evaluation before being able to suggest an answer to the question of the subject of the verb, σωθήσεται.

Reference to Adam and Eve must be put within the larger context of the general comments made by the author about men and women. Beginning with 1 Tim 2:8, the author says that he desires for men to pray in a particular way and for women to dress in a particular fashion. The woman's dress is said to reflect in some way her spiritual inclination, to be maintained through a discipline of quietness. Then the author turns to Adam and Eve, with respect to the order (πρῶτος...εἶτα) of creation and the order of deception.[13] Although it must be conceded that "the woman" of v. 14 could be Eve, the inferring of Eve as the subject of the future verb in v. 15 does not carry great conviction. The attitudinal[14] force of the future form of the verb in v. 15 is one of expectation, that is, it grammaticalizes or conveys not a temporal conception (past, present or future) but a marked and emphatic expectation towards a course of events. Since Eve's fortunes have already been determined, they are beyond any further expectation, so this solution is unlikely.

To extrapolate further that the consummate act of the woman, Mary—that is, giving birth to Christ—is spoken of here requires an even larger leap of exegetical faith, one not warranted on the basis of the context. It first requires that there be a clear and logical progression in the argument from Eve to Mary, one not indicated in the text. Furthermore, it requires association of "childbirth" with one particular childbirth, with stress upon the article to specify a particular instance. The word translated here "childbirth" is not used elsewhere in the New Testament, much less to speak of Jesus' birth (an obscure reference at

London: A. & C. Black, 1963; repr. Grand Rapids: Baker, 1981) 69; D. Guthrie, *The Pastoral Epistles* (TNTC; 2nd edn; Grand Rapids: Eerdmans, 1990 [1957]) 88; A.T. Hanson, *The Pastoral Epistles* (NCB; Grand Rapids: Eerdmans, 1982) 74.

11 See, for example, G.D. Fee, *1 and 2 Timothy, Titus* (Peabody: Hendrickson, 1988) 74–75. Cf. his *Gospel and Spirit: Issues in New Testament Hermeneutics* (Peabody: Hendrickson, 1991) 52–65.

12 See M. Dibelius and H. Conzelmann, *The Pastoral Epistles* (Hermeneia; Philadelphia: Fortress Press, 1972) 48, on the basis of the qualifying clause; D.J. Moo, "1 Timothy 2:11–15: Meaning and Significance," *Trinity Journal* 1 (1980) 70–73 esp. 71; J.L. Houlden, *The Pastoral Epistles: 1 and II Timothy, Titus* (London: SCM Press, 1976) 72; N. Brox, *Die Pastoralbriefe* (RNT; 4th edn; Regensburg: Pustet, 1969) 137.

13 See Kelly, *Pastoral Epistles*, 68–69.

14 See S.E. Porter, *Verbal Aspect in the Greek of the New Testament, with Reference to Tense and Mood* (Studies in Biblical Greek 1; New York: Peter Lang, 1989) 409–16 esp. 414, on the force of the future form as grammaticalizing expectation.

best).[15] The *protoevangelium* of Gen 3:15 does not use this language, and neither is Jesus' birth referred to in this way until much later (in the second century by Irenaeus). This highly theological view puts too much emphasis upon the particularizing function of the article, as well. Although the article may be used to specify a particular item, and in fact does so on occasion in the pastoral epistles,[16] this is only one of its several uses; it could be generic as well, as it probably is in v. 8 with reference to "the" men in every place.[17]

Most plausible, it seems to me, is to take 1 Tim 2:15 as a concluding statement of the entire section (1 Tim 2:8–15).[18] Within the section, Adam and Eve are used for illustrative purposes, with the idea that even though Adam was first created, it was Eve or "the woman" (here an anaphoric use of the article, "the woman referred to above, that is, Eve") who was first deceived. The argument implies that all women as a result are "deceived." But the one who is "saved" (see below) is the woman who remains in faith and love and holiness. Before we can be any more specific about who this woman is, as well as determining the sense of the entire verse, several of the other items in v. 15 must be examined.

B. *The Sense of the Verb Σῴζω*

To say something more specific about the concept of salvation an examination of the use of σῴζω must be made. Determination of the meaning of σῴζω as it is used in 1 Tim 2:15 is complicated by several factors, however, including the question of which corpus of writings to examine for suitable parallel usage. The pastoral epistles constitute the immediate context. But should the entire Pauline corpus be included? In other words, should continuity between the agreed-upon authentically Pauline material and the questionably Pauline material be assumed on the basis of verbal parallels? If continuity is assumed, the difficulty in determining the meaning of σῴζω is reduced to a large extent, since in virtually all authentically Pauline contexts σῴζω denotes a salvific spiritual act, perhaps eschatological in consequence (e.g. Rom 5:10; 1 Cor 7:16). In the deutero-

---

15 Fee, *1 and 2 Timothy, Titus*, 75.

16 Lock, *Pastoral Epistles*, 33, who cites: τὸ μυστήριον, ἡ πίστις, ἡ διδασκαλία; see also pp. xvi–xvii for more examples. He is followed apparently by Oden, *Pastoral Epistles*, 101–102; Payne, "Libertarian Women," 181.

17 Guthrie, *Pastoral Epistles* (2nd edn), 88. On the use of the article, see now S.E. Porter, *Idioms of the Greek New Testament* (Biblical Languages: Greek 2; 2nd edn; Sheffield: JSOT Press, 1994) 103–105.

18 Some interpreters have even taken it as the climax of the section: D.M. Scholer, "1 Timothy 2:9–15 and the Place of Women in the Church's Ministry," in *Women, Authority and the Bible* (ed. A. Mickelsen; Downers Grove, IL: InterVarsity Press, 1986) 196; contra S.T. Foh, *Women and the Word of God: A Response to Biblical Feminism* (Grand Rapids: Baker, 1979) 128, who calls v. 15 "a puzzle and a sort of non sequitur."

Pauline material the same may well hold true also, especially in the pastoral epistles, which provide an essential minimum corpus for examination, and the one considered here. Besides 1 Tim 2:15, which will be examined below, the examples of the use of σῴζω in 1 Timothy include the following: 1:15: one of the "faithful sayings"[19] is that Christ Jesus came into the world to save (σῶσαι) sinners; 2:4: reference is to our saviour (σωτῆρος) God, who wants all men to be saved (σωθῆναι) and to enter into knowledge of truth; 4:16: Timothy is told that by upholding and maintaining the teaching he will save (σώσεις) himself and those who hear him, a context in which perseverance is taken by several commentators to imply final salvation.[20] Examples in 2 Timothy include 1:9: it is God who saves (σώσαντος) us and calls with a holy calling; and 4:18: the Lord will rescue me from every evil work and save (σώσει) me into his heavenly kingdom. Although some interpreters debate about the sense of 2 Tim 4:18, this seems to be unnecessary fretting since the goal of salvation is said to be the heavenly kingdom. The only example in Titus is 3:5: according to the mercy of our saviour God (σωτῆρος) he saved (ἔσωσεν) us through (διά) a washing of rebirth and renewing of the Holy Spirit, a context in which final salvation is united with past events.

In the light of the above cumulative evidence and in particular in the context of 1 Tim 2:15, σωθήσεται is virtually guaranteed a salvific sense (the passive voice is probably a divine or theological passive, that is, God is the agent of salvation). This is confirmed both by the verb being introduced by contrastive δέ,[21] which puts v. 15 in juxtaposition to the sinful state of "the woman" in v. 14, and by the use of the following ἐάν clause (see below). The sense of "be kept safe" (NIV early edition, later changed; NASB; Moffatt; TEV footnote)[22] must be rejected as an accommodation to the apparently harsh theology of v. 15, a proposal which introduces a sense not clearly established for this word in the pastoral epistles. As Houlden says, "the salvation referred to must not mean physical safe-keeping in childbirth but that assured on the Last Day."[23]

---

19 On this issue, see G.W. Knight, III, *The Faithful Sayings in the Pastoral Letters* (Kampen: Kok, 1968; repr. Grand Rapids: Baker, 1979).

20 See Fee, *1 and 2 Timothy*, 109; cf. Guthrie, *Pastoral Epistles* (2nd edn), 111, who compares the sense with that in Phil 2:12; G. Fohrer, σῴζω, *TDNT*, 7.995.

21 This is recognized by many commentators, including Spîcq, *Épîtres pastorales* (4th edn), 382; D.J. Moo, "The Interpretation of 1 Timothy 2:11–15: A Rejoinder," *Trinity Journal* 2 (1981) 205; Payne, "Libertarian Women," 180.

22 So, for example, J.B. Hurley, *Man and Woman in Biblical Perspective* (Grand Rapids: Zondervan, 1981) 222: "Eve and women in general will be saved or kept safe from wrongly seizing men's roles by embracing a woman's role."

23 Houlden, *Pastoral Epistles*, 72; see also Spîcq, *Épîtres pastorales* (4th edn), 383; Fee, *1 and 2 Timothy*, 75; G. Holtz, *Die Pastoralbriefe* (Berlin: Evangelische Verlagsanstalt, 1965) 70; Scholer, "1 Timothy 2:9–15," 196; N.J.D. White, *The First and Second Epistles to Timothy and the Epistle to Titus* (5 vols.; Expositor's; repr. Grand Rapids: Eerdmans, n.d.)

C. *Denotation of the Term Τεκνογονία*

With respect to the word τεκνογονία (often translated "childbirth"), as mentioned above, it only appears once in the entire New Testament, although the cognate verb form appears in 1 Tim 5:14. In the light of the apparently rather narrow and even sexually-discriminatory meaning of this word as it is used in this context, it is not surprising that there have been several attempts to try to show that it cannot be confined simply to the idea of childbearing. For example, some interpreters, trying to expand its meaning, have proposed that it might well refer to a woman's normal responsibilities and duties, including but not specifically restricted to the act of bearing children. Moo says that "τεκνογονία, which may indicate child-*rearing* as well as child-*bearing*, may represent, by *synecdoche*, the general scope of activities in which Christian women should be involved." He looks to 1 Tim 5:14 for support of this proposal.[24] Other interpreters have gone even further and construed the term in a less tangible and more theological sense as the idea of a woman's performing her proper role of maintaining moral and spiritual virtues, and being kept from falling into error, in particular the error of Eve, which was lording authority over her man.[25] This view is made exceptionally difficult by the distance of v. 15 from v. 12, rendering an apparent connection between the two less than self-evident. And the most expansive view is that τεκνογονία is simply a figure for good works in general.[26] This last interpretation is much too broad to be established in any meaningful way, especially from the linguistic context of 1 Timothy.

That these solutions cannot be correct is further borne out in two ways. The first way is by examining use of the cognate verb form in 1 Tim 5:14. In that context the author specifies that he desires for younger women to carry out certain duties and responsibilities: γαμεῖν, τεκνογονεῖν, οἰκοδεσποτεῖν, etc. It is to be noticed that the three words form a logical and conceptual continuum, in which marriage is differentiated from the bearing of children, which is differentiated from the managing of one's household. It is difficult to see how

4.110; Dibelius–Conzelmann, *Pastoral Epistles*, 47–48; Kelly, *Pastoral Epistles*, 69–70; Lock, *Pastoral Epistles*, 31; Moo, "1 Timothy 2:11–15," 72; Payne, "Libertarian Women," 178.

24 Moo, "Interpretation," 72; following W. Ramsay, *The Teaching of Paul in Terms of the Present Day* (2nd edn; London: Hodder & Stoughton, n.d.) 170–75, who is very disappointing here; Spîcq, *Épîtres pastorales* (4th edn), 383–84; J. Jeremias, *Die Briefe an Timotheus und Titus* (Göttingen: Vandenhoeck & Ruprecht, 1975) 22; Hanson, *Pastoral Epistles*, 74; Brox, *Pastoralbriefe*, 136; C.K. Barrett, *The Pastoral Epistles* (Oxford: Clarendon Press, 1963) 56–57, a position which tends to neglect the sense of the verb σῴζω. This view is rightly criticized by Payne, "Libertarian Women," 178–79.

25 See S. Jebb, "A Suggested Interpretation of 1 Tim 2:15," *ExpTim* 81 (1969–70) 221; Hurley, *Man and Woman*, 222.

26 Discussed by Spîcq, *Épîtres pastorales* (4th edn), 384.

"childbearing" forms an inclusive term with household management or any other duties. It is equally illegitimate to include "childrearing" within a larger semantic range for τεκνογονία, since the author apparently uses τεκνοτροφέω (1 Tim 5:10) to denote this function.[27] Secondly, there is no moral, spiritual or theological quality directly (or even tangentially) attributed to any of these actions in this context. They are all listed within the confines of performance of specific and definable duties. This is confirmed by examination of use of τεκνογονία in extra-biblical Greek literature, although it must be admitted that the word is not widely used in other than Christian writers. Apart from later Christian writers, in all four contexts in which this word is used, where the meaning can be determined with any degree of certainty it denotes the specific act of bearing children.[28]

D. *Function of the Preposition Διά with the Genitive Case*

The next grammatical issue warranting examination revolves around the preposition διά. With its object in the genitive case, the preposition may have a number of different sense relations. One of the least likely suggestions is by Scott. On the basis of what he sees as the totally "preposterous" sense of the passage—that a woman is saved through childbirth—he takes διά as denoting a condition: "She will be saved *even though* she must bear children." As a result the woman will be saved, so he posits, despite the continuing mark of divine judgment, if she lives the "true Christian life."[29] But Scott has perhaps gone too far here. He has constricted himself into arguing for an understanding that not only has failed to garner support from any other commentator I am aware of, but fails to find any significant support in the major grammarians as well. Taking the preposition with the sense of "in the experience of" is an attempt by Falconer to mitigate what he sees as the uncompromizable Pauline idea of salvation by faith alone, while at the same time maintaining a sense of attendant circumstances.[30] His grammatical conclusions are therefore dictated by his theology, and he does little to defend this position apart from appealing to

---

27 See Dibelius–Conzelmann, *Pastoral Epistles*, 75.

28 Hippocrates (5th–4th centuries B.C.), *Epistulae* 17: ἢ τοὔμπαλιν γάμους ἢ πανηγύριας ἢ τεκνογονίην ἢ μυστήρια ἢ ἀρχὰς καὶ τιμὰς ἢ ἄλλο τι ὅλως ἀγαθόν; Galen (2nd century A.D.), *De Instrumento Odoratus* 49: ὑπὲρ ὧν ἐπὶ πλέον ἔν γε τῷ περὶ τεκνογονίας λόγῳ διερχόμεθα; Joannes Philoponus (6th century A.D.), *De Opifici Mundi* 301: εἰ δὲ κακὸν πᾶσα μῖξις, οὐκοῦν καὶ ἡ τεκνογονία κακὸν καὶ τὰ ἀποτελέσματα ταύτης, οἱ ἄνθρωποι; Simplicius (6th century A.D.), *Commentarius in Epicteti Enchiridion* 96: καὶ ἡ τῶν ζώων σύνοδος εἰς τεκνογονίαν ὁρᾷ. This list was secured using the Thesaurus Linguae Graecae data-base and Ibycus computer system. It confirms Fee's claim (*1 and 2 Timothy*, 75).

29 E.F. Scott, *The Pastoral Epistles* (New York: Harper & Bros., n.d.) 28.

30 R. Falconer, "1 Timothy 2:14, 15: Interpretative Notes," *JBL* 60 (1941) 376; White, *First and Second Epistles*, 110.

supposed Jewish thought regarding the necessity of having children.

In contrast to these theological explanations are the recognized grammatical categories of either some temporal or some instrumental sense of the preposition διά with the genitive case. The temporal sense would be one of duration: "during the time of childbearing." Although this is a grammatical possibility, the major difficulty with this view is that the most convincing examples that grammarians cite of the temporal use of διά have clear temporal words, for example, day, year, night (Acts 1:3; 5:19; 24:17; Gal 2:1).[31] Furthermore, if the salvific sense of σῴζω is accepted, as there is good reason to do (see above), the temporal view of the use of the preposition is virtually eliminated. Hence, the temporal view tends to be found only in translations where the sense of "preservation" for σῴζω is maintained (e.g. NIV early edition; Moffatt; TEV footnote). The instrumental sense of the preposition must finally be recognized as the most likely in this grammatical context,[32] whether it be more specifically (1) "by means of" or (2) "through the channel of" childbearing.[33] The only other place in the pastoral epistles where σῴζω is collocated with διά (Titus 3:5) has the instrumental sense (see above). It might on occasion be required to differentiate these two senses more exactly, but it is sufficient here to note only that they share the common feature that "childbearing" is the instrument (the means or the channel) by which salvation is accomplished.

E. *Shift in Number of the Verbs*

The next important grammatical issue in 1 Tim 2:15 revolves around the shift in number from the singular use of σωθήσεται to the plural use of μείνωσιν. The shift has resulted in several proposed explanations. Unwarranted because of its unjustified speculation is Bartsch's proposal that the author's use of the plural reflects quotation of a source-document on church order.[34] Unlikely also is the idea that husbands and wives are the subject of the plural verb, on the basis of the conceptual sphere purportedly being one of marriage.[35] There is little in the

31 A possible though highly debatable exception is 1 Pet 3:20: διεσώθησαν δι' ὕδατος.

32 The best discussion of the grammatical issues is found in C.F.D. Moule, *An Idiom Book of New Testament Greek* (2nd edn; Cambridge: Cambridge University Press, 1959) 55–58 esp. 56–58. His thought that 1 Tim 2:15 might be temporal is answered above.

33 (1) Dibelius–Conzelmann, *Pastoral Epistles*, 48; Spîcq, *Épîtres pastorales* (4th edn), 383; (2) Lock, *Pastoral Epistles*, 33; Moo, "1 Timothy 2:11–15," 72; *idem*, "Interpretation," 206, following M.J. Harris, "Appendix: Prepositions and Theology in the Greek New Testament," in *NIDNTT* (ed. C. Brown; 3 vols.; Grand Rapids: Zondervan, 1975–79) 3.1182; Holtz, *Pastoralbriefe*, 71.

34 H.W. Bartsch, *Die Anfänge urchristlicher Rechtsbildungen* (Hamburg, 1965) 73, cited in Hanson, *Pastoral Epistles*, 74.

35 White, *First and Second Epistles*, 110; Spîcq, *Épîtres pastorales* (1st edn), 74; Brox, *Pastoralbriefe*, 137.

context to suggest or support this development in thought. More likely is a third proposal that the plural refers by way of an awkward grammatical shift to the products of the act of childbirth, the children themselves.[36] A fourth proposal is that the plural expands to include all of the individual examples of the women referred to in 2:11–15a by representative or generic classification.[37] If these women remain in faith, love and holiness, then they will be saved.

Although most interpreters adopt the third proposal above, this does not seem satisfactory in the grammatical context, with proposal four being the most likely. Houlden claims, however, that the shift to the plural with reference to women from the singular reference in the verses above is awkward,[38] but it is no more awkward than to suggest with proposal three that the children are the subject. The resolution of this ambiguity of reference is of surprisingly great consequence. If the plural verb refers to the children, the implication is that they in some way through their abiding faithful and holy behaviour establish their mother's salvation. Since the children never constitute a focus of attention—or even merit direct reference—in this section, such a shift is implausible without some explicit marker. The fourth alternative, on the other hand, has several contextual reasons in its favour. Within the context of 1 Tim 2:8–15, plural reference to "women" is explicitly made in vv. 9 and 10.[39] Whereas in vv. 11–14 reference is made in the singular, using the singular with generic or representative force in relation to the actions of the first woman, in v. 15 the author expands reference from the representative case to the larger sphere of all "women," stating that women's abiding faithfulness and holy behaviour in some way establish "her" or the representative woman's salvation.

F. *Third Class Conditional Construction*

The last grammatical issue of significance considers the use of the conditional construction in v. 15. The plural verb μείνωσιν is the main verb of the protasis of a third class (ἐάν) conditional structure,[40] in which the apodosis precedes the protasis in clause order. Conditional constructions have proved notoriously difficult for grammarians on account of both conceptual and grammatical

36 For example, Houlden, *Pastoral Epistles*, 72–73; Jeremias, *Briefe an Timotheus und Titus*, 22.

37 Scholer, "1 Timothy 2:9–15," 196.

38 Houlden, *Pastoral Epistles*, 72–73.

39 Kelly, *Pastoral Epistles*, 69. This does not require that a Semitic construction be seen in the collective use, contra M. Wilcox, *The Semitisms of Acts* (Oxford: Clarendon Press, 1965) 127. Cf. L. Rydbeck, *Fachprosa, vermeintliche Volkssprache und Neues Testament: Zur Beurteilung der sprachlichen Niveauunterschiede im nachklassischen Griechisch* (Uppsala: University of Uppsala; Stockholm: Almqvist & Wicksell, 1967) 27–45.

40 On conditional constructions, see Porter, *Verbal Aspect*, 291–320. On the second class conditional, pp. 306–11. Cf. *idem*, *Idioms of the Greek New Testament*, 254–67.

considerations. With respect to conceptual factors, questions arise regarding the implications of the structure with respect to reality, the kinds of implications attendant upon the protasis and the range of conclusions to be drawn from the apodosis, and the sorts of temporal relational implications to be seen. With respect to grammatical factors, questions arise regarding the use of indicative and non-indicative moods, and the various ways in which conditional constructions can be formulated. What is perhaps especially surprising about discussion of 1 Tim 2:15 is that the conditional construction is rarely the focus of serious attention.[41] Recent research indicates that the entire conditional construction must be considered, in which a logical relationship of consequence (not necessarily a temporal or sequential relationship) is established between the protasis and the apodosis. Furthermore, the construction functions in terms of positing a condition with various degrees of strength on the basis of the attitudinal force of the mood form used in the protasis, and drawing logical implications on the basis of the attitudinal force of the mood form used in the apodosis.

The instance in 1 Tim 2:15 of a so-called third class conditional, with the subjunctive in the protasis,[42] makes no implication whether in fact "they remain," only that "they might remain." Regarding the action of the apodosis in relation to the protasis, interpreters often take one of two approaches. Some are tempted on the strength of the future verb form to see the apodosis as action future to the protasis. Others are tempted on the strength of the aorist subjunctive to see the protasis as action antecedent to the apodosis. The temporal analysis that results from these two formulations is roughly the same but they leave unanswered the larger question of the logical relation between the protasis and the apodosis, considered much more important in the light of recent research into conditional structures.[43] A more plausible analysis here for the relation of the protasis and apodosis is either cause and effect or ground and inference. By the first, the understanding is that the women abiding in faith and love and holiness constitute the necessary cause, with the effect that the woman in question will be saved by childbearing. By the second, the understanding is that the women abiding in faith and love and holiness form the ground, from which the legitimate inference can be drawn that the woman in question will be

---

41 Exceptions are Falconer, "1 Timothy 2:14, 15," 377–78, although he attributes it to an author who wishes to "give a Christian infusion to a sentiment which was current in Judaism" (p. 378); Brox, *Pastoralbriefe*, 137; and Spîcq, *Épîtres pastorales* (4th edn), 384, who states, "il accentue l'objectivité de la condition supposée."

42 See J.L. Boyer, "Third (and Fourth) Class Conditions in New Testament Greek," *GTJ* 3 (1982) 163–75.

43 See Porter, *Verbal Aspect*, 317–19, for analysis of these attempts to establish temporal relations between the protasis and the apodosis.

saved by childbearing.[44] Neither category is fully satisfactory, however, especially in the light of the instrumental use of διά in the apodosis. This grammatical analysis indicates, however, that there is an intricate relationship between the protasis and the apodosis, a relationship that has been neglected. As Guthrie says, "Indeed, it is not too much to claim that the former part of the verse must be interpreted in the light of the latter half."[45] Nevertheless, most scholars have placed the majority of their emphasis upon the apodosis, with the result that they heighten the supposed theological difficulties by making it look as if the author is *simply* stating that salvation comes by childbearing. But the presupposed condition of remaining in faith and love and holiness must not be overlooked. The conditional structure, especially the protasis, does draw the comments of v. 15 towards conformity with established authentic Pauline teaching regarding salvation. But it still does not eliminate the ineluctable force of the apodosis regarding salvation by means of childbearing.

4. *Conclusion*

In conclusion, it seems to me that the author of 1 Timothy establishes two parts to his argument in 2:15.[46] The two parts may well be in tension, except that both focus on the woman's actions. The fundamental assumption for the women of this author's audience is that they will lead lives of faith in Christ, love towards fellow Christians and holiness in their married life,[47] with self-control. Although Scott does not believe that "self-control" is a distinctly Christian virtue, as he concedes the others are,[48] Scholer convincingly shows how the concept is applied here to the early Christian concern for reputation.[49] This makes it likely that the author is addressing the Christian women of his audience, and by implication all Christian women. He goes further, however, and equates a woman's earthly function of bearing children with her eschatological or salvific reward.

The plausibility of this analysis is reinforced by brief reference to the context of the entire book of 1 Timothy. The author of 1 Timothy seems to be fighting against a group distinguished by several characteristics. They were promoting doctrine (1 Tim 1:3) that resulted in the telling of all sorts of silly myths and the emphasizing of genealogies (1:4), holding to stories about deceitful spirits and

44 Porter, *Verbal Aspect*, 319–20.

45 Guthrie, *Pastoral Epistles* (1st edn), 78–79.

46 See Kelly, *Pastoral Epistles,* 69, who appreciates the two prongs to the statement.

47 These glosses are based upon Kelly, *Pastoral Epistles*, 70.

48 Scott, *Pastoral Epistles*, 28–29.

49 Scholer, "1 Timothy 2:9–15," 198; cf. Guthrie, *Pastoral Epistles* (2nd edn), 90; Moo, "1 Timothy 2:11–15," 73, quoting Spîcq, *Épîtres pastorales* (4th edn), 384.

demons (4:1), and forbidding marriage and other practices (4:3). Consequently, they elicited his instructions concerning care of the home, the raising of children, and the marriage of widows (5:9–10, 13–16). Instead of being engaged in right behaviour, the women were habitually spending time gossipping in each other's houses (5:13), giving opportunity for those outside the church to slander those in it (5:14; cf. 6:1). It is easy to conclude that the encouraging of ascetic practices, combined with shunning of the women's domestic roles, resulted in sexual abstinence or similar practices which were considered by the author to have missed the mark (cf. 1:3–7; 6:20–21).[50] In the light of this ascetic tendency, the author endorses the resumption of normal practices between men and women, including sexual relations that result in giving birth to children. The inevitable result of such an exegetical conclusion is to make most modern readers highly uncomfortable. But regardless of what we may believe today about the roles and relations of men and women, and despite our best efforts to dismiss or obscure what the text says linguistically through ideologically or theologically dictated exegesis, the author of 1 Timothy apparently believed that for the woman who abides in faith, love and holiness, her salvation will come by the bearing of children.

---

50 See Scholer, "1 Timothy 2:9–15," 197–98; K. van der Jagt, "Women are Saved through Bearing Children: A Sociological Approach to the Interpretation of 1 Timothy 2:15," in *Issues in Bible Translation* (ed. P.C. Stine; London: United Bible Societies, 1988) 288.

INDEX OF ANCIENT SOURCES

INDEX OF MODERN AUTHORS

STUDIES IN BIBLICAL GREEK is an occasional series of monographs designed to promote and publish the latest research into biblical Greek (Old and New Testaments). The series does not assume that biblical Greek is a distinct dialect within the larger world of *koine,* but focuses on these corpora because it recognizes the particular interest they generate. Research into the broader evidence of the period, including epigraphical and inscriptional materials, is welcome in the Series, provided the results are cast in terms of their bearing on biblical Greek. Primarily, however, the Series is devoted to fresh philological, syntactical and linguistic study of the Greek of the biblical books, with the subsidiary aim of displaying the contribution of such study to accurate exegesis.

The series editor is:

D. A. Carson
Trinity Evangelical Divinity School
2065 Half Day Road
Deerfield, IL 60015

